the LIVING and the UNDEAD

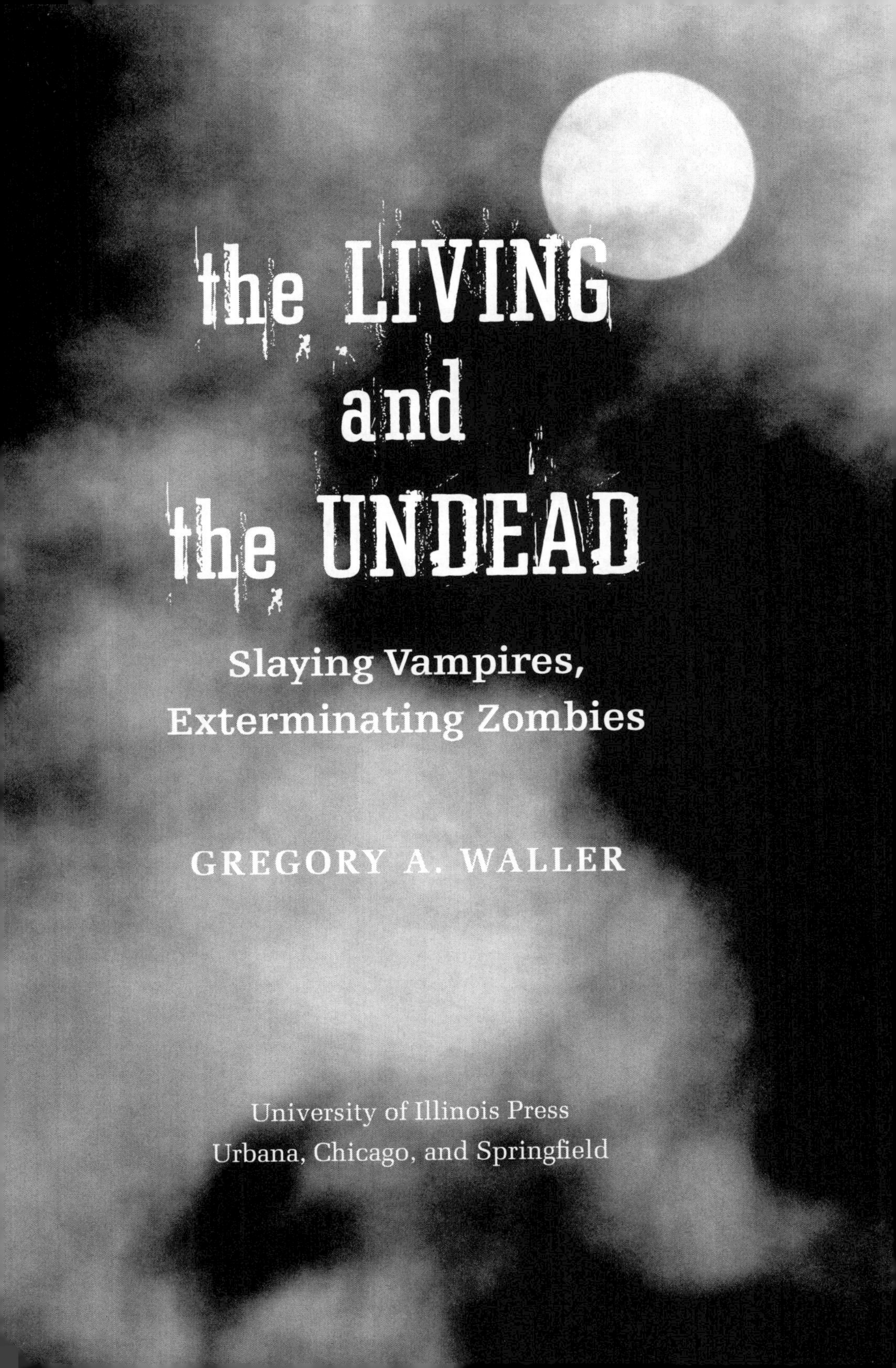

the LIVING and the UNDEAD

Slaying Vampires, Exterminating Zombies

GREGORY A. WALLER

University of Illinois Press
Urbana, Chicago, and Springfield

To my parents

First Illinois paperback, 2010

Manufactured in the United States of America
P 5 4 3 2 1

This book is printed on acid-free paper.

The Library of Congress cataloged the cloth edition as follows:
Waller, Gregory A. (Gregory Albert), 1950–
The living and the undead.
Bibliography: p.
Includes index.
1. Vampire films—History and criticism. I. Title.
PN1995.9.V323 1985
791.43'09'09375 84-24027
ISBN 0-252-1208-9 (alk. paper)

Paperback ISBN 978-0-252-07772-2

Contents

Preface

The Living and the Undead had its origins not in a lifetime of fandom or in early memories of glimpsing monsters on a black-and-white screen. This book was born in the classroom, when, apropos of films like *Nosferatu, A Symphony of Horror* (1922) and *Dracula* (1931), I began to ask undergraduates in my courses on film and popular genres: how do you kill a vampire? It didn't strike me then how different a question this was than asking students: which characters garnered your sympathy and became objects of identification? Or, how did you experience the decidedly mixed and potentially quite disturbing or transgressive pleasures of vampire stories? Affect and identification, in fact, rarely figure in *The Living and the Undead,* though these topics became a central concern in much subsequent writing about horror, including Linda Williams's work on "body genres," Noel Carroll's *The Philosophy of Horror* (1990), Carol Clover's *Men, Women, and Chainsaws* (1992), Cynthia A. Freeland's *The Naked and the Undead* (2000), and Adam Lowenstein's *Shocking Representation* (2005).

Still, almost everyone in these classes knew the answer to my ostensibly more straightforward and oddly "factual" question, or at least they knew *an* answer. Students were ready to debate the finer points of weaponry, techniques, and strategies, even quick to distinguish between means of protection (cross, garlic) and means of eradication (sunlight, wooden stakes), between targeting the head or the heart. No one pointed out the oddness or perversity of deeming it heroic when one of the living (almost always a man) drove a stake into the heart of a distinctly human-looking vampire who might well be a peacefully sleeping beautiful young woman or mature man of aristocratic mien. This quite striking instance of common knowledge seemed to me all the more worth thinking about precisely because knowing how to kill a vampire was utterly useless information, not to be taken seriously or to make its way onto an SAT exam. Only for fictional characters and paranoid psychopaths could such arcane knowledge ever come in handy.

I wasn't curious then about precisely how generations of students came to acquire vampire lore or what they actually thought about the movies, books, television programs, fanzines, games, and comics that delivered this information. In other words, I never considered an ethnographic approach to the reception of vampire stories and, more broadly, to horror as a popular genre—a methodology that would come to generate valuable scholarship on fan cultures. Students' matter-of-fact familiarity with vampire lore led me instead back to the stories themselves, which very often offered spectacular moments of bloody violence as well as scenes of instruction regarding what Professor Van Helsing in *Dracula* so memorably calls the "wild work" of destroying the undead. This dirty, necessary labor seemed to me as essential to the story as the seductive, ravenous, or calculatedly malevolent work undertaken by the vampire looking to satisfy a thirst, capture a consort, or expand a dominion.

Part of the impetus behind *The Living and the Undead* was that despite all of the attention that Count Dracula and his kindred had attracted—with good reason and interesting results, as Ken Gelder ably demonstrates in *Reading the Vampire* (1994)—the vampire's human enablers, victims, and adversaries had been given short shrift by commentators in and out of the academy. For these were unmistakably stories not only about monsters but also about killing monsters, rarely a simple or unambiguous task. From this starting point, more questions emerged: how and when and why to undertake this potentially gruesome and dangerous responsibility? Who to entrust with wielding the stake? What did this violence signify? Was it the climactic, entirely justifiable act in a passionate play of survival? Was it the last, decidedly primitive recourse after other, more ostensibly modern strategies failed? Was it a fruitlessly homicidal or even pathologically genocidal gesture? An excuse for sadism? A testament to age-old patriarchal privilege? A sign of human ingenuity or of unquestioning adherence to tradition? Was it an act of purification? A means of differentiation or purgation? Was it, itself, a source of infection rather than redemption? These are serious, troublesome, ideologically loaded questions about violence, the monstrous, boundary making, and the limits of heroism. My aim in this book was to take seriously the dramatically enacted and hardly uniform answers that popular fictions provided to these questions.

To this end, when researching *The Living and the Undead,* I sought to be as comprehensive as possible, ranging primarily across the spectrum of English-language popular culture from the 1890s to the 1980s, taking in juvenilia and paperback originals, low-budget movies and *Masterpiece Theater,* widely known classics and obscure titles. My focus, however, centered on a set of interrelated films, novels, and telefilms, (with one stage play), stretching from Stoker's *Dracula* (1897) to the second film in George A. Romero's zombie series, *Dawn of the Dead* (1979), and notably including Hammer's Count Dracula films, Richard Matheson's *I Am Legend* (1954), Stephen King's *'Salem's Lot* (1975), Murnau's *Nosferatu,* and Werner Herzog's *Nosferatu the Vampyre* (1979). Attending in detail to how the encounter between the living and the undead was worked out, embellished, and resolved (or not resolved) in each of these stories occupies the bulk of this book, which obviously would have taken a different shape had I written it after the release of memorable movies like *Near Dark* (1987), *Braindead* (1992), *The Addiction* (1995), *28 Days Later* (2002), *Vampire Hunter D: Bloodlust* (2005), and *Let the Right One In* (2008). For me, it is not so much a question of how these post-1985 films might fit into some schema I have established but, rather, how they extend, transform, reiterate, and re-inscribe an ongoing set of narrative possibilities and thematic concerns.

In designating a particular body of related texts collectively as the *story of the living and the undead,* I was attempting to engage then-current theorizations of genre. This particular story, preoccupied with the passing on of knowledge, infused with the air of mortality, and self-conscious about the desire for closure, looked to be a prime site to explore the historicity and messiness of genre and to track popular culture's degree of variation and difference as well as its reliance on repetition and similarity. Subsequently, Rick Altman, Steve Neale, James Naremore, and others have convincingly argued that genres are discursive constructs, not so much up for grabs as potentially contested and capable of re-articulation while always being historically grounded, variable, and hybrid. We can see this process at work quite dramatically with horror over the past twenty years, evidenced by the proliferation of subgenres and short-term cycles, the marketing strategies of DVDs, the increased repackaging of older product, and the wealth of genre-related discourse on and off the World Wide Web. What I have called the story of the living and the undead stands as an admittedly heuristic construct, a "genre" identified for the purposes of analysis. I was able to point to certain ways that these novels, films, and made-for-television productions were linked, one to another, by lines of adaptation, influence, or affinity, but the real test is whether the reader finds it productive to group the tales of Stoker, Romero, and the rest together as instances in an ongoing story of the wild work that links and defines the living and the undead.

To explore this genre, *The Living and the Undead* relies on close textual readings of books, films, and television productions, examining them in terms of narrative strategies, thematic emphases, and formal qualities, and putting them into dialogue with a broader discourse concerning violence and community. This method was in some measure a reaction against what I took to be the devaluation and underestimation of horror and other contemporary popular narratives. At the same time, I was frustrated as much by the hyperbole common in fanzines and the abstract models of gendered spectatorship offered by psychoanalytic film theory as by a version of ideological criticism that hinged on the reductive distinction between what qualified as "progressive" and what was deemed unproblematically reactionary in the contemporary horror film. Thus, attending with equal care to the scene-by-scene details and the larger narrative arc of Romero's gory sequel to *Night of the Living Dead* as well as to Murnau's acclaimed silent film seemed to me fully warranted and was a way to challenge, indirectly at least, a certain bias against and oversimplification of modern horror movies as well as a way of re-viewing a hallowed classical tradition. In this regard, Joan Hawkins offers a particularly insightful take on the relations between "high" and "low" horror in *Cutting Edge: Art-Horror and the Horrific Avant-Garde* (2000).

In examining how the story of the living and the undead has been told and retold across different media over almost a century, I imagined a hypothetical viewer or reader who comes to know these stories one-by-one, roughly in chronological order, reading *Dracula* (1979), for instance, in light of *Dracula* (1973) and *Horror of Dracula* (1958), and on backwards to Stoker's original text and its nineteenth-century antecedents. I was less concerned with pointing out, for instance, certain fairly obvious topical references to the Vietnam War in *Night of the Living Dead,* than in analyzing this film's full spectrum of human work and undead labor and its intertextual relations, via *I Am Legend,* to a tradition of vampire stores. By the same token, I was more interested in speculating about how we can understand *Dracula* (1931) as a retelling of Stoker's novel and

Dracula: The Vampire Play (1927) and as one iteration in a cluster of stories pitting a master vampire against a small cohort of humans than in examining the making of this film or situating it as a product of the Hollywood studio system, and, more generally, of America during the early Depression years. These particular historical topics would, in fact, be well treated in later research by, among others, Rhona J. Berenstein (*Attack of the Leading Ladies: Gender, Sexuality, and Spectatorship in Classic Horror Cinema* [1995]), David J. Skal (*Hollywood Gothic* [2004]), and Robert Spadoni (*Uncanny Bodies: The Coming of Sound and the Origins of the Horror Genre* [2007]).

The Living and the Undead is directly concerned with how the revivified and mobilized undead circulate, driven by appetite and desire, while the living attempt to defend the borders of the nation, the community, the home, the family, and the self. But what about the cultural circulation of these texts themselves? How were these novels and movies marketed, distributed, exhibited, and reviewed? Even before the advent of digital technologies, how were they repackaged and repurposed for various audiences, delivery systems, and commercial opportunities? These questions did not drive my research project, though they have come to seem to me increasingly important. To cite only two possible lines of inquiry: *Dracula*'s ascent up the ladder of literary respectability and *Night of the Living Dead*'s ubiquitous availability on 16mm and all subsequent audio-visual formats would make for rich case studies of the circulation of horror as a popular genre with an increasingly global reach through the twentieth century.

More than two decades after the publication of *The Living and Undead* the particular variant of the horror story that it explores is unquestionably alive and well, and vampires have continued to attract their share of critical attention in perceptive studies like Nina Auerbach's *Our Vampires, Ourselves* (1997) and Stacy Abbott's *Celluloid Vampires: Life after Death in the Modern World* (2007). All of the retellings of *Dracula* I consider—even more obscure titles like *El Conde Dracula* (1970) and the PBS miniseries *Count Dracula* (1977)—have been released in digital format. At the same time, the more-or-less direct lines of descent I noted have continued to proliferate. A third screen version of *I Am Legend* with full blockbuster packaging premiered in 2007, and after appearing as a mini-series in 1979, *'Salem's Lot* was adapted by the BBC as a radio drama in 1995 and surfaced in 2004 again as a mini-series, this time produced by Warner Bros. for the TNT network. Stoker's *Dracula* served as the source for

Francis Ford Coppola's *Bram Stoker's Dracula* (1992), as well as for a 2006 BBC telefilm and for Guy Maddin's *Dracula: Pages from a Virgin's Diary* (2002), based on a production by the Royal Winnipeg Ballet. (Less directly informed by the novel are other post-millennium "Dracula" films like *Bram Stoker's Dracula's Curse* [2006], *Bram Stoker's Dracula's Guest* [2008], *Dracula 2000* [2001], *Dracula II* [2003], and *Dracula III: Legacy* [2005].) Among the many published sequels to *Dracula* is Dacre Stoker and Ian Holt's *Dracula: The Un-Dead* (2009), authorized by the Stoker estate. Versions of the novel previously difficult to access have also become more readily available, including Orson Welles's 1938 Mercury Theatre radio dramatization of *Dracula* and Stoker's own unproduced five-act stage adaptation, *Dracula: Or the Un-Dead, A Play in Prologue and Five Acts.* Digital technology has made it easier to distribute versions of *Nosferatu: A Symphony of Horror* with significantly different soundtracks (including the original score), while *Shadow of the Vampire* (2003) takes as its narrative premise the production of Murnau's 1922 film. Thanks in part to the vagaries of copyright law, Romero's living dead have likewise had a thriving screen life. *Night of the Living Dead* and *Dawn of the Dead* have both been remade, and Romero has continued the saga with *Day of the Dead* (1985), *Land of the Dead* (2005), and *Diary of the Dead* (2007), while *The Return of the Living Dead* (1985), another "authorized" sequel, spawned four additional installments from 1988 to 2005.

Of course, new titles specifically related to the set of novels, films, and telefilms I examine in this book count for only a fraction of the vampires and zombies set loose on the marketplace since 1985, particularly when we look beyond film to take into account series fiction, graphic novels, and video/computer games. Given the focus of *The Living and the Undead,* the new variation of prime relevance is not the *Twilight* franchise (2005–present), Anne Rice's *Vampire Chronicles* (1976–2003), or even HBO's *True Blood* (2008–present), but rather those stories that foreground the dedicated and preternaturally capable vampire hunter, equipped with an arsenal of specialized weapons and facing off against a virtually never-ending supply of opponents. Based on a Marvel Comics character, the *Blade* trilogy (1998, 2002, and 2004 films, then continued as a short-lived television series), for example, relies on the special effects and choreographed fight sequences of the big-budget action film, as does the CGI-driven period piece *Van Helsing* (2004), with the aged professor now a hard-bodied superhero. *Vampires* (1998, with a 2002 sequel set in Mexico), in contrast, puts its hard-boiled, wisecracking slayer in the modern

Southwest, a terrain increasingly overrun by the undead, as the unwitting visitors to a remote Mexican strip club discover in *From Dusk Till Dawn* (1996, with two later installments released in 1999). While the most well-known hunter is likely the redoubtable teenage heroine of *Buffy the Vampire Slayer* (1997–2003), the most interesting play on this theme may be serial narratives produced in Japan, like *Hellsing* (first a manga [1997–2008], then a thirteen-episode anime television series [2001–2], then a direct-to-video animated series [2006–present]) and, most widely seen and influential, *Vampire Hunter D.* Originally a series of novels (1983–present) by Hideyuki Kikuchi, which began to appear in English translation in 2005, *Vampire Hunter D* was adapted as a feature-length animated film in 1985, with a second film (*Vampire Hunter D: Bloodlust*) appearing in 2000.

As Jamie Russell's encyclopedic—and exemplary—*Book of the Dead: The Complete History of Zombie Cinema* (2005) attests, the zombie branch of the undead also shows no signs of becoming culturally or commercially extinct, regardless of how many stumbling creatures are decapitated or otherwise exterminated in films like *Undead* (2003), *Shaun of the Dead* (2004), and *Planet Terror* (2007). From the perspective of *The Living and the Undead,* what looks to be most fascinating about the resilience of the sometimes absurdly mundane living dead is the ongoing resonance of these creatures and the apocalyptic world they bring into being. The prospect of a land overrun with legions of the living dead—call it Zombieland after the 2009 movie—forms an especially telling contrast with contemporary fears of global terrorism, which is often represented as being threatening precisely to the extent that it appears to be an intricate system of technologically equipped, single-minded true believers able to infiltrate and wreak havoc on the everyday. Zombies en masse—un-terrorists, as it were—continue to serve as a threatening Other that is quite distinct from the intricately rendered and sometimes highly evolved vampire families, clans, subcultures, communities, and societies in stories such as the *Underworld* trilogy (2003, 2006, 2009), *Near Dark, Vampire Hunter D, The Lost Boys* (1987), *Interview with the Vampire* (1994), *Blade,* and *True Blood*—all of which depict alternative undead social configurations well beyond the fantasies of Stoker's King-Vampire. Needless to say, there is still much wild work to be done.

Acknowledgments

Thanks to Robert Hemenway and John G. Cawelti of the University of Kentucky and Ann Lowry Weir and Susan L. Patterson of the University of Illinois Press for their advice and encouragement, to Bruce F. Kawin and Mark M. Hennelly, Jr., for their helpful comments on the manuscript, to the University of Kentucky Research Foundation for grants that helped defray the cost of preparing the manuscript, to Philip Booth for granting permission to reprint part of "Burning the Tents," which was originally published in the *American Poetry Review*, and to the Hollywood Book and Poster Company, the Museum of Modern Art Film Study Center, and the Margaret Herrick Library of the Academy of Motion Picture Arts and Sciences for assistance in obtaining stills. Special thanks to Richard Angelo, Walter C. Foreman, and Armando Prats—good colleagues, good readers, and good friends. My greatest debt is to Robin, Moby, and Graham Waller, who bore with my wild work and taught me daily about the world of the living.

INTRODUCTION

Count Dracula: There is work to be done.
Dracula (1897)

Professor Van Helsing: There is work, wild work to be done.
Dracula (1979)

CHAPTER

1

Stories of the Living and the Undead

THE DISEASE CONTINUES, even though we know the simple objects traditionally required to effect a cure: cross, garlic, and stake—sacred talisman, natural herb, and forged weapon. The vampire lives—as Transylvanian aristocrat, seductive siren, anonymous walking dead, superior natural creature, or satanic master-villain, even as bumbling anachronism or as cultured, romantic hero or as troubled, isolated victim of immortality. Such distinctions, however, have little value for Professor Abraham Van Helsing, the prototypical vampire hunter first introduced in Bram Stoker's *Dracula* (1897). Van Helsing refers to his antagonists simply as the "Un-Dead"—in contrast to both the living and the "common dead"[1]—and also as the "nosferatu," who, in his words, "do not die like the bee when he sting once" (D, 243). Appropriately enough, the vampire in all its forms is the most often resurrected and the most durable of all the monstrous threats that roam the dark landscape of the horror story, as if the undead have drawn continuing life from generations of readers and viewers. With a legacy that stretches back into legend and folklore and continues through the popular culture of the past 150 years, the vampire has figured prominently in the onslaught of horror during the 1970s, from Marvel Comics' *Tomb of Dracula* to R-rated exploitation movies like *The Velvet Vampire* (1971); from made-for-television movies like *The Night Stalker* (1972) to acclaimed works like Anne Rice's *Interview with the Vampire* (1976) and Werner Herzog's *Nosferatu the Vampyre* (1979).

Given the universality, durability, and popularity of the vampire, it is no surprise that Count Dracula and the panoply of other undead creatures have become the object of critical investigation as well as the object of parody. One form the investigation takes is the general survey that purports to trace the vampire's appearances in "legend, fact, and art," to quote the subtitle of Basil Copper's *The Vampire* (1974). Preeminent among such works are Montague Summers's *The Vampire: His Kith and Kin* (1928) and *The Vampire in Europe* (1929), which Summers offers as "the first serious study in English of the Vampire, and kindred traditions from a general, as well as a theological and philosophical point of view."[2] Summers's compendium of historical accounts, tales, anecdotes, and passing references to the undead serves as a basis for superficial surveys like Copper's *The Vampire* and Bernhardt J. Hurwood's *Vampires* (1981), which exhibit little interest in the "theological and philosophical point of view." Of much greater usefulness than these pastiche popularizations are Donald F. Glut's *The Dracula Book* (1975), an encyclopedic survey of Dracula's appearances in film, theater, fiction, television, and comic books, and David Pirie's *The Vampire Cinema* (1977), a critical history of vampire films that is based on the assumption that "the function of the vampire movie is precisely to incarnate the most *hostile* aspects of sexuality in a concrete form."[3]

Pirie's history of the genre is predicated on the explanatory model offered by Ernest Jones in *On the Nightmare* (1931; revised edition, 1951). Jones, one of the most influential of the first generation of Freudian psychoanalysts, argues that the "latent content" of legends and superstitions about the vampire "yields plain indications of most kinds of sexual perversions," including necrophilia and "oral sadism" and that the "essential elements" of the "vampire belief" are "repressed desires and hatreds derived from early incest conflicts."[4] To a great extent, Jones's assumptions also inform James Ursini and Alain Silver's *The Vampire Film* (1975). After a cursory glance at the vampire in legend, history, and literature, Ursini and Silver focus on the undead in film, those creatures who "rise up out of men's hidden fears *and* desires" and who "represent the arch-need of man to purge himself of his severest repressions." For Ursini and Silver, "obviously, the core of the fiction is the character of the vampire itself, whether described as a vortex of malevolence, lust, and savagery or, alternately, as the unwilling victim who becomes a tormented, driven, even tragic figure."[5] The organization of *The Vampire Film* reflects the belief that the core of the vampire story is the vampire itself: the book is divided into sections on the "male vampire," including Dracula and the "sympathetic male vampire," and the "female vampire," including Elisabeth Bathory and Carmilla Karnstein. The titles of many of the movies that belong to this genre—*Countess Dracula*; *Dracula, Prince of Darkness*; *Dracula's Daughter*; *Count Yorga, Vampire*—do indeed suggest that "the core of the fiction is the character of the vampire itself."

Yet in such stories the vampire is always defined and depicted in relation to those human beings who become its victims or allies or antagonists. In short, the undead, as Van Helsing insists, must be understood in the context of the living, even when such monstrous creatures seem to be the antithesis of what we deem to be human. My interest, therefore, is not in merely cataloguing the various forms the vampire has taken in folklore and art or in listing the countless guises that Count Dracula has assumed in the twentieth century; my principal interest is not even in vampires per se. Rather, I am concerned with stories of the confrontation between the living and the undead, stories in which the resolution of conflict often depicts the survival of the fittest and, in fact, defines what fitness consists of. The "core of the fiction," to use Ursini and Silver's phrase, is this confrontation in which the living as well as the undead can come to embody and enact our "hidden fears and desires."

In this study I will examine how a group of texts—primarily novels and feature-length films, but also short stories, plays, and telefilms—present this confrontation between the living and the undead. Although I discuss a large, diverse number of works, I have not attempted to analyze or even to categorize all the stories of this type that have appeared since the publication of John Polidori's *The Vampyre* in 1819. Many minor works as well as innovative artistic achievements like Carl-Theodor Dreyer's *Vampyr* (1932) and commercial successes like *Dark Shadows* (a daytime soap opera featuring the vampire Barnaby Collins, produced by Dan Curtis for ABC television between 1966 and 1971) receive at best a passing glance.[6] Several of the texts I examine do not include creatures specifically identified as vampires; yet all of these stories center on a violent confrontation between the living and the undead that ultimately determines who is to survive.

The primary group of stories under consideration comprises a series of related texts in that almost every one announces its lineage and points the reader or viewer not only back to its predecessors but also toward the larger, ongoing story. For example, Tod Browning's *Dracula*

(1931), Philip Saville's *Count Dracula* (1977), and the other works I will discuss in chapters 3–5 are all identified in their introductory credit sequences as adaptations of Stoker's *Dracula*, while Herzog's *Nosferatu the Vampyre* (1979) is a homage to and a critical revision of F. W. Murnau's *Nosferatu, a Symphony of Horror* (1922), which is itself based upon Stoker's novel. Richard Matheson, on the other hand, identifies one major context for *I Am Legend* (1954) by having his protagonist actually read *Dracula* in search of information and inspiration, and a similar situation occurs in Stephen King's *'Salem's Lot* (1975), though these two American novels offer diametrically opposed responses to Stoker's *Dracula. I Am Legend*, in turn, is the direct antecedent and the "inspiration" for George A. Romero's apocalyptic horror film, *Night of the Living Dead* (1968), which depicts the undead as flesh-eating zombies rather than as bloodthirsty vampires. In *Dawn of the Dead* (1979), Romero continues the story.

Of course, the significance of allusions and borrowings and even explicit statements of relationship ("based upon," "adapted from," e.g.) varies from text to text. My point here is to note that such elements inform us or remind us of how each of these works participates in an ongoing series of narratives; precisely how we are thus directed will be one of the areas I will examine in this study. Our awareness of this fact helps direct our reading and rereading of these stories. And each of these storytellers is, like the poets Harold Bloom describes in *The Anxiety of Influence*, "caught up in a dialectical relationship (transference, repetition, error, communication)" with his predecessors.[7] A close, extended look both at the stories that I have mentioned and at other related texts will allow us to see the shape and the particular significance of the entire series, as well as the unique achievement of works like Stoker's *Dracula*, Herzog's *Nosferatu the Vampyre*, and Romero's *Dawn of the Dead*.

This group of stories of the confrontation between the living and the undead does not constitute a major, immediately recognizable genre comparable to the western or the detective story. I would label this series of works, from *Dracula* to *Dawn of the Dead*, a subgenre of the horror story, though we could also see the series as a formula, following the definition of formula that John Cawelti provides in *Adventure, Mystery, and Romance* (1976).[8] More important than the choice of terminology is our acceptance of the fact that these stories do indeed constitute a body of related material, a series of narrative variations on several interrelated themes. I do not propose to formulate a new theory of genre or to survey the immense quantity of contemporary critical literature on genre. I do believe, however, that my study of the living and the undead corroborates and extends certain propositions offered in, for example, Cawelti's examination of popular storytelling and Tzvetan Todorov's structural analysis of the "fantastic," as well as the discussions of movie genres in works like Andrew Tudor's *Image and Influence* (1974), Leo Braudy's *The World in a Frame* (1976), and Thomas Schatz's *Hollywood Genres* (1981).[9] While these and other discussions of genre in film and fiction provide an important framework for the study of the vampire story, the vampire story—with its insistence on the importance of traditional wisdom, symbolic and sacred objects, and ritualized action—can teach us a great deal about the role of the conventional in all genres, subgenres, and formulas of popular art. In certain of the stories I will discuss, ignorance of the generic rules of the game often means death—or worse, the agony of undeath—while knowledge of and full commitment to convention and tradition often guarantee the survival of the living. One function of characters like Stoker's wise, experienced Professor Van Helsing is to inform the uninitiated and convince the skeptical of this all-important point.

Let me briefly indicate here, with due acknowledgment to the critics mentioned above, several topics that seem to me to be particularly significant in the study of popular genres. For Cawelti, to discuss a popular formula is to identify and describe the definitive, essential "aspects" of the formula: the initial situation, the "pattern of action," the setting, the main character roles, and the relations between these characters.[10] Such an approach necessarily emphasizes the degree of "standardization" and of the conventional in generic narratives. Operating under similar assumptions, Schatz finds the "determining, identifying feature" of the gangster film and other Hollywood genres to be "a network of characters, actions, values, and attitudes." This network he calls the "generic community," whose system of values is visually and narratively encoded in a specific iconography.[11] When we focus on the aristocratic European vampire, the defenseless, virginal female victim, the Van Helsingesque patriarchal figure of authority, and other character roles that appear in text after text, we immediately become aware of the importance of convention in stories of the living and the undead. It is the same as when we consider, for example, the place of Christian faith and modern skepticism in the generic community created by these stories. It is the degree of standardization, after all, that provides us with what Braudy calls the "pleasures of familiarity" in the generic text,[12] and that gives rise to Silver and Ursini's *The Vampire Film* and to most critical studies of the iconography and ideology of popular art.

The pleasures of familiarity, however, must be understood in relation to the pleasures of originality, for the generic text always involves variation as well as standardization, innovation as well as convention. As Stephen Neale observes, once we conceive of genre as "process," then "repetition is never simply the return of the identical and difference is never simply the eruption of the absolutely new."[13] It is precisely the play of repetition and difference that I find to be at once the most entertaining and the most significant feature of popular genres.

We may note here, by way of illustration and preview, the interplay of difference and repetition, of originality and familiarity, in the story of the living and the undead. Our pleasure of familiarity is mirrored by the characters who must become familiar with traditional wisdom and the ways of ritualized violence so as to determine the extent to which variation and innovation is possible or desirable or necessary. For example, in order to survive, the young heroes of Hammer Studio's vampire films of the 1960s all must acquire knowledge of tradition, arm themselves with sacred weapons, and ritualistically destroy Count Dracula. In effect, those human beings who hunt the vampire must realize that stakes and garlic have a particular iconographic significance and that the present struggle—the story they are living—must be understood in relation to previous struggles, previous stories. The vampire hunters in films like *Taste the Blood of Dracula* (1970) intentionally or unintentionally alter the given ritual yet still manage to triumph. In certain cases the living triumph only because they are innovative. The relationship between repetition and variation, convention and innovation, that underlies the working of all popular genres is, in stories of the living and the undead, a matter of life and death for the characters and a topic of direct, explicit interest for the informed reader/viewer.

As Todorov argues in *The Fantastic*, a discussion of the conventional and unconventional aspects of a genre can become merely a list, a classification of "elements" that disregards the fact that the individual work forms a "coherent whole." Genre, according to Todorov, is an "inventory of options" that is transformed with each telling of the story or rather, with our experience of each version of the story.[14] Somewhat similarly, Stanley Cavell, in a recent study of what he calls the "Hollywood comedy of remarriage," proposes that the idea of a genre as an object with certain properties be replaced by the idea of a genre as a "story" with certain "clauses and provisions," a story that remains "provisional" and subject to new tellings—new "interpretations"—until it reaches a "state of absolute explicitness, of expressive saturation."[15]

It seems to me that Todorov's and Cavell's suggestions quite correctly acknowledge and direct us toward the complex interrelation between the individual text, the reader, and the genre. The notion of an ongoing transformation of options and the image of genre as a provisional story inform much of my discussion of the confrontation between the living and the undead. These concerns are best explored, I believe, not by listing character types or iconographical details, but by examining a series of individual texts, one after the other in order to determine how each text participates in and continues the ongoing story. This approach allows for a detailed study of the interrelation between text, reader, and genre, as well as a consideration of what Bloom calls the "creative revisionism" and "*mistranslation*" that is at the heart of artistic "influence."[16] At the same time, this format provides the opportunity for us to trace the transformation of this genre's "inventory of options" and the exploration of its "clauses and provisions."

For both Todorov and Cavell, one important way to identify the structure or the unique configuration of a genre, particularly a narrowly circumscribed body of material like the Hollywood comedy of remarriage or the literature of the fantastic, is to examine the genre in the context of "adjacent genres."[17] Such a critical maneuver acknowledges the extent to which popular genres form a continuum (a fact often made evident in the 1930s and 1940s by the casting of such stars as James Cagney and Humphrey Bogart and made evident in the contemporary film by the self-conscious mixing of genres in movies as different as *Dirty Harry* [1971] and *Mommie Dearest* [1981]). Ever since Universal Films released both *Dracula* and *Frankenstein* in 1931, then rereleased the two movies as a double feature, and brought Count Dracula, Frankenstein's creature, and other monsters together in films like *House of Frankenstein* (1944) and *House of Dracula* (1945), the story of Frankenstein and his creation has remained an essential comparison point for the vampire story. And during the past fifteen years, the story of the living and the undead has increasingly found itself in various ways adjacent to other types of horror, to stories of satanic evil, for example, or homicidal psychopaths or predatory animals. Other equally interesting, if less obvious, points of comparison become apparent when we consider the story of the living and the undead as a narrative account of violent conflict and the struggle for survival. In my conclusion I consider the relationship between the works I discuss and other versions of the story of the struggle for survival, like World War II combat films and disaster stories of the late 1960s and 1970s.

Placing stories of the living and the undead in the context of adjacent genres helps to demonstrate both the uniqueness and the larger cultural significance of these stories. So, too, does a comparison of the story of the living and the undead with nonfiction works of sociology and social psychology. My intent in comparing Sigmund Freud's *Totem and Taboo* (1913) and Stoker's *Dracula*, for instance, is neither somehow to valorize popular fiction by placing it in the company of serious nonfiction nor to identify any direct influence of one text on another. Rather, I seek to situate the series of works I consider in a larger history of ideas and shifting ideological assumptions.

That the story of the living and the undead, like all popular genres, itself has a history and that this genre bears some relation to our history I assume without question. This relation cannot, however, be reduced to a simple explanatory equation.[18] Neither can the changes in the story of the living and the undead be easily explained in terms of an entirely consistent progression toward some readily apparent end. Changes in our sense of what constitutes the genre result from the process of repetition and variation that I have already mentioned. This process becomes most apparent in works like Romero's *Night of the Living Dead* and Badham's *Dracula*, which directly undertake what Braudy calls the "creative destruction and complication" of their generic inheritance and which use "our expectations against themselves, and, in the process, reveal to us expectations and assumptions that we may never have thought we had."[19]

Romero's *Martin* (1977) is an excellent example of the creatively destructive text that Braudy describes. This stylistically self-conscious contemporary story of an American teenage murderer, who may actually be a vampire or may only believe or fantasize that he is one, complicates—"re-vamps," to use Romero's word—not only our assumptions about the undead but also about the living.[20] In *Martin* the vampire hunter is a monomaniacal, dictatorial, egotistical old man, who is obsessed with preserving the rigid and seemingly absurd conventions he has inherited from the "Old Country" and with simplifying all ambiguity and complexity he encounters in the New World. By pounding a stake into the boy's heart, the old man attempts to force life to conform to his expectations and to treat the present as, in Neale's phrase, "simply the return of the identical." The death of the teenager does not regenerate the economically depressed, deadeningly ugly modern world or restore its broken families or rebuild its decaying churches. And unlike this modern-day nosferatu who slashes his victims with razor blades and shards of glass, the questions raised by *Martin* are not so easily disposed of. As a result, Romero forces us to become a more informed, wary, self-conscious audience—an audience that realizes that movies can be about movies and movie-going even when they are not literally about filmmaking.

This distinction between the self-conscious text, critical of the conventionality of conventions, and the uncritical text (which is surely not unself-conscious of its identity as horror film or gangster movie or western) can become the basis for a history of popular genres, an easily charted line of progress from the simple and repetitive primitives to the ironic, complicated, and complicating moderns. Borrowing from Christian Metz's *Language and Cinema* and art historian Henri Focillon's *The Life of Forms in Art*, Schatz proposes "a rather consistent pattern of schematic development" along these lines. Hollywood genres, according to Schatz, progress "from transparency to opacity—from straightforward storytelling to self-conscious formalism."[21] A comparison of Browning's *Dracula* (1931) and Terence Fisher's *Horror of Dracula* (1958) with *Martin* and films such as Roman Polanski's *The Fearless Vampire Killers or Pardon Me, but Your Teeth Are in My Neck* (also released as *Dance of the Vampires* [1967]), Paul Morrissey's *Blood for Dracula* (also released as *Andy Warhol's Dracula* [1974]), and even Stan Dragoti's *Love at First Bite* (1979) proves that this pattern of development is indeed present in the vampire story. (This pattern also holds true for the horror story in general, as a comparison of *Frankenstein* [1931] and *The Curse of Frankenstein* [1957] with *Targets* [1968], *It's Alive* [1974], and *The Funhouse* [1981] immediately makes clear.)

Yet the number of works that do not neatly fit into this explanatory formula suggests that the evolution of popular genres is not simply or universally a historical movement toward creative destruction and "self-conscious formalism." Andrew Tudor in *Image and Influence* convincingly argues that the "evolutionary analogy" can be "usefully applied to change in the popular genres," but only if we acknowledge that such change is generally "conservative" and "slow" and also "cumulative" in that "innovations are added to an existent corpus rather than replacing redundant elements."[22] The notion of cumulative change—which is linked for me with the idea of genre as an ongoing story and an "inventory of options"—is particularly important, for it helps account for a book like *'Salem's Lot* (1975), which employs and endorses the generic conventions that Matheson in 1954 and Romero in 1968 had creatively destroyed. An awareness of the conservative, slow, and cumulative evolution of the story of the living and the undead, in turn, enables us to assess more accurately the role of works like Fisher's *Horror of Dracula* and Romero's *Night of the Living Dead* that have revolutionized the genre.

Unfortunately, the all-too-common tendency to underestimate individual generic texts and to oversimplify the history of a genre is matched only by the tendency to disregard the complex relationship between a genre and the social, political, and cultural values and institutions that make up our world. In response to such oversimplifications, Tudor concludes that it is impossible to locate "single, distinct causal factors to explain the development" (and the appearance of individual examples) of a genre, for "popular culture is conceived to be *simultaneously* the cause, justification, and consequence of various patterns of social behaviour."[23] Similarly, as Tudor and the other critics I have cited fully realize, the cultural role of popular genres cannot be reduced to one simple function. Cawelti notes that genre stories "relate to the processes of culture" in a variety of ways: these stories can, for example, confirm "some strongly held conventional view," as well as explore the boundary between "the permitted and the forbidden"—functions that are fulfilled by Hamilton Deane and John L. Balderston's *Dracula: The Vampire Play* (1927) and by Hammer's Dracula films.[24] *Night of the Living Dead*, on the other hand, exemplifies what Braudy describes as the genre film's ability to express problems that have not been "solved or hardly even identified" by the "explicit politics" of society.[25]

As these examples begin to suggest, stories of the living and the undead perform a variety of social, psychological, and cultural functions as they depict the strengths and weaknesses of the living in the face of the threat posed by the undead.[26] Questions about the role played by these stories and about the relationship between their world and our world inevitably bring us back to the interrelated topics I have briefly described here: the process of repetition and variation, the historical evolution and the internal transformations of the story as it is retold and reinterpreted, and the relationship between this story and adjacent genres and between the individual text, the audience, and the genre.

In *The Vampire in Europe* Montague Summers includes several brief but exemplary (and purportedly factual) narrative accounts of the confrontation between the living and the undead. Here are my paraphrases of three such accounts, the first two from William of Newburgh's *Historia Rerum Anglicarum* (a history of England from 1066–1198, written during the twelfth century) and the third from the Marquis D'Argens's *Lettres Juives* (1727).

1. After having died and been "decently buried," a man returned from the grave to terrify and attack his wife, then his brothers and his friends and neighbors as well. Soon, in every house in the small town the people kept an all-night watch, but the dead man then "began to wander abroad in plain daylight." Finally, "well-nigh scared out of their senses," the inhabitants of the town appealed to their archdeacon, who in turn informed the bishop and "consulted with a number of learned priests and reverend theologians." Following the bishop's advice, the priests and theologians opened the coffin containing the man, placed a "chartula of episcopal absolution" on the breast of the corpse, and resealed the coffin. The dead man never again left his grave.[27]

2. A man given to a "depraved and dishonest life" died without making his final confession, after having caught his wife in bed with a "lusty youth." "By the power of Satan in the dark hours," the dead man "was wont to come forth from his tomb," terrifying all the inhabitants of the district. Soon "the air became foul and tainted as this fetid and corrupting body wandered abroad," and a terrible plague broke out, decimating the local population. While the parish priest met with "a number of wise and devout men" together with other "leading citizens," two younger brothers whose father had died of the plague set out to avenge his death. "Mad with grief and anger," they dug up the vampire's corpse and struck it with a sharpened spade. "A stream of warm red gore" from the wound proved that the monster had "battened in the blood of many poor folk." The brothers dragged the corpse outside of the town and burned it in a large pyre while the parish priest and "the chief men of the district" watched. "No sooner had that infernal monster been thus destroyed than the plague, which had so sorely ravaged the people, entirely ceased, just as if the polluted air was

cleansed by the fire which burned up the hellish brute who had infected the whole atmosphere."[28]

3. In a Hungarian village a farmer died and three days after his death he returned to his son's home asking for food. First the son died, after refusing to give food the second time the vampire visited him, then nine other people of the village died, each telling of "a fearful dream" in which the dead man "seemed to glide into the room, catch them by the throat biting hard and suck the blood out of the wound." Since the apothecary could do nothing to save the victims, the local magistrate requested help from the "Commander of the Imperial forces," who arrived with two other military officers and the "common executioner." Opening the grave of the farmer, they found his eyes open and "glaring horribly" and his mouth "stained with fresh blood." The executioner then hammered a sharp stake through the vampire's heart, and blood gushed from "every orifice" of the corpse, which was then burned to ashes. "Garlic and whitethorn" were placed in the coffins of the vampire's victims, and "thenceforth the village was freed from any molestation."[29]

I do not offer these narratives (for the sake of convenience I will refer to them as Summers's stories) as archetypal or even typical narrative accounts of the confrontation between the living and the undead, although they do share certain structural characteristics and thematic emphases with several of the twentieth-century novels and films I will discuss later. And I am not—like Summers—interested in establishing the veracity of these three accounts. True (!) or false, they are above all stories of the life-or-death struggle between the living and the undead, stories of a deadly disequilibrium that gives way to stability and of an unexpected conflict that is ultimately resolved by the unequivocal triumph of the living over the undead. Let us briefly consider what Summers's stories suggest about the confrontation, the combatants, and the sort of questions we can ask concerning more recent and more complex stories.

The first and third of these accounts are patently social fables that emphasize the inability of the threatened family members and villagers to protect themselves, as well as the efficacy of accepted, hierarchical religious, military, and/or political authority. Without the intercession of the bishop and the imperial commander—who come from outside the threatened area and must be contacted through local figures of authority—the villagers will be driven mad by their fears or killed off one by one in their sleep. The saviors of society in the second story, however, are two young brothers motivated by the desire for vengeance, and these residents of the community are quite explicitly set apart from the ruling class, whose piety seems to do it little good. Here, personal actions have important public consequences, just as the private sins of the "depraved" man ultimately affect and infect the entire society.

In these three stories, as in all the works I will discuss, the identity—social status, age, and occupation—and the motives of the hunter are of the utmost significance; it is very different to owe one's safety to "priests and theologians" or to the "common executioner" than to two young brothers, "mad with grief and anger." Those human beings who challenge the undead act to ensure the survival of the living and often come to embody the particular fitness that enables man to win his struggle against the monster. In turn, the victims, potential victims, and impotent onlookers embody our vulnerability. Like these three stories, other versions of the confrontation between the living and the undead insist that we take into account not only the identity of the hunter and the victim, but also the relationship between the hunter, the victim, and the status quo, with its sanctioned authorities and its hallowed institutions. For example, Stoker in *Dracula* contrasts the newly formed community of courageous, mutually dependent vampire hunters with the selfishness and skepticism of late-Victorian society as well as with Count Dracula and his vampiric brides. Herzog in *Nosferatu the Vampyre* and Romero in his living dead films even more completely divorce their heroes from the ill-fated, deeply flawed status quo. One of my primary concerns, then, will be to examine the way stories of the living and the undead, above all through their presentation of man as hunter and victim, explore the nature of the status quo and the relationship between the public and the private, civic duty and personal desire. As we will soon see, several of these stories also consider the viability of—indeed, the necessity for—collective action and the possibility that the living can create a new community, akin to that type of social organization Ferdinand Tönnies calls Gemeinschaft.

All the works I will discuss define the strengths and weaknesses of the living in the context of the undead, who may appear as the antithesis or in some fashion the double of man. The aristocratic European vampire—the Dracula figure, Stoker's King-Vampire—is no doubt the most common image of the undead being, but even the three accounts from Summers's *The Vampire in Europe* suggest that the particular features of the monster and the danger it poses can vary a great deal from text to text: the vampire may be a creature who emerges from the grave to harass and terrify his family and neighbors or to drink the blood of the living or to spread a deadly pestilence throughout his native village. By noting the variation as well as the repetition in nineteenth- and twentieth-century representations of the undead, we can begin to chart the way these creatures speak to our understanding and our fear of evil and chaos, of desire and egotism, of slavish dependence and masterful control.

While it is important to situate the various portraits of the undead, from Stoker's King-Vampire to Romero's stumbling zombies, in relation to other representations of the monstrous threat—as a single creature (like Freud's image of the primal father) or as an overwhelming mass (like certain images of the mob)—the most essential context for the undead are the human beings these creatures stalk, feed on, and struggle against. Whatever their physical appearance, their special powers and unnatural appetites, or their particular sort of immortality, the undead betray their origins and remain recognizably, disturbingly, human; just as the vampires in Summers's stories are, in effect, local citizens, still somehow identifiable as fathers, husbands, farmers, or neighbors.

The confrontation between the living and the undead in these three stories exemplifies what Robin Wood calls the "simple and obvious basic formula for the horror film: normality is threatened by the Monster." For Wood, it is "the relationship between normality and the Monster that constitutes the essential subject of the horror film."[30] To the extent that they rely on this formula, horror stories, including the vampire stories I have paraphrased above, provide definitions of normality and the monstrous, as well as demonstrations of how easily normality can be threatened. For example, Murnau's *Nosferatu*—a film that Wood analyzes in detail—relies on this formula to prove the vulnerability and the inherent shortcomings of bourgeois society. Murnau, following Stoker and followed in turn by Browning (*Dracula* [1931]), Badham (*Dracula* [1979]), and Herzog (*Nosferatu the Vampyre*), also links the relationship between normality and the monster with the relationship between sanity and madness—particularly through the character of the vampire's human servant, Renfield, whose desires for immortality or power or for the security of being a slave to an all-powerful master become "proof" of his madness (though these are all thoroughly human desires, needless to say).

As my later discussions will make clear, the three stories from *The*

Vampire in Europe and a number of other stories of the living and the undead do not share the critique of normality undertaken in different ways by Murnau, Badham, Herzog, and Romero. Yet in Summers's stories, all life in the village and district is disrupted and endangered by the undead creature who wanders freely, infects the atmosphere, and enters the bedrooms and the dreams of the local citizens. As Wood suggests, the monster's threat (which in these three accounts seems almost to be a result of sheer spitefulness) generates the story. Once the living have triumphed, the district, the village, and the home are rendered safe and normal enough to no longer warrant our attention. I place much emphasis throughout this book on the precise way in which the return to normality is represented, for this image often defines what is most important in and to the world. Even when the blame is laid on Satan (as in the second of Summers's stories), these stories still show how monsters emerge from within the village and how the distance—literally and figuratively—between the normal and the monstrous collapses—collapses just as easily, we could say, as the distance between life and death. In a number of texts the monster's threatening actions and the loss of clear separation between normality and the monstrous are linked to scenes of invasion, assault, rape, and seduction and to an emphasis on the role of human beings as willing victims or conscious allies of the undead. All such scenes force us to take note of the origin of the monster (a topic often discussed in these stories): Is the threat truly exterior to us and our world, or is the image of the monster as invader a convenient way of displacing the threat from inside to outside? In this regard, the conventional notion that the vampire must be invited inside the safe dwelling (and thus into the consciousness) of the potential victim takes on a great deal of significance, as King makes clear in *'Salem's Lot.*

To Wood's formula, which directs us toward the importance of the threat and the relationship between normality and the monster, we can add or perhaps superimpose the pattern that Tudor offers for the "basic horror narrative." Horror movies, according to Tudor, conform to a "'seek-it-out-and-destroy-it pattern,'" for "the whole genre revolves around the creation or the discovery of an *it*, *its* recognition, seeking, and destruction."[31] Such a pattern is, for example, readily apparent in all three of Summers's stories. Tudor's formulation has the advantage of focusing our attention on the actions of those human beings who "seek-it-out-and-destroy-it," whereas Wood's definition of the genre emphasizes humans as victims and targets of the monster's threat. In all three accounts from *The Vampire in Europe*, the process of seeking and destroying involves actions—for example, digging up the vampire's grave—that are extraordinary and potentially dangerous, if not illegal and sacrilegious. This process differs in all three cases, depending, as I noted earlier, on exactly who is the destroyer and also on what the act of destruction entails. It is in the fleshing out of the narrative pattern Tudor describes that stories of the living and the undead reveal much of their ideological significance. Vary the identity of the hunter, the type of weapon wielded, or the mode of destruction, and the process of seeking and destroying the undead can range from a holy crusade into the primitive (Stoker's *Dracula*) to a methodical, futile exercise in genocide (Matheson's *I Am Legend*).

What remains constant in almost all examples of this genre, however, is that the threat posed by the undead and the defensive and retaliatory action undertaken by the living are presented in such a way as to bring us face to face with gushing blood and burning flesh (thereby linking us with the two young brothers, who see the "warm red gore" well out of the pierced vampire, rather than with the "leading citizens," who are off discussing the problem). Thus in the second and third of Summers's stories, the vicious attacks by the vampire are answered by the hunters' fires of purification and bloody acts of destruction and mutilation. In contrast to the marauding undead and the easily terrified and physically weak human victims, the young brothers are heroes, preservers of life, and so in a different sense are the executioner with his stake and the priests and theologians with their "chartula of episcopal absolution." By showing us the process of recognizing, seeking, and destroying the monster, stories of the living and the undead reveal the possibilities, if any, for individual heroism and collective effort and the efficacy of socially sanctioned, predetermined means of handling threatening disturbances—what the airmen in Christian Nyby's *The Thing* (1951) refer to with disdain as "standard operating procedure." In these stories the living must act to survive the threat posed by the undead, and through their actions in this life-or-death confrontation they demonstrate humankind's capabilities. Together, *Dracula*, *Nosferatu*, *Night of the Living Dead*, and the other works I will discuss offer an ongoing exploration, demonstration, and assessment of humanity's fitness.

It is above all in the conclusion of these works that we get the clearest sense of what it takes to survive and of the relationship between normality and the monster. For one thing, almost all of these stories are organized so that the most significant confrontation occurs at the end of the narrative, after earlier skirmishes in the course of recognizing and seeking out the undead (though even this convention is varied and challenged by Matheson and Romero, among others). I will spend considerable time discussing how stories of the living and the undead end, not only because these endings are so important narratively and thematically, but because the sense of an ending is especially resonant in stories involving vampires and the living dead.

With their insistence on flawed, tainted immortality and unquenchable, unnatural thirst, most stories of the living and the undead make us admit the absolute necessity for the end of "molestation" and terror, for the closure and peaceful stasis of what in *Dracula* is called "true death." Such stories seem to me to be inevitably about the nature and the function of endings in stories as in life. In particular, these works are about the conflicting desires for continuation and immortality, on the one hand, and for an ending that satisfactorily resolves all conflicts, on the other. Examining this genre lets us explore the ideological and psychological role of resolution in popular narrative and reconsider the commonly drawn distinction between "open" and "closed" endings.

Like Stoker's *Dracula* and Murnau's *Nosferatu*, the three brief accounts I quoted from *The Vampire in Europe* leave no possibility for a sequel: the monstrous threat has "entirely ceased," and the life of town, village, and family, we assume, can again take up its usual, uneventful course (under the protection of archdeacon or imperial officers), perhaps even strengthened by its ordeal. And this ordeal need not be repeated—unlike, for example, the annual rituals enacted for the expulsion of evil that Sir James George Frazer describes in *The Golden Bough*.[32] In Summers's stories the destruction of the undead is much more emphasized than the resumption of normality, which is almost taken for granted. But the concluding sequences to these stories do, in fact, account for the fate of the living, the monster, and the world that has been threatened. All three of these interrelated elements must be considered when we describe the degree of closure and the quality of resolution in any given story. Badham's *Dracula* and Romero's *Dawn of the Dead*, for instance, leave unsatisfied the desire for an unambiguous end to the threat, even as they question whether normality is worth saving or resuming—assuming that it could be saved or resumed, which in these films seems unlikely, if not impossible. Romero's open ending, however, is an affirmation of new, if dangerous, possibilities for the human survivors, while Badham's ending is above all an ironic comment on the failure of the vampire hunters and of the late-Victorian values they embody. Once again, it is by tracing the process of repetition and variation that we can best appreciate and analyze individual works and best follow the evolution of the entire genre.

For example, unlike Stoker's novel or Browning's adaptation of *Dracula*, in most stories of the living and the undead that have appeared during the 1970s and 1980s, the apparent or "true" death of the monster seems at best a remission, rarely a complete end to the disease, as the concluding sequence in Herzog's *Nosferatu the Vampyre* so stunningly demonstrates: because of a beautiful, pure woman's willing sacrifice, Nosferatu the vampire—in the shape of Count Dracula—dies, blinded and convulsed by the rays of the rising sun. Yet almost simultaneously, a new vampire is born, as Jonathan Harker is transformed into Nosferatu. "Bring me my horse," he declares to a servant, "I have much to do, now." In the final image of the film the new Nosferatu gallops into an endless wasteland of shifting sands and fleeting clouds, leaving the stationary camera and the viewer far behind as he disappears into the horizon. This conclusion shares and therefore perpetuates what is by 1979 a conventionalized lack of finality, but Herzog's ending differs dramatically from open-ended stories like *'Salem's Lot* and *Dawn of the Dead* in its image of the survival of the undead, as well as in its suggestions about the role of the viewer in the movement toward closure. In large part, the function of *The Living and the Undead* is to make precisely this type of discrimination, based on the rich interplay between genre, individual text, and reader.

Like Herzog's Nosferatu, Stoker's Count Dracula also insists that "there is work to be done" (D, 47), for both of these vampires—unlike the plague-bearing, bloodthirsty creatures in Summers's stories—make plans, wage campaigns, and articulate their desires and the goals that obsess them. The work that the undead must do—and hence the threat they pose to the living—is surely one of the most noteworthy aspects of these horror stories. To describe the vampire's activity as work, however, is both revealing and insufficient. Work for the undead can often be a purposeful mission and an act of creation or colonization. At times—as in *I Am Legend*, for example, or *Night of the Living Dead*—the work of the undead is merely the monotonous fulfillment of basic biological need, but in many stories the vampire is, so to speak, a connoisseur, and bloodsucking is an aesthetic occasion that provides pleasure as much as physical nourishment. Because of

Stoker's influence, as filtered through stage adaptations of *Dracula*, Universal horror films of the 1930s and 1940s, and Hammer films twenty years later, the vampire seems perpetually about to caress and violate the beautiful, reclining body of a mesmerized, and in some fashion willing, virginal young woman. (To this image of work as an act of seduction or quasi-mystical initiation we may compare the ravaging brutality of the creatures in *'Salem's Lot* or the Hungarian vampire described in *The Vampire in Europe*, who rips open his victims' throats and laps up their blood like some starving, predatory animal.) Yet the vampire's attack in Stoker's *Dracula* extends much further than the seductive deflowering of a passive maiden. In the stories I will discuss, the undead come to threaten not only the solitary woman or man or child: when the sun sets, the family, the society, even the entire world can and do have their lifeblood drained.

And so the living must also work—to challenge, mutilate, and destroy an often ancient adversary to defend themselves, to survive, to protect, and even perhaps to redeem that which they deem most valuable in the world. "It must be steadily borne in mind," Summers concludes after describing the destruction of a vampire in eighteenth-century Greece, "that the people had to cope with a most malignant and terrible foe and in order to destroy him they were obliged to employ rough and terrible methods."[33] To employ such methods is to undertake what Van Helsing calls the "wild work" of destruction—bloody, dangerous work that is primitive by our civilized standards. (At times this wild work clearly resembles the ritualized destruction of a scapegoat, whose death restores or revitalizes society.) Stories of the living and the undead place beleaguered human beings in a position in which they are "obliged"—as Summers puts it—to carry out such work, regardless of how abhorrent and unthinkable they find the rough and terrible methods to be.

Just as the stumbling, zombielike creatures in *I Am Legend* are vastly different from the commanding, cosmopolitan Count Draculas of Bela Lugosi and Christopher Lee, so, too, the rough and terrible methods employed by the living vary from text to text, as even the three brief accounts quoted earlier demonstrate. A "chartula of episcopal absolution" is not the same as a funeral pyre, a sharpened spade, a stake, or a handful of whitethorn and garlic. The choice of weapons is always significant (even when the weapon is not already symbolic, like the cross), for it begins to suggest what resources the living have at their disposal, what sort of assistance they can count on, and what qualities and values they need if they are to survive. The vampire hunters in Summers's stories and all subsequent hunters in this genre are to a great extent defined by their weapons and by the particular rough and terrible methods they employ. Their actions against the monster can be taken as a commentary on the role of ritual and convention and on the degree, if any, that traditional methods can be varied. By focusing, as these stories themselves do, on the wild work of the living and the weapons they wield against the undead, we again confront the process of repetition and difference, which here involves the relationship among tradition, authority, and prescribed methods, on the one hand, and innovation, independence, and imaginative individual action, on the other.

In *Dracula*, for example, Stoker quite clearly contrasts the wild work of the living (carried out under the authoritative direction of Van Helsing) with both the self-serving, destructive work of Count Dracula and the mundane work of a supposedly safe, unruffled world. The young, upper-middle-class men and women in Stoker's novel initially take work to refer to daily personal and household tasks and to the labor required by one's occupation. Yet, as Dracula's invasion of England proceeds, the term becomes more and more associated with the quest to destroy the vampire and protect his victims. The living give up their ordinary, everyday vocations and avocations and undertake the "work" of "destruction" (D, 222), the "bloody work" (D, 207), the "butcher work" (D, 375). Such activity is not a source of livelihood, but of life itself—and of salvation as well. Wild work in Stoker's *Dracula* is proven to be an absolutely necessary sacred duty, regardless of how barbaric, superstitious, and unscientific it seems. "We must so work," Van Helsing tells his young allies, "that other poor souls shall perish not, whilst we can save" (D, 243). Bloody acts of butchery are thus revealed to be good works that serve both God and man; these vampire hunters find justification through wild work.

Not all stories of the living and the undead follow *Dracula* in presenting wild work as a holy crusade that serves God and the community (*I Am Legend* and *Dawn of the Dead*, for instance, thoroughly reject Stoker's presentation of "butcher work" as good works), though throughout the genre, the bloody confrontation between man and monster is linked with questions about the role of faith and the status of science in the modern world—in the broadest sense, with the relationship between civilization and the primitive. Furthermore, all of the stories since *Dracula* can be seen in part as implicit commentaries on what C. Wright Mills, among many other social critics, has characterized as the "conditions of modern work." As we shall see, in most cases the work of both the living and the undead is not an alienating, dissatisfying, economic necessity; it is not, in Mills's words, "a sacrifice of time, necessary to building a life outside of it."[34] Here work is life, and the living are given the opportunity to take meaningful action that will determine their own destiny.

The "butcher work" of destroying vampires in Stoker's novel is an act of violence, as are Count Dracula's attacks on innocent maidens and conscience-stricken madmen. Stephen Neale correctly observes that "what defines the specificity" of the horror film—and, I believe, of most forms of the horror story—"is not the violence as such, but its conjunction with images and definitions of the monstrous."[35] Stories of the living and the undead both explore the nature and the function of violence and the monstrous and also juxtapose the violence directed against the undead with the violence carried out by these creatures. In so doing, these stories offer a range of opinion and a dramatic rendering of what violence has come to mean in the twentieth century: from, for example, the image of obligatory, sacrificial, ritualistic holy butchery in Stoker's *Dracula*—an act that ennobles, matures, or otherwise positively transforms the hunter and restores or redeems the world—to Matheson's and Romero's demythologization of the wild work in *Dracula* and their rejection of heroic violence that almost magically manages to destroy the prey without ever negatively affecting the hunter. Let us now turn to these particular works and other stories of the living and the undead to trace the conjunction of violence and the monstrous, the role of work, the relationship between normality and the monster, and the other topics that this genre ponders, explores, and brings to life as narratives for our entertainment.

NOTES

1. Bram Stoker, *Dracula* (1897; rpt. New York: New American Library, 1978), p. 207. All future references to Stoker's *Dracula*, abbreviated D, will be included parenthetically in my text.
2. Montague Summers, *The Vampire: His Kith and Kin* (1928; rpt. New Hyde Park, N.Y.: University Books, 1960), p. xxiv.
3. David Pirie, *The Vampire Cinema* (London: Hamlyn, 1977), p. 100.
4. Ernest Jones, *On the Nightmare* (1951; rpt. New York: Liveright, 1971), pp. 98, 120, 130.

5. James Ursini and Alain Silver, *The Vampire Film* (New York: A. S. Barnes, 1975), pp. 54–55. This emphasis on the "character of the vampire" as the "core of the fiction" is also found in Leonard Wolf's impressionistic *A Dream of Dracula: In Search of the Living Dead* (New York: Popular Library, 1972), which ranges from Gilles de Rais and Mick Jagger to Stoker's *Dracula* and William Beaudine's *Billy the Kid vs. Dracula* (1966). Much more than Wolf's study, Ornella Volta's *The Vampire*, trans. Raymond Rudorff (1962; rpt. New York: Award Books, n.d.) focuses on the deeds of actual vampirelike criminals (necrophiliacs, "necro-sadists," and so on) and on the undead creatures present in folklore and myth.

6. Although I make several references to *Vampyr* in later chapters, I have not included a separate analysis of this film adaptation of Sheridan Le Fanu's *Carmilla* because *Vampyr* is not a retelling of Stoker's *Dracula* (as are the films I discuss in Part Two and Part Three), nor is it a story set in modern America involving legions of the undead (as are the works I discuss in Part Four). For the same reason, I do not examine in detail other adaptations of *Carmilla* (such as Roger Vadim's *Blood and Roses* [1960] and Roy Ward Baker's *The Vampire Lovers* [1970]) and the many European variations on the story of the living and the undead, from nineteenth-century romantic poetry and prose, Spanish vampire films, and Jean Rollins's series of sexually explicit films in the late 1960s and early 1970s to German films like Harry Kumel's *Daughters of Darkness* (1970) and Ulli Lommel's *Tenderness of the Wolves* (1973).

For further information on *Vampyr*, see Dreyer's script for the film (included in *Carl Theodor Dreyer: Four Screenplays* [Bloomington: Indiana University Press, 1970]) and two detailed discussions of the film: Mark Nash, "*Vampyr* and the Fantastic," *Screen* 17 (Autumn 1976), 29–67; and David Bordwell, *The Films of Carl-Theodor Dreyer* (Berkeley: University of California Press, 1981), pp. 93–116. In particular, I wholeheartedly recommend Bordwell's insightful, convincing analysis of Dreyer's cinematic, narrative, and thematic concerns in *Vampyr*. This essay is a model of film criticism at its best.

7. Harold Bloom, *The Anxiety of Influence: A Theory of Poetry* (New York: Oxford University Press, 1973), p. 91. Bloom's attempt to move beyond the "failed enterprise of seeking to 'understand' any single poem as an entity in itself" (ibid., p. 43) constitutes a unique program in contemporary literary theory. He proposes that "criticism is the art of knowing the hidden roads that go from poem to poem" (ibid., p. 96), roads that he maps out as six "revisionary ratios" in *Anxiety of Influence.* Though the process of "creative revisionism," as Bloom defines it, does seem to help explain the relationship between Herzog's *Nosferatu the Vampyre* and Murnau's *Nosferatu*, for example, I would agree with Frank Lentricchia, who convincingly criticizes Bloom's "elitism" and his exclusion of the "extraliterary" (*After the New Criticism* [Chicago: University of Chicago Press, 1980], pp. 319–46). My decision to examine stories of the living and the undead can itself be taken as a response to what Lentricchia calls Bloom's emphasis on the "strong" poet's "splendidly isolated dialogue with his strong ancestors" and on the equally strong critic's revision and correction of this dialogue (ibid., p. 343). Bloom states this position most clearly

in *The Breaking of Vessels* (Chicago: University of Chicago Press, 1982), pp. 27–32.

8. In discussing the classical detective story, Cawelti defines a formula as "a conventional way of defining and developing a particular kind of situation or situations, a pattern of action or development of this situation, a certain group of characters and the relations between them, and a setting or type of setting appropriate to the characters and action" (*Adventure, Mystery, and Romance: Formula Stories as Art and Popular Culture* [Chicago: University of Chicago Press, 1976], p. 80).

9. For a survey of the use of genre in literary criticism and theory, see Paul Hernadi, *Beyond Genre: New Directions in Literary Classification* (Ithaca, N.Y.: Cornell University Press, 1972). Heather Dubrow's *Genre* (New York: Methuen, 1982) is a useful short introduction, and Claudio Guillén's chapters on the picaresque in *Literature as System: Essays toward the Theory of Literary History* (Princeton: Princeton University Press, 1971) are a particularly effective example of genre criticism in practice. Stephen Neale's *Genre* (London: British Film Institute, 1980), one of the most noteworthy recent theoretical discussions of popular film genres, is an attempt to "relocate the discussion of and the importance accorded to genre," particularly "in light of the overlapping but by no means homogeneously co-existent fields of semiotics, psychoanalysis, and post-Althusserian Marxism" (p. 5).

10. Cawelti, *Adventure, Mystery, and Romance*, pp. 80–98.

11. Thomas Schatz, *Hollywood Genres: Formulas, Filmmaking, and the Studio System* (New York: Random House, 1981), pp. 21–22. For a critique of the "concept of iconography" as it has been applied in the study of popular film genres, see Neale, *Genre*, pp. 7–17.

12. Leo Braudy, *The World in a Frame: What We See in Films* (Garden City, N.Y.: Anchor Books, 1977), p. 105.

13. Neale, *Genre*, p. 13.

14. Tzvetan Todorov, *The Fantastic: A Structural Study of a Literary Genre*, trans. Richard Howard (1973; rpt. Ithaca, N.Y.: Cornell University Press, 1975), pp. 101, 141. See Christine Brooke-Rose's discussion of Todorov in *A Rhetoric of the Unreal* (Cambridge: Cambridge University Press, 1981), pp. 55–71.

15. Stanley Cavell, *Pursuits of Happiness: The Hollywood Comedy of Remarriage* (Cambridge, Mass.: Harvard University Press, 1981), pp. 30–32.

16. Bloom, *Anxiety of Influence*, pp. 42, 71.

17. Cavell, *Pursuits of Happiness*, p. 31. See also Todorov, *Fantastic*, pp. 41–57.

18. My assumptions throughout this study challenge what I find to be simplistic assertions about the ahistoricality of popular genres, such as those present, for example, in Thomas Sobchack, "Genre Film: A Classical Experience," *Literature/Film Quarterly* 3 (1975), 196–204.

19. Braudy, *World in a Frame*, pp. 109–11.

20. George A. Romero, Afterword to *Martin* (New York: Stein and Day, 1977), p. 209.

21. Schatz, *Hollywood Genres*, pp. 37–38.

22. Andrew Tudor, *Image and Influence: Studies in the Sociology of Film* (New York: St. Martin's, 1974), pp. 228, 225–26.

23. Ibid., pp. 195, 232. Tudor's *Image and Influence* serves as a necessary critique of the reductive bias common to many "vulgar Marxist" analyses of popular culture. For example, Judith Hess concludes that "American genre films" (presumably *all* American genre films) "serve the interests of the ruling class by assisting in the maintenance of the status quo." From Hess's perspective the horror film depicts a world split between the masses and the "hereditary aristocracy," and its "message is clear; science must not be allowed to replace traditional values and beliefs . . . the existing class structure prevents chaos." Vampire stories are often concerned with traditional values and beliefs, but they do not all deliver this simple, reactionary message ("Genre Films and the Status Quo," *Jump Cut* 1 [May-June 1974], 1, 16, 18; rpt. in *Film Genre: Theory and Criticism*, ed. Barry K. Grant [Metuchen, N.J.: Scarecrow Press, 1977], pp. 53–54, 58).

24. Cawelti, *Adventure, Mystery, and Romance*, pp. 35–36.

25. Braudy, *World in a Frame*, p. 124.

26. One important additional function of popular art, as Tudor notes, is to "find ways to justify the unjustifiable" (*Image and Influence*, p. 218); another is to provide, in Schatz's phrase, "an array of ideological strategies for negotiating social conflicts" (*Hollywood Genres*, p. 29); a third is to offer what Will Wright in a study of the western calls "a model of social action" (*Sixguns and Society: A Structural Study of the Western* [Berkeley: University of California Press, 1975], p. 188).

27. Montague Summers, *The Vampire in Europe* (1929; rpt. New Hyde Park, N.Y.: University Books, 1961), pp. 80–81.

28. Ibid., pp. 85–88.

29. Ibid., pp. 149–50.

30. Robin Wood, "Return of the Repressed," *Film Comment* 14 (July-Aug. 1978), 25–32; rpt. in *The American Nightmare: Essays on the Horror Film*, ed. Robin Wood and Richard Lippe (Toronto: Festival of Festivals, 1979), p. 14. Wood's "formula" is convincingly explained and applied in the other essays that appear in this volume.

31. Tudor, *Image and Influence*, p. 209. A more recent attempt to define the formula of horror stories, employing a "morphological" method, such as Cawelti develops in *Adventure, Mystery, and Romance*, is William M. Clements, "Formula as Genre in Popular Horror Literature," *Research Studies* 49 (June 1981), 116–23.

32. See Sir James George Frazer, *The Golden Bough: A Study in Magic and Religion*, abr. ed. in 1 vol. (1922; rpt. New York: Macmillan, 1951), pp. 633–86.

33. Summers, *Vampire in Europe*, p. 250.

34. C. Wright Mills, *White Collar: The American Middle Classes* (New York: Oxford University Press, 1956), pp. 224, 228.

35. Neale, *Genre*, p. 21.

PART ONE

The Moral Community and the King-Vampire

Professor Van Helsing: We, too, are not without strength. We have on our side power of combination—a power denied to the vampire kind.

Dracula (1897)

It is our purpose to study the sentiments and motives which draw people to each other, keep them together, and induce them to joint action.

Ferdinand Tönnies
Community and Society

CHAPTER

2

Into the Twentieth Century

WRITTEN AT NEARLY the beginning of our century, Bram Stoker's *Dracula* (1897) is the single most influential of all stories of the living and the undead; indeed, it is among the most influential of all horror stories. Yet Stoker's novel is not the first such story published in English—that distinction is generally accorded to John Polidori's *The Vampyre* (1819). *Dracula* is not even the only Victorian vampire story to be adapted for the movies and to be often reprinted in the twentieth century, for there is Sheridan Le Fanu's *Carmilla* (1871), which today remains much more than a long-forgotten curiosity piece. Nonetheless, *Dracula* provides the best and most appropriate introduction to the series of works I will discuss. Rather than being a footnote to or an imitation of *Dracula*, the story of the living and the undead as it develops in the twentieth century is an ongoing process of retelling and revisioning Stoker's narrative and in various ways modifying, reaffirming, or challenging the assumptions that inform *Dracula*. Accordingly, we will enter the genre, so to speak, through Stoker's novel, and *Dracula* will serve as a reference point throughout the discussion.

This chapter begins with a reading of *Dracula* and concludes by placing Stoker's novel in the context of *The Vampyre* and *Carmilla*, of several vampire stories published between 1890 and 1925, of Stoker's other horror stories, and of the "myth of the father of the primal horde" that Freud explores in his studies of culture and group psychology. Comparing *Dracula* with these works and reading these stories in light of Stoker's novel help both to define the specific features of the confrontation between the living and the undead in *Dracula* and to suggest this genre's "inventory of options" as twentieth-century stories like F. W. Murnau's *Nosferatu* (1922), Hamilton Deane and John L. Balderston's *Dracula: The Vampire Play* (1927), and Tod Browning's *Dracula* (1931) begin to appear.

In Stoker's hands the story of the living and the undead becomes the story of how, in the face of the enormous threat posed by the vampire, the living form a new community and together carry out the ritualized violence necessary to rid the world of the undead. In the course of discussing *Dracula*, I will set Stoker's image of the community against Ferdinand Tönnies's classic distinction between Gemeinshaft and Gesellschaft, and compare the assumptions about violence in *Dracula* with Freud's speculations concerning collective violence and Hannah Arendt's remarks about creative violence. Let us begin, however, at the beginning of Stoker's narrative with Jonathan Harker's journey to Transylvania, an episode that could be said to parallel the reader's entrance into this novel and this entire genre—for, during this opening journey, the sightseer becomes a confused and frightened witness to horror and the innocent traveler a potential victim. Jonathan's adventures in Count Dracula's homeland are a particularly effective example of what Walter M. Clements calls the "Polyphemous type" of horror formula, which involves "an encounter with an alien being or state in an exotic locale and an escape—at least physically—from the alien force."[1] Presented in Jonathan's own first-person account, the type of formula Clements identifies becomes for Stoker a means of emphasizing the visitor's realization—resembling both an awakening and a lapsing into nightmare—that monsters exist and that evil has an almost irresistible appeal.

At the same time Jonathan's journey to Transylvania, a business trip that draws this middle-class, commonsensical solicitor into the "imaginative whirlpool" that is the "East" (D, 12), demonstrates the vulnerability of the isolated modern man who is immersed in the primitive. Initially, Jonathan is an open-eyed if somewhat condescending tourist, filling his journal with facts and personal observations about the scenic beauty of nature and the quaint local color of paprika-spiced food and picturesque peasants. Armed with factual knowledge of the area gleaned from the books and maps of the British Museum, enlightened by the tenets of lukewarm Anglicanism, well-versed in law and real estate, Jonathan is a late Victorian with modest expectations who has no trouble in perceiving and actively pursuing his "duty." His own "queer dreams" (D, 12) and the many cryptic warnings of superstitious local inhabitants go unheeded, for "there was business to be done" and nothing must be allowed "to interfere with it" (D, 15).

The redefinition of duty and the transformation of this innocuous excursion into a spiritual quest that will lead through temptation and suffering to redemption begin when Jonathan becomes not merely a tourist, but truly a stranger in a strange land. (As Count Dracula so fully realizes, "A stranger in a strange land, he is no one" [D, 30].) After leaving the company of terrified peasants and entering the coach that will transport him over the Borgo Pass to Dracula's castle, Jonathan becomes increasingly passive and isolated, trapped alone inside the coach by the forbidding darkness and the roving wolves outside. Carried on a circuitous route into the night that destroys his sense of both spatial direction and chronological time, Jonathan enters a world in which "reality" and the most "awful nightmare" inextricably merge to create a "paralysis of fear" (D, 22–23). Ironically, for Jonathan the castle and its English-speaking host herald a return to the normality of business and social intercourse (even though the British Museum maps do not note the "exact locality" of Castle Dracula [D, 12]). Thus this naive young man enters the vampire's domain "freely" of his "own will" (D, 25) and is easily led to adopt the Count's "night-existence" (D, 34). However, once Jonathan begins to glimpse the threat that Dracula poses, "safety and the assurance of safety" disappear, and the man of real estate begins to doubt even his own sanity (D, 44).

As is the case in so many horror stories, both false, opiatic security and well-intentioned, if imprudent, exploration render the potential victim even more vulnerable. After Jonathan realizes the impossibility of communicating with his fiancée, Mina, and the rest of the outside world, the castle becomes a labyrinthine prison that, when explored, leads past innumerable closed doors to a room where, "in old times, possibly some fair lady sat to pen . . . her ill-spent love-letter" (D, 44). Alone in the ancient "fair lady's" room, far removed from all traces of the business and morality of late nineteenth-century England, Jonathan encounters the three brides of Dracula, who embody that which he most desires and most fears. "In an agony of delightful anticipation," he passively waits with eyes closed for the "voluptuous" brides to satisfy his "wicked, burning desire" as he feels the "hard dents of two sharp teeth" upon his exposed neck (D, 46, 47). Only by the grace of Dracula is Jonathan's physical desire left unfulfilled and thus his soul—for the time being—saved.

Isolated and left to his own devices and dreams, Jonathan does in a sense become "no one," for all the fragile foundations of his public identity begin to disintegrate in Castle Dracula, where he is without the "protection of the law" (D, 53). "Action!" is what saves Jonathan (D, 55); even though he fails in his courageous attempt to destroy the monster, Jonathan manages to escape from the castle after the Count departs. However, survival—at this point in the novel—is not the same as victory. Jonathan alone is no match for the vampire. The eager solicitor and expectant fiancé is merely a pawn who unwittingly fulfills his part in Dracula's ambitious strategy.[2]

Jonathan's journey to Transylvania (chapters 1–4 of the novel) serves as the necessary prelude to the other journeys that figure prominently in *Dracula*—the Count's invasion of England, the trek to Lucy Westenra's tomb, and the final holy crusade that moves eastward to rid the world of the undead.[3] Similarly, this opening section of the novel introduces several interrelated motifs that form the ideological structure of Stoker's narrative: the dangerous, hypnotizing appeal of physical beauty; the saving quality of action; the disorienting departure from modern civilization; and the troubling convergence of nightmare and wish-fulfillment. Yet perhaps most important is the overwhelming impression of Jonathan's "dread loneliness" (D, 44), for comparable images of isolation and vulnerability are found throughout *Dracula*: the ship captain binding himself to the wheel of the *Demeter* after his crew has all died, Renfield alone in his madman's cell, Lucy Westenra sleepwalking in a moonlit graveyard with "not a sign of any living thing about" (D, 101), Mina Harker forced to suck blood from the breast of the vampire while her husband sleeps beside her.

Thus the organization of the novel as a collection of letters, memoranda, journals, and diary entries is appropriate, even though Stoker is not very successful in capturing the subtleties of dialect and accent. For as the first-person narration shifts from character to character, revealing ironic misperceptions and cross-purposed actions, the limitations of each individual perspective are exposed.[4] Unlike the protagonists and victims of much twentieth-century horror, the narrators in *Dracula* are not guilt-ridden, apathetically faithless, or "evil" in any traditional sense; yet, because they are isolated individuals each telling and living his or her own story, the modern civilized world they inhabit is particularly susceptible to the vampire's assault. As Jonathan's journey begins to suggest, the foreign threat that stretches out of the past to invade the present can only be countered by a community, a group of human beings who can, in Mina's words, "all work together" (D, 301).[5]

One type of group in *Dracula* is the Russian crew of the *Demeter*, the ship that unknowingly transports the vampire to England. Organized into a strict hierarchy, these men appear to be competent and experienced. Yet, as the crew becomes increasingly aware of a strange presence aboard the ship, a "panic of superstitious fear" spreads (D, 92), and in its wake come the potential for mutinous violence and then "madness" and suicide. One by one the group disintegrates, until finally only the Captain is left alive, terrified, but determined to "baffle" the "fiend" by tying himself to the wheel and praying to "God and the Blessed Virgin and the saints" (D, 95). Regardless of his courageous allegiance to his duty, however, the Captain fails, and his failure is a reminder that the isolated individual cannot halt the progress of the vampire. More important, the Captain's faith—much deeper than anything Jonathan demonstrates in Transylvania—assures neither protection nor salvation: "only God can guide us in the fog, which seems to move with us," he writes, "and God seems to have deserted us" (D, 94). The failure of the *Demeter*'s crew suggests that a highly organized, all-male group cannot combat Dracula, even when this group is itself from the East and when its pious leader senses the magnitude of the evil he confronts and is willing to sacrifice himself in the name of duty.[6]

No more effective than the crew of the *Demeter* is an even more basic social unit, the family. From Mina's first letter to Lucy, courtship and marriage figure prominently in *Dracula* (not least in the actions of the vampire and his brides), but until the final page of the novel there are virtually no extended families in Stoker's vision of middle- and upper-class England. Both the American Quincey Morris and Dr. John Seward, who runs the asylum where Renfield is kept, have no parents—no blood relatives at all, in fact, though both are young men (Seward, for all of his professional responsibility, is only twenty-nine years old). And the closest person Mina and Jonathan have to a parent is Jonathan's employer and benefactor. Although the Harkers are left materially secure when this kindly old man dies, leaving his home and business to Jonathan, Mina admits that "it really seems as though we had lost a father" (D, 164). Arthur Holmwood's father also dies of natural causes during the novel, but not before his long illness forces Arthur, who remains true to his filial "duty" (D, 124), to leave the side of his fiancée, Lucy Westenra, rendering her more vulnerable to Dracula's nocturnal visits. Lucy receives even less aid from her mother than from her fiancé, for Mrs. Westenra's weak heart and overall physical fragility force the others to keep Lucy's situation a secret from her. So when Mrs. Westenra, with the best of intentions, opens a window and removes a garland of garlic flowers from Lucy's neck, she allows the vampire free access to her daughter. The ultimate irony, however—and the scene which summarizes the status of the traditional family in the novel—occurs when a wolf under Dracula's control appears at Lucy's window. Terrified, Mrs. Westenra again inadvertently tears the garlic flowers from Lucy's neck and then falls dead upon her daughter's reclining body: "dear mother's poor body, which seemed to grow cold already . . . weighed me down" (D, 151).

Lucy is isolated and imprisoned in the bedroom of her family home, the most familiar and yet in *Dracula* the most easily invaded domain. Terrified and helpless, she appeals to God to "shield me from harm this night!" (D, 152), but her prayer seems to go unanswered. Literally burdened by her mother's corpse, Lucy suffers the attack that ultimately transforms her into a vampire. Her fate is even more disturbing than Jonathan's because she has not journeyed to the mysterious East. Except for her sleepwalking excursions, Lucy remains at home—protected, loved, watched over. Still she is repeatedly drained of blood and then finally captured by Dracula, an apparently unstoppable predator who appears almost always in nonhuman form during this section of the novel (chapters 5–16), mocking by his success the well-intentioned, hopelessly inadequate plans and precautions of the living.

Into the vacuum left by dead or dying parents steps Dr. Abraham Van Helsing, a surrogate father who redeems Lucy, unites the orphaned children, and is thus himself rescued from a "barren and lonely" life (D, 191). (Stoker assumes without question that a strong paternal figure is not just important, but essential; left to their own devices, the young people will not live long enough to gain maturity.) Jonathan is only a lawyer and Seward only a scientist, but Van Helsing is a Renaissance man in an age of specialization, and his credentials are indeed impressive. By occupation, he is a lawyer, "a philosopher and a metaphysician, and one of the most advanced scientists of his day" (D, 121). Along with his age and gender, what qualifies him to be a paternal figure and guide, however, is his temperament. With an "absolutely open mind" (D, 121), Van Helsing can acknowledge and respect the "mysteries in life" that lie beyond the understanding of science (D, 197), mysteries that include both God and Dracula. Being aware of these mysteries, the Professor also realizes what Jonathan and Lucy so painfully come to understand, that "to be alone is to be full of fears and alarms" (D, 165). To an "iron nerve" and "indomitable resolution" that are like those of the Captain of the *Demeter*, Van Helsing also adds the "kindliest and truest heart" (D, 121) and the abiding faith of a benevolent Christian patriarch. Significantly, Van Helsing, like Dracula, is a foreigner. Both the height of wisdom and the depth of evil are alien to the placid superficialities of modern England, and thus the stage is set for a melodramatic one-to-one confrontation between two worthy opponents with the future of British civilization at stake.

Yet this confrontation never occurs. Even with all of Van Helsing's secular and spiritual qualifications, he alone cannot destroy the "King-Vampire" (D, 374).[7] And this fact is essential, because *Dracula* is, perhaps above all, the story of the formation and growth of a community, a story that proves that the foremost source of strength the living possess is, as Van Helsing realizes, the "power of combination" (D, 244). In this emphasis on community, *Dracula* differs substantially from Mary Shelley's *Frankenstein*, nineteenth-century ghost stories, and even from many twentieth-century stories of the living and the undead. For example, as I will discuss in chapter 3, the narrative structure and ideological implications of Browning's 1931 version of *Dracula* set this film far apart from Stoker's novel. Closely following Deane and Balderston's melodramatic 1924 stage adaptation of the novel, Browning repeatedly pits Van Helsing directly against Dracula, until in the final sequence the elderly Doctor, with no assistance, drives a stake he himself has fashioned through the vampire's heart, thereby preserving the world of the living. Stoker, who served for years as stage manager of the Lyceum Theater and as Henry Irving's personal secretary, was thoroughly familiar with Victorian melodrama, but in the novel there are heroes rather than a hero, and while Van Helsing is necessary, he is not by himself sufficient to banish the "devil in callous" (D, 243).

Initially, the community of the good forms around Van Helsing, the sole person to understand the cause of Lucy's mysterious "illness" and to realize that only a concerted effort will defeat Dracula. As father and guide, Van Helsing provides the patient wisdom and practical instruction that console Arthur's grief, channel Quincey's instinctive propensity for rash action, and expand Seward's limited "scientific" perspective. Well before Van Helsing arrives in England, however, these three young men share a long-standing friendship and a love for Lucy Westenra that does not diminish when she rejects the marriage proposals of Quincey and Seward and elects to wed Arthur. If anything, their concern for Lucy increases after Van Helsing is summoned by Seward to diagnose Lucy's "illness." Yet even their transfusions of blood cannot save the stricken young woman. Through the commingling of their blood with Lucy's, the selfless and well-intentioned suitors all symbolically marry the object of their wholly legitimate desire, but it is Dracula who enters the marriage bed and truly possesses the innocent virgin. By deflowering Lucy—regardless of the garlic flowers that Van Helsing, the surrogate father, places in her bedroom—the more experienced Count captures the prize that Quincey, Seward, and Arthur seek but never speak of. Lucy "dies," soon to be reborn as a woman and a vampire, and the young men's naive chivalry, selfless concern, and boys' school friendship will not suffice to restore her purity.

The all-important first stage in the transformation of these young men into an effective force of good occurs when Van Helsing leads Quincey, Seward, and Arthur to Lucy's tomb. Van Helsing provides the physical tools with which to kill the vampire, the historical and folkloric knowledge of the undead, and the exemplary faith required to believe in that which seems impossible. England, it would appear, has become too civilized to acknowledge, much less be able to destroy an evil that is as ancient as it is malignant. Guided by Van Helsing, the group leaves the nineteenth century and civilization as they know it, for the four men must journey from the well-lit but false security of the home and the mental institution into the night, leaving the industrialized "life of a great city" (D, 215) for the darkness of nature. Illegally the men enter the tomb, and sacrilegiously they desecrate Lucy's corpse, for their duty transcends English law and Anglican tenets, which contain no guidelines for the "thorny paths" (D, 211) that the group must traverse.

These paths lead to Lucy, who, with blood staining her lips and the "purity of her lawn death-robe" (D, 217), holds a small child to her breast. Through Dracula's embrace the would-be wife and mother has become aggressive and animalistic, driven by the most basic physical needs to feed off rather than nurture children. Like the vampire brides Jonathan encounters in Transylvania, Lucy is a beautiful siren, and Arthur very nearly succumbs to her "voluptuous wantonness" (D, 217) and overt sexual invitation. She is Dracula's creation; more than a nightmarish distortion of Victorian femininity, the undead Lucy is a woman whose beauty and physical desires are totally divorced from morality and the social conventions that govern and limit female behavior.[8] Perhaps most disturbing of all is that the undead Lucy, this "nightmare of Lucy" (D, 220), is still recognizably, unmistakably Lucy Westenra—calling her a cat or a dog or a devil (as Seward does in his account of the scene) cannot change this fundamental fact. To regain Lucy's "unequalled sweetness and purity" (D, 222) and to free her from hunger and render her completely passive and nonthreatening, the men must not merely kill her, but also butcher and mutilate her body. If Dracula's attacks on Lucy are loosely veiled sexual encounters in which sex and death merge in the unity of passionate, forbidden love, the "mercy-bearing stake" wielded by Arthur enters his fiancée's body with the violence of rape, as she "quivers" while her blood "wells and spurts" (D, 222). By cutting off her head and filling her mouth with garlic, Van Helsing and Seward complete the desecration of Lucy's physical beauty and ensure the salvation of her soul.

The mutilation and murder of the undead Lucy are ritual acts that preserve society, yet in committing these deeds the group is forced to become almost as "foreign" as Dracula, moving far beyond the legal boundaries, moral beliefs, and scientific assumptions of late nineteenth-century England. The journey to Lucy's tomb, supervised by Van Helsing, has proven the efficacy of and the necessity for ritualized action and unwavering faith, just as Lucy's funeral, managed with "obsequious suavity" (D, 170) by professional undertakers, demonstrates the bankruptcy of communal ritual in the modern world. Baptized in Lucy's blood, Arthur, Seward, and Quincey in effect lose their virginity and enter the world of experience. The individual men are forged into a community when they are initiated into the "primitive," a domain where life is governed by the rhythm of sun and moon and where the spiritual struggle of Good and Evil is the basis of reality. After their bloody, "unhallowed work" (D, 205), the three young men each shake hands with Van Helsing and vow to undertake the "great quest" to destroy the King-Vampire, a "terrible task" fraught with "danger" and "pain" (D, 223–24). Nonetheless, the group is still incomplete and unable to defeat Dracula.

With the inclusion of Jonathan and Mina Harker, the community of the good gains the two people it lacks. Appropriately, each member of the group contributes unique skills and qualities of mind or character necessary for the larger unified effort. And as in many popular narratives that focus on the possibility of collective action, the individuals who constitute Stoker's ideal community are quasi-allegorical representatives of various human types and social classes: age allies with youth, and men with women; law and commerce join forces with science and medicine; the rising middle class unites with the landed aristocracy (since Arthur Holmwood becomes Lord Godalming upon the death of his father); England, potentially stagnating by virtue of its insularity, is invigorated by the energetic heroism of America and enlightened by the far-reaching wisdom of the continent.[9] Only this grand alliance will preserve civilization and thereby inherit the twentieth century. In a gesture that ritualistically formalizes their "solemn compact," these diverse people join hands, forming a circle around a table upon which rests a golden crucifix (D, 244).

Before this group can begin its pursuit of the vampire, however, the hunters must collate "every scrap of evidence" into a "connected" chronological narrative (D, 231). Mina's letters to Lucy, no less than Seward's diary, are essential, for each individual account contributes significantly to the larger narrative. ("This is the merit of entire, or collected, narrative," a character in Stoker's *The Jewel of the Seven Stars* [1912] declares, "isolated facts, doubts, suspicions, conjectures, give way to a homogeneity which is convincing."[10]) This project allows the entire group to trace the events of the past and prepare a course of action for the future, while at the same time it solidifies the community by demonstrating the limitation and vulnerability of all individual perspectives.[11] Perhaps most important, the incorporation of the separate accounts into a "connected" narrative is an act of confession. Jonathan must acknowledge his desire for Dracula's brides; Seward must reveal the shortcomings of his scientific assumptions as well as his most personal feelings about Lucy; and so on. "We have told our secrets," Van Helsing later declares (D, 241). What was private becomes public in a cleansing act of "absolute trust" (D, 229) that promotes the security and interdependence of the community.

Armed with knowledge and strengthened by their confessions, the men set out to trap the vampire, but they have still failed to perceive the fundamental import of Lucy's story. With "manlike," "chivalrous" concern for Mina's safety (D, 248), the men exclude her from their active efforts, thereby isolating her from the group and leaving her open to Dracula's attack. All the while, ironically, Jonathan and Van Helsing congratulate themselves on the eminent correctness of their decision.[12] Only because of Renfield's heroic resistance to Dracula are the men able to rescue Mina before she suffers the same fate as Lucy. By reverting to the codes of chivalry and underestimating both Dracula and Mina, the men jeopardize their entire undertaking.

For Mina's role in the community is essential. Indeed, she is as adamant as Van Helsing about the need for "working together" (D, 229). As Jonathan admits, "It is due to her energy and brains and foresight that the whole story is put together" (D, 254); and later her methodically deductive analysis of the collated narrative reveals the route Dracula must take back to his castle. In addition to the practical benefits of her "man's brain" (D, 241), Mina's "mother-spirit" consoles the men with "sweet sympathy" (D, 236). Her importance to the community, however, extends much further than these specific contributions, for she is more than a paragon of "bravery and unselfishness" (D, 313). As Van Helsing declares, Mina "is one of God's women, fashioned by His own hand to show us men and other women that there is a heaven where we can enter, and that its light can be here on earth" (D, 194).[13] This statement is not merely a generous compliment, for Mina is indeed the clearest proof that God has not deserted this "sceptical and selfish" world (D, 194). Even before the young men fully acknowledge Mina's spiritual importance, Dracula seems to realize that by capturing "God's women"—and especially Mina, the men's "best beloved one" (D, 293)—he can sever the ties between heaven and earth. Thus, to treat Mina chivalrously is not enough; she must be worshiped as the very heart of the community, lest she, like Lucy, become a creature of the night rather than the light. After Mina has been tainted by Dracula's blood and wears the mark of his "unclean" seduction on her forehead like a scarlet letter, she insists that the men promise to kill her if she becomes one of the undead, since her "soul is at stake" (D, 335). To seal the pact, she asks that they conduct the "Burial Service," and so the "little group of loving and devoted friends kneel round that stricken and sorrowing lady," as Jonathan reads "the simple and beautiful service from the Burial of the Dead" (D, 337).

After this ceremony—"bizarre," as Seward reflects, in its blend of "horror" and "sweetness" (D, 337)—the holy crusade to the East can begin, for the community is now fully unified and spiritually prepared. The men kneel as one in a circle that excludes all that is "sceptical and selfish" (D, 194). That Jonathan's words are borrowed from Anglican ceremony ironically emphasizes that the community of the good can seek no practical aid or spiritual guidance from priests or organized religion. Because modern England has no direct experience with Evil,

Dracula suggests, its crumbling old churches have become merely picturesque artifacts and potential havens for the vampire, like the chapel at Carfax, Dracula's English estate. Thus Van Helsing and the young people who oppose Dracula must turn their backs on the nineteenth century and rediscover a "primitive" communal life that derives its energy and unity from ritual murder, group confession, and ceremonial worship.

Unlike many other popular novels and films that chart the formation of a community, in *Dracula* the group is not threatened from within by the weakness or egotism of one or more of its members. Consider, for example, how different the novel would be if Renfield—a fallible madman who desires both power and the security of being a slave—had been included from the start in the group that combats the vampire. Yet Stoker's community of the faithful must still battle against the disintegrating force of egotism, because Dracula is the arch-individualist, whose singleminded antisocial actions are rooted in a "selfishness" of cosmic proportions (D, 347). (The various limitations on Dracula's freedom that Van Helsing enumerates, such as the inability to cross running water except during slack or flood tide and the immobilizing effect of a branch of wild rose, almost suggest that Nature has erected her own obstacles to Dracula's egotism.) According to Van Helsing, the ultimate goal of Dracula—proud product of a "conquering race" (D, 38)—is to become the "father or furtherer of a new order of beings" (D, 308), and to this end the vampire conducts his invasion of England "systematically and with precision" (D, 233). This "new order," an "ever-widening circle of semi-demons to batten on the helpless" (D, 60), can never constitute a moral community like the circle of vampire hunters, however, for Lucy and the other undead must remain enslaved to their individual physical needs and to Dracula, their sole master. As Franco Moretti puts it, the King-Vampire's "nature forces him to struggle to be unlimited, to subjugate *the whole of society.*"[14] With the same aristocratic disdain he shows for the peasants in Transylvania, Dracula yells at Van Helsing and the young men: "You and others shall yet be mine—my creatures, to do my bidding and to be my jackals when I want to feed" (D, 312). Thus the confrontation between Good and Evil that is so apparent in *Dracula* increasingly becomes synonymous with the struggle between the values of a selfless, unified community and the destructive excesses of egotistical individualism.

Somewhat analogous to the opposition between the selfless community and the supreme egotist in *Dracula* is the distinction Arendt so convincingly draws in *On Violence* (1970) between "power" and "strength." Power, she argues, "is never the property of an individual; it belongs to a group and remains in existence only so long as the group keeps together." Strength, on the other hand, "unequivocally designates something in the singular, an individual entity" that is "essentially independent."[15] By uniting and acting in concert, Stoker's vampire hunters become and remain powerful—the violence they must commit is justifiable as a means to preserve their power against the threat posed by Count Dracula, the embodiment of individual strength and independence. The confrontation and eventual triumph in *Dracula* of Van Helsing, the Harkers, and Lucy's suitors over the King-Vampire dramatizes—in the language and conventions of the horror story—what Arendt identifies as the basic fact in the relationship of power and strength: "It is in the nature of a group and its power to turn against independence, the property of individual strength," she concludes, and in this confrontation the power of the group will inevitably triumph (OV, 44). (An even more schematic illustration than *Dracula* of Arendt's thesis is Christian Nyby's *The Thing* [1951], a film I will return to in chapter 7.)

On Violence, needless to say, is concerned with historical reality—the political life of the twentieth century—and not with vampires, extraterrestrial invaders, and other imaginary "individual entities" who wield enormous strength. Yet *Dracula* and a great many other horror novels and films address, explicitly as well as implicitly, the same network of relationships among power, strength, and violence that Arendt and other political theorists explore. If, in *Dracula* as much as in *On Violence* (and, as I will later suggest, in Freud's studies of group psychology), the clash between the group and the independent individual is inescapable—and "the strength of even the strongest individual can always be overpowered by the many" (OV, 44)—Stoker is much more optimistic than Arendt about the role of violence in this "overpowering." Violence, according to Arendt, can never be redemptive or "creative"; while it can "destroy power," it is "utterly incapable of creating it" (OV, 56). Her critique of the admirers of Frantz Fanon's *The Wretched of the Earth* can also stand as a critique of certain assumptions that underlie *Dracula* and many subsequent works of popular art, westerns, and war movies as well as horror stories. "It is true," she admits, "that the strong fraternal sentiments collective violence engenders have misled many good people into the hope that a new community together with a 'new man' will arise out of it. The hope is an illusion for the simple reason that no human relationship is more transitory than this kind of brotherhood, which can be actualized only under conditions of immediate danger to life and limb" (OV, 69). *Dracula* concludes—long after the immediate danger is passed—with the realization of this very hope, as the collective violence of the vampire hunters directly gives rise to peace and prosperity, marriage and new birth. In this respect at least, it is the living as well as the undead in *Dracula* who speak to our fears of failure and guilt. And it is also the living who embody our wish that personal acts of sacrifice and heroism will have significant public consequences and that justified violence can also somehow be creative violence.

Not all acts of violence (even acts of self-defense) in *Dracula*, however, are successful, much less creative. Because of the particular nature of this "brotherhood" and the power that they collectively possess, the group of vampire hunters succeed in protecting and regenerating their world through the wild work of bloody, wholly justified violence. Van Helsing, the Harkers, and Lucy's suitors together triumph because they form what I have called a moral community that is both fully opposed to the egotism and evil of the undead and completely divorced from and at times even antipathetic to the institutions, laws, and modern beliefs of late Victorian society. Obviously Stoker has his literary antecedents in the many works of nineteenth-century British literature that consider the nature of social relations. In particular are those texts that extol the unique virtues of the small, cohesive, morally and spiritually self-sustaining, quasi-"organic" community—as an enclave in the industrialized, utilitarian present (Charles Dickens's *Hard Times*), for example, or as a hallmark of life during the "simpler" Middle Ages (Thomas Carlyle's *Past and Present*). In the late nineteenth century it was not Herbert Spencer in his *Principles of Sociology*, however, who comprehensively examined the phenomenon of community, but rather German sociologist Ferdinand Tönnies who, as Raymond Williams observes in *Keywords*, "influentially formalized" in 1887 the contrast between Gemeinschaft (community) and Gesellschaft (society).[16] There is no evidence that Stoker was familiar with Tönnies's theories—and in any case I am not concerned with establishing direct influence, only with situating *Dracula* and the other stories of the living and the undead in a more inclusive history of ideas and shifting ideological assumptions—yet the community of vampire hunters in *Dracula* shares several important features of Gemeinschaft as Tönnies describes it in the first section of his study.

"The essence of the Gemeinschaft," for Tönnies, is "the unity of unequal beings,"[17] a unity dependent on "mutual affirmation" and "reciprocal, binding sentiment" (CS, 38, 47). Conversely, in Gesellschaft, "everybody is by himself and isolated"; people "are essentially separated in spite of all uniting factors," and social relations take the form of "potential hostility or latent war" (CS, 65, 77) because each isolated person is concerned with furthering his or her own self-interest. Tönnies repeatedly insists that Gemeinschaft is "natural" and "organic," for the community is based on models found in the "relations of kindred individuals" (CS, 37)—parent and child, brother and sister, husband and wife. Of the various types of Gemeinschaft that Tönnies considers, it is "Gemeinschaft of mind" (as distinguished from Gemeinschaft of kinship or geographic locality) that comes closest to paralleling the vampire hunters in *Dracula*, for Gemeinschaft of mind—"the truly human and supreme form of community"—is characterized by "co-operation and co-ordinated action for a common goal" (CS, 42). Communities of this sort, like guilds and religious fraternities, arise from "similarity of work and intellectual attitude" and are "united by a spiritual bond and the co-operation in a common task" (CS, 43). Unity and successful cooperation, however, require not equality but the recognition and acceptance within the community of a "superior" form of authority. All embodiments of such authority in Gemeinschaft find their prototype in "the father who is engaged in protecting, assisting, and guiding his family" (CS, 41). In the community bound by spiritual friendship and a common goal, authority takes the form of the wise, priestly master, who may also share particular leadership qualities of the aged patriarch and the courageous feudal lord.

While *Dracula* is not a novel of ideas in which a deep-thinking character or an omniscient narrator offers abstract speculations about the nature of society and social relations, Stoker does depict the formation of a community that seems to exemplify certain key characteristics that Tönnies attributes to Gemeinschaft. In *Dracula* this community is not formed expressly as a utopian social experiment or as a self-conscious political and cultural alternative to the status quo. Until Dracula intrudes into the normal turn of events, Mina, Seward, and the others seem destined (and perfectly happy) to proceed with their private lives and professional careers, looking forward to marriage, but never considering their place in British society and their potential vulnerability. For self-defense, however, the living must unite, since as isolated individuals they are vulnerable, and the society to which they belong offers them no protection. (Recall the role of Jonathan's journey to Transylvania as Stoker's introduction to this modern dilemma.) No one in *Dracula*, for example, even considers calling upon the legitimate social authorities to help save Lucy or to destroy the vampire. "What is to be done," Van Helsing declares, "is not for police or of the customs. It must be done by us alone and in our own way" (D, 324). As I have already suggested, without Van Helsing—who is analogous to the wise authority figure in Tönnies's Gemeinschaft of mind—Lucy's friends and suitors will fall one by one into the ranks of the undead. With Van Helsing's guidance, however, the hunters are baptized in blood and forge a community spiritually bound by shared sentiment and therefore capable of the cooperative action necessary to achieve their common goal of seeking out and destroying Dracula. This superior form of Gemeinschaft is man's last and best hope, Stoker implies, but such a community will only arise when man is forced to confront and do battle with a threat the magnitude of the King-Vampire, when life, in other words, becomes quite literally a struggle for survival.

Although the series of communal rituals in *Dracula* that I discussed earlier make it clear that all of the vampire hunters draw strength from the realization that they live in and for the group, Van Helsing, Mina, and the rest rarely pause in the midst of their struggle to consider the nature of the social contract they have entered into. They do not, for example, call themselves a community, but rather a "little group of loving and devoted friends" (D, 337). For Tönnies, it should be noted, friendship stands as a "definite and meaningful" form of Gemeinschaft of mind (CS, 42). Somewhat comparably, for Stoker friendship serves as a model for the ideal relationship of people in a group, because love and devotion among friends can exist and thrive in *Dracula* untroubled by sexual relations (apparently the domain of the hungry undead) and familial ties (which can literally entrap as with Lucy and her mother). The vampire hunters never cease to be friends, mutually concerned and mutually dependent, but when they carry their quest eastward to a "world of dark and dreadful things" (D, 361) in the novel's final three chapters, the group also becomes, in Van Helsing's words, "as the old knights of the Cross" (D, 325). Concerned with more than their own survival, these hunters are "pledged to set the world free" (D, 326);

they are bound by a social and spiritual purpose and strengthened by abiding faith and the example of Christ's sacrifice.

What Mark M. Hennelly calls the "circular structure" of *Dracula* leads to the pointed contrast between Jonathan's ill-fated business trip that begins the novel and the moral community's final, successful journey to Transylvania.[18] Whereas Jonathan is summoned by Dracula and transported to the castle, the vampire hunters themselves plan and undertake the pursuit of the King-Vampire. Jonathan is easily imprisoned and manipulated by the Count because the young solicitor is so completely a product of what Van Helsing mockingly dubs the modern "enlightened age" (D, 326). Alone and forced to rely on his own instincts and imagination, Jonathan can at best escape (and not slay the monster), but he must then be nursed back to health after an attack of "violent brain fever" (D, 109). The hunters, in contrast, know full well that they must travel far beyond "even the sign of habitation" (D, 376), and they realize that their faith, however deep and true, is not by itself sufficient to ensure their victory. Mina and the men may trust in superstition and believe that they are "instruments of ultimate good" (D, 321)—"ministers of God's own wish" (D, 325)—but they must act and not passively wait for divine intercession. Thus the group comes armed with stakes, knives, Winchester carbines, and, perhaps most important, with what Dracula calls the "feelings of the hunter" (D, 28).

Solicitor, doctor, young aristocrat, assistant schoolmistress—all are now "hunters of wild beast" (D, 312), following a "rough," "ancient" path (D, 369) into a primitive world of wolves and swirling snow, journeying farther and farther from civilization as they move closer to the "awful den of hellish infamy" (D, 359). To track and trap the beast, the community must split into three separate couples, each pair out of communication with the others. Hence the danger implicit in isolation again becomes a factor, particularly for Van Helsing when he leaves Mina so that he can destroy the three vampire sisters who sleep in the chapel of Castle Dracula. Unlike Jonathan and Arthur in their encounters with undead sirens, Van Helsing enters the chapel knowledgeable, mature, and fully committed to the wild work at hand. Yet he, too, is tempted by the "radiantly beautiful" and "exquisitely voluptuous" brides of Dracula. No man by himself, it would seem, not even the aged, fatherly guide, can resist this "sweet fascination" that fosters life-threatening paralysis (D, 374), as if the physical beauty of the undead women, in and of itself, could suck the will and energy out of the defenseless, solitary, sexually aroused man. Only Mina's distant wail "full of woe and pity" awakens (and thus rescues and redeems) Van Helsing from his "open-eyed sleep" and allows him to proceed with his task. As at Lucy's tomb, Van Helsing once again hears the "horrid screeching" of the stake and sees the "plunging of writhing form, and lips of bloody foam" as his "butchery" spiritually frees the undead women (D, 374–75). Van Helsing's destruction of Dracula's brides provides a suspenseful prelude to the final confrontation in the novel between the living and the undead. More significantly, however, the sequence reaffirms the legitimacy of and the necessity for violence if the world is to be saved. Transfixion and decapitation—gruesome, barbarous acts of mutilation and desecration—are presented as the sole way to halt the vampire's assault on the living and simultaneously to grant the undead a merciful, human, "true" death. In *Dracula*, the end (quite literally the end of an evil, un-human existence) unquestionably justifies the violent means. But Van Helsing's "butcher work"—unlike, for example, the acts of self-defense in *Night of the Living Dead* and most other contemporary horror films—is also legitimated because of *how* it is carried out, because it is formally correct and true to the prescriptions laid down in "traditions and superstitions" (D, 244). And in this sense, the destruction of the undead is a ritual act that combines both punishment and mercy, just as it separates the hunters from the modern world and ultimately solidifies their communal ties.

Like his brides, Dracula, at least from Mina's viewpoint, is also granted an instantaneous "look of peace" before his "final dissolution" (D, 380). But the slaying of the King-Vampire—the single most important act in the novel, the act that will "set the world free"—is very different from Van Helsing's solitary, ritualistically correct butchery of the three brides. As the sun sets, the vampire hunters converge from different directions to surround the cart that carries Dracula's coffin. Armed gypsies escort the cart, yet these mercenaries are no match for the outnumbered moral community. While Van Helsing, Mina, Arthur, and Seward aim their Winchesters to hold the gypsies at bay, Jonathan and Quincey (the Englishman whose marriage bed has been violated and the American man of action) fight their way to the cart, toss down the coffin, and rip off its lid. Simultaneously, Jonathan slashes the Count's throat with his Kukri knife and Quincey plunges his Bowie knife into the heart of the vampire. By puncturing the heart and separating the head from the body, Jonathan and Quincey reenact the traditional remedy, and the King-Vampire crumbles into dust. Yet the weapons they wield are personal objects and practical tools (hence the emphasis on the fact that the two knives are vastly different in design and origin) in a way that Van Helsing's stakes are not. As I noted in the previous chapter, those human beings who hunt the undead are defined in part by their weapons, which suggest the resources the living have at their disposal and the possibilities for independent action. By using their own knives instead of stakes that have been "hardened by charring in the fire" and "sharpened to a fine point" (D, 220)—can there be any other purpose besides transfixion for such carefully wrought objects?—Quincey and Jonathan prove that the particular details, if not the general formula, of the ritual can be altered and adapted to accommodate specific circumstances and the individual hunter. Henceforth, for the vampire hunters and other beleaguered human beings in twentieth-century horror films and fiction, violence is inextricably linked to questions of individual imagination and ingenuity, of personal strength and weakness, and of the variation that convention will allow.

Quincey dies from wounds inflicted by the gypsies who futilely try to guard Dracula, but the community of the faithful, through their suffering and their heroic quest, preserve and redeem a world that has not so much fallen as it has slipped unknowingly into the selfishness and skepticism of modernity. (One major lesson learned from the journey to Transylvania is, as Jonathan realizes, that "the old centuries had, and have, powers of their own which mere 'modernity' cannot kill" [D, 44].) Before he dies, Quincey, as well as his devoted friends, is finally rewarded by tangible proof that God has not "deserted" this community. Earlier, when the touch of the holy wafer had burned the "mark of shame" on Mina's brow, Van Helsing avowed that the "scar shall pass away when God sees right to lift the burden that is hard upon us" (D, 302), and the entire group then "knelt down together, and, all holding hands, swore to be true to each other" (D, 303)—keeping their faith in the face of God's apparent rejection of the victimized Mina. In the end, as the men kneel in communal worship with their eyes on Mina, the "red gleams" of the setting sun bathe her now "stainless" face in "rosy light" (D, 381). And thus several skeins of imagery in the novel are finally woven together: Mina, one of the true "lights" in life (D, 190), escapes from the enlightened modern world and braves the darkness so that she can be purified by the rays of natural/divine rosy light that revoke Dracula's profane "baptism of blood"

(D, 347). "A deep and earnest 'Amen' broke from all" (D, 381), for the community has selflessly fulfilled its purpose—by saving Mina, it has preserved the link between heaven and earth.

Unlike many twentieth-century stories of the living and the undead, *Dracula* is a closed rather than an open-ended narrative. By the end of the novel all known undead have been destroyed, and, except for Renfield, who dies alone calling out "God! God! God!" (D, 295), the victims of the vampire are granted eternal peace. It is a mark of Stoker's optimism (perhaps as much as his naiveté) that the community emerges not just untainted, but strengthened psychologically and spiritually by the butchery they must commit and the nightmares they are forced to endure. Seven years after the destruction of Dracula, as Jonathan's brief concluding note informs us, Seward and Arthur have both become "happily married," and Van Helsing, like a grandfatherly patriarch, has begun to tutor Quincey, the Harkers' young son. Embodying the future, the boy is unmistakably a product of the past, for his "bundle of names links all our little band of men together" (D, 382).[19] What young Quincey will learn from Van Helsing is history written by the victors—how "some men so loved her [Mina], that they did dare much for her sake" (D, 382). The story of the vampire hunters is, as Jonathan admits, "wild" and without actual "proof," and it will therefore require the kind of open-mindedness and faith that proved to be so important in the battle with the King-Vampire. If Mina's son is able to believe without actually seeing, then he will come to share his mother's realization that "the world seems full of good men—even if there *are* monsters in it" (D, 230). Perhaps Quincey will also learn an even more fundamental lesson taught by the "wild" story of the vampire hunters: only after the community unites and goes "through the flames" (D, 382) can the family once again thrive and new life begin.

No new life is born or old civilization revitalized in John Polidori's *The Vampyre*, the first English vampire story. Published in 1819, *The Vampyre* was immediately a popular success, and the story was quickly adapted for both the English and continental stage (farce and opera versions soon followed).[20] Within the year, *The Vampyre* was translated into French and German, and henceforth, according to E. F. Bleiler, "the remainder of the nineteenth century fiction based on vampirism is heavily in debt to Polidori's work."[21] Yet in several important respects, *The Vampyre* is the antithesis of Stoker's *Dracula*. Lord Ruthven, Polidori's Byronic vampire, successfully feeds on the innocent and then escapes. He is not only triumphant but also seemingly invincible, and human society can do absolutely nothing to challenge, much less destroy him. Aubrey, the young orphaned gentleman, who alone in England knows the truth about Lord Ruthven's vampirism, is able to pass on his hard-earned knowledge before he dies, but "it was too late. Lord Ruthven had disappeared, and Aubrey's sister had glutted the thirst of a VAMPYRE!"[22] With these lines, Polidori's story abruptly ends, offering an exclamatory, upper-case, melodramatic climax, while at the same time denying the ideological satisfaction of retributive justice which in *Dracula* gives birth to a revitalized resumption of normality.[23]

The upper-class society in *The Vampyre* contains no wise and pious Van Helsing, for it puts no value on wisdom or piety. It contains no vampire hunters or potential hunters at all, in fact—only the corrupt, the corruptible, and the naively innocent, all easy prey for the aristocratic vampire. Through Aubrey's foolish curiosity and "high romantic feeling" (V, 266), Lord Ruthven is able to seduce and destroy the only two women who are "unaffected by crowded drawing-rooms and stifling balls" (V, 271): Ianthe, a Greek peasant girl, the epitome of "innocence, youth, and beauty" (V, 271); and Miss Aubrey, Aubrey's "melancholy" sister, whose soul was eternally "conscious of a brighter realm" (V, 278). Only by sucking the blood of these "young and beautiful" women (V, 261) can Lord Ruthven survive, and thus his survival assures that the world, drained of its virtues and innocence and youthful beauty, will sink further into the vanity fair of "fashionable vice" (V, 268), "violent excitement" (V, 265), and superficial frivolities. Yet Lord Ruthven, like Count Dracula, is motivated by more than just the desire to survive. Dracula dreams of a "new order," a world formed in his own image and subservient to his will, while Ruthven seems satisfied to seduce the innocent and to subvert and mock "drawing-room" society. With "malicious exultation" (V, 275), Polidori's vampire doles out charity that inevitably corrupts, ruining those who may only be guilty of being rash or thoughtless. Viewing the world through a "dead grey eye" (V, 265), Lord Ruthven is the vampire as embittered, jaded rake, oblivious to sentiment and melancholy.

Polidori's villain undoubtedly served as the model for later nineteenth-century vampires like James Malcolm Rymer's Varney the Vampyre, but Stoker's Count Dracula is obviously a more compelling, complex, and threatening creature than Lord Ruthven.[24] For my purposes, of greater interest than Count Dracula's literary ancestry is the fact that Stoker's community of vampire hunters has no parallel in *The*

Vampyre. Lord Ruthven's victims die isolated, and no social or legal authority, no blood relations, no friend or fiancé steps forward to challenge the vampire. Like Aubrey, London society possesses "great wealth," but it lacks responsible "guardians" (V, 266). Polidori's villain can "disappear" not because he has supernatural powers, but because he knows the rules of the game and is so completely assimilated into a corrupt "fashionable world" that thrives on "violent excitements." Ultimately, in *The Vampyre* upper-class society is beyond the power of faith and ritual; it is as "dead grey" as the eye of Lord Ruthven.[25]

With all its idiosyncrasies, *The Vampyre* does share one important detail with later nineteenth-century stories of the living and the undead, for Polidori, in an introductory survey of the vampire "superstition," asserts that the undead monster must feed "upon the blood of the young and beautiful" (V, 261). Hence Lord Ruthven's victims are Ianthe and Miss Aubrey—"beautiful and delicate" (V, 270) virginal young women—and a tradition is established that leads from *The Vampyre* and *Varney the Vampyre* to *Dracula* and into the twentieth century. In these works young women are the prize in the struggle between the living and the undead; these women are literally life-giving and to possess them is to win, to survive (hence the final line of *The Vampyre*: "Lord Ruthven had disappeared, and Aubrey's sister had glutted the thirst of a VAMPYRE!"). Yet in each work the young women carry different ideological significance. Compare, for example, Mina Harker's various roles within the moral community as "one of God's women" in *Dracula* to the role in *The Vampyre* of Ianthe and Miss Aubrey, who represent for Aubrey and the reader the only examples of innocence and purity in a world of affectation and vice. Thus when Lord Ruthven possesses these women, draining their blood, he destroys the "flower of life" (V, 274), making the world of the living even more barren and unnatural, flowerless.

In Le Fanu's *Carmilla* (1871), which offers a very different sense of the monster's relationship to the status quo and of the possibilities for the living to defend themselves, the vampire again stalks only young women, in particular, Laura, the naive, nineteen-year-old narrator of the story. What immediately makes *Carmilla* noteworthy, however, is the fact that like the victims, the vampire in this story is also a beautiful young woman—two-hundred-year old Mircalla (also called Carmilla and Millarca), Countess Karnstein, last descendent of a bloodthirsty, corrupt aristocratic family. True to her ancestry, Carmilla feeds off of peasant girls, while she seduces and drains the life from daughters of the upper class—nourishment is not always synonymous with pleasure.[26]

Through Laura's first-person account, we follow her response to the vampire's seduction. Thus Le Fanu focuses on the individual victim who is courted and possessed, initiated into a realm of sexuality that she can only describe in oxymorons, since this realm lies so far outside her limited experience. As a result, the boundary between sentimentalized adolescent girl's friendship and forbidden, deadly sexuality is never entirely clear. Immediately attracted to Carmilla, Laura simultaneously feels "something of repulsion"[27] and melancholy, which is both "sad" and "sweet" (C, 51). Somewhat like Jonathan Harker tempted by Dracula's brides in Transylvania, Laura "experienced a strange tumultuous excitement that was pleasurable, ever and anon, mingled with a vague sense of fear and disgust." "I was conscious," she writes, "of a love growing into adoration, and also of abhorrence. This I know is paradox, but I can make no other attempt to explain the feeling" (C, 36). Carmilla attacks by night, invading Laura's dreams and her bed, piercing the girl's breast with long needle-sharp teeth. By day, the exhausted Carmilla caresses Laura and seduces her with words: "I live in your warm life, and you shall die—die, sweetly die—into mine. I cannot help it; as I draw near to you, you, in your turn, will draw near to others, and learn the rapture of that cruelty, which yet is love" (C, 35), a love that must be "selfish . . . a cruel love—strange love" that "will have its sacrifices. No sacrifice without blood" (C, 47). When spoken by a vampire, the hyperbolic, fatalistic avowals of romantic love become ironic, chillingly literal possibilities—"murderous enjoyment" in the guise of "artful courtship" (C, 83).

Although she can transform herself into a "sooty-black animal that resembled a monstrous cat" (C, 48), Le Fanu's languid seductress never becomes a snarling monster like Stoker's undead Lucy Westenra. Yet in both works, the same striking image is used to shock the mesmerized victim (Laura and Arthur Holmwood) into recognition and to reveal the true nature of these vampiric women, who must wear their sexual experience, their hunger, and their unnatural crimes like a stain, more horrifying than any scarlet letter: "I saw Carmilla," Laura writes, "standing, near the foot of my bed, in her white nightdress, bathed, from her chin to her feet, in one great stain of blood" (C, 53). Like Lucy Westenra, whose "lips were crimson with fresh blood" that "stained the purity of her lawn death-robe" (D, 217), Carmilla belongs to the nightmarish darkside of Victorian sexuality, as surely as does

Robert Louis Stevenson's Mr. Hyde and Charlotte Brontë's Bertha Rochester.

Carmilla is not, however, the undead progeny of some foreign count; she herself is the source of the "mysterious disease" (C, 46) that threatens to destroy the archaic, picturesquely Gothic, male-dominated world in *Carmilla.* Although Laura is English and the story is not set in some distant past, she lives in a small "feudal residence" in Styria with her kindly but aged father and assorted maids and governesses. Laura's mother has long been dead, and, aside from the peasantry, there are very few teenage girls in this "lonely and primitive place" (C, 17), and the only men are her father's elderly acquaintances. Thus the beautiful little castle she inhabits, with its swan-filled moat and antique drawbridge, seems to enclose a father's fantasy of unchallenged possession, affection, and stasis: a juvenile, doting nineteen-year-old daughter with no mother or suitors and few friends, living with her elderly father in a world of his making that seeks to exclude sexuality and maturity. The situation of Bertha, Carmilla's previous victim, directly parallels Laura's, for Bertha is an orphaned teenage girl, the ward of the aged General Spielsdorf.

Laura's father's paternalism, more than his willingness to accept a "natural explanation" for inexplicable occurrences (C, 57), places his daughter in danger. With "kindness and chivalry" (C, 26), he invites Carmilla into his castle, because the frail young woman is apparently innocent and dependent, and thus no threat to the status quo. By isolating Laura in a storybook Gothic setting and denying her the opportunity to mature, he creates an impressionable, naive young woman who responds fully to the pleasure and pain of Carmilla's caresses. Thus once again the nineteenth-century vampire story offers a veiled commentary on the status of the family and on the failure of parental responsibility: Aubrey's "guardians" in *The Vampyre* act only as financial executors; Mrs. Westenra removes the garlic that protects her daughter; Laura's father creates the perfect environment for Carmilla's "strange love" and then invites the vampire in; and even Carmilla, we are told, belongs to a "bad family" (C, 73).

Yet unlike Aubrey's sister and Lucy Westenra, Laura survives, for her father, in league with other men of the region, manages to destroy the vampire. Bertha, Carmilla's previous victim, is not so lucky; she is visited by "appalling dreams" and eventually dies. Her guardian, General Spielsdorf, fully convinced that he has been the victim of a "preternatural conspiracy" (C, 62), vows to commit a "pious sacrilege" that will "subserve the vengeance of Heaven" and "relieve our earth of certain monsters" (C, 63–64). To this end he journeys, with Laura and her father, to the ruins of Karnstein Castle, Carmilla's ancestral home, and attacks the vampire with a hatchet. Carmilla easily parries the blow and escapes, for in *Carmilla* as in *Dracula* the single man, however "righteous and merciful" his purpose (C, 23), cannot alone destroy the vampire. To avenge their own errors of judgment and to "deliver this region from a plague that has scourged its inhabitants for more than a century" (C, 80–81), General Spielsdorf and Laura's father must ally themselves with Baron Vordenburg, a "fantastic old gentleman" (C, 80) who "devoted himself to the minute and laborious investigation of the marvelously authenticated tradition of vampirism" (C, 83) and with a "good priest" who performs "solemn rites" that protect Laura from further attacks (C, 81).

The actual destruction of Carmilla, summarized by Laura from an "official" report of the "formal proceedings" (C, 82), is anticlimactic, particularly when read in the context of *Dracula*. With the General, Laura's father, the Baron, the priest, and two "medical men" present, Carmilla is destroyed and mutilated in strict accordance with "ancient practice": staked, beheaded, and burned, her ashes thrown into the river and carried away by the water. Unlike, for example, the snarling vampires in Hammer films who claw and scratch until the end, Carmilla puts up no struggle. Indeed, the ritual violence that saves Laura and rids the region of the Karnsteins' "atrocious lusts" (C, 73) is merely a "formal proceeding," not a heroic gesture or a baptism in blood, and not the wild work of a newly formed moral community. Through their allegiance to "ancient practice," the old men of this rural world—doctor, father, General, scholar, Baron, priest—destroy the "perfidious and beautiful" (C, 82) female creature who has threatened their young women; through their alliance of social, religious, and scientific authority, these men reaffirm the power and the validity of a patriarchal ruling class that can only see female sexuality as an aberration.

Because of the combined actions of the men who control her world, Laura survives. Once safely returned to the confines of her father's castle, Laura learns from Baron Vordenburg about the "authenticated tradition of vampirism" (C, 83) and the specific details of Carmilla's history. Le Fanu thus provides, like Stoker, certain essential components of a closed ending: the status quo is defended and reaffirmed, and the monster is not only killed but explained, *understood* by the survivors. Yet *Carmilla*'s concluding paragraph returns us to the object of Carmilla's "artful courtship" and "horrible lust" (C, 83), with Laura, now much older, reflecting back on the events she has narrated. "To this hour," Laura confesses, "the image of Carmilla returns to memory with ambiguous alternations—sometimes the playful, languid, beautiful girl; sometimes the writhing fiend I saw in the ruined church; and often from a reverie I have started, fancying I heard the light step of Carmilla at the drawing-room door" (C, 85).

Carmilla survives—not in Laura's nightmares, but in her memories and daydreams. For the men, Carmilla is either a "beautiful girl" or a "fiend," a virgin or a vampire. Only Laura is able to acknowledge Carmilla's "ambiguous alternations," and thus perhaps to acknowledge her own ambiguous response to the vampire's "strange love." In "fancy," at least, there is a world of sentiments and sensations apart from the father, yet as close as the drawing-room door. As we will see, both Laura's final confession and the disappearance of Lord Ruthven in *The Vampyre*—conclusions very much at odds with the resolution of Stoker's *Dracula*—have analogies with several open-ended twentieth-century stories of the living and the undead.

While *The Vampyre*, *Carmilla*, and *Dracula* differ so completely in the way they resolve the confrontation between the living and the undead, the most obvious feature shared by these nineteenth-century stories is the figure of the seductive, aristocratic vampire who survives by drinking the blood of the innocent. This similarity, in turn, makes more evident the extent to which Count Dracula's egotism, power, and ambition set him apart from Lord Ruthven and Carmilla. Less variation is apparent, for example, in the characterization of the vampire's young female victims—though the particular value assigned to these women differs in each of these three stories, as does the image of family relations and patriarchal authority. By attacking the young women, the vampire in fact threatens the family, society, and the status quo. In responding to this threat, the living prove their fitness (in *Carmilla* and *Dracula*) or their unfitness (in *The Vampyre*). What becomes even clearer after we see the impotence and corruption of society in Polidori's story and the relatively easy success of the male ruling class in *Carmilla* is the emphasis Stoker places on a new moral community—divorced from modern society—that is willing and able to carry out the bloody wild work of destruction. The formation of such a community is unnecessary in *Carmilla* and impossible in *The Vampyre*.[28]

A brief survey of vampire stories published between 1890 and 1925 further highlights by way of contrast the uniqueness and the significance of *Dracula* and also suggests the genre's "inventory of options" as it moves into the twentieth century. As would be expected, some of these vampire stories obviously parallel certain aspects of the works of Polidori, Le Fanu, and Stoker, for these stories also focus on the status of the family and the corrupting power of the aristocracy. In Count Stenbock's *The Sad Story of a Vampire* (1894), for example, the vampire is Count Vardalek, who, like Carmilla, is invited into a Styrian castle by a short-sighted elderly widower with two young children. After his twelve-year-old son is kissed and destroyed by the vampire, the father dies of grief, and the undead creature "utterly disappears."[29] Thus Stenbock neatly draws together the aristocratic, invincible villain from *The Vampyre* and the "strange love" that can lay waste to "hearth and home" from *Carmilla*. In *The Sad Story of a Vampire* the family cannot survive, for no one can alter the course of events once the vampire becomes a guest in the castle; neither doctor nor priest can save the young boy's life.

An isolated, incomplete family is also decimated in Victor Roman's *Four Wooden Stakes* (1925), in which a young man's grandfather, father, and two elder brothers all die within five years from a mysterious wasting disease. Alone and terrified, Remson, the survivor (for there are no women in this household), implores a friend to come and solve the "damnable mystery that hovers over this house."[30] Together, the men discover that Remson's grandfather was bitten by a vampire bat in South America and was eventually transformed into a vampire, who in turn fed upon his own son and grandsons, turning them into undead creatures as well.[31] Following the instructions given in an old encyclopedia, the two men sharpen stakes, enter the family crypt, and destroy Remson's blood relations in a scene that recalls the destruction of Lucy Westenra in *Dracula*. As the stake is driven into the heart of the grandfather-patriarch, "the blood gushed out of the open wound, up and over us, staining the walls and our clothes."[32] Freed of his ancestors and siblings, Remson survives. His grandfather's transfixed corpse disintegrates into dust, but four bloodstained wooden stakes remain—a testimony to the courage of the two hunters and an appropriate synecdoche for what Van Helsing calls the wild work of the living.

Stenbock's multilingual, world-weary Count Vardalek and Roman's snarling, utterly malevolent fiend are but two of the forms the vampire assumes in stories of this period. In addition, for example, Countess Sarah in F. G. Loring's *The Tomb of Sarah* (1900) is, like Dracula's brides, a siren with a "crimson sensual mouth" and a "soft soothing voice" who tempts a rural priest.[33] Less directly tied to the lamia figures of Romantic literature are the female vampires in M. E. Braddon's *Good Lady Ducayne* (1896) and E. F. Benson's *The Room in the Tower* (1912). Braddon's social fable is closer to Dickensian satire than to Gothic horror, for Lady Ducayne is an "aristocratic witch in her withered old age," who is literally kept alive by blood her Italian doctor secretly removes from young working-class girls.[34] Benson's vampire, Mrs. Julia Stone, is also "old and withered and white-haired," but she is driven by a "vitality that foamed and frothed with unimaginable evil." (Note that one immediately apparent change that Carl-Theodor Dreyer made in adapting *Carmilla* into *Vampyr* [1932] was to substitute an old, almost asexual female vampire for Le Fanu's youthful-looking, seductive Carmilla.) Less an "aristocratic witch" or a wicked benefactress than a stern, demanding, possessive mother figure, Mrs. Stone haunts a recurrent dream of the narrator of *The Room in the Tower*. When this dream is finally realized, the aged, hungry vampire, "spotted and stained with mold," leaves her grave to enter the narrator's bedroom, so that she may "feast."[35] In *Mrs. Amworth*, published in 1920, Benson again offers a female vampire: Mrs. Amworth is a high-spirited, congenial, middle-aged widow, who by night preys upon the inhabitants of a secluded, peaceful English village. Benson's stories in particular seem to be conscious attempts to expand the possibilities of the genre by introducing vampires who are quite obviously not titled foreigners or voluptuous temptresses. In this respect these stories are the precursors of certain contemporary vampire novels, like Stephen King's *'Salem's Lot* and Robert R. McCammon's *They Thirst* (1981), in which the roving undead represent all strata of modern society.

Except for Stenbock's *The Sad Story of a Vampire*, in all of the stories I have mentioned, the monster is destroyed or at least publicly identified (as with Mrs. Stone, whose blood-filled coffin is unearthed) or thwarted (as with Lady Ducayne, who is blackmailed into ending her wicked schemes). In *The Tomb of Sarah* and *Mrs. Amworth*, as in *Four Wooden Stakes*, two men must unite to carry out the "terrible work" of exterminating the undead. In each case, the dominant vampire hunter shares certain traits with Stoker's Professor Van Helsing. The major hunter in Loring's story, for instance, is a church restorer—experienced, well versed in local superstitions, pious, and committed to a violent "war of extermination" against the increasingly beautiful Countess Sarah.[36] Curiosity and scientific open-mindedness, on the other hand, are the key characteristics of Francis Urcombe, the psychic investigator and former professor of physiology who destroys Mrs. Amworth. Both of these men—like Remson in *Four Wooden Stakes* and the elderly priest in F. Marion Crawford's *For the Blood Is the Life* (1911)—must have help. Thus as much as these stories by Stoker's contemporaries and immediate successors explore and alter the identity of the vampire (without pursuing, however, Stoker's conception of the King-Vampire) and of the victim, they all insist that no one man alone can destroy the undead; even the pious and the brave and the knowledgeable require "assistance," moral as well as physical support.[37] Working in pairs with no hesitation and no second thoughts, these men recognize and carry out their duty, whether they work for self-preservation (as in *Four Wooden Stakes* and *For the Blood Is the Life*) or for the protection of a small rural village (as in *The Tomb of Sarah* and *Mrs. Amworth*). In addition, these stories resemble more recent works like *Dracula, A.D. 1972* (1972) and other Hammer vampire films in that they culminate most often in the personal triumph of the living amid the spouting blood and "unearthly screams" of the undead, that is to say, in the dangerous, victorious act of destruction, rather than in the return to normality or the regeneration of the world. In stories like *The Tomb of Sarah* and *Four Wooden Stakes*, assistance is necessary to slay the beast, but it does not serve as the foundation for a moral community such as Stoker envisions; without the threat posed by a King-Vampire, there is apparently no need for such a community—two brave men are sufficient.

Much closer in structure and ideology to *Dracula* is Stoker's last novel, *The Lair of the White Worm* (1911).[38] In both works the appearance of evil in the form of an ancient, thoroughly malevolent threat to specific individuals and by implication to all of England is once again a "blessing in disguise,"[39] since it necessitates a human response that ultimately leads to the affirmation and triumph of the good. Certain details of the "bedrock struggle between good and evil" (WW, 56) in *The Lair of the White Worm* have direct analogies with *Dracula*, as the following brief synopsis suggests: Adam Salton, a young man born and raised in Australia, returns to the "heart of the old kingdon of Mercia" (WW, 11)—the ancient center of modern Britain—to meet his long-lost grand-uncle. Adam is instructed in local history, legend, and superstition by an elderly friend of the family, Sir Nathaniel di Salis, and falls in love with and then marries Mimi Watford, a beautiful young woman who combines "strength of character" with "sweetness of disposition" (WW, 129). Together these three people must combat and eventually destroy the evil of both Edgar Caswell, an irredeemably egotistical aristocrat obsessed with acquiring occult knowledge and with exercising his hypnotic power over Mimi's innocent sister, and Lady Arabella March, epitome of the predatory female, who is actually the white worm, an enormous, age-old monster with "no soul and no morals" (WW, 135) that emerges from a "mysterious orifice" in the earth to threaten the modern world (WW, 148).

Like the young men in *Dracula*, Adam Salton is a "willing and attentive pupil" (WW, 19), who is also capable of heroic, selfless action—particularly for the protection of his wife. Mimi Watford, inspired and illuminated by "divine light" (WW, 69), is quite obviously the spiritual sister of Mina Harker; both women demonstrate the necessity for faith in "God's justice" (WW, 186), yet both fully realize that faith must be accompanied by the ability and by the willingness to think and act. Like Adam (and like Stoker's vampire hunters), Mimi is motivated by an "unselfish, unchanging devotion for those she loved" (WW, 192). In their attempt to understand and destroy evil, this young couple is instructed and guided by Sir Nathaniel, the Van Helsing figure in *The Lair of the White Worm*. Sir Nathaniel is learned and experienced, his common sense matched by an overwhelming sense of duty, for he knows what all of Stoker's selfless heroes must realize: that with the gain of knowledge and experience, "our power to help others has grown—and our responsibility in equal proportion" (WW, 163). Evil must be completely destroyed to preserve Mimi and the "common weal" (WW, 74), and to this end, Sir Nathaniel insists that the hunters must "think and work patiently, fearlessly, and unselfishly" (WW, 48).

Just as similar qualities of mind and character link the defenders of the good in *Dracula* and *The Lair of the White Worm*, the embodiments of evil in both novels share the same essential characteristics and even the same purpose. Edgar Caswell, for example, is not a vampire, but his "partly hypnotic, partly mesmeric" powers are in the service of an "inflexible will" (WW, 17). He aspires toward the forbidden knowledge and dominance that Dracula has already achieved, but above all, as Stoker repeatedly emphasizes, Edgar is an aristocrat from a tainted family whose egotism and selfishness know no bounds. Lady Arabella March, motivated by similar desires, is a less sympathetic and less convincing siren than the undead Lucy Westenra. Lady Arabella, as Adam realizes, combines "the heartlessness of a *cocotte* and the want of principle of a suffragette. She has the reserved strength and impregnability of a diplodocus" (WW, 140). Edgar Caswell may represent the dangerous distortion of the "masculine," but Lady Arabella is quite literally the white worm—an antediluvian creature "without heart or consideration for anything or anyone" (WW, 153) that dwells amid the charnel house stench of dank underground caverns, ready to feed upon mankind and pollute the earth.

In the end, all three hunters contribute to the complete eradication of evil—Mimi with her faith, Sir Nathaniel with his knowledge and clear thinking, and Adam with his fearless action and military experience (dynamite is planted in the worm's lair). Yet the redemptive violence must be sparked by a tremendous, "appallingly bright" flash of lightning (WW, 213), which levels the overreaching tower on Edgar's estate and ignites the dynamite. Thus both man's selfless work and the lightning that seems to signify God's burning wrath are necessary for the "absolute destruction" (WW, 218) of evil. As in *Dracula*, the final triumph is announced and the struggles of the living justified by the sun's "red rays," which bring "relief" and the "promise of a new order of things" (WW, 216) and even reveal that the explosions have unearthed valuable deposits of china clay on Adam's estate. The earth has been freed from the evil legacy of the past and has delivered its material treasures to the worthy. "All's well that ends well," Sir Nathaniel declares to Adam as they turn away from the rotting fragments of the white worm, now overrun with "insects, worms, and vermin of all kinds" (WW, 219–20), and head back "home" for breakfast with Mimi—domesticity and material comforts can now reign supreme. At last, the heroic survivors can, in Leonard Wolf's words, "breathe the humid air of British Decency."[40]

With its death-wielding "mysterious orifice" (the home of the feminine serpent) and its madness-inducing tower (the home of masculine egotism) *The Lair of the White Worm* suggests more than a little about Stoker's personal fears and obsessions. And the characters, narrative structure, and ideology of the novel throw certain elements of *Dracula* into high relief—the role of "God's women" and of the wise, paternal elder, for example, as well as the necessity for the violent destruction of the monster and the equation of excessive egotism with social, moral, sexual, and spiritual evil. Yet, for my purposes, the distinctions between these two novels are even more revealing. Needless to say, the King-Vampire and his brides are far more fearsome and attractive than the various embodiments of evil in *The Lair of the White Worm*. However one evaluates Stoker's literary skills, his Dracula has struck at the heartblood of the popular imagination in the twentieth century. Likewise, though the three interdependent people who constitute the force of good in the later novel share the same degree of commitment and courageous selflessness as Van Helsing, the Harkers, and Lucy's suitors, yet *The Lair of the White Worm* contains none of *Dracula*'s insistence on the ritualistic, primitive basis of the community of hunters. Adam, Mimi, and Sir Nathaniel are never tempted by the evil they combat; they are never forced to undertake journeys that completely alienate them from modern society; and their wild work resembles a carefully planned military campaign more than a holy crusade of butchery and mutilation. These defenders of the good are never baptized in blood, and thus they are not rewarded with the birth of new life and with tangible proof that God is merciful as well as wrathful—Mina is redeemed, Mimi has never been tainted. When the smoke clears in *The Lair of the White Worm*, the world has been rendered comfortable, and no prayers of thanksgiving or legends of heroic struggle are necessary. Breakfast can at last be served, and the monstrous evil threat seems in retrospect no more than an irritating interruption.

It is therefore Stoker's presentation both of Dracula and of the group of vampire hunters led by Van Helsing that most clearly distinguishes *Dracula* from *The Lair of the White Worm* and the nineteenth- and early twentieth-century vampire stories I have discussed. Dracula is not just a vampire, not just an evil predatory aristocrat, but the King-Vampire whose threat extends much further than the single family or the rural village. And for Stoker, neither a solitary hero nor a pair of brave men nor a ruling class alliance can dispose of Dracula; only a newly forged moral community can destroy the King-Vampire.

Given Stoker's presentation of the living and the undead, perhaps the closest analogue to *Dracula* is not *Carmilla* or *The Vampyre*, but rather, as Maurice Richardson has suggested, Freud's description of the "primal horde" in *Totem and Taboo* (1913). In "The Psychoanalysis of Ghost Stories," Richardson describes *Dracula* in the following terms: "Mina is saved and Lucy avenged by a noble brotherly band led by Dr. Van Helsing. . . . Apart from Van Helsing, who represents the good father, the set-up reminds one rather of the primal horde as pictured somewhat fantastically perhaps by Freud in *Totem and Taboo*, with the brothers banding together against the father who has tried to keep all the females to himself."[41] In the wake of Ernest Jones's chapter on vampirism in *On the Nightmare*, several psychoanalytic commentaries on *Dracula*, including Richardson's article, have appeared.[42] Nonetheless, it seems to me that a more thorough comparison of *Dracula* and Freud's theory of the primal horde is needed, not only because Richardson's suggestion has become, in James Twitchell's words, "almost a donnée of *Dracula* criticism,"[43] but because *Totem and Taboo*, like Freud's other studies of civilization and human society, addresses the relationship of fathers and sons, of the individual and the group, of the leader and the mass, of violence and the possibility for human community.[44] These same concerns, I would argue, inform *Dracula* and a significant number of stories of the living and the undead in the twentieth century.

Drawing upon Charles Darwin's speculations about the social organization of primeval man into hordes, each governed by a single powerful male, William Robertson Smith's analysis of sacrifice and the sacrificial meal in "primitive" culture, and J. A. Atkinson's hypothesis about paternal tyranny and patricide in the primal horde, Freud formulated in *Totem and Taboo* what he later referred to as the "scientific myth of the father of the primal horde."[45] This myth is also discussed in Freud's other major works of social psychology: *Group Psychology and the Analysis of the Ego* (1921), *The Future of an Illusion* (1927), *Civilization and Its Discontents* (1930), and *Moses and Monotheism* (1939). Freud returns to the myth so often because the "story" of the primal horde and the fraternal community offers the underlying pattern for and marks the "beginning of so many things—of social organization, of moral restrictions and of religion" (TT, 142).

This story is a condensed narrative account of "what in reality took centuries to achieve" and involved "all primeval men, including, therefore, all our ancestors" (MM, 102).[46] In the beginning (or once upon a time), "the strong male was the master and father of the whole horde, unlimited in his power, which he used brutally. All females were his property, the wives and daughters in his own horde as well as perhaps also those stolen from other hordes. The fate of the sons was a hard one; if they excited the father's jealousy they were killed or castrated or driven out. They were forced to live in small communities and to provide themselves with wives by stealing them from others" (MM, 102). Eventually, the outcast sons joined together and collectively killed their tyrannical father; "united, they had the courage to do and succeeded in doing what would have been impossible for them individually" (TT, 141). Being "cannibal savages," the brothers then devoured their dead father, each thereby assuring his "identification with the father by incorporating a part of him" (MM, 103). After a period in which the brothers futilely fought among themselves for the right to become the sole master of the horde, a "union" arose among them, a "sort of social contract" that required "renunciation of instinctual gratification" through the creation of incest taboos and laws of exogamy (MM, 104). A "community of brothers" (GP, 69), the "fraternal clan," then took the place of the primal horde, and "society was now based on complicity in the common crime" (TT, 146). The crime also brought guilt, however, because of the sons' ambivalent attitudes toward their father—admiration and love mixed with jealousy and hatred.

In *Civilization and Its Discontents* Freud identifies this "primal guilt" as the "beginning of civilization" (CD, 83) because the sons offered "deferred obedience" to their dead father by instituting totemism, man's "first attempt at a religion" (TT, 144), with the totem animal, venerated, feared, and protected by taboos, serving as a substitute for the father. Essential in this totemic system is the sacrificial totem meal (for Freud the prototypical festival) in which the clansmen slaughter and devour the totem animal in a "repetition and a commemoration" of the murder of the father (TT, 142). Totemism, Freud insists, is a testament to the "ambivalence implicit in the father-complex" (TT, 145), an "ambivalence present to a greater or less amount in the innate disposition of everyone" (TT, 60). Eventually the fraternal clan with its totemic religion was superseded, as "humanized" gods took the place of the totem animal—first, "great mother deities" and a matriarchal social structure, then the male gods of polytheism and a "restitution of the patriarchal order" (MM, 105). In the new "patriarchal order," the family, Freud concludes, "was a restoration of the former primal horde and it gave back to fathers a large portion of their former rights" (TT, 149). Yet no one father could approximate the power and control the primal father once wielded. Hence the decline of the father deities and the rise of "God Himself" (TT, 150), the "one and only father deity whose power is unlimited" (MM, 106). For Freud, as Herbert Marcuse so convincingly argues in *Eros and Civilization*, "in the development of civilization, freedom becomes possible only as *liberation*. Liberty *follows* domination—and leads to a reaffirmation of domination" and the "restoration and glorification of authority."[47] Man cannot, apparently, escape from the tyranny of the primal father or from the "primal guilt" of his murder. "There probably exists in the mental life of the individual," Freud speculates, "not only what he has experienced himself, but also what he brought with him at birth, fragments of phylogenetic origin, an archaic heritage" (MM, 125). In this sense all men know that "once upon a time they had a primeval father and killed him" (MM, 129). For the individual as for all of humankind, "the beginnings of religion, morals, society and art converge in the Oedipus complex" (TT, 156).

Since for Freud the triumph of the fraternal clan over the primal horde marked the "first beginnings of a moral and social order" (MM, 153), all subsequent manifestations of group or communal behavior reflect our "phylogenetic origins" in this prehistoric conflict. "In so far as men are habitually under the sway of group formation, we recognize in it the survival of the primal horde" (GP, 70). Just as the outcast brothers were eventually forced to band together and murder the primal father, so the "replacement of the power of the individual by the power of a community constitutes the decisive step of civilization" (CD, 42). To maintain its power and cohesiveness, however, the community (group, civilization) must insist upon the restriction (repression, supression, sublimation) of the individual's sexual and aggressive instincts. In other words, the very instincts that led the brothers to commit patricide were then restricted by the fraternal clan's development of totemic religion. According to *Civilization and Its Discontents*, what was true for the fraternal clan remains true for all examples of "human life in common" (CD, 42), including the family, the "germ-cell of civilization" (CD, 61).

Through the totem animal of the fraternal clan and the omniscient God of later patriarchal society, civilization perpetuates the image of the primal father, who is "the model after which later generations have formed their figure of God."[48] "Human groups," Freud writes in *Group Psychology and the Analysis of the Ego*, "exhibit once again the familiar picture of an individual of superior strength among a troop of equal companions, a picture which is also contained in our idea of the primal horde" (GP, 69). In the relationship between the leader and his followers, then, human groups are a "revival of the primal horde" (GP, 70); whether human being or God, "the leader of the group is still the dreaded primal father; the group still wishes to be governed by unrestricted force; it has an extreme passion for authority" (GP, 76).

According to Richardson, the parallels between Stoker's vampire novel and Freud's description of the primal horde are straightforward: Dracula is the primal father who seeks to extend the dominion of his horde by capturing Lucy and Mina, and the "noble brotherly band" of vampire hunters are the outcast sons who ultimately destroy their tyrannical father.[49] Richardson, like the other critics who follow this line of inquiry, does not pursue these parallels, except to note that Dracula "seems almost conscious" of the situation, for he yells at the hunters: "Your girls that you all love are mine already, and through them you and others shall yet be mine—my creatures, to do my bidding and to be my jackals when I want to feed" (D, 312). The new order Dracula seeks to create is indeed very much like Freud's primal horde, for the King-Vampire envisions a world of human beings reduced to indistinguishable undead creatures, all servile objects for the gratification of his appetite. (In later chapters I will consider the relationship between Freud's primal horde and twentieth-century images of the undead, like Romero's in *Night of the Living Dead.*) In this world Dracula clearly occupies the position of the primal father whose actions are not limited by taboos against incest and murder; with Lucy Westenra, he is both father and lover and so, too, with his brides/daughters in Transylvania.[50] Like the figure of the leader that Freud discusses in *Group Psychology and the Analysis of the Ego*, Dracula "need love no one else," even as he maintains his quasi-hypnotic control over his followers. Both Freud's leader and Stoker's King-Vampire possess "a masterful nature, absolutely narcissistic, self-confident and independent" (GP, 71). Dracula is not merely a "father-figure," as Royce MacGillivray suggests;[51] he is an avatar of the primal father.

Bound by friendship, past experiences, and a common love for Lucy Westenra, Arthur Holmwood, Quincey Morris, and John Seward qualify as a "noble brotherly band." Unlike Freud's fraternal clan, however, Lucy's suitors in *Dracula* can neither accurately assess their dilemma nor destroy their tyrannical antagonist until a wise father, Van Helsing, instructs and guides them. The presence of both Van Helsing and Mina Harker as all-important members of the moral community in *Dracula* qualifies any complete identification of the vampire hunters with the community of outcast brothers who slay the primal father. However, Stoker's portrait of a moral community linked by "libidinal ties" supports Freud's contention that "it is impossible to grasp the nature of a group if the leader is disregarded" (GP, 65).[52] Three scenes from *Dracula* that I discussed earlier dramatize Stoker's concept of community and emphasize "the importance of the leader in the psychology of the group" (GP, 35): the men's nocturnal journey to destroy the undead Lucy ("we all kept somehow close together," Seward writes, "with Van Helsing slightly in front as he led the way . . . . entering [the tomb] first himself. The rest of us followed, and he closed the door" [D, 214]); the service for the Burial of the Dead with the "little group of loving and devoted friends kneeling round that stricken and sorrowing lady" (D, 337); the men again kneeling around Mina offering thanksgiving as the "rosy light" removes the stain of Dracula's embrace (D, 381). Often, as at Lucy's tomb, Van Helsing quite literally leads—he opens doors and the young men follow. Mina, especially in the two scenes referred to here, is the focus of what Freud would call the young men's "libidinal ties." By kneeling around Mina, one of "God's true women," the men are acknowledging that God is their ultimate leader. Stoker, it would seem, cannot conceive of a "community of brothers" who, without the leadership of fatherly guide or God, can end the tyranny of the primal father.

Another important difference between Stoker's story and Freud's "scientific myth" is that the vampire hunters in *Dracula* experience none of the remorse that plagues the patricidal sons, for Van Helsing and the others feel very little, if any, "emotional ambivalence" toward Dracula. (Mina's sympathy for the Count during the final chase suggests her capacity for selfless, Christ-like mercy, much more than veiled sexual attraction to the vampire.) The King-Vampire arouses only the young men's hatred and perhaps unspoken envy. All the love and admiration for the dead primal father that leads to the beginning of totemism in *Totem and Taboo* is directed in *Dracula* toward Van Helsing. For Stoker, fathers are either good or evil, and thus his young men are spared the traumas bred of ambivalent emotions, and the moral community is allowed to murder Dracula without suffering guilt. (By way of contrast, consider Jonathan and Renfield's agonizing guilt when they feel that they have betrayed Mina.) In Freud's reconstruction of prehistory, the murdered father of the primal horde is like a vampire who still survives—in his sons' guilt and "deferred obedience," in the totem animal, and ultimately in the social and religious structure of civilization. In this respect, the "scientific myth" of the primal horde is an open-ended narrative of variation in repetition—the tyrannical primal father cannot be destroyed once and for all. At the closed ending of *Dracula*, the vampire is dead, and he haunts neither conscience nor nightmare ("every trace of all that had been was blotted out" [D, 382]). The victorious hunters cannot devour their victim's corpse even if they wanted to, for the King-Vampire "crumbled into dust and passed from our sight" (D, 380); thus the hunters will assimilate and carry into the future neither his evil nor their own guilt.

The story that Van Helsing will pass on to young Quincey Harker will not commemorate the frightening power of the King-Vampire, but rather the heroic work of the living, "how some men loved her [Mina] that they did dare much for her sake" (D, 382).

Yet perhaps in the most important respect Freud and Stoker are telling the same story, for their narratives insist that an act of violence is necessary either to originate or to renew civilization. Regardless of the psychic cost or the physical danger to the community of hunters, Dracula and the primal father *must* be killed. What is at stake is nothing less than the social, sexual, and spiritual future of mankind. Thus in their narratives both Freud and Stoker challenge the idea that "collective violence" can never be "creative" and never give birth to what Arendt calls a "new community together with a 'new man'" (OV, 69). "Human life in common is only made possible," Freud asserts in *Civilization and Its Discontents*, "when a majority comes together which is stronger than any separate individual and which remains united against all separate individuals" (CD, 42). Eventually, from the dust of the King-Vampire and the blood of the primal tyrant comes the restoration or the creation of a new patriarchy based on the family and on God the father. Baptized in blood, "human life in common" triumphs through the wild work of butchery over the supreme individual, and for Stoker as much as for Freud, "this replacement of the power of the individual by the power of a community constitutes the decisive step of civilization" (CD, 42).

NOTES

1. William M. Clements, "Formula as Genre in Popular Horror Literature," *Research Studies* 49 (June 1981), 118. Clements does not mention *Dracula* as an example of this particular formula. In fact, he labels the other major horror story formula as the "Dracula Type," for it involves "the discovery of the source of unexplained phenomena and the destruction of that source" (ibid., p. 120). I would suggest that Stoker juxtaposes these two formulas to contrast the vulnerability of the isolated individual with the strength of the alliance of vampire hunters. In this context see also Noel Carroll's description of the "Discovery plot," which he argues is the "most serviceable narrative armature in the horror film genre" ("Nightmare and the Horror Film," *Film Quarterly* 34 [Spring 1981], 23).

2. Interestingly enough, Jules Verne published in 1892 a novel entitled *Le château des Carpathes* (*Carpathian Castle*), concerning the mysterious adventures at an ancient castle in Transylvania. Verne mentions vampires and

other local "superstitions," but *Le château des Carpathes* is actually a tedious Gothic novel of the Anne Radcliffe school, in which all the seemingly extraordinary and terrifying events are explained. In fact, these events are here entirely the product of modern, electrically powered machinery. Unlike *Dracula*, in *Le château des Carpathes* there is no need for faith and ritual, and the "traditional" is merely another word for the superstitious and ignorant. See also Arthur Conan Doyle's "The Adventure of the Sussex Vampire," in which Sherlock Holmes proves the innocence of a woman who is falsely accused of being a vampire. "What have we to do," Holmes asks Watson, "with walking corpses who can only be held in their grave by stakes driven through their hearts? It's pure lunacy" (in *The Annotated Sherlock Holmes*, ed. William S. Baring-Gould [New York: Clarkson N. Potter, 1973], 2: 463).

3. Mark M. Hennelly, Jr., discusses the novel as an "allegory of rival epistemologies in quest of a gnosis" ("*Dracula:* The Gnostic Quest and Victorian Wasteland," *English Literature in Transition* 20, no. 1 [1977], 13). Hennelly's article is the most perceptive and helpful discussion of *Dracula* in the context of Victorian literary tradition.

4. Which is not to argue, as Carol A. Senf does, that Stoker's novel is a Jamesian exercise in "unreliable" narrators ("*Dracula:* The Unseen Face in the Mirror," *Journal of Narrative Technique* 9 [1979], 160–70).

5. As Dennis E. Poplin observes, "Community" is "one of the most confusing terms sociologists use" (*Communities: A Survey of Theories and Methods of Research*, 2d ed. [1972; rpt. New York: Macmillan, 1979], p. vii). Poplin outlines three major definitions: community as a closely knit minority group, such as the members of the same profession or religious organization; community as a "unit of social and territorial organization"—village, town, city, and so on; and community as a "moral or spiritual phenomenon" (ibid., p. 1). As I will suggest in this chapter, the community of vampire hunters depicted in *Dracula* somewhat resembles what Poplin calls a "moral community." Drawing upon the work of Robert A. Nisbet and other sociologists, Poplin concludes that the members of a "moral community" share the following characteristics: a "deep sense of belonging to a significant, meaningful group"; a "sense of pursuing common goals" and a sense of "oneness with other community members"; a "compelling need to participate"; and a "regard" for "each other as whole persons who are of intrinsic significance and worth" (ibid., p. 6). For an excellent introduction to the sociological study of community, see also Maurice R. Stein, *The Eclipse of Community: An Interpretation of American Studies* (New York: Harper and Row, 1964).

6. In a chapter originally written for *Dracula* and later published separately as a story entitled "Dracula's Guest" (in *Dracula's Guest* [1914; rpt. New York: Zebra Books, 1978], pp. 9–25), Stoker provides another picture of an all-male group. This story is set in Germany, where Jonathan Harker, on his way to Transylvania, casually dismisses the fears of local inhabitants, since "Walpurgisnacht doesn't concern Englishmen" (ibid., p. 13), and travels alone into a rural valley, curious to see a deserted and purportedly haunted village. After night falls, a violent storm forces Jonathan to take refuge in a tomb. As he passes out, he seems to see the dead rising from their graves, and he awakens

to discover a wolf poised on his chest, ready to feed. Physically trapped and semiconscious, Jonathan is rescued by a troop of soldiers and escorted back to Munich. In the story's ironic conclusion, however, we discover that the soldiers searched for Jonathan only because they had received a note from Dracula promising them bountiful remuneration if they insured the safety of his long-awaited guest. The soldiers are no potential force of good, just hired hands who do not even manage to kill the wolf; as much as Jonathan, they are easily manipulated pawns of the aristocratic Count Dracula.

7. Compare Van Helsing, who in Stoker's novel and even more in Browning's *Dracula* (1931) and Fisher's *Horror of Dracula* (1958) best fulfills the role of the vampire hunter, with the Serbian figure of the *dhampir*. According to the Serbian tradition summarized by Ornella Volta, the *dhampir* is the only man capable of destroying a vampire. In a one-on-one confrontation, the *dhampir*—who inherits his particular power from his father—battles with the vampire while the beleaguered villagers can only watch in silence and immobility (*The Vampire* [1962; rpt. New York: Award Books, n.d.], pp. 118–19).

8. Phyliss A. Roth argues that Lucy and Mina are both images of the "mother," and therefore both the men's incestuous desires and their matricidal desecration are part of the novel's "hostility toward female sexuality" ("Suddenly Sexual Women in Bram Stoker's *Dracula*," *Literature and Psychology* 27 [1977], 113).

9. For a discussion of the make-up of this alliance, see Richard Wasson, "The Politics of *Dracula*," *English Literature in Transition* 9, no. 1 (1966), 24–27; and Hennelly's survey of Stoker's "allegorical characters" ("Gnostic Quest," pp. 18–23). In the course of considering *Dracula* as a version of the pastoral, Thomas P. Walsh offers another view of these "allegorical characters" ("*Dracula:* Logos and Myth," *Research Studies* 47 [Dec. 1979], 233–35).

10. Bram Stoker, *The Jewel of the Seven Stars* (1912; rpt. New York: Zebra Books, 1979), p. 116. Janet M. Todd convincingly argues that "communication is indeed the essence of their [the vampire hunters'] fellowship" ("The Class-ic Vampire," in *The English Novel and the Movies*, ed. Michael Klein and Gillian Parker [New York: Ungar, 1981], p. 199).

11. As Bruce F. Kawin notes, since this collated narrative does not include "Dracula's perspective," it does not offer "an inside or direct understanding of the supernatural," and thus the horror of "Dracula's nature" remains unexplained (*The Mind of the Novel: Reflexive Fiction and the Ineffable* [Princeton: Princeton University Press, 1982], p. 193). Kawin's remarks on *Dracula* are part of a perceptive examination of the "many examples of complex framing structures and of reflexivity" in horror literature (ibid., p. 181).

12. By excluding Mina from the hunt for Dracula, the men are following what might be identified as a fundamental principle of "male bonding," at least as Lionel Tiger defines this process in *Men in Groups*. "Male bonding," according to Tiger, is "the spinal column of a community, in this sense: from a hierarchical linkage of significant males, communities derive their intra-dependence, their structure, their social coherence, and in good part their continuity through the past to the future" (*Men in Groups* [New York: Vintage, 1970], p. 78). Yet for Stoker, the all-male hunting group can only succeed after

it recognizes the spiritual and practical importance of Mina and includes her in its efforts.

13. As Carrol L. Fry notes, Mina and Lucy are both examples of the "'pure woman,' the staple heroine of popular fiction from Richardson to Hardy" ("Fictional Conventions and Sexuality in *Dracula*," *Victorian Newsletter* 42 [Feb. 1972], 20). Yet Fry, like Judith Weissman in "Women and Vampires: *Dracula* as a Victorian Novel," *Midwest Quarterly* 18 (July 1977), 392–405, overlooks the differences between Lucy and Mina and oversimplifies Mina's role in *Dracula*.

14. Franco Moretti, *Signs Taken for Wonders: Essays in the Sociology of Literary Forms*, trans. David Forgacs (London: Verso Editions, 1983), p. 92. In an insightful analysis that draws on both Marxism and Freudianism, Moretti argues that Dracula is "a saver, an ascetic, an upholder of the Protestant ethic"; "like capital, Dracula is impelled towards a continuous growth, an unlimited expansion of his domain" (ibid., p. 91). The King-Vampire, from this perspective, is a fit representative for "the nineteenth-century bourgeois" of "monopoly," and the vampire hunters are "a bunch of fanatics who want to arrest the course of history" (ibid., pp. 93–94).

15. Hannah Arendt, *On Violence* (New York: Harcourt, Brace, 1970), p. 44. All future page references to *On Violence*, abbreviated OV, will be included parenthetically in my text.

16. Raymond Williams, *Keywords: A Vocabulary of Culture and Society* (New York: Oxford University Press, 1976), p. 66.

17. Ferdinand Tönnies, *Community and Society*, trans. and ed. Charles P. Loomis (New York: Harper & Row, 1963), p. 46. All future page references to *Community and Society*, abbreviated CS, will be included parenthetically in my text.

18. Hennelly, "Gnostic Quest," p. 17.

19. What Jonathan does not mention in his epilogue is that his son might also be a product of the past because Mina has suffered the vampire's baptism, and so the blood of Count Dracula runs through the child's veins. Thus Hennelly argues that the young Quincey's inheritance of the "vitality of the Count" and the vampire's "ancient blood-knowledge" is a necessary "transfusion" that will allow for the revitalization of the "Victorian wasteland" ("Gnostic Quest," p. 23). I assume that just as the hunters are not stained by the blood of the creatures they destroy, so Mina, too, is rendered stainless and free of Dracula's evil, polluting influence once the King-Vampire is destroyed and she is bathed in the purifying beams of "rosy light."

20. For an account of the translations and adaptations of *The Vampyre*, see Montague Summers, *The Vampire: His Kith and Kin* (1928; rpt. New Hyde Park, N.Y.: University Books, 1960), pp. 290–303.

21. E. F. Bleiler, Introduction to *Three Gothic Novels*, ed. E. F. Bleiler (New York: Dover, 1966), p. xxxix.

22. John Polidori, *The Vampyre*, in *Three Gothic Novels*, p. 283. All future references to *The Vampyre*, abbreviated V, will be included parenthetically in my text.

23. In contrast, the first stage adaptation of Polidori's story, Charles Nodier's

Le Vampire, mélodrame in trois actes (1820), concludes with the rescue of the vampire's intended victim and the destruction of Lord Ruthven: "l'Ange exterminateur paraît dans un nuage, le foudre éclate et les Ombres s'engloutissent avec Rutwen. Pluie de feu" (quoted in Summers, *Vampire: His Kith and Kin*, p. 293).

24. Stoker's Count Dracula actually has less in common with Lord Ruthven than with, for example, Mr. Richards in Edward Bulwer-Lytton's *The Haunted and the Haunters* (1859), one of the most famous Victorian ghost stories. Richards is not a vampire, but a man who has learned to control life, to live for centuries. Like Dracula, Richards dreams of becoming the Lord of future generations, for he is an "absolute egotist," a Master who with a "will of intense, creative, working evil" challenges natural law and human society (*The Haunted and the Haunters*, in *Thirteen Famous Ghost Stories*, ed. Peter Underwood [New York: Dutton, 1977], pp. 150, 136).

25. Again, the contrast to nineteenth-century theatrical versions of the vampire's story is very much apparent. According to Summers, Alexandre Dumas's *Le Vampire* (1851) concludes with Lord Ruthven locked forever in his tomb as "multitudes of rejoicing angels are seen" and the victims of the vampire are united in heaven "in happiest benison" (*Vampire: His Kith and Kin*, p. 302).

26. Alain Silver and James Ursini discuss several film adaptations of *Carmilla* in the context of other portraits of the female vampire (*The Vampire Film* [New York: A. S. Barnes, 1975], pp. 97–121). Bruce Kawin notes that *Dreadful Hollow*, one of Faulkner's best unproduced screenplays, contains a vampire who is "a magnetic and terrifying figure, comparable not to Dracula but to Sheridan Le Fanu's seductive, relentless Carmilla" (*Faulkner and Film* [New York: Ungar, 1977], p. 142).

27. Sheridan Le Fanu, *Carmilla*, in *The Dracula Book of Great Vampire Stories*, ed. Leslie Shepard (Secaucus, N.J.: Citadel Press, 1977), p. 33. All future references to *Carmilla*, abbreviated C, will be included parenthetically in my text.

28. As James B. Twitchell points out in *The Living Dead: A Study of the Vampire in Romantic Literature* (Durham, N.C.: Duke University Press, 1981) the most important influence on *Carmilla* was probably not Polidori's *The Vampyre*, but Samuel Taylor Coleridge's "Christabel." Though "Christabel" contains no explicit references to vampires, several critics have called attention to Coleridge's use of vampire lore in the poem. According to Twitchell, for example, "Christabel" reflects Coleridge's interest in "the process of psychic energy transfer, dark eroticism, and the infection of evil" and the poem is best interpreted in Freudian terms, as an "Oedipal reading of the lamia myth" (pp. 47–48). Perhaps the most striking difference between "Christabel" and *Carmilla* is that in the poem the aged, widowed father of the innocent young victim is never awakened to the threat posed by the vampiric female creature who has entered his household. In the end, the father rejects his daughter's warning and takes the serpentine lamia figure as a sort of surrogate wife and daughter. No "formal proceedings" and no alliance of the male ruling class destroy the threatening female creature who seduces the innocent.

Like *Dracula*, *Carmilla* is for Twitchell a late (and relatively simple) variation on nineteenth-century Romantic preoccupations with "vampirism as a mode of discussing energy exchange" (ibid., p. 129) and "human interaction" (ibid., p. 62). In this literary tradition of "only accepted masterpieces" (ibid., p. ix), Twitchell includes John Keats's "Lamia" and "La Belle Dame Sans Merci," Edgar Allan Poe's *Ligeia* and *The Fall of the House of Usher*, Percy Bysshe Shelley's *The Cenci* and George Byron's *Manfred*, as well as works like Coleridge's "The Rime of the Ancient Mariner" and Oscar Wilde's *The Picture of Dorian Gray*, in which vampirism serves as an "elaborate metaphor of the relationship between artist, artifact, and audience" (ibid., p. 142). By 1902, Twitchell concludes, the vampire "myth had been worn almost to the bone" (ibid., p. 178), and thus he dismisses almost all twentieth-century vampire stories as little more than "vulgarized" hackwork full of "gothic stuffing" (ibid., p. 193).

Needless to say, vampirism as "elaborate metaphor" and as psychosexual "myth" remains important in contemporary works like Ingmar Bergman's *Persona* (1966) and John Rechy's *The Vampires* (1971). (See, for example, Bruce Kawin's comments on vampirism in *Persona* in *Mindscreen: Bergman, Godard, and First-Person Film* [Princeton: Princeton University Press, 1978], pp. 123–32.) And while *Dracula* may be, in Twitchell's words, "the consummate retelling of the vampire story" (*Living Dead*, p. 134) and the "culmination of the Romantic interest in the vampire" (ibid., p. 140), Stoker's novel does not exhaust the possibilities of the vampire story. *Dracula*, in fact, generates and demands the countless retellings of this story that have appeared in the last eighty-five years. To evaluate *Dracula* solely in terms of certain "accepted" nineteenth-century literary "masterpieces" is to ignore the fact that Stoker's novel is one of a series of stories about the bloody, violent confrontation between the living and the undead. Only in the context of its sequels as well as its antecedents, in the context of the twentieth as well as the nineteenth century, can the uniqueness of *Dracula* and the significance of the entire genre be measured.

Twitchell focuses more directly on the psychoanalytic implications of vampire stories in "The Vampire Myth," *American Imago* 37 (1980), 83–92, in which he argues that "the vampire is the most complete condensation of the problem and the resolutions of pre-adolescence" (p. 92). The same approach is apparent in his "*Frankenstein* and the Anatomy of Horror," *Georgia Review* 37 (Spring 1983), 41–78, a convincing essay in which Twitchell is much more willing to pay attention to the particular shape *Frankenstein* has taken in the movies.

29. Count Stenbock, *The Sad Story of a Vampire*, in *The Dracula Book of Great Vampire Stories*, p. 122.

30. Victor Roman, *Four Wooden Stakes*, in *The Dracula Book of Great Vampire Stories*, p. 253.

31. The vampire in *Four Wooden Stakes* therefore remains true to what Summers refers to as "the tradition of the vampire who . . . seeks the destruction of his own kin" (*Vampire: His Kith and Kin*, p. 164).

32. Roman, *Four Wooden Stakes*, p. 260.

33. F. G. Loring, *The Tomb of Sarah*, in *The Dracula Book of Great Vampire Stories*, p. 163.

34. M. E. Braddon, *Good Lady Ducayne*, in ibid., p. 136.

35. E. F. Benson, *The Room in the Tower*, in ibid., pp. 193, 197. Like Benson's *The Room in the Tower*, M. R. James's *Count Magnus* (1904) focuses on the haunting of one man by an undead creature. In James's story, an inquisitive, middle-aged antiquarian mysteriously dies after he becomes increasingly interested in the life of Count Magnus, a sixteenth-century Swedish nobleman known for his violent temper and experiments with the black arts.

36. Loring, *Tomb of Sarah*, p. 160.

37. Ibid.

38. Certain details in Stoker's *The Jewel of the Seven Stars*, like the striking image of the beautiful heroine suddenly appearing in her "white nightdress stained with the blood in which she knelt" (p. 44), call to mind aspects of *Dracula*. But the quasi-detective/adventure story Stoker tells in *The Jewel of the Seven Stars* about an attempt to resurrect a mysterious, beautiful, mummified Egyptian queen shares much less with *Dracula* than does *The Lair of the White Worm* and the stories collected in *Dracula's Guest*.

39. Bram Stoker, *The Lair of the White Worm* (1911; rpt. New York: Paperback Library, 1966), p. 142. All future references to *The Lair of the White Worm*, abbreviated WW, will be included parenthetically in my text.

40. Leonard Wolf, *A Dream of Dracula: In Search of the Living Dead* (New York: Popular Library, 1972), p. 254.

41. Maurice Richardson, "The Psychoanalysis of Ghost Stories," *Twentieth Century* 166 (Dec. 1959), 428.

42. See, for example, Joseph S. Bierman, "*Dracula:* Prolonged Childhood Illness, and the Oral Triad," *American Imago* 29 (1972), 186–98; C. F. Bentley, "The Monster in the Bedroom: Sexual Symbolism in Bram Stoker's *Dracula*," *Literature and Psychology* 22 (1972), 27–34; Roth, "Suddenly Sexual Women in Bram Stoker's *Dracula*," 113–24; Twitchell, "The Vampire Myth," 83–92; and Moretti, *Signs Taken for Wonders*, pp. 98–104.

43. Twitchell, *Living Dead*, p. 135.

44. Edwin R. Wallace IV, in *Freud and Anthropology: A History and Reappraisal* (New York: International Universities Press, 1983), offers a comprehensive study of *Totem and Taboo*. Wallace examines the works of philosophy, anthropology, and physical science that influenced Freud, as well as the effect of Freud's own clinical work on the formulation of his social and anthropological theories. *Freud and Anthropology* also contains a critique of *Totem and Taboo* and a survey of the critical response to this work.

45. Sigmund Freud, *Group Psychology and the Analysis of the Ego*, trans. James Strachey (New York: Bantam, 1960), p. 86. All future page references to *Group Psychology and the Analysis of the Ego*, abbreviated GP, will be included parenthetically in my text, as will references to *Totem and Taboo: Some Points of Agreement between the Mental Lives of Savages and Neurotics*, trans. James Strachey (New York: Norton, 1950), abbreviated TT; *Civilization and Its Discontents*, trans. James Strachey (New York: Norton, 1961), abbreviated

CD; and *Moses and Monotheism*, trans. Katherine Jones (New York: Vintage, 1958), abbreviated MM.

46. In *Moses and Monotheism* Freud (and his translators) refer to his narrative account of these primeval events as an "argument" (MM, 102), a "story" (MM, 102), a "historical survey" (MM, 106), and a "reconstruction of prehistory" (MM, 155). And, as I have already noted, he calls this narrative a "scientific myth" in *Group Psychology and the Analysis of the Ego*. Although Freud insists that the events he "reconstructs" actually occurred in man's prehistory, his shifting terminology suggests that "stories," "myths," and "histories" (and also "arguments"?) are all "reconstructions," all versions of the same underlying structure.

47. Herbert Marcuse, *Eros and Civilization: A Philosophical Inquiry into Freud* (New York: Vintage, 1955), pp. 59, 63.

48. Sigmund Freud, *The Future of an Illusion*, trans. W. D. Robson-Scott (Garden City, N. Y.: Doubleday, n.d.), p. 76.

49. Richardson, "Psychoanalysis of Ghost Stories," pp. 428–29.

50. If Freud's comments about children's tendency to "displace" their hostility toward and fear of the father onto an animal substitute are correct, then Dracula's ability to transform himself into a bat or wolf might well be linked to his role as primal father. See *Totem and Taboo*, pp. 129–32.

51. Royce MacGillivray, "*Dracula*: Bram Stoker's Spoiled Masterpiece," *Queen's Quarterly* 79 (Winter 1972), 522–23.

52. See Freud's discussion of the role of libido in group psychology in *Group Psychology and the Analysis of the Ego*, pp. 29–31.

PART TWO

Dracula Retold

Let us think of the common inheritance of the members of a genre as a story, call it a myth. The members of a genre will be interpretations of it, or to use Thoreau's word for it, revisions of it, which will also make them interpretations of one another.

Stanley Cavell
Pursuits of Happiness

CHAPTER

3

Dracula: The Vampire Play (1927), *Dracula* (1931), and *Dracula* (1979)

ONE OF THE MOST OBVIOUS yet most interesting and significant ironies as vampire stories move from the nineteenth into the twentieth century is that, for all of the efforts of Stoker's moral community, Count Dracula lives, rising in film and fiction after his absolute destruction at the end of Stoker's *Dracula*, then suffering another "true death" in Hamilton Deane and John L. Balderston's *Dracula: The Vampire Play* (1927), Tod Browning's Universal film, *Dracula* (1931), and Terence Fisher's Hammer film, *Horror of Dracula* (1958), among other works that would conclude the saga of the King-Vampire once and for all. As quickly proven by a glance at anthologies like M. L. Carter's *The Curse of the Undead* (1970), at critical studies like David Pirie's *The Vampire Cinema* (1977), at encyclopedic surveys like Donald F. Glut's *The Dracula Book* (1975), and even at the programming schedules for independent television stations and cable TV movie channels, other vampires have thrived in the twentieth century. Of course, none of these undead creatures—male and female, of all ages and classes and backgrounds—has the stature and the notoriety of Count Dracula, who is to vampires what Sherlock Holmes is to private detectives, not the prototype but the definitive exemplar.[1] These two products of late Victorian England, of the nineteenth century's last gasp, now exist apart from any specific text; they are recognizable by people who have never heard of Bram Stoker or Arthur Conan Doyle, or, for that matter, Queen Victoria and the British Empire.

Even more than Holmes, Dracula has been removed from his original context to reappear as the aristocratic, foreign predator in countless other works, including, for example, Universal's *House of Frankenstein* (1944) and *House of Dracula* (1945), Hammer's *Dracula Has Risen from the Grave* (1968) and *Taste the Blood of Dracula* (1969), Marvel Comics' *Tomb of Dracula* (first issue in 1972) and *Dracula Lives!* (first issue in 1973), and Pinnacle Books' paperback "Dracula Horror Series" beginning, appropriately enough, with *Dracula Returns!* (1973). In most cases these works share very little, if anything, with Stoker's story of the confrontation between the living and the undead. Raymond Rudorff's *The Dracula Archives* (1972), on the other hand, is presented as an account of the events that preceded Jonathan Harker's journey to Transylvania in *Dracula*. Following Stoker (who himself was utilizing techniques that Wilkie Collins had mastered and popularized in *The Moonstone* [1868]), Rudorff's novel is a collection of first-person narratives in the form of diaries, letters, journalistic accounts, and so on, all of which together depict a pseudohistory as complex and ingenious as Kaspar Gutman's story of the Maltese Falcon. Full of allusions to and imitations of Stoker's novel, *The Dracula Archives* is a "prequel" to *Dracula* that traces the Count's lineage to historical figures like Vlad the Impaler and Countess Elisabeth Bathory and follows the adventures of several characters (often modeled on Stoker's characters) who unwittingly participate in the resurrection of Dracula.[2] An equally ingenious, gamelike blend of imitation, allusion, pseudo-scholarship, and fiction-about-fiction (purporting to deliver the "real" facts, the "true" story) is Fred Saberhagen's *The Dracula Tape* (1975), in which Dracula, like John Gardner's Grendel, offers his own first-person account of the events Stoker depicts so one-sidedly in *Dracula*. Witty, urbane, honorable, and logical in his own defense, Dracula here easily outwits his dull and "sadistic" opponents.[3]

By imitating *Dracula*'s mode of narration or by shifting the novel's viewpoint from the living to the undead, *The Dracula Archives* and *The Dracula Tape* become critical commentaries on Stoker's novel, in the same sense that successful extended parody comments on and illuminates its source. Saberhagen's novel might even be termed a retelling of *Dracula*, covering the same events in the same order as Stoker does, yet with Count Dracula as narrator, resembling a defendant at last able to testify in his own behalf or a concerned historian determined to set the record straight. In this and the following two chapters I will focus on other retellings of *Dracula*, on adaptations of

Stoker's novel for theater, film, and television—but not in order to assign evaluative ratings based on a bias toward literature and a dogmatic perspective that would condemn all so-called infidelity to the sacrosanct original (as if the act of criticism was equivalent to delivering a verdict in divorce court). My interest is in the complex play of permutation and constancy, in the uniqueness of each retelling as well as its place in an ongoing tradition, in the significance of variation and repetition that only a comparative analysis can reveal, and, above all, in the important questions that these versions of *Dracula* raise about violence, ritual, and the status quo, and about the nature of victims and hunters—both living and undead.[4]

Between Stoker's novel and Tod Browning's much-parodied 1931 *Dracula* stands *Dracula: The Vampire Play in Three Acts*, "dramatized," as the title page declares, "by Hamilton Deane and John L. Balderston from Bram Stoker's World Famous Novel, *Dracula*."[5] (In an appendix, I offer an act by act summary of this play.) Deane's first dramatization of the novel appeared in 1924, and after successful runs in England, the play was sold in 1927 to American producer Horace Liveright. According to Glut, Liveright "suggested that the play be revised to make it more modern," so Deane collaborated with Balderston on a new version, which opened in New York City in October 1927.[6] Deane and Balderston's adaptation was a major commercial success for both New York and the touring companies and was published, complete with detailed production notes, in 1933 by Samuel French.

In modernizing *Dracula*, Deane and Balderston went little further than to provide Jonathan Harker with an automobile and to reveal that Count Dracula journeyed to England in a "three-engined German plane." Twentieth-century technology serves only to extend the vampire's potential hunting ground, while the living still rely on traditional weapons: wolfsbane (in lieu of garlic), cross, and stake. This nonstop trans-European night flight stands out as an obvious addition to Stoker's narrative, and so, too, do several scenes of comic relief, featuring a flirtatious maid and a bumbling attendant at Seward's "Sanatorium." Of much greater interest, however, are the major deletions, condensations, and alterations Deane and Balderston introduce in their attempt to dramatize Stoker's novel for the popular theater of the 1920s, a theater which obviously fostered its own standards of stage convention and suspenseful horror and which implicitly promoted its own ideological entertainment.

A comparison of the characters in *Dracula: The Vampire Play* and Stoker's *Dracula* begins to suggest how different these two works are in their presentation of the confrontation between the living and the undead and also in their sense of what constitutes fitness. For example, Deane and Balderston retain Dracula's attacks on two young Englishwomen, but focus almost completely on Lucy Seward (here the daughter of the middle-aged Dr. Seward and the fiancée of Jonathan Harker). Lucy's friend, Mina Weston, the first victim of the vampire, never appears on stage, although she is mentioned in all three acts: in Act I, Seward describes her fatal illness to Van Helsing; in Act II, Lucy learns of the undead Mina's attacks on children; and in Act III, Van Helsing describes how he released her from her unholy existence by driving a stake into her heart. Mina's story is purely secondary and supplementary, an off-stage subplot that illustrates the effects of Dracula's attacks and, more important, demonstrates the knowledge, courage, and capability of Van Helsing, who alone can identify Mina's disease and wield the stake that provides her with salvation.

While we only hear about Mina's story, we see Lucy Seward on stage throughout the play, yet Lucy remains as one-dimensional as her friend—"so young, so beautiful, so pure," as Renfield declares (DVP, 46), and also so easily victimized. The stage directions only stipulate that Lucy be a "beautiful girl of twenty," who looks "weak" and "unnaturally pale" (DVP, 18). By having Lucy already seriously ill and subject to quickly shifting "alternate moods" when the play begins, Deane and Balderston insist that she is completely dependent, if not on Van Helsing and her father, then on Count Dracula. (In fact, the only other woman in the play is Lucy's maid, and this character may be physically healthy, but she is also under Dracula's hypnotic power. The Count, it would seem, easily holds dominion over all women who once gaze into his eyes.) Dressed in a "semi-revealing" negligee (DVP, 91), Lucy appears in the first two acts as a passive object of concern and of desire. When she finally does exhibit a bit of vitality in Act III, it is only a sign of her vampiric appetites. With a crucifix, Van Helsing exorcises Lucy's unnatural "ardor," and the aggressive, sexually assertive "animal" once again becomes a beloved invalid who describes—with anguish and embarrassment—the vampire's embrace. Lucy's on-stage confessions do not save her, of course, for the men are responsible for providing her salvation. Unlike Stoker's Mina Harker, Lucy plays no active role in the counterattack against Dracula. She runs "hysterically" from the library, leaving her fate entirely in the hands of "my lover, my father, my dear friend" (DVP, 65). As Dracula is destroyed, Lucy reappears. Released from the vampire's control, she does not thank God, as does Renfield. Instead, Lucy calls out for her father and Jonathan, thereby reaffirming her full acceptance of what this play presents as the normal and natural order of sexual and familial relations, an order that Dracula has disrupted.

In place of the four young men who hunt for the vampire in Stoker's novel, Deane and Balderston provide Lucy with only one suitor, Jonathan Harker, "a typical Englishman of the Public School class, but in manner direct, explosive, incisive and excitable" (DVP, 7). Jonathan is neither lawyer nor doctor; he is, as the stage directions suggest, quite simply the Young Man—courageous, willing to sacrifice all for love, impulsive, committed to action, easily influenced, and obviously in need of guidance. The play opens with an "agitated" Jonathan insisting to Dr. Seward that "surely there must be something *more* we can do for Lucy" (DVP, 8). Seward, Lucy's fifty-five-year-old father in this play, has no suggestions. His daughter's illness falls far outside his traditional medical experience, and, more important, Seward is a "typical specialist who lives in a world of text books and patients, not a man of action or force of character" (DVP, 8). Separately or together, the fiancé and the father can do little to alter the course of events, except provide blood transfusions for Lucy. Unlike Seward, Van Helsing knows what needs to be done for Lucy's sake, and, while Seward is initially skeptical ("Of course Lucy's trouble can't be *that*!" [DVP, 28]), Jonathan immediately accepts, once and for all, the Professor's strange theories. As long as Jonathan is told what to do, he proves to be a useful assistant (more helpful than Seward, who is ill-equipped for action). When Jonathan is alone with Lucy, however, he very nearly falls prey to her unnatural advances, but Van Helsing steps in with his crucifix to save the young man's life.

As a reward for his "manner direct" (and perhaps also as a sort of rite of passage), Jonathan is allowed to hammer in the stake that Van Helsing positions over Dracula's body. Protected and directed by a wise, older guide, the young man ultimately wins back his beloved by vanquishing his monstrous rival. *Dracula: The Vampire Play* thus offers a particularly tidy resolution to potential psychological conflicts among the father, the daughter, and the fiancé that are raised only by implication: Seward is allowed to witness the death of an apparently irresistible intruder who sought to steal away his only child; Jonathan is allowed to destroy a dominating older aristocrat who sought to control his fiancée and turn her against him. Dracula—a version of the possessive father as well as the aggressive lover, and thoroughly evil, too—dies, and Lucy calls out for her father and her young lover in the same breath, as if she does not have to choose between them, as if the destruction of the vampire signals the end of rivalry and jealousy.

Lucy, Seward, and Jonathan are the beneficiaries, but it is Van Helsing who makes this conclusion possible, who creates it through word and deed. For example, like his prototype in Stoker's novel, Deane and Balderston's Van Helsing serves as the source of information for the beleaguered human beings, and for the audience as well. In Act I, after a series of mysterious, apparently unrelated events (Renfield's raving "madness," Lucy's descriptions of her "bad dreams," Dracula's sudden appearance on stage), Van Helsing sternly informs Seward and Jonathan about the characteristics of the undead, the probable cause of Lucy's illness and Renfield's madness, and the "dangerous work" that must be undertaken (DVP, 28). At once a lecture, a call to arms, and a sermon against the shortsightedness of modern science, this exposition unquestionably establishes Van Helsing as the leader of the living. "I must be master here," he insists, "or I can do nothing" (DVP, 30). Although this master is gray-haired and pious, he is not the grandfatherly patriarch of Stoker's novel, but more akin to a "Dutch Sherlock Holmes" (DVP, 35) in his single-mindedness and his distance from the other characters.

As the stage directions make clear, Van Helsing's "incisive speech, always to the point," reflects his overall "air of resolution," but this resolution finds its fullest expression in his "resourceful action" (DVP, 11). Offstage, he provides blood for Lucy, transfixes Mina, and leads the men to Carfax in search of Dracula's coffins. On stage, Van Helsing at several points assumes the role of a director: situating Jonathan and Seward, "arranging" Lucy on the couch, switching off the lights at the end of Act I in an attempt to capture the still unidentified intruder, and setting another trap in Act III, this time with Renfield as bait for the vampire. As at the conclusion of the play when Van Helsing positions the stake over Dracula's heart and hands Jonathan the hammer, the master provides the all-important objects necessary for the struggle with the undead. In Act I he uses wolfsbane to demonstrate Renfield's connection with the vampire, and later he seals Lucy's room with this "preventive medicine" (DVP, 17). In Act II, when he is alone with Dracula, Van Helsing brandishes the host, and with it forces the snarling vampire offstage. In Act III he thrusts forward a crucifix to protect

Jonathan from his now tainted betrothed. Thus in *Dracula: The Vampire Play* one man provides all the essential information, supplies the necessary objects, and leads the living into battle with the vampire. Jonathan has good reason to tell Van Helsing: "God must have sent you here to help us. Without you there'd be no hope" (DVP, 40).

Van Helsing is Renfield's "only hope" as well, as this madman realizes when he falls on his knees and begs the older man: "Save my soul! Save my soul! I am weak. You are strong. I am crazy. You are sane" (DVP, 44). By the end of the play Renfield is indeed saved, for he "rises to his full height, and becomes a sane person" (DVP, 104)—in this world, sanity and salvation are as inseparable as insanity and evil. Renfield is a much more prominent character in the play than in Stoker's novel. He escapes from his cell and invades the Seward house in all three acts, each time dominating the onstage action with his exaggerated shifts in mood, his maniacal laughter, and his cryptic pronouncements. Renfield is most obviously an example of madness/insanity/lunacy, a state of mental disorder that is linked in some way to the power of Count Dracula. Since Renfield is a "repulsive youth" (DVP, 12)—rather than the middle-aged man in Stoker's *Dracula*—he is directly contrasted to Jonathan, a youth who is "handsome in appearance" (DVP, 7). However, like Jonathan, and Lucy for that matter, Renfield is shown as being under the domination of an older male figure. Just as all of the women in the play fall under the vampire's spell, all of the young people are incapable of independent action—they are controlled (for better or worse) by their elders, by their "masters." That one of the basic distinctions in *Dracula: The Vampire Play* is between age and youth is emphasized by the fact that the Count is "aged fifty," Seward is "about fifty-five," and Van Helsing is "in the early fifties" (DVP, 5). Furthermore, because Seward is not a "man of action," Van Helsing and Count Dracula alone decide the fate of this world, with the young people as pawns or prizes.

Deane and Balderston's Count Dracula (played by Bela Lugosi in the initial New York run of the play) has no desire to spawn a new order of beings, but only to gain another bride for his harem in Transylvania. To this end, he invades not England and the modern world in general, but one single household, entering the library with "bows in courtly fashion" (DVP, 22). While Dracula acts his role with enough of a "distinguished, Continental" manner to fool Seward and Jonathan (DVP, 5), he is also—like Van Helsing—a director who manipulates the maid, Lucy, and Renfield almost as if these characters are his marionettes.

Yet duplicity and a certain skill in manipulation are characteristic of a great many villains of the popular theater. To reveal that this "polished" aristocrat is in fact a "devil" and not merely another foreign lothario, Deane and Balderston employ a range of lighting and sound effects, stage tricks, and special props. For example, dogs endlessly howl off stage to signal the presence of the Count; green spotlights illuminate his face as he secretly enters the house; traps allow for his mysterious disappearances; and in the form of a bat he crashes against the windows and flies across the stage. (The "Notes on Production" provide a detailed guide for all these effects, particularly for the construction and use of the "flying bat," an effect which "should be as carefully rehearsed as the play itself" [DVP, 89].) Through these effects in *Dracula: The Vampire Play*, Dracula becomes associated with certain techniques of theatrical spectacle, just as F. W. Murnau links his vampire with specific cinematic techniques in *Nosferatu, a Symphony of Horror*, and Philip Saville with certain video techniques in *Count Dracula* (1977). In each case these techniques separate the undead from the world of the living (which is represented with some attempt at verisimilitude in mise-en-scène and action), while at the same time they make the vampire the most visually interesting character in the work, one worth watching because we never know precisely how and when he will rupture the predictable surface of "realistic" representation.

By presenting Count Dracula and Stoker's other characters in the manner I have outlined, Deane and Balderston necessarily alter the thematic focus of the novel—limiting the magnitude and the range of the threat posed by the vampire, omitting almost completely the role of faith, ritual, and community for the vampire hunters, and emphasizing certain simple, reassuring distinctions between men and women, young and old, sane and insane, good and evil, heroes and victims. What these two veterans of the popular stage turn Stoker's *Dracula* into is a compact, well-made play about vampires and madness that is presented in a thoroughly conventional, easy-to-follow, symmetrical form.[7] For example, each act, as I have indicated, includes an interruption by Renfield, as well as appearances by Lucy and Count Dracula. After the curtain falls at the end of Acts I, II, and III.1 with Dracula in control (either outwitting the hunters or embracing Lucy), the destruction of the vampire in the brief final scene becomes particularly satisfying.

To destroy Dracula, Van Helsing, Seward, and Jonathan may not have to journey to the wilds of Transylvania, but these hunters must leave the confines of Seward's home (the setting for all but the final scene of the play) and venture into the darkness of an old vault, far from "all the powers of society" (DVP, 29). Once they locate the coffin, the actual murder of the sleeping vampire is relatively easy, and the only special effect is a "low groan" from backstage. No blood taints the living, whose violence is formally correct and unquestionably justified. Lucy and Renfield, the two observers of this action, are immediately "released from the evil power" (DVP, 104); the transformation is so sudden as to suggest that without Dracula there is no raving madness or unnatural appetites. Renfield thanks God, Lucy calls for her father and Jonathan, and Van Helsing—now become the priest—scatters the dust of the vampire's remains. The curtain falls as normality rises with its recognizable gestures and its full acceptance of God, the family, and natural death.

As I noted in chapter 2, Jonathan Harker's epilogue to Stoker's *Dracula* is essential in establishing the closed ending of the novel by insisting on the absolute destruction of the undead and the psychic health and material happiness of the living. For their finale, Deane and Balderston offer a curtain speech that is intended to "throw the chill back into their [the audience's] marrows and send them out of the theatre quaking" (DVP, 105). Van Helsing, appearing alone on stage, seems about to waylay the prospect of any "bad dreams" that Dracula and Renfield might cause us, but the Professor concludes by telling the audience that indeed "*there are such things*" (DVP, 74). This half-serious attempt to link the theatrical world and the "real" world, the characters and the audience, is ironically a ploy that draws attention to the artifice and conventionality of footlit stages and curtain falls. Nonetheless, Van Helsing's insistence in this curtain speech that the threat persists suggests at least one way in which the closure of *Dracula* will be opened up in the twentieth century.

The introductory credits of Tod Browning's *Dracula* (1931)—probably the single most well-known version of Count Dracula's story—announce the film as "*Dracula* by Bram Stoker. From the play adapted by Hamilton Deane and John L. Balderston." Based to some degree on a Broadway play and starring the two actors who were featured in the stage production (Bela Lugosi as Dracula and Edward Van Sloan as Van Helsing), Browning's film has often been criticized for what Roy Huss calls its "static staginess" and its failure to exploit certain "cinematic" possibilities, such as varying camera set-ups, "montage" editing, and "suggestive" lighting effects.[8] Even though such criticisms are generally based upon simplistic, prescriptive assumptions about the nature of the "cinematic" and the "theatrical,"[9] they do begin to suggest the extent to which Browning and screenwriter Garrett Fort borrow from *Dracula: The Vampire Play*, particularly for the characterization and the alignment of the major figures and for the mise-en-scène of the scenes set in Seward's home.

Yet for all of its use of static tableaus and theatrical entrances and exits, Browning's *Dracula* is obviously not merely a filmed version of Deane and Balderston's play. For example, Browning's reliance on readily identifiable sound effects to create the sense of off-screen space and his use of dissolves to provide spatial and temporal transitions (rather than to create metaphoric juxtapositions) are typical of American movies during the early 1930s. So, too, is his dependence on intrusive close-ups and medium shots, particularly of the vampire, for dramatic emphasis. And like almost all Hollywood adaptors of Broadway productions, Browning and Fort attempt to open up the theatrical text—filming what is only discussed in the play, greatly expanding the number and the magnitude of the sets (interior as well as exterior, natural settings), and reinstating sequences from Stoker's novel that Deane and Balderston had omitted.[10] Thus Browning's *Dracula*, unlike *Dracula: The Vampire Play*, begins with a journey to Castle Dracula in Transylvania and includes the Count's sea voyage to England, as well as images of London, Seward's sanitarium, Carfax Abbey, Renfield's cell, and even Van Helsing's study.

Such images do not situate this horror film within the context of identifiable, quotidian reality (as Murnau's on-location images often do in *Nosferatu* [1922]). But they do expand the highly circumscribed boundaries of Deane and Balderston's three-act, three-set play and provide us with additional information about the principal characters and about the values involved when the living confront the undead. None of the sets or locations in Browning's *Dracula* is merely background, merely a place; all tell us a great deal about the characters who visit or inhabit or own them. (We should never cease to marvel at the enormous amount of information the cinematic image can convey—casually, indirectly, without the narrative pause that literary description so often requires.)

Transylvania, with its rocky, inhospitable countryside, isolated peasant village, and ancient, impregnable castle, is the obvious example of the significance of the locations in Browning's film, for this strange land is rarely mentioned, much less shown, in *Dracula: The Vampire Play*. Unlike in Stoker's novel, in *Dracula* (1931), it is Renfield who journeys to Transylvania. With this young traveler we encounter a land in which the terrified, pious, superstitious human beings live in a state of constant watchfulness. Language here is only used for issuing warnings, repeating local legends about the vampire, and reciting prayers. Armed with religious talismans, this rural civilization expends all its energy in protecting itself. It cannot hope to conquer and exploit its environment, and so it seems less picturesque than pitifully anachronistic in contrast to Western societies, which measure progress in terms of industrialization and imperialism. With its luxurious music hall, freely traveled paved streets, and landscaped sanitarium, England could almost be on another planet than Transylvania, though the vampire proves to us that his wild and primitive homeland is within easy striking distance of the modern world.

The heart of Transylvania is Castle Dracula, which exerts an influence greater than any feudal estate. The very magnitude of this fortress is a mark of its dominance. Unlike the peasants' homes, the castle's rooms are huge, with no ceilings in sight, as the walls rise thirty feet or more. Before Renfield enters the vampire's domain, Browning carries us with a series of dissolves into the seemingly endless, mist-filled, cavernous crypt area of Castle Dracula. Then, after several brief detail shots of, for example, the vampire's wives emerging from their coffins, the Count appears, standing motionless while the camera moves toward him like a supplicant. (It will be similarly drawn toward the vampiric Mina later in the film.) No scene in *Dracula: The Vampire Play* even approximates Browning's emphasis here on the commanding power of the Count and on the utter barrenness of his undead existence. Furthermore, the presence of Dracula's three white-robed wives—who do not appear in the play—directly links vampirism with voracious, "perverse," destructive sexuality. Browning's Dracula does not simply desire to carry off two pretty Englishwomen, he seeks to create more wives who sleep in coffins and rise to satisfy unnatural desires. And the Count in *Dracula* (1931) takes Renfield as his victim/paramour as well, kneeling to embrace/feed off the defenseless young man in an act that prefigures Dracula's seduction of the young women in England.

Because we see and therefore know Count Dracula better even than do the Transylvanian peasants and the informed Van Helsing, the real horror in *Dracula* (1931) is the ease with which this monster can enter and move through British society (in contrast to Renfield, who fails so abysmally in his business trip to Transylvania). In scenes that, again, have no source in *Dracula: The Vampire Play*, the vampire seems not at all out of place at night on the streets of London. Just prior to his first encounter with Lucy and Mina, Dracula murders a lower-class young woman who sells flowers on a foggy street, and this brief, seemingly digressive episode pointedly suggests how successfully the formally dressed vampire can thrive in the open, unprotected modern world. Thus before Browning finally takes us to Seward's asylum for a series of interior scenes that are derived to a great extent from Deane and Balderston's play, *Dracula* (1931) has allowed us to gauge both the nature of the vampire and the type of threat this foreign aristocrat poses to a secular society that does not arm itself with religious talismans and traditional beliefs.

By showing us images of London, Browning is also able to draw clear distinctions between the two major female victims of the vampire: Mina Seward (called Lucy Seward in the play, Mina Harker in Stoker's novel) and Lucy Western (called Mina Weston in the play, Lucy Westenra in the novel), a character who serves in Deane and Balderston's play only as an offstage validation of Van Helsing's theories and as a lesson about what might befall Miss Seward. Once again, the story of the living and the undead provides an occasion for assessing what makes women both uniquely valuable and particularly vulnerable.

Regardless of the policeman who strolls next to Dracula below the window of her London home, Lucy of Browning's film is easy prey for the vampire, not only because she recites somber poetry and is immediately fascinated by the Count's melancholia and Old World mien, but also because she is to some degree independent, with no father or lover to protect her. Mina, on the contrary, is first seen at a concert in the company of both her father and John Harker, her fiancé. Fully (and falsely) confident of her own role as daughter and wife-to-be in an upper-middle-class, male-dominated environment, Mina mockingly chides her friend's deviations from the normal: the Count is "fascinating," Lucy declares as she sits before her mirror and vanity table. Mina laughs and tells her friend that "you need someone a little more normal . . . like John." The film bears out Mina's criticism, even though we will later see this young woman leave her father's home to embrace the vampire. After Dracula's attack, the undead Lucy appears on screen only once. Closely resembling Dracula's white-gowned wives in Transylvania, Lucy glides past a cemetery like a mannequin on wheels while a child cries in the distance. Although Van Helsing vows to release Lucy's soul, this redemptive act is neither shown as in Stoker's *Dracula* nor reported as in *Dracula: The Vampire Play*. Lucy is, in effect, an expendable victim (with her admittedly romantic sensibility and her slight degree of independence, she is perhaps even more dangerous alive than undead), while Mina—who lacks the intelligence, faith, and the all-important spiritual significance of Stoker's heroine—must be saved if the world is to be returned to normal.

Unlike Stoker's orphaned women, Mina in Browning's *Dracula* has a father, but the elderly Dr. Seward plays no part in the salvation of his daughter. At first, in the name of "modern medical science," Seward unconvincingly counters Van Helsing's strange speculations. Soon, however, as both the pastoral calm of his sanitarium and the security of his home break down, Seward cedes his authority to Van Helsing. Whereas in the play Seward participates in the final confrontation with the vampire and shares in the triumph of the living, he disappears from the film just when the danger to his daughter is greatest and when the active pursuit of Dracula begins. We could say that once the vampire gains access to Mina's bedroom, any protection her father might provide is completely negated—thus indirectly Dr. Seward is also a victim of Dracula, who causes the destruction of an already incomplete family.

If Mina's father seems easily taken in by the Count's formal attire and aristocratic manners, John Harker quickly sizes up Dracula as a potential rival or at least as a bad influence. The complete fiancé, John lives only for Mina (he has no home of his own, no family, no vocation) and is, needless to say, prepared to do anything to protect her. Yet his concern, born of worshipful love, only renders Mina more susceptible to the vampire, and John alone can no more protect his fiancée than he can drive away the large bat that hovers over the terrace next to Mina's bedroom. Unlike his counterpart in *Dracula: The Vampire Play*, who instinctively and immediately accepts Van Helsing's guidance, Browning's young man wants to "call the police" and take Mina away with him so that she can be "safe." Even more naively, John suggests that she merely "forget" her dreams of Dracula's embrace, and later he accepts with relief Mina's suspiciously rapid "cure," which is in fact only the devious ploy of a dissembling vampire. Much more than Lucy's suitors in Stoker's novel or Jonathan in *Dracula: The Vampire Play*, Browning's John Harker is the young man as vain fool, untutored and almost untutorable, and therefore a danger to the welfare of the living.

Faced with Seward and John Harker, it is no wonder that Browning's Van Helsing declares: "I must be master here or I can do nothing." This line is derived from Deane and Balderston, as is much of the characterization of Van Helsing in *Dracula* (1931). Van Helsing is master from his first appearance in the film, when he—dressed in a white labcoat—examines Lucy's body in a large operating room (while other doctors watch from a gallery of seats) and then views Renfield's blood under a microscope. Costume and decor in these two scenes (which have no analogue in the novel or the play) immediately establish Van Helsing as an authoritative man of science. Later he reveals that he has devoted a "lifetime to the study of many strange things, little known facts which the world is perhaps better off for not knowing."[11] As the stern, unemotional master, Van Helsing issues orders and provides explanations (although he is not our sole source of information about vampires in the film, as he is in *Dracula: The Vampire Play*). Yet his knowledge and strength of will are not tempered by the sentiment and Christian wisdom of Stoker's paternal guide. The crucifix, for Browning's hero, is only a weapon—more effective than wolfsbane, but less effective than a stake. Set apart from the vulnerable women and ineffectual men of England through his personal attributes and often through Browning's staging, Van Helsing is the sole human being capable of defeating the vampire. Thus when these two foreigners first confront each other in the parlor of Seward's home, the other characters stand apart, unaware that the parlor—another embodiment of the normal—has become the setting for a struggle that will determine their fate. And when Dracula and Van Helsing match wills in the parlor for the second time, none of the Englishmen is even present in the room.

These two confrontations are based on similar scenes in the play, but Browning omits Deane and Balderston's climactic showdown in Act III, when Dracula is able to escape from Van Helsing, Seward, and Jonathan, who have used crucifixes to corner the vampire in the library. Instead, the Count in *Dracula* (1931) enters Mina's bedroom with the assistance of a maid he has hypnotized; then, as Dracula reaches for his victim, Browning cuts to Carfax Abbey just as the vampire and his new bride are about to enter the massive, old building. After Dracula has abducted Mina, Van Helsing and John pursue the vampire back to his English estate, a home in the modern world that very clearly calls to mind Castle Dracula. But no communal action is required, much less celebrated in Browning's *Dracula*. While John futilely searches for Mina, Van Helsing discovers and opens the two coffins, breaks apart a coffin lid to fashion a stake, and hammers the stake into the vampire's body. He accomplishes what the frightened Transylvanian peasants never dared to attempt. John comes upon Mina only after Van Helsing has freed her from Dracula's control—she awakens as if from a trance. Van Helsing then places John's arm protectively around Mina's shoulder. The couple leaves the Professor behind as they slowly climb a steep stairway, ascending toward the light in an image that clearly evokes a wedding march and that contrasts with Count Dracula's solitary ascent out of the underground crypt of Castle Dracula early in the film.[12] No prayers of thanksgiving are offered, and the young lovers, it appears, have not changed because of their ordeal. By slaying the seducer who comes in dreams, the aged foreign master has made England once again safe for marriage. And Browning, even more than Deane and Balderston, has brought center stage what R. H. W. Dillard calls the "heroic man"—the utterly unique, wise elder who guards and rescues the living.[13] Unlike the final affirmation of the family and the birth of new life in Stoker's novel or the restoration that marks the end of *Dracula: The Vampire Play*, in Browning's version of *Dracula* the final image associates the return to normality with the reunion and marriage of John and Mina, a legitimate heterosexual relationship that answers and narratively supersedes Dracula's relationship with his wives and with Renfield. Like Dracula, Lucy and Dr. Seward are excluded from this image, as is Van Helsing, who remains in the shadowy subterranean vaults with death and the vampire and all those "strange things . . . which the world is perhaps better off for not knowing."

Since Browning's *Dracula* does not include the vampire hunters' holy crusade to Transylvania, Carfax Abbey—Count Dracula's Gothic lair in England—becomes a sort of repository for all that most threatens the normal world. Whereas Deane and Balderston only take us into the Abbey's dark vaults for the play's concluding scene, Browning repeatedly uses cross-cutting to contrast the vampire's English domain with the Seward's brightly lit, well-furnished home, which is not intended to be a fortress and so can provide no true safety. Thus not only Dracula and Van Helsing but also Renfield, who has been strangled by Dracula, his false master, are left behind in the vaults as John and Mina move away from death, seductive dreams, and violence and literally rise toward the light—civilization triumphing over the apparent causes of its discontents.

It is appropriate that Renfield is included in the final sequence of the film, because this English "madman" figures much more prominently in *Dracula* (1931) than in any of the other cinematic versions of Stoker's novel or in *Dracula: The Vampire Play*, even though Browning borrows extensively from the play in his characterization of Renfield. As I noted earlier, it is Renfield and not John Harker who first journeys to Castle Dracula, thereby contributing to the vampire's invasion of England. And in Browning's film, unlike *Dracula: The Vampire Play*, Renfield as well as Dracula must die, thereby severing all links between Transylvania and England. Perhaps most important, however, Renfield embodies Browning's conception of madness, a disease directly caused by the vampire. In the novel Renfield has been committed to Seward's asylum long before Dracula leaves Transylvania, and thus Stoker implies that England harbors insanity that can be manipulated by the vampire. In Browning's film Renfield begins as a rather effete, fashionably dressed, modern Westerner—naive and blind to all but business concerns, to be sure, but not insane. Yet after Dracula's bite, Renfield is transformed into a glazed-eyed fanatic, grovelling to fulfill the wishes of his new master. When the ship bearing Dracula arrives in England, Renfield stares up from the dark hold, and an off-screen voice declares: "He's mad. Look at his eyes. Why the man's crazy!" Like the rats that accompany Nosferatu in Murnau's film, madness in Browning's *Dracula* is a plague that the vampire introduces into a "healthy" society.

Hence Seward's sanitarium is first seen—in direct contrast to Castle Dracula and Carfax Abbey—as a spacious, sunlit resthome, with carefully attended, well-behaved patients recuperating in manicured gardens. This establishing shot ends, however, with the camera moving from a view of the grounds to reveal Renfield, screaming in his barred cell. The bars cannot prevent this madman, the only obvious mentally ill patient in the asylum, from entering the domain of the normal. Like Dracula, Renfield repeatedly invades the parlor, alternately taunting the men and trying to save Mina, in a series of scenes adapted almost verbatim from *Dracula: The Vampire Play*. While the Count transforms his wives into somnambulistic puppets, he transforms Renfield into a schizophrenic, who instantaneously shifts from one extreme mood to its opposite, torn between his allegiance to his master and his moral concern for Mina, avatar of the normal. Seward, the pro-

Naive and blind to all but business concerns, the fashionably dressed modern Englishman (Dwight Frye) freely enters the massive Old World domain of Count Dracula (Bela Lugosi) in *Dracula* (1931).

Van Helsing (Edward Van Sloan) wields the cross against Count Dracula (Bela Lugosi) as these two masterful foreigners do battle in the Sewards' parlor, an embodiment of the normal in Browning's *Dracula* (1931). The staging and lighting in this publicity photo reflect the influence of *Dracula: The Vampire Play* on Browning's film. (Museum of Modern Art/Film Stills Archive)

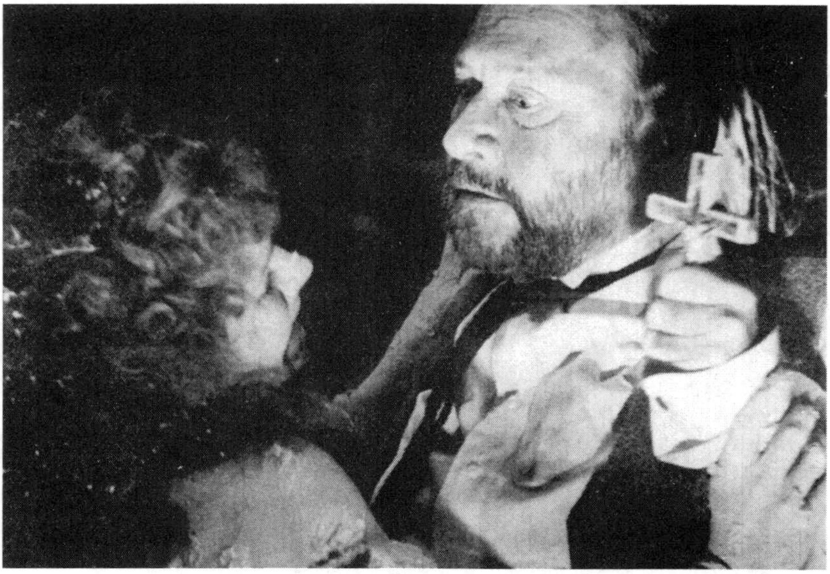

In *Dracula* (1979), Dr. Seward (Donald Pleasence), ineffectual father and incompetent alienist, relies on the cross for protection against the undead Mina Van Helsing (Jan Francis), Victorian child-woman become chalky white walking corpse.

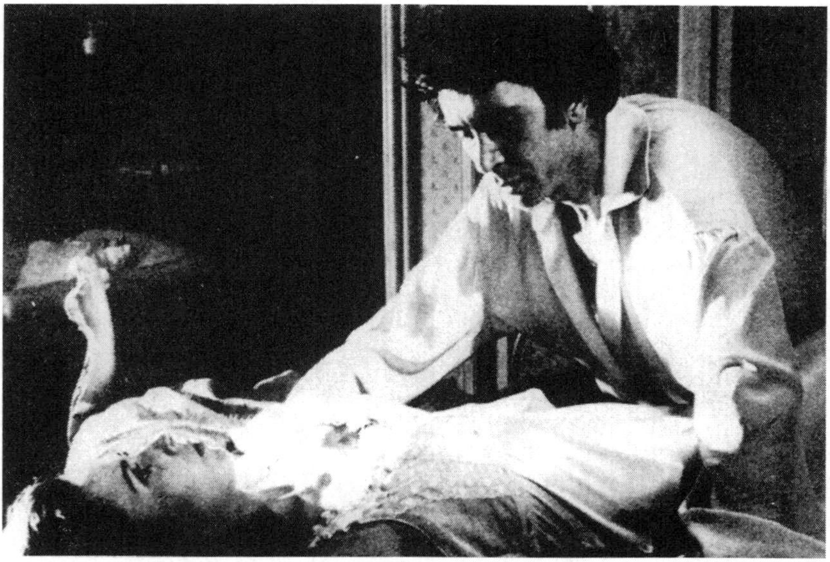

Lucy Seward (Kate Nelligan), erstwhile "New Woman," awaits the caresses of Count Dracula (Frank Langella), her aristocratic lover in Badham's *Dracula* (1979). This image of the commanding male vampire and the passive (and seemingly willing) victim is a mainstay in the story of the living and the undead, though in Badham's film the vampire's embrace offers sexual ecstasy and grand romance rather than pain and infection.

In Badham's revisionist 1979 adaptation of *Dracula* the prescribed rituals and traditional weapons of the living will not suffice; the cross bursts into flames at the touch of Count Dracula (Frank Langella).

Jonathan Harker (Trevor Eve) removes his fianceé (Kate Nelligan) from the arms of her undead lover, while Van Helsing (Laurence Olivier) prepares to transfix Count Dracula (Frank Langella) in *Dracula* (1979)—for the vampire hunters, a necessary, justifiable, heroic act; for Lucy, an abduction that would return her to the mundane modern world.

Ironic reversal of generic convention in *Dracula* (1979), as the vampire (Frank Langella) thrusts the stake through the vampire hunter (Laurence Olivier). In Badham's open-ended retelling of *Dracula*, Van Helsing dies without any assurance that his wild work has avenged his daughter's fate and restored harmony to the world.

moter of mental health, has no cure for this foreign-bred insanity; the Doctor can only attempt—unsuccessfully in every case—to keep Renfield locked up.

Browning's most interesting suggestion in *Dracula* is that those who struggle against the vampire and his abnormal creations could also be considered insane. (Deane and Balderston lay the groundwork for such an interpretation with their presentation of Renfield, and in the novel Van Helsing at one point tells Seward that "all men are mad in some way or the other" [D, 128].) Thus John, still trusting in the power of love and in his own ability to protect Mina, accuses Van Helsing of "driving her crazy." And Renfield, after overhearing Van Helsing's plans for destroying Dracula, ironically declares: "Isn't this a strange conversation for men who aren't crazy?" Once Van Helsing has finally convinced the others to face the "incredible" facts and to follow his course of action, an attendant at the sanitarium tells a nurse that "they're all crazy except you and me, and sometimes I have my doubts about you." Browning's implication, though never fully explored or directly faced in *Dracula* (1931), is that to believe in Van Helsing, and hence to accept the existence of "strange things," to trust in the power of wolfsbane and crucifix, and to acknowledge the necessity for purgative violence, is to be "crazy"—only insanity can restore normality. Once the normal world is restored in the film, however, all vestiges of madness can and must be left behind. Perhaps that is why Van Helsing must ultimately remain in the cavernous vaults with the corpses of Dracula and Renfield, while John and Mina climb toward the light, never glancing back.

A close comparison of John Badham's *Dracula* (1979) with Deane and Balderston's play and Browning's film immediately suggests how each of these works of popular art reflects, embodies, and perpetuates certain assumptions about storytelling that inform the aesthetic and commercial environments from which these texts emerge. This point is most clear in the case of the two film adaptations of *Dracula*. Both are examples of the mainstream, commercial American feature film, yet they are not just two distinct movies, but products of two different historical occasions, two different forms of "pressure," to use Stephen Neale's word.[14]

Perhaps the most obvious instance of such pressure is the way prevailing censorship codes—formal and informal—affect the presentation in these two films of sexual activity and graphic violence, separately and in combination, and of other actions as well, including the act of dying. For example, no images in *Dracula* (1979) seem further from Browning's *Dracula* than Badham's close-ups of Mina suffocating in agonizing death throes. And these images render this victim somehow more human than the heroines in *Dracula* (1931), whose suffering we never actually see. Particularly for Browning, such censorship codes inevitably reinforce taboos about what must remain unseen (not invisible or nonexistent, just hidden from sight) and promote certain attitudes concerning religion, justice, and other controversial topics. Badham is freer, but only within the bounds of a Motion Picture Association of America R-rating that allows for on-screen transfixion while prohibiting the representation of explicit sexual activity. Another obvious distinction is that black-and-white cinematography is as natural for Browning as color is for Badham—the state of the art in filmmaking apparatus and the prevailing standards of technology in the motion-picture industry govern these decisions (which are hardly choices for either filmmaker). These same factors also enable Badham to utilize a much more sophisticated, multileveled soundtrack than Browning, a soundtrack, complete with Count Dracula leitmotif, that comments upon as well as supplements the images. Finally, in one other important, but less obvious way, these two versions of *Dracula* are characteristic of two very different periods of Hollywood filmmaking. For all its insistence on strange things and extraordinary occurrences, Browning's *Dracula* is never intentionally confusing, misleading, or ambiguous: establishing shots introduce and identify each new location (the first image of Seward's sanitarium, for example, includes a large sign with the name of the establishment), and transitions between sequences are painstakingly indicated by dissolves, clearly matched cuts, and fade-outs.[15] Badham, on the contrary, consistently omits traditional establishing shots (he does not guide us into Seward's asylum, but begins inside the madhouse with an unestablished detail) and employs abrupt cuts to unidentified locations or apparently unrelated details, ironic matches between actions and objects, and transitions (again often ironic) where we hear the sound and dialogue of a scene before we actually see the visual source of the sound. All these techniques in Badham's *Dracula* involve the play of mystification and clarity, a play that at times infuses the process of storytelling itself with a gamelike air of surprise, ambiguity, and irony. To different degrees, the narrative strategies and the technological possibilities for the use of sound and color available to Badham have important thematic implications, just as do the prevailing censorship codes.

For all their distinctions, both films are identified in the opening credits as being "Based on the Play by Hamilton Deane and John L. Balderston and the novel, *Dracula*, by Bram Stoker." (Badham's film was adapted from a commercially successful 1977 revival of *Dracula: The Vampire Play*, featuring Frank Langella as the Count, with sets and costumes designed by Edward Gorey.[16]) This acknowledgment is true, of course; these two extremely different films are based on the same source material. Yet "based on," like "adapted from," is so vague as to be meaningless. The process of retelling and the manifold relationships between the source(s) and the adaptation defy easy categorization, not to mention facile evaluations about so-called fidelity to the original. Badham's *Dracula* does include characters derived from Stoker, scenes and dialogue from Deane and Balderston, even details found only in Browning's film (like the visual metaphor of the spider's web). This most recent *Dracula*, however, is not merely a repetition of previous stories or one more performance of an unchanging text that precedes and will outlive all such performances. On the one hand, Badham's film is very clearly a modernization of earlier *Dracula*s (the characterization of Lucy Seward being the most apparent example); on the other hand, the film's set design and art direction situate the story as a period piece, not as a contemporary adventure like Stoker's novel was in 1897 and *Dracula: The Vampire Play* in 1927. With ironic hindsight and at times with a sense of loss, *Dracula* (1979) looks back on the stories upon which it is based and also on the beginning of our century.

Unlike the other works discussed thus far in this chapter, Badham's *Dracula* seems to me at times to adopt a critical, revisionist stance toward its sources—though hardly to the degree of Richard Matheson's *I Am Legend* and Roman Polanski's *The Fearless Vampire Killers*. Through his treatment of generic conventions, Badham implicitly comments on, for example, Deane and Balderston's assumptions about madness, Browning's image of the sanitarium, and, most important, on the endings of all three earlier *Dracula*s. Such revisionism is a major characteristic of American genre films during the last fifteen years.[17] As much as in the other ways I have mentioned, in its self-conscious sense of text, genre, and audience, Badham's *Dracula* is a film of the 1970s. (And, needless to say, I as a viewer am as attuned to revisionism, irony, and reflexivity as the filmmakers born in my generation.) This retelling of *Dracula* forces us to consider the role and the effect of revisionism in a genre in which the human beings are so often required to follow, without question, authoritative wise men who prescribe traditional, even ritualized, modes of action.

Nowhere are Badham's alterations of his source material more evident than in the scenes set in Seward's asylum, for madness in *Dracula* (1979) is neither an isolated symptom of disease in a selfish and skeptical society, as for Stoker, nor a hysterical aberration introduced into placid, sane England by a foreign vampire, as for Browning. Similarly, Seward's asylum is, for Badham, neither an institution presided over by a dedicated young alienist, curious to learn and eager to help his patients, nor a bucolic sanitarium burdened with an uncontrollable madman. The asylum in Badham's *Dracula* is a massive, imposing building with an adjoining graveyard, set alone on a seaside promontory. It is an institution where madness, having been identified and segregated from society, is imprisoned. After the film opens with the futile attempt of the *Demeter*'s crewmen to toss the box containing Dracula overboard during a raging storm at sea, Badham cuts directly to the large central room of Seward's asylum in which different tiers of cells are linked by a network of walkways, suspended like a spider's web. This building, which looks so formidable and grand from the outside, can no more keep out the natural world than Mina's bedroom window can keep out Dracula. Inside the asylum the thunder echoes and bursts of lightning illuminate the mass of inmates—male, female, young, and old all glimpsed in a series of brief images, each shot a fragment of dizzying motion and cacophonous sound. In the face of this chaotic outburst (which is the antithesis of the collective, concerted human effort that defeats the King-Vampire in Stoker's novel), Seward is powerless; he can only call in vain for his assistant to administer laudanum.[18] Yet drugs are no more effective than straightjackets, manacles, and incarceration. The inmates' screams, laughter, and incomprehensible language echo into the Sewards' elegantly furnished living quarters, which are under the same roof, but demarcated and protected from the madmen by a locked gate.

Just as the sound of the asylum rings through Dr. Seward's private residence, the images of madness and institutionalization that Badham uses to introduce us to England echo through all the film's later images of the modern world. Poised at the threshold of the twentieth century, with automobiles and pony carts sharing the same roads, this world is also poised on the verge of collapse. Beneath the well-kept graveyard where Mina, the vampire's first victim, is buried with religious formality, lie deserted mines, subterranean tunnels now reclaimed by the decomposing forces of nature and by rats, bats, and the undead, the creatures of the night. Even the beautifully evoked scenes of village life and everyday activity in the mines and on the docks suggest a society unalterably divided along the lines of social and economic class. Badham quickly reveals that Seward and Jonathan Harker (here a hard-working solicitor in love with Lucy Seward) have little, if any, control over the world that they as middle- and upper-middle-class professionals apparently possess. There is no status quo here worth reasserting, and *Dracula* (1979) implies—with a cynicism worthy of its decade—that this world cannot be redeemed by sacrifice or by the forging of a new, alternate community. Hence the appeal to Mina and Lucy and, I assume, to the viewer as well, of Frank Langella's Count Dracula, last "descendant of a conquering race," who acts with complete self-command and self-assurance and who offers passionate sexual fulfillment that is inseparable from the promise of aristocratic power and privilege.

In contrast to Deane and Balderston, Badham, like Browning, emphasizes the distinction between the two young women who surrender to the vampire's embrace. Mina—here presented as the much-beloved daughter of elderly Professor Van Helsing (an important and ingenious alteration in the story to which I will later return)—is fair, frail, and dependent, a Victorian child-woman who often resembles a Pre-Raphaelite maiden. While recuperating from a long illness, Mina is drawn from the apparent security of the Seward household, where she rests with a framed photograph of her father on the table beside her bed, into the stormy night to a cave on the shore and the arms of Dracula. She offers no resistance and no challenge to the vampire, for she has no strength of will and no young man to risk his life for her. Mina suffers a horrible death. Her face is distorted with pain as she gasps for air, suffocating while Seward and Lucy, her surrogate parents, can do absolutely nothing to help. Reborn as a vampire, Mina does not become a voluptuous siren, but rather a half-decomposed, chalky white, walking corpse, who feeds off of infants, lives in the dank, deserted mines, and finally reaches out to give her Papa one final, deadly embrace. This gesture is her undoing, and it suggests how much Mina remains dependent until the end, when a crucifix that Seward thrusts forward forces her backward into the long stake her father holds. She dies—again—in her father's arms, and the next day he cuts out her heart to assure her eternal rest.

Badham contrasts Mina's dependency and frailty throughout the film with Lucy Seward's independence and assertiveness. Whereas Mina needs her father in life and in undeath, during the chaotic outbreak in the asylum Seward calls for his daughter, Lucy, and she is more calm, capable, and authoritative than her father. Unlike Stoker's heroine, who can joke about being taken for a "New Woman" (D, 99), Badham's Lucy is unmistakably a "New Woman," seemingly more at home in the twentieth than the nineteenth century. When first seen, Lucy is entertaining Mina with news of Jonathan's career and insisting that "women ought to have some say on things. After all, we are not chattel." (Even more impressive is that these young women can laugh together as they repeat this declaration of independence, thereby mocking pompous didacticism and not the value of independence.) Within the confines of her social and familial situation, Lucy has more than "some say" about her own destiny. She is governed neither by Jonathan nor by her buffoonish, ineffectual father. In particular, Badham stresses Lucy's guilt-free, modern attitude toward sexual relations. She is no passive female objet d'art. She takes the initiative with her fiancée, leaving her bed for a nighttime rendezvous with Jonathan, and she asks Count Dracula to waltz with her during the dinner party at which the elegant foreigner is first introduced to the Sewards. Lucy *can* choose, yet in a world of limited choices (she dreams of no brilliant career, no exotic destination) being independent and modern can be synonymous with being able to dance the tango with your lover in your father's Victorian parlor. Then into the parlor strides Dracula, immediately dominating the soirèe and the image and offering Lucy a clear choice—she extends her hand towards him: "Dance with me."

In Badham's *Dracula* the captain of the *Demeter* and the other men whom Dracula kills (except for Renfield) have tried to destroy him, and Mina is easily controlled and led to her fate through no choice of her own. Only Lucy—"stronger than most women," as Dracula immediately notes—chooses her fate. Before the vampire enters her bedroom, she journeys to Carfax Abbey against the wishes of her fiancé and her father. What Lucy receives is grand romance such as Emma Bovary can only dream of and sexual ecstasy that is visualized in exploding colors, far brighter than the natural world, colors that dissolve into one another with the two lovers silhouetted in black, completely united in flesh and blood. Although Carfax Abbey is the one set in the film that recalls Browning's *Dracula*, for Badham the ancient, cavernous Abbey is not only a decrepit locus from which evil emanates and a spider's web designed to trap the unwary; more important, the Abbey, which is even further set off from society than Seward's asylum, is the perfect setting for the birth of grand romance. Isolated from quotidian reality and from all the trappings of the twentieth century, yet open to the moonlight, the Abbey is less a deteriorating and dangerous relic than a palatial, candlelit haven. Exercising her right as a "New Woman," Lucy makes the choice that will apparently end all choosing, a choice that ends her independence and initiates her into the most complete form of aristocratic nobility: "I am king of my kind," Dracula declares to Lucy, "and you will be my queen."

Unlike her counterpart in Stoker's novel (Mina Harker), Lucy in *Dracula* (1979) is not the spiritual center of the world—if, in fact, this world has a spiritual center or realizes that it lacks such a center. And far from being guilt-ridden, on only one occasion does Lucy ever waver in her committed devotion to Dracula. Yet Lucy, who would not be chattel, is still the prize for which the men and Dracula struggle. After she has become blood of the vampire's blood, Lucy cringes as she watches Van Helsing's mutilation of Mina; then she sets out again for Carfax. Jonathan, Seward, and Van Helsing must block her path, physically restrain her, and ultimately lock her up in one of the asylum's cells—like Renfield, who eats insects and babbles about the Master's powers. Lucy's independence, which was prized and even exploited by her lover and her father, has become threatening and dangerous, a symptom of madness. She has become, in her father's words, a "wild thing." Thus when Lucy, now a devious vampire, tries to trick Jonathan into a fatal embrace, she does not play the role of a wanton, provocative siren, but rather of a chastened, apologetic fiancée, who lulls Jonathan with promises of devoted love, almost as if she has been somehow weakened and cured by her incarceration in the asylum. No one, however, is cured in Seward's asylum, which is a prime example of the "Institutional Psychiatry" that Thomas Szasz so rigorously condemns in *The Manufacture of Madness* (1970) and other works. Seward's institution is a prison that relies on laudanum and straightjackets to control all the people identified and feared as embodiments of the monstrous, alien Other—a category that includes Lucy once she has chosen Dracula over Jonathan and her father. While the vampire in Browning's *Dracula* must place Mina in a hypnotic trance in order to take her away from Seward's sanitarium, in Badham's film Dracula bursts through the stone walls of the asylum and literally carries Lucy away, abducting her, or more correctly, liberating her from a male-dominated society that imprisons and suppresses all that it deems mad.

While Badham's heroine differs dramatically from the central female characters in *Dracula: The Vampire Play* and Browning's *Dracula*, women who have no desire for independence and are initially unwilling victims of the vampire, all three works in different degrees place the defense of society (the family, the parlor, the patriarchal order) in the hands of Van Helsing and Jonathan Harker. In Badham's *Dracula* Seward is a Dickensian caricature of harmless gluttony and bumbling ineptitude, who has no role in the final confrontation with Dracula, although Seward does assist in destroying the undead Mina. Van Helsing, played by Laurence Olivier in Badham's film, has more than enough knowledge and commitment to combat Dracula, but Van Helsing is an old man, physically weaker and more aged than the unflinching, authoritarian heroes of Browning's film and *Dracula: The Vampire Play*. By altering his sources so that Mina becomes Van Helsing's daughter, Badham insists that this vampire hunter must pay a personal price and suffer through the agony of his daughter's sudden death and then her horrifying rebirth. Having been forced to see and touch the living corpse that calls him "Papa," Van Helsing can cut open Mina's breast to remove her heart, even though she looks calm and beautiful in her facsimile of true death. Out of revenge for Mina's plight and presumably for what he himself has been forced to undergo, Van Helsing is driven to destroy Dracula; the Professor's motives are selfish and personal. And with these changes in the character of Van Helsing, Badham's *Dracula* is left without any selfless hero whose success is in part due to the fact that he has no personal involvement and no grudge to settle—a selfless hero such as Browning's Van Helsing, who does all the necessary wild work while Jonathan searches for his fiancée.

In *Dracula* (1979) Van Helsing can use religious icons to drive the vampire from the Seward's house when the two foreigners confront each other amid elegant Victorian furnishings, but Van Helsing is not able single-handedly to end the reign of the King-Vampire. Even when the men encounter Mina in the mines, Seward must wield a cross to save Van Helsing's life. Thus Jonathan in Badham's film must take an active role in the hunt and not merely be handed his lover, the prize of a wise and powerful elder's violent labors. Jonathan is here an active figure from the first time he appears in the film, driving up the beach to the wrecked *Demeter*. "I've got business on board. I am a solicitor," Jonathan announces as he climbs aboard the ship and gives orders and legal opinions. He is introduced as the very picture of a young man who has charted the direction his life will take and who works confident of success and advancement. Like Stoker's young solicitor, Badham's Jonathan Harker deals with (and trusts in) contracts, deeds, private property, and real estate. Yet his client turned adversary is an aristocratic vampire, who has a very different sense of what constitutes a binding tie and what characterizes the "real." For Badham as for Stoker, the law must be violated and forgotten, left behind just as Jonathan's modern automobile must be left behind in *Dracula* (1979) after it crashes during the final chase.

Since both Van Helsing and Jonathan in Badham's *Dracula* have been tempted and betrayed by their best-beloved women and have been taunted and mocked by the egotistical, aristocratic vampire, these two men must together undertake the "wild work" that is necessary. Just as in *Dracula: The Vampire Play* and Browning's *Dracula*, the aged foreigner and the young Englishman leave Seward's asylum and journey to Carfax Abbey. Although the two earlier works end in the Abbey's vaults with the triumph of the living, in Badham's *Dracula* the Count wins the confrontation at Carfax. The sequence in which he triumphs can be taken as a critique of *Dracula: The Vampire Play* and Browning's *Dracula*.

For Badham it is not enough that the two hunters venture into the vampire's domain, wield the correct weapons, and follow prescribed formulas. Van Helsing and Jonathan enter the Abbey, illuminating skeletons and debris with their lantern as they proceed into the underground chambers. Often, a moving, hand-held camera follows their exploration and at times assumes their point of view, suggesting that the camera—and the viewer—are participants in this expedition. (The camera is also hand-held when it approaches Mina's grave before Van Helsing cuts open his daughter's breast. For the rest of the film, however, the camera movement is smooth and unobtrusive, dramatically isolating specific details and following the characters' movements, but not exploring or participating in their world.) Thus we, too, are surprised when Jonathan tears off the lid of Dracula's earth-filled shipping box, and there is no sleeping, immobilized vampire for Van Helsing to transfix. The sequence is even more effective if we are familiar with

Dracula: The Vampire Play and Browning's *Dracula*, where the Count is indeed in his coffin and offers no resistance once the living have committed themselves to redemptive violence. Dracula suddenly materializes out of the darkness, almost toying with Van Helsing and Jonathan and challenging them with a demonstration of his powers: when Jonathan thrusts forward a large wooden cross, Dracula grabs it and it bursts into flames; when the young man in anger swings a shovel at his foe, the vampire instantaneously becomes a bat that latches itself to Jonathan's face. By knocking down a beam, Van Helsing allows light into the crypt, causing the bat to flee and thereby saving Jonathan. But while the living survive, more mutually dependent than ever, this sequence demonstrates their weakness and vulnerability—Jonathan is bloodied and scarred by the bat, and Van Helsing is exhausted after this unsuccessful struggle. The two men will pay an even greater price in their final confrontation with Dracula, a confrontation in which prescribed ritual action and traditional weapons—garlic, cross, and stake—will not suffice.

While Van Helsing and Jonathan in Badham's *Dracula* do not track the vampire to Transylvania, their quest does take them beyond the geographical as well as the cultural and scientific boundaries of early twentieth-century England. Leaving Seward (incompetent modern medicine and dubious mental health) and the crowded dock (the world of commerce and work-as-labor) behind, Van Helsing and Jonathan pursue and board the ship that transports Dracula and his bride toward a new life in the Old World. After descending into the darkened cargo hold, both men actively engage in the wild work, ripping the lid off of the coffin-shaped box to reveal Lucy nestled in the arms of her king. While Jonathan carries his snarling, struggling fiancée aside, Van Helsing positions the stake on the chest of the unconscious vampire. Dracula, however, is awakened by Lucy's anguished screams; he grabs the stake and impales Van Helsing, pinning the old man like an insect to the side of the hold. Jonathan futilely fires his revolver at Dracula, smacks Lucy aside as she claws and screams at him, and hurls a grappling hook at the vampire, who catches it with ease and tosses it aside, then advances to strangle the young man. With one final effort, Van Helsing grabs the hook and throws it into Dracula's back, and, when Jonathan releases the pulley rope attached to the hook, the vampire is pulled upward, bursting through the closed doors of the hold into the sunlight. Gnashing and swirling, Dracula hangs defenseless from the top of the mast, while below Lucy cringes and covers her face as the sunlight strikes her red eyes. Once the sun burns its marks of mortality on him, Dracula's frantic resistance stops—his passive, rapidly decaying body apparently signifying the end of a life that has spanned centuries. Below, in the hold, Lucy stares up with eyes that now seem to be human, then she glances toward Van Helsing's corpse and reaches out to touch Jonathan, who lies near her—drained by the struggle—with his eyes half-closed. Shot from below (roughly from Lucy's point of view), a black object that could be either Dracula's cape or a large bat breaks loose from the mast and rises away from the ship after Lucy has moved her hand away from Jonathan. As the sound of a howling wolf is heard, the camera moves in to an extreme close-up of Lucy's face: her eyes open as her lips form a slight smile. While the credits appear, superimposed over the images, the cape/bat continues to rise into the sky, moving farther from the ship and the camera. After a brief extreme long-shot shows the ship from high overhead, Badham cuts back to the black object; now a moving small shape far distant from the camera, the cape/bat disappears into the white expanse of the sky.

The final sequence of Badham's film merits the detailed description presented here because it contrasts so thoroughly with the conclusions of the other adaptations of *Dracula* I have thus far discussed. For Badham, both Jonathan and Van Helsing must act to destroy Dracula, and both hunters must suffer the consequences of the struggle. Faith and sacred objects (such as crosses or holy wafers) play no role in this confrontation, and a grappling hook takes the place of a stake. In this respect, as in the conclusion of Stoker's novel, Badham's *Dracula* challenges the primacy of the stake not just as preferred but as required weapon and thus insists that the attack against the monster is a unique, personal act—an affirmation of the human as opposed to the ritualistic. What Jonathan and Van Helsing manage to do is to force Dracula into the burning sunlight, pictured here as a sort of elemental force, exemplified by several shots Badham inserts of the sun's fiery red surface, an inferno of explosive energy. Most important, however, is that Badham does not offer an affirmative, closed ending wherein the destruction of the vampire leads to the restoration of the status quo or to the birth of new life or even to the sheer pleasure of triumphant survival.

The ambiguity surrounding Dracula's final fate is, of course, the most obvious indication of the film's denial of a closed ending. We see Dracula decay and age, thus fulfilling Jonathan's desire to emasculate his handsome, irresistible rival. Yet the escape and final disappearance of the black object, the high overhead view of the ship as if from the point of view of this object, and the wolf's howling are hardly subtle hints that Dracula has survived the best that Jonathan and Van Helsing can offer. (By 1979, after immensely popular works like *The Amityville Horror* [1977] and *Halloween* [1978] had appeared, this type of open ending in horror stories had become a conventional feature that seemed to signal the possibility of a sequel in which the story continues.) In this respect, Badham's *Dracula* is fully in keeping with the many recent horror stories in which the threat, whether animal or supernatural evil or homicidal maniac, may disappear or be temporarily checked, but is rarely eradicated completely: hidden from the view of the hunters, survivors, and victims, one litter of deadly rats in James Herbert's *The Rats* (1974) remains alive after thousands have been killed, and so the threat persists, ineradicable, and what is worse, often unseen except by the viewer or the reader. Unlike the monstrous creatures in *The Rats* or in Barbara Peeters's *Humanoids from the Deep* (1979), Badham's Count Dracula perhaps deserves to survive, for, as Lucy realizes, he is no creature of "unmixed malignity" and is more handsome, dynamic, commanding, and independent than his human foes.[19] In addition, as Alain Garel notes in an article in *Image et Son*, the Count's escape is in keeping with the emphasis throughout Badham's *Dracula* on this aristocratic vampire's powers of transformation. Before our eyes he becomes a wolf or a bat and thus becomes both more and less than merely human. Such transformations—into a wolf on the *Demeter*, for example—allow Dracula to survive, to adapt, and to change without aging. Such is the case, it seems to me, in his confrontation with Jonathan and Van Helsing at Carfax Abbey, where the cross cannot repulse the vampire as it did earlier in the film. Badham's Dracula has more than a flawed, vulnerable immortality; he has what Garel so aptly calls "permanence."[20] One possible reading of the film's conclusion is that the Count has triumphed even over the powers of the sun. If this be true, then his freedom is complete and his permanence is assured, for he has become flawless.

Coupled with the final images of Dracula, the final images of Lucy also contribute to the ambiguity and hence to the open ending of the film. The sunlight that causes her to recoil in pain is not the rosy beams of heaven-sent light that purify Mina in Stoker's novel, rendering her both able and capable of bringing forth a new generation. And unlike the defenseless heroines of *Dracula: The Vampire Play* and Browning's *Dracula*, Badham's Lucy does not awaken as if from a bad dream and resume her life where it was so rudely interrupted by the undead foreigner. On the other hand, Lucy does physically return to normal; to all appearances, she herself has not become the embodiment of the threat (in contrast, for example, to Jonathan Harker at the end of Herzog's *Nosferatu the Vampyre*). Her eyes, which were blood-red discs, are now again clear. Yet Lucy neither clings to her savior-lover nor weeps over Van Helsing's corpse. She lies still, the only witness (except the camera and the viewer) to what seems to be Dracula's magical transformation. Her final smile suggests satisfaction, pleasure, and awareness. It matters little if Lucy is actually witnessing the escape of her paramour or, like Laura at the conclusion of Sheridan Le Fanu's *Carmilla*, remembering the vampire's caress. In either case, Lucy is cut off or has escaped from the world she once inhabited, as if she, like us, can hear the howling of the wolf, the music of the night, which is, in fact, not only the last sound heard in the film, but also the first sound, before any credits, any images at all appear on the screen.

Notwithstanding the importance of Lucy and Dracula in Badham's open ending, the most interesting aspect of the film's conclusion is the fate of Van Helsing and Jonathan Harker. The hunters' triumph is dubious at best, and not only because they may have failed to end the reign of the King-Vampire. Ironically, Van Helsing becomes a victim of the stake, a fate his own daughter suffered at his hands, and he dies—unlike Stoker's Quincey Morris—without any assurance that his work has satisfied the demands of retributive justice and restored harmony to the world. Earlier, Van Helsing insisted to Jonathan that "if we are beaten, then there is no God," yet the film's ambiguous ending neither affirms nor denies the existence of God.

In some respects, however, Jonathan's final situation is worse than Van Helsing's. The young solicitor-turned-hunter has demonstrated courage and strength of will, yet his descent into the darkened hold and his violent actions do not regenerate him. In the end, Jonathan is left motionless and drained of energy like a vampire's victim; he is still separated from Lucy, and now his eyes are closed to the light as well as the darkness. Without recourse to traditional faith, Jonathan remains exhausted and isolated—cut off from England and from Van Helsing and unable to console or be consoled by Lucy. For Badham, once one has descended into the darkness, faced the foe, and become the violent aggressor, there is no readily available, easily mounted staircase that stretches upward into the light and no one on whom to lean for support and reaffirmation of your own humanity.[21]

Although Frank Langella's self-consciously dramatic flourishes and graceful, dynamic movement as Count Dracula in Badham's *Dracula* differ substantially from Bela Lugosi's mysteriously deliberate and solemn performance as the vampire in Browning's film, these two films do share certain thematic emphases that are derived from Deane and Balderston's *Dracula: The Vampire Play*. While Browning and Badham return to Stoker's novel for details that are not included in *Dracula: The Vampire Play*, their film versions of *Dracula* offer the same cast of characters as Deane and Balderston's play, as well as similar conceptions of the threat posed by the vampire. That *Dracula: The Vampire Play*, Browning's 1931 film, and Badham's 1979 film are vastly different stories of the living and the undead suggests how much narrative and ideological variation is possible in texts that address similar thematic concerns and depict basically the same characters and the same series of episodes.

Consider, for example, how all three of these works not only prominently feature the "madman" Renfield, but also situate the relationship between madness, vampirism, and normality in the foreground, and thus demonstrate how the story of the living and the undead can become a vehicle for exploring the nature of madness (a topic traditionally relegated to works of horror, from Edgar Allan Poe's *The Black Cat* and Charlotte Perkins Gilman's *The Yellow Wallpaper* to Alfred Hitchcock's *Psycho* and Stanley Kubrick's *The Shining*). Madness has a much less significant role (even quantitatively) in Stoker's novel and in other film adaptations of *Dracula* that I will later discuss, like Terence Fisher's *Horror of Dracula* and Dan Curtis's *Dracula*. *Dracula: The Vampire Play*, *Dracula* (1931), and *Dracula* (1979) in very different ways force us to see and to acknowledge the relationship between an unnatural, ancient threat that invades our world and a threat that comes from within us and our society. As I have suggested, Badham offers ironic, troubling images of Seward's asylum and of the entire process of institutionalization (this asylum is, in fact, the quintessential embodiment of the modern world in *Dracula* [1979]), images that challenge several of the most important assumptions that inform Deane and Balderston's play and Browning's film. In these three works we can begin to trace one way that conceptions of madness and normality have evolved in twentieth-century popular culture, as the clear-cut psychological and sociological distinctions that underpin our increasingly secular world in *Dracula: The Vampire Play* and *Dracula* (1931) have eroded or have become suspect or have disappeared entirely in *Dracula* (1979).

We could also say that these three works cast doubt on certain ways we have of distinguishing between the monstrous and the human, for Deane and Balderston also introduce a different sense from Stoker's of the King-Vampire's stature and motivation. In the three versions of *Dracula* I have discussed in this chapter, Dracula—for all his diabolical machinations and animal appetites—enters the Sewards' home as a refined, exceedingly proper guest; his goal is to seduce and possess Seward's daughter, who will then take her privileged place as his latest bride or perhaps his queen. (The easily captured first victim in these three works only offers the vampire physical sustenance and a momentary diversion.) This Dracula dreams of no "ever widening circle of semi-demons" (D, 60). One ranting, servile Englishman is apparently satisfactory for his purposes. Such details in *Dracula: The Vampire Play* diminish the magnitude of Dracula, lessen his "strength," in Hannah Arendt's sense of the term. While the Count does not suddenly exhibit guilt, melancholy, and other signs of human psychology, Dracula for Deane and Balderston (and hence to some degree for Browning and Badham as well) is brought closer to humankind—as if the King-Vampire had to be somewhat domesticated, if not completely defanged, before he could make his appearance in the footlit, realistic illusions of the popular commercial theater. Badham's image of an irresistibly handsome, skillful, graceful Count Dracula carries this process to a logical conclusion. While the opening scenes of Browning's film depict the barren, inhuman existence and unnatural, destructive sexuality of the aristocratic vampire, *Dracula* (1979) suggests that once we no longer fear (or even truly acknowledge) the Old World aristocracy, then we can see the once-monstrous, parasitic aristocrat as a heroic, appealing nobleman, who offers romantic ecstasy and immortal privilege that will allow his chosen lover to escape from the modern world.

Complementing their redefinition of Count Dracula, Deane and Balderston substantially reduce the novel's cast of characters, as *Dracula* becomes a relatively uncomplicated three-act drama that is much closer to a drawing-room murder mystery than to a David Belasco or Steele MacKaye theatrical extravaganza. With only five principal characters, *Dracula: The Vampire Play* necessarily foregoes Stoker's insistence on the formation of a community to repulse and defeat the vampire. Quincey Morris, the brave, self-sacrificing American, and Arthur Holmwood, the young English aristocrat, do not appear in Deane and Balderston's play or in the films of Browning and Badham, and Seward becomes Lucy's middle-aged father. Transforming Seward from Lucy's twenty-five-year-old suitor to her fifty-five-year-old father also causes the relationship between the young and the old to become a much more primary concern in *Dracula: The Vampire Play* than in Stoker's novel. This change refocuses *Dracula* so that the failure of the father and the doctor/psychiatrist becomes a central point in the story, much more central than it is for Stoker. As a modern alienist who cannot cure or control the patients and inmates in his asylum and as a single male parent who cannot protect or control his own daughter, Dr. Seward becomes the foil to Van Helsing and Jonathan Harker and, of course, to Count Dracula. Products of an age that had begun to feel the effects of the psychoanalytic movement, *Dracula: The Vampire Play* and *Dracula* (1931) bring the father to the fore, then dramatize his impotence, as if both to acknowledge and to answer Freud's vision of the father's primacy and his neverending influence. By identifying Van Helsing as Mina's father (and also by casting a more youthful and more energetic actor as Count Dracula), Badham reinforces this theme, and in so doing he denies the living recourse to an authoritative fatherly figure who is not a father.

Perhaps the most significant distinction between Stoker's novel and the three retellings of *Dracula* that I have discussed here does not concern the vampire, the victim, the madman, or the father, however, but rather the vampire hunters and the violent action they undertake. These twentieth-century versions of *Dracula* secularize what in the novel is a holy crusade and a sacrificial quest by downplaying or omitting Stoker's emphasis on faith, ritual, collective violence, and the journey into the primitive. (In this respect, these texts are more modern than *Dracula* [1897], in Stoker's pejorative use of the word.) At the same time, Deane and Balderston, Browning, and Badham replace Stoker's moral community with two vampire hunters, Jonathan Harker and Van Helsing, and, as a result, *Dracula: The Vampire Play*, *Dracula* (1931), and *Dracula* (1979) become commentaries on the possibilities of individual masculine heroism rather than of communal action. Though these three adaptations all share a common concern with the personal attributes, characteristics, values, and actions of the young man and the elderly professor, as I have suggested, these texts sketch extremely different portraits of Jonathan and Van Helsing (and of the vampire's female victims as well). Finally, Deane and Balderston, Browning, and Badham offer—within a similar narrative framework—contrasting and even antithetical images of how and why the vampire hunters struggle to survive and of what finally separates the living from the undead. As we will see in the next chapter, with Terence Fisher's *Horror of Dracula* comes not only another retelling of Stoker's novel and another depiction of the relationship between the living and the undead, but also a shifting of emphases and an opening up of options that leads the story of Count Dracula as far from Deane and Balderston as from Stoker.

NOTES

1. Leonard Wolf's *A Dream of Dracula: In Search of the Living Dead* (New York: Popular Library, 1972) remains the most interesting book-length discussion of Count Dracula's precursors and his image and influence in the twentieth century.

2. See also Peter Tremayne's vampire novels, which contain various allusions to and elaborations of Stoker's *Dracula*. Tremayne's *Bloodright* (1980) and *Dracula, My Love* (1983), for example, are presented as newly discovered manuscripts that tell of Count Dracula's existence before the events that Stoker describes.

3. Having survived the best that Van Helsing and company can offer, the vampire hero of *The Dracula Tape* reappears in Saberhagen's *The Holmes-Dracula File* (1978) and *An Old Friend of the Family* (1979). The 1978 novel, with its twisting, convoluted plot, brings Holmes and Dracula together, as these two "men of honor" protect England from the threat posed by heinous, greedy, all-too-human villains.

4. Brief plot summaries and credits for the various cinematic adaptations of *Dracula*, as well as for other vampire films released before 1979, are found in Michael J. Murphy, *The Celluloid Vampires: A History and Filmography, 1897–1979* (Ann Arbor, Mich.: Pierian Press, 1979).

5. Hamilton Deane and John L. Balderston, *Dracula: The Vampire Play in Three Acts* (New York: Samuel French, Inc., 1933). All future page references to this play, abbreviated DVP, will be included parenthetically in my text. Nancy Garden reprints a playbill for the premiere performance of a stage adaptation of Stoker's novel entitled *Dracula or The Un-Dead*. This play was written by Stoker himself and was performed 15 May 1897 as a means of copywriting the novel. The playbill lists a prologue and five acts, comprising forty seven

scenes, with the beginning and the conclusion set in Transylvania (*Vampires* [New York: Bantam, 1977], pp. 74–75).

6. Donald F. Glut, *The Dracula Book* (Metuchen, N.J.: Scarecrow Press, 1975), p. 82.

7. John Russell Taylor's description of Eugene Scribe's "pièce bien faite," the well-made play that was to have a major influence on popular theater in England and America, is also applicable to *Dracula: The Vampire Play*, with Deane and Balderston's succession of "scènes à faire": "There is not one moment in the whole evening when the audience is not in a state of eager expectation, waiting for something to happen, for some secret to be uncovered, some identity revealed, some inevitable confrontation actually to occur" (*The Rise and Fall of the Well-Made Play* [New York: Hill and Wang, 1967], p. 15).

8. Roy Huss, "Vampire's Progress: *Dracula* from Novel to Film via Broadway," in *Focus on the Horror Film*, ed. Roy Huss and T. J. Ross (Englewood Cliffs, N.J.: Prentice-Hall, 1972), pp. 51–53. See also, for example, John Brosnan, *The Horror People* (New York: New American Library, 1977), p. 30.

9. I discuss this prescriptive aesthetic in more detail in *The Stage/Screen Debate: A Study in Popular Aesthetics* (New York: Garland Press, 1983).

10. See Barrie Pattison, *The Seal of Dracula* (New York: Bounty Books, 1975), pp. 15–18. For background on the production of the film and on Lugosi's performance in *Dracula: The Vampire Play*, see Arthur Lennig, *The Count: The Life and Times of Bela 'Dracula' Lugosi* (New York: G. P. Putnam's Sons, 1974), pp. 66–109. The visual style of *Dracula* (1931) no doubt owes a great deal to the film's cinematographer, Karl Freund, who had filmed several noteworthy German silent films (including *The Golem* [1920], *Metropolis* [1927], and a number of films directed by F. W. Murnau) and who would direct *The Mummy* (1932) and *Mad Love* (1935). David Pirie goes so far as to argue that in *Dracula* (1931), "Freund's brilliance is continually undercut by Browning" (*The Vampire Cinema* [London: Hamlyn, 1977], p. 53).

11. Van Helsing in Browning's *Dracula* bears a very marked resemblance to Dr. Waldman in James Whale's *Frankenstein*, a film also released by Universal in 1931. Waldman, also played by Edward Van Sloan, is the representative of and spokesperson for institutionalized, socially accepted science in *Frankenstein*. With absolute certainty, Waldman and his colleagues at the Goldstadt Medical College are able to distinguish between the normal and the abnormal. R. H. W. Dillard, "Even a Man Who Is Pure in Heart: Poetry and Danger in the Horror Film," in *Man and the Movies*, ed. W. R. Robinson (Baltimore: Penguin, 1969), pp. 60–96, offers an excellent examination of the role of the Van Helsing/Waldman figure in the "morality play" structure of Hollywood horror films of the 1930s.

12. Again, the parallels with Whale's *Frankenstein* are illuminating. In both films normality is associated with marriage, but *Frankenstein* ends with the foolish, elderly Baron Frankenstein firmly in control of the situation, offering a toast to the future as a continuation of the past ("An heir to the House of Frankenstein!"), while his once-rebellious son has been reduced to an invalid who is cared for by his new wife.

13. Dillard, "Poetry and Danger," p. 69.

14. Stephen Neale, *Genre* (London: British Film Institute, 1980), p. 10. Even the idea of what constitutes feature-length differs from 1931 to 1979. Browning's film is seventy-five minutes long, shorter than almost all feature films of the 1970s except for certain X-rated movies; Badham's *Dracula* at 109 minutes is nearly fifty per cent longer.

15. David Bordwell reaches a similar conclusion when he contrasts Browning's film with Dreyer's *Vampyr*. Bordwell argues that unlike *Vampyr*, which relies on Dreyer's sophisticated manipulation of "narrative uncertainty," *Dracula* (1931) offers "causation" that is "lawlike and certain," and as a result, Browning's narrative is "perfectly coherent" (*The Films of Carl-Theodor Dreyer* [Berkeley: University of California Press, 1981], pp. 94–95).

16. Reviewers of this 1977 revival of *Dracula: The Vampire Play* focused above all on Gorey's contribution to the production. Walter Kerr, for example, argues that the "settings and costumes are detaching us from the story about to be told," so that, in effect, "it's not 'Dracula' that's being offered us, but a lavishly satirical *comment* on 'Dracula'" ("Parody In and Out of Focus," *New York Times*, 28 Oct. 1977, sec. 3, p. 1). The year 1977 also saw the production in New York of *The Passion of Dracula* (written by Bob Hall and David Richmond), another theatrical adaptation of Stoker's novel.

17. See, for example, John G. Cawelti, "*Chinatown* and Generic Transformation in Recent American Films," in *Film Criticism and Theory*, ed. Gerald Mast and Marshall Cohen, 2d ed. (New York: Oxford University Press, 1979), pp. 559–79.

18. Donald Pleasence, who plays Seward in Badham's film, plays an even more incompetent alienist and a more menacing proponent of mental health in John Carpenter's *Halloween* (1978), which is not to say that Pleasence is typecast, but that these two roles provide variations on the same theme. The exploration of this theme and the presentation of the alienist/psychologist/psychiatrist as figure of authority are similar in *Dracula* (1979) and *Halloween* (although these two films offer radically different pictures of the monster), especially when these two late 1970s films are contrasted with, for example, Hitchcock's *Psycho* (1960), in which the psychiatrist is confident, socially respected, and full of tidy explanations (that are undercut by the film's final images).

19. "Unmixed malignity" is a phrase used to describe the monster in the Scottish folktale, *Nuckelavee*, reprinted in *Wolf's Complete Book of Terror*, ed. Leonard Wolf (New York: Clarkson N. Potter, 1979). Even less "malignant" than Badham's Dracula is Le Comte de Saint-Germain, the suave, cultured, irresistibly handsome and dashing vampire-hero in Chelsea Quinn Yarbro's series of "novels of historical horror": *Hotel Transylvania* (1979), *The Palace* (1979), *Blood Games* (1980), *Path of the Eclipse* (1982), and the stories collected in *The Saint-Germain Chronicles* (1983). Yarbro's "honorable" vampire is so far from being a force of evil that in *Hotel Transylvania* he rescues the "exquisite" heroine from a coven of sadistic aristocrats who worship Satan. In the end the Count and his bride prepare to live together in the "eternal passion" born of "blood that is taken with love" (New York: New American Library, 1979, p. 274). A similar situation occurs in Tremayne's *Dracula, My Love*, in

which the strong-willed, much-exploited heroine chooses to accept Dracula's offer of immortality rather than to assist Van Helsing in destroying the undead. By way of contrast with Yarbro and Tremayne, it should be noted that, however infatuating the vampire appears to the young women in Badham's *Dracula*, the first image of Dracula in human form in the film is a close-up of his muddy hand emerging from a shipping crate on the storm-tossed *Demeter*. This hand then reaches up and rips the throat of a seaman who is attempting to toss the crate overboard. To be sure, Dracula murders in self-defense, but the act is particularly vicious, efficient, and animalistic, done with the same hand that will later beckon Lucy forward to an eternal life of passion and privilege. In this respect, consider Richard Eder's assessment of the 1977 Broadway revival of *Dracula: The Vampire Play*, starring Frank Langella as the Count: "It is elegant, taut, only very faintly camped up, and visually stunning—it also tends to be bloodless." Langella, Eder concludes, is a "beautiful and sensual Dracula . . . but he notably lacks terror" ("Horrors," *New York Times*, 21 Oct. 1977, sec. 3, p. 1).

20. Alain Garel, "Permanence de Dracula," *Image et Son* 345 (Dec. 1979), pp. 12–16.

21. Compare the fate of Lucy, Jonathan, and Van Helsing in Badham's *Dracula* with the fate of the living in *Vampire*, a 1979 made-for-television movie, directed by E. W. Swackhamer and probably intended to exploit the interest in vampires generated by works like Badham's film and King's *'Salem's Lot*. *Vampire*, set in present-day San Francisco, is not an adaptation of Stoker's novel but has many obvious parallels with the retellings of *Dracula* that I have been discussing. All of these works pit a young man and a wise elder against an aristocratic, foreign vampire who has captured a much-valued woman. In *Vampire* the Van Helsing figure is a deeply religious ex-policeman; the young man is a successful architect who must drive a stake into the heart of his beautiful wife after she has become a vampire; and the major female victim is a divorcee working nights to support her young son, and she—unlike Badham's Lucy—never freely chooses to accompany the vampire. Both *Vampire* and Badham's *Dracula* conclude with the hunters leaving the confines of modern civilization in an attempt to rescue the captive woman and destroy the threat. *Vampire* is open ended because the unambiguously evil vampire manages to escape from the hunters and disappear into the night. ("It's not over," the young man says, and the old man replies, "I know that. I know that, son.") Yet the woman is rescued, freed from her false sexual desire and her allegiance to the vampire by the selfless courage of the two men and by the power of the cross and holy water. In the final image of *Vampire* the three scarred survivors move together into the night, their faith and mutual dependence only strengthened by their confrontation with evil (as if Swackhamer has prepared both us and his characters for a television series based on this film). Badham's *Dracula* offers no such affirmation.

CHAPTER

4

Horror of Dracula, Hammer's Dracula Films, *El Conde Dracula*

IN RED GOTHIC LETTERS the opening credits of Terence Fisher's *Horror of Dracula* (released in America in 1958, released in England in 1957 with the title *Dracula*) appear superimposed over a stone statue of a hawk, quite possibly intended to represent Dracula, the aristocratic predator. After the last credit disappears, the camera moves down toward a formidable recessed door, the entrance to an underground chamber. A dissolve carries us through the door and inside the confined, gray crypt to a stone sarcophagus bearing the nameplate "Dracula." From above, off screen, bright red blood drips onto the letters, signaling the beginning of Hammer's vampire saga, dramatically bringing Dracula into a world of color, and underlining the importance of red, the color of Jonathan Harker's leather-bound diary, Lucy Holmwood's lips, Dracula's bloodshot eyes, and Van Helsing's bloodstained hands. This opening image is no doubt less shocking today than it was for a 1950s audience that associated film vampires and horror in general with a black-and-white world first defined by Tod Browning's *Dracula* and other Universal films during the 1930s and 1940s.[1] Yet for me at least, *Horror of Dracula*'s opening sequence remains effective, primarily because, like the introductory shots in Werner Herzog's *Nosferatu the Vampyre*, it serves no obvious narrative purpose. Fisher never reveals why the blood falls onto the crypt nor where it falls from, and the blood is no sacrificial offering to the Count, no miraculous agent that will restore him to life (as it will be in the introductory images of later Hammer productions like *Lust for a Vampire* [1970]). In a less explicit way, however, this blood, like all blood in vampire films, is the life—the trickling red drops add motion and color to a still-life gray image, just as Dracula later in the film will suddenly bring his promise of eternal life into the quiet, darkened bedrooms of Lucy and Mina.

As in Stoker's novel, in the first section of *Horror of Dracula* after the opening credits, Jonathan Harker journeys alone to Castle Dracula and proves unable to resist the temptations he encounters and to combat the unique powers of his aristocratic host. Yet Fisher and screenwriter Jimmy Sangster's Jonathan Harker is no young solicitor whose business trip goes terribly awry.[2] He is, rather, a man approaching middle age who poses as a librarian so that he can gain access to the castle and "forever end this man's reign of terror." With his knowledge of how to destroy the vampire and his commitment to carry out this task, Jonathan seems at first a protagonist to be reckoned with, a man who does not wait for Dracula's invasion of the modern world, but instead dares to seek out the unsuspecting monster in its own lair. (Compare Jonathan in Fisher's film with David Gray in Dreyer's *Vampyr*, who travels into the domain of the vampire not as a hunter, but as a man of "imagination," "lured as usual by fantasy toward the unknown.") Nonetheless, Jonathan fails miserably; not only does Dracula escape, but also the would-be hunter is himself transformed into a vampire. Ironically, his mission of purification ends when Van Helsing hammers the stake intended for Dracula into Jonathan's own undead heart.

For both Fisher and Stoker, Jonathan's adventures at Castle Dracula demonstrate the capability of Dracula, as he triumphs with relative ease over a flawed human being—vampirism here is presented almost as an alternate or even a superior mode of existence. Human weakness is perhaps more evident in *Horror of Dracula* than in Stoker's *Dracula* because Fisher's Jonathan Harker has knowledge and purpose, and yet he still fails. His failure, in fact, becomes the standard by which we measure Van Helsing's success later in the film, just as the moral community's holy crusade contrasts with the failure of the young solicitor in Stoker's novel. One major reason for Jonathan's inability to carry out his intentions is suggested by the extremely stylized acting of John Van Essyn, who plays Jonathan in the film. For Van Essyn, acting is a matter of striking identifiable poses as, for example, the writer who ponders each sentence in his diary entries, or the visitor who is completely surprised by his first glimpse of Dracula, or the man of feeling who must wield a stake. The contrast of Van Essyn's acting style with the more varied and dynamic performances of Christopher Lee as Count Dracula and Peter Cushing as Van Helsing is immediately apparent, and as a result Van Essyn's Jonathan seems unprepared for the task at hand—too readily surprised, too preoccupied with words instead of action, too easily betrayed and rendered vulnerable by his own facile emotions.

As well as underestimating Count Dracula, Jonathan allows himself to be tempted by a female vampire. Stoker's solicitor leaves the safety of his locked room to explore the castle at night and confronts Dracula's brides in a sequence that has, in C. F. Bentley's words, the "irreal quality of a masturbatory fantasy or erotic dream."[3] Jonathan in Fisher's film also leaves his bedroom only to deliver himself over to a young woman who begs for his protection. His vanity, his naive code of masculine chivalry, and his stilted posturing make Jonathan an easy mark. "With you to help me I would have a chance," the vampire implores Jonathan, "You must help me! You must! You are my only hope." With a smile that betokens less sexual anticipation than brotherly concern, Jonathan protectively draws the woman to his breast to console her. However, in the next image, shot from behind Jonathan's back, Fisher allows us to see the vampire's fangs and the gleam of hunger in her eye. The joke is on Jonathan; he cannot see and act because he is too preoccupied with indulging his all-too-human emotions. (As *Horror of Dracula* so clearly suggests, one primary appeal of Dracula's world is that while it allows for hate and desire, it has no place for sentimentality.)

When Jonathan, after he has been infected by the vampire, has a final opportunity to fulfill his mission of destroying Dracula, he fails because of these same emotions. As the sun is about to set on Jonathan's final day as a human being, he enters the vampires' underground resting place, armed with hammer and stakes. He first sees Dracula, asleep and defenseless, but, instead of seizing the opportunity, Jonathan goes to the female vampire's open coffin. With her bloodstained mouth, she no longer looks the part of the dependent woman who begged for his protection, and Jonathan drives the stake into her chest. His personal desire to punish her (the redemptive power of the stake is not mentioned or even implied at this point in the film) for preying upon his male weaknesses and for distracting his thoughts from his fiancée seems to take precedence over his social and spiritual responsibility to rid the world of Dracula. With the stake imbedded in her chest, the female vampire shrieks and ages. Shaken by the murder and by the vampire's transformation, Jonathan pauses long enough to allow Dracula to take the offensive.

Though Jonathan often acts like an inexperienced young man, he is clearly much older than his counterpart in Stoker's novel or in the other works I have discussed. As a result, *Horror of Dracula*, unlike Browning's or John Badham's film adaptations of *Dracula*, does not emphasize the difference in age between Jonathan Harker and Van Helsing. In Fisher's film these two men are roughly the same age; they are neither young men nor white-haired elders. Even though Jonathan and Van Helsing are friends, who both possess the knowledge necessary to destroy Count Dracula, Fisher insists that the two vampire hunters are almost complete opposites. In fact, the most obvious function of Jonathan's ill-fated adventures in *Horror of Dracula* is to define by contrast Van Helsing, the successful hunter who shares none of his friend's hesitancy, emotionalism, and vulnerability. For example, whereas Jonathan's diary entries (presented in voice-over narration) include his own fearful misgivings as well as the factual details of his journey, Van Helsing records the results of his lifelong research on vampires into a dictaphone machine, the only bit of modern technology in the entire film. (In Stoker's novel, a similar machine is used by Dr. Seward.) No personal commentary intrudes as Van Helsing informs us of "certain basic facts" about the vampire: "One. Light. The vampire is allergic to light. Never ventures forth in the daytime. Sunlight fatal. Repeat. Fatal." Van Helsing has no diary and no photos of his fiancée that catch Dracula's attention because he has no personal life. While Arthur Holmwood, the only other man of any consequence in the film, is immediately defined by his role as husband and brother and by the decor of his upper-middle-class Victorian-styled home, in Van Helsing's private residence, we see only one room, a combination study and parlor, shorn of personal touches. From this room, the doctor issues forth, a fully committed man who lives in and for his work, a no-nonsense specialist who cannot be tempted or in any other way deflected from his purpose.

Fisher's Van Helsing provides practical information and well-considered explanations of the apparently inexplicable, but, unlike Stoker's patriarchal professor, the "eminent" doctor in *Horror of Dracula* is neither a wise foreigner nor a surrogate father. Instead, he is a man of action—physically agile, strong, and quick, much more like the undead foe he battles than the doddering old men who provide the mostly tedious touches of comic relief in Fisher's film. (Appropriately, two of these old men, a kindly policeman and a corrupt border guard, embody the legitimate social authority, to which no one even thinks of applying for help after Dracula's attacks.) Fisher, in fact, very clearly sets Van Helsing apart from all the other human beings in the film, from the easily victimized Holmwood family as much as from the peasant villagers who dare not attack the predatory aristocratic vampire ("Some things are best left alone," an innkeeper warns Van Helsing). Van Helsing, of course, must have some assistance—"with God's help we'll succeed," he tells Arthur—but he alone drives in the stakes that rescue Jonathan and Lucy from their undead purgatory, and he alone exterminates Count Dracula. In Lucy's tomb, her brother Arthur cowers against a wall and covers his eyes while Van Helsing commits the desecration that will "liberate her soul and give it eternal peace." Van Helsing knows that "there is no other way," even though Lucy's blood is quite literally on his hands. He can and does wipe off the blood, for he is completely confident that his actions are justified and necessary "to rid the world of this evil." In *Horror of Dracula* Van Helsing is the hero, the sole hero, not just because he has faith, knowledge, and the willingness to face the vampire, but because he alone does the dirty work, while the rest of the living, guiltless, reap the benefits.

The world that the vampire threatens in *Horror of Dracula* ultimately becomes identified not with a single young woman and her widowed father or with all of modern civilization, but with one upper-middle-class nineteenth-century family; in this case, the Holmwoods, Arthur, his wife Mina, and younger sister Lucy (here Jonathan's fiancée), and the family's maid Gerta and her child, Tania. According to Van Helsing, Dracula attacks Lucy, then Mina, because he seeks to avenge and to replace the bride Jonathan destroyed at Castle Dracula. In effect, the Holmwoods are innocent victims, preyed upon only because of their association with Jonathan, even though they have no idea of his role as vampire hunter. Their ignorance, needless to say, makes them susceptible to the undead, and so, too, in an important sense, does their intimacy with each other and their unthinking acceptance of familial roles. Only Van Helsing's direct intervention prevents the complete decimation of the Holmwood household.

As in Badham's *Dracula*, in *Horror of Dracula* the vampire's embrace transforms his victim into an invalid by day and an expectant lover by night, until she dies and rises completely shorn of her social and moral inhibitions. Dracula enters the Holmwood house through the French doors in Lucy's bedroom, for it is in the bedroom, not the parlor or study, that the fate of the family is decided. When we first see Lucy, she is already bedridden, a young girl with pigtails and a high-collared nightgown who looks less like a bride-to-be than like a naive child.[4] At night, however, after her concerned relatives leave her bedside, Lucy comes to life, opening the French doors and removing the cross from around her neck, then lying back on her bed and loosening the collar of her nightgown as she waits, almost mesmerized, for Dracula. Her actions are secretive and private; she is no longer a child and no longer a dependent member of the family.

After her death Lucy ventures into the night as a predator, seeking out Tania as her first victim. Dressed in a nightgown, with her hair hanging loose and her fangs bared, Lucy calls to Tania in the woods, promising the little girl: "I know somewhere nice and quiet where we can play." "Aunt Lucy" leads Tania by the hand back toward the coffin/bed in her crypt, but she leaves the child when Arthur—a more appealing victim—appears, amazed at his sister's resurrection. "Arthur, dear brother," Lucy whispers as she approaches him, "let me kiss you." In Stoker's *Dracula*, a comparable situation occurs, but in the novel Lucy entices her betrothed, not her brother. The violation (or at least the possibility of violation) of sexual taboos is thus more prominent in *Horror of Dracula* than in *Dracula: The Vampire Play* or Browning's *Dracula*, for Fisher's Lucy would "kiss" and "play" with her own brother and with a young child who lovingly regards her as an aunt. Arthur, Tania, and the sexual status quo are protected, however, by the dramatic intrusion of Van Helsing, who appears suddenly, almost magically materializing in the same way that Count Dracula does so often in the film. As Lucy reaches for her awestruck and defenseless brother, Van Helsing thrusts his arm into the framed image. The silver cross he clenches in his hand separates brother and sister and burns its imprint onto Lucy's forehead. The cruciform scar disappears only after Van Helsing transfixes Lucy and thereby renders her truly dead—that is to say, passive and virginally beautiful and hence no longer a threat to her brother's household.

Once Van Helsing has purified the undead Lucy, Dracula invades the master bedroom of the Holmwood house to seduce Mina, Arthur's wife. Ironically, Mina is easily open to attack because she so unquestioningly accepts her role as a dutiful and devoted wife. Following the instructions in a note purportedly sent by Arthur, Mina leaves her home at night alone. Dracula, it turns out, has arranged the rendezvous; he will be her new husband. After the first meeting, the vampire can enter Mina's bed while Van Helsing and Arthur stand outside the house keeping watch, because Mina has allowed Dracula to take refuge in the cellar of her home. Through this ingenious plot twist, Fisher suggests that the Count can "live" in the Holmwoods' upper-middle-class house. Suddenly, a medieval castle or a crumbling, deserted abbey is no longer necessary; any house with a dark, accessible cellar will do. The modern world of Harkers and Holmwoods, it seems, already has a place for the vampire. Furthermore, *Horror of Dracula* implies that the women of this world need Count Dracula to occupy the beds left vacant by easily fooled husbands and wandering fiancés. In Fisher's version of *Dracula*, the vampire's assault/seduction of Lucy and Mina becomes an attack on the patriarchal family, which relies on strictly defined female sexual roles, and on the home, which provides neither privacy nor protection for the family. When Arthur finally accepts the fact that his household and therefore the very foundations of his life (he has no occupation in the film; he is nothing but a father and a brother) are under siege, he by himself can do nothing. He must depend completely on Van Helsing. "I'll do anything you say," Arthur declares, ceding his authority to the specialist, for in *Horror of Dracula* the father is as impotent as the bumbling, old government official who cannot prevent Dracula from entering or leaving the country.

After Van Helsing discovers the vampire's coffin in the Holmwoods' cellar, Dracula abducts Mina and rushes back to his castle, a home that has proven scarcely more secure than the Holmwood house. Arthur and Van Helsing pursue the vampire into his own territory, following the path that Jonathan had taken in the beginning of the film. While Stoker's vampire hunters hurry to complete their wild work before the sun sets, in *Horror of Dracula* it is Dracula who is under "natural" pressure to find refuge, for sunrise is imminent and nature is here on the side of the living. In a startling image that seems to owe more to Poe than to Stoker, Dracula drops the catatonic Mina into an open grave and begins to shovel dirt onto her white-robed body. She suddenly awakens, screaming in the midst of her own nightmarish premature burial. Arthur rushes to his wife's aid, leaving Van Helsing, who has no such personal responsibility as husband or brother, to dash into the castle alone in pursuit of the vampire.

More than Browning's film or any other version of *Dracula*, Fisher's film emphasizes the similarities between Dr. Van Helsing and Count Dracula, two superior beings whose physical strength and agility match their single-minded sense of purpose and their ability to demand and receive allegiance. (The similarity is even more marked because Fisher's Dracula cannot transform himself into mist or animal.)[5] In the library, the same room in which Jonathan succumbed to the female vampire and was easily overcome by Dracula, the master vampire and the master vampire hunter confront each other. From the failure of Van Helsing's ally, Jonathan Harker, to the abduction of his patient, Mina, *Horror of Dracula* leads inexorably to the final struggle for survival between the vampire and the sole man capable of destroying the undead "propagator" of "unspeakable evil."

In the large library room with a circular zodiac tile pattern prominent on the floor (perhaps somehow related to the idea that Dracula is part of an "unholy cult"), Van Helsing and Dracula struggle in hand-to-hand combat that brings them quite literally face to face. (Badham, as I noted in the previous chapter, uses a similar image to underscore the vampire's superhuman strength.) Van Helsing survives, first, because he feigns unconsciousness and because Dracula—for all his glazed red eyes and canine fangs—is not simply a predatory animal. Taken in by Van Helsing's ploy, Dracula pauses with a decidedly human look of satisfaction before finishing off his apparently defenseless prey. This momentary pause allows Van Helsing to push away the surprised vampire and escape. Like an ingenious, acrobatic swashbuckler (and most unlike Stoker's elderly professor, not to mention Badham's Van Helsing), Fisher's Van Helsing runs down a long table and leaps to grab a heavy curtain that covers a large, arch-shaped window. The curtain falls and sunlight streams into the room; like beams of fire, the rays burn Dracula's foot to ashes. (This emphasis on the power of sunlight owes more to F. W. Murnau's *Nosferatu* than to Stoker's novel.) Holding two candlesticks in the form of the cross, Van Helsing forces the vampire into the destructive, purifying light. Dracula's body collapses inward and disintegrates in a real death—ashes to ashes and dust to dust.

The living survive in *Horror of Dracula* only because of Van Helsing, and Van Helsing survives because of his cunning and physical strength as much as because of his knowledge and his ability to improvise a plan of attack. Significantly, given the conventions of this genre and, more specifically, the role of weapons in Browning's *Dracula*, Van Helsing in Fisher's film does not enter Castle Dracula armed with the hallowed and effective objects he has used earlier in the film—garlic, cross, and stake: his crucifix was left behind in Dracula's coffin in the Holmwoods' cellar; garlic is at best a preventative measure; and a stake would apparently be useless against a foe who is not in the comatose sleep of the undead. Alone and with no talismans to protect him, Van Helsing triumphs because he lets in the sunlight. Unlike Henry Frankenstein (a character Peter Cushing had played in Hammer's *The Curse of Frankenstein* [1956]), Van Helsing does not seek to harness the immense power or discover the secrets of nature. His function is to allow bright sunlight, and later fresh air as well, into a closed, undead environment, thereby restoring the natural order that Dracula has violated. If God does provide the "help" that Van Helsing earlier says he will need, then it comes in the form of sunlight that can obliterate evil. Whether or not this natural force is also a supernatural force, it can only be effective if Van Helsing forces Dracula into the light. The candlestick cross thus becomes a crucially important object that signifies more than just Van Helsing's ingenuity. Unlike the holy wafers in *Dracula* or the gold cross Lucy wears earlier in *Horror of Dracula*, the two candlesticks are not sanctified, symbolic, Christian objects that can be employed as defensive weapons against the vampire. Van Helsing transforms the candlesticks into a cross; in his hands and through his faith and commitment, everyday objects—indeed, the very furnishings of Castle Dracula—become magically charged with power. Neither the candlestick cross nor the sunlight nor Van Helsing is alone sufficient to end Dracula's existence. All three elements are necessary—the human, the natural, and the supernatural. In lieu of Stoker's moral community, who must act collectively under the guidance of an elderly patriarch, Fisher offers us one man who by himself can let in the sunlight, forge his own weapon, and wield the cross. Van Helsing does not disregard tradition, he transforms it.

The heroic vampire hunter in *Horror of Dracula* may not literally be a foreigner, like his counterpart in Browning's *Dracula*, but in both films the man who destroys the undead and thereby "rids the world of this evil," is, in fact, excluded from the key image that reveals the newly saved world of the living and in so doing epitomizes what is most worth protecting and preserving in life. In Fisher's film, after Dracula turns to dust and ashes, we see a close-up of Mina's hand as she sits outside Castle Dracula in the sunlight. The cruciform mark of her adulterous impurity and of Dracula's violation, the mark that had earlier been burned onto Mina's hand when she touched a cross, now disappears in the sunlight, and her wedding ring is very much apparent. The same light that incinerates Dracula purifies Mina. In the next image, a medium shot of the couple, Arthur kisses his wife's hand as he sits with his arm protectively around her and his coat draped over her shoulders. This couple may not be safely ensconced in the comfort of their own parlor after the battle with the vampire, but the Holmwoods are reunited. Arthur has rescued his wife from the grave, and she leans on him for protection and consolation. Their marriage survives, and with it at least the possibility for the restoration of the values of home and family. While *Horror of Dracula* does not conclude with the celebratory new birth and complete affirmation of the family that is emphasized in the epilogue to Stoker's novel, Fisher does place Mina and Arthur in the sunlight at the end of the film. (Contrast this final image to the concluding scene—also a "happy ending"—in *Dracula: The Vampire Play*, in which all the survivors remain inside the crypt at Carfax Abbey.) Their marriage is visually associated with the restored natural order, so as to underline the fact that in *Horror of Dracula* the Holmwoods' marriage is natural and legitimate as opposed to the unnatural appetites and desires of the undead.

Yet the Holmwoods are not the final thing we see in *Horror of Dracula*, as, for example, the betrothed couple of Jonathan and Lucy are the final image of Browning's *Dracula*. Fisher cuts from Mina and Arthur back to Van Helsing, who is still inside the library. His victory complete, Van Helsing opens the window so that the fresh air can blow away the ashy remains of Dracula's decomposed corpse. Van Helsing's triumph ensures the survival of the Holmwoods, but the vampire hunter does not join Arthur and Mina after the battle, perhaps because the qualities that enable him to defeat Dracula separate him from the more domestic and interdependent world of the Holmwoods. Van Helsing is not in any obvious way polluted by the ritual murders he commits or infected by his contact with Dracula; nonetheless, he remains outside the human community, a solitary, single-minded man in a world where the traditional marriage is clearly associated with the natural order of things. Van Helsing's work is his life, and his work ends with the airing out of Castle Dracula.

All that is left of the vampire is a large gold ring, and the camera holds on a close-up of this single token of Dracula's aristocratic legacy as the final credits roll. Only the Count's ring remains, lying empty on the floor, while outside with her husband Mina still wears her gold wedding band.

Seeing *Horror of Dracula* today, after Hammer's lucrative resurrection of the Count in, for example, *Dracula, Prince of Darkness* (1965) and *Dracula Has Risen from the Grave* (1968), this final image seems to open up Fisher's narrative, suggesting—however illogically—the possibility that Dracula will return and that Van Helsing's victory is therefore illusory or at best temporary. A similar signet ring even appears on Dracula's finger after he has been restored to life through an elaborate black mass in *Dracula, A.D. 1972*. Whether or not Fisher envisioned a sequel to *Horror of Dracula* in 1958, when he directed *Dracula, Prince of Darkness* seven years later, he used the final struggle between Van Helsing and Dracula in the earlier film as a prologue to this new story of the Count. Thus *Horror of Dracula* becomes part of an ongoing saga in which the triumphs of both the living and the undead are always temporary, as the struggle for control of the world (usually pictured as a village and surrounding wooded countryside) continues. Since Hammer's later vampire films are not adaptations of Stoker's *Dracula* (though these films are identified as being "Based on the characters created by Bram Stoker"), they fall outside the scope of this chapter. However, a brief survey of Hammer's extremely successful and influential Dracula series in the 1960s is necessary to provide a context against which to consider the three film adaptations of *Dracula* released during the 1970s, as well as several of the contemporary works I will discuss in chapters 7 and 8.[6]

The Brides of Dracula (1960), also directed by Terence Fisher and starring Peter Cushing (but not Christopher Lee), was Hammer's first vampire film after *Horror of Dracula*. A voice-over introduction to the film informs us that, although Count Dracula was destroyed, "his disciples live on to spread the cult and corrupt the world." Thus Van Helsing continues his solitary crusade against the undead by instructing the often-skeptical living in the habits and weaknesses of the vampire cult, by protecting potential victims with his cross, and by performing "acts of healing" with his hammer and stake. The closest figure to a King-Vampire in the film is Baron Meinster, a rakish youth intent on establishing a harem, beginning with his own mother, who in the past condoned and fed her son's evil habits. Unlike in *Horror of Dracula*, the vampire in *The Brides of Dracula* does not threaten the bourgeois family or the private home; his targets are, purely and simply, pretty, virginal village girls or young teachers at a secluded girls school—just the sort of women who, in a Gothic romance as opposed to a horror film, might dream of a young, handsome, eligible aristocrat's embrace that would raise them to the status of baroness. Against Baron Meinster and his voracious brides, Van Helsing is completely alone. A local priest shies away from the "sacrilege" Van Helsing must commit; a foolish doctor dismisses the "superstitions" about vampires. Surrounded by terrified villagers, incompetent male authority figures, and women who are either potential victims or willing allies of the vampire, Van Helsing is the only human being capable of preventing the "corruption" of the world.

Alone, at night, he ventures to the vampire's lair, a deserted windmill far removed from civilization (the location is perhaps Fisher's allusion to the end of James Whale's *Frankenstein*). After grappling with an aged hag, who is the vampire's devoted human servant, Van Helsing loses his cross and is overpowered and bitten by the Baron, while the brides look on. The Baron then leaves to abduct Marianne Danielle, a teacher at the girls school. Van Helsing cauterizes the bite on his neck with a red-hot poker and cleanses the wound with holy water. As in *Horror of Dracula*, Van Helsing ultimately triumphs because of his ability and willingness to think and act quickly and ingeniously: having returned to the windmill with Marianne, the Baron must again battle Van Helsing, who now uses the holy water as a weapon against the vampire. During this struggle, fire breaks out and the windmill is engulfed in flames, allowing the vampire to escape. With the same agility and quick thinking he used to destroy Count Dracula, Van Helsing leaps onto one of the windmill's vanes, thus causing the shadow of a cross to fall on the Baron. As the would-be Dracula dies, Van Helsing watches with his arm protectively around Marianne—a gesture that affirms his essential humanity. The vampire hunter has withstood pain and proven again the supremacy of the living over the undead. The film's final long shot of the burning windmill, its vanes forming a fiery cross, is an image of militant Christianity and of fire as a means of purification. The image is also a tribute to Van Helsing, for without him the windmill would not become a cross and the night would remain the domain of the undead.

The Brides of Dracula celebrates Van Helsing's triumph and suggests that, after all his isolation and all the violence he must commit, he is reintegrated into human society through his final connection with Marianne. To the extent that *The Brides of Dracula* singles out Van Helsing as a victorious hero, the film also insists that the rest of the living are vulnerable and incapable even of self-defense. It is particularly surprising, therefore, that in Fisher's next vampire film, *Dracula, Prince of Darkness*, Van Helsing appears only in the opening sequence, a masked reprise of his battle with Dracula in *Horror of Dracula*, here described by a voice-over narrator as the "final and absolute destruction" of the "King of the Undead."

This narrator is wrong, however, since Dracula rises again to confront, in Van Helsing's stead, two men who bear more than a little resemblence to the two vampire hunters in *Horror of Dracula*. Like Arthur Holmwood in Hammer's first vampire film, Charles Kent in *Dracula, Prince of Darkness* is forced to act in order to rescue his wife from the vampire; bad luck and his own naive carelessness turn Charles from a harmless tourist into a determined hunter. Instructing and guiding the young man is Father Sandor, older and more insistently authoritarian than Peter Cushing's Van Helsing. In his first appearance in the film, Sandor prevents a group of what he calls "superstitious frightened idiots," including the local priest, from driving a stake into the corpse of an innocent young woman. Like Van Helsing, the grey-haired Sandor is set apart from the foolish masses, even isolated from the other monks in his order. With his imposing physical appearance and his total dedication, Father Sandor is the Christian soldier armed with rifle and cross (and later hammer and stake), who travels through the world knowing full well "what has to be done." He never wavers, never suffers remorse or feels temptation; he has no debilitating heart ailment like Father Merrin in *The Exorcist*, no crisis of faith like Father Callahan in *'Salem's Lot*.

Sandor's role as vampire hunter in *Dracula, Prince of Darkness* is best defined when he destroys Charles's sister-in-law, Helen, who sheds her nagging bitchiness and prim inhibitions once she becomes a vampire. The sequence of Helen's destruction is very much like the "formal proceedings" in Le Fanu's *Carmilla*, except that this female vampire snarls and writhes as a group of monks try to hold her down on a table, with her arms spread as if for crucifixion (or for gang rape). Unlike the other men present, Sandor shows no fear or hesitation as he pounds the stake into Helen's heart: "This is a shell and what it contains is pure evil," Sandor tells Charles, "when we destroy it, we destroy only the evil." Nonetheless, Charles covers his eyes. But the wise guide is proven correct, just as he was correct earlier in preventing the desecration of the young woman's corpse. With a bloodstained stake in her heart, Helen no longer resists; she is truly dead, and Sandor delivers the requisite blessing over her fully human corpse. What this sequence demonstrates is that evil is indeed "pure evil," and that it can be isolated, then destroyed by the bloody ritual of transfixion, an act of violence whose beneficent effects are immediately and readily apparent.

If *Dracula, Prince of Darkness* insists on the efficacy of stake and cross and places the defense of the living in the hands of a monk who believes in and can carry out the violent ritual, the film—like many of Hammer's productions—also reveals the dangers of ritual. Once destroyed by Van Helsing, Count Dracula can only be restored to life through a ritual enacted by a servant, Clove, who is in his way as dedicated and free of guilt as Father Sandor. Clove hangs the body of Charles's milquetoast older brother Alan upside down over an open sarcophagus that contains the ashes of Count Dracula. With one smooth stroke, the vampire's human servant slashes Alan with a knife so that his blood drips onto the ashes until Dracula rematerializes. As David Pirie points out in *A Heritage of Horror*, this ritual is particularly ironic, since "Alan's blood gives life to Dracula and so, in a mystical sense, Alan *becomes* Dracula; the mild pompous Victorian is transformed into the wildly sensual voracious anti-hero who immediately claims Alan's wife Helen as his first victim."[7]

Once the actions of Clove and the blood of Alan recreate the vampire before our eyes (reminding us in a graphic manner that all monsters are, in fact, our creations), Count Dracula proves far more difficult to destroy than his brides, who ultimately succumb to the stake. As in *Horror of Dracula*, in *Dracula, Prince of Darkness* the hunters must do more than merely follow a prescribed ritual if they are to defeat the King-Vampire. Their victory in the latter film, however, is curiously hollow—a temporary triumph that relies more on luck than on skill, courage, or faith. Fighting on what seems to be the frozen moat surrounding Castle Dracula, the Count easily overpowers Charles, while Charles's wife, Diana, and Father Sandor watch, unable to help the young man. In frustration Diana fires Sandor's rifle at the vampire, and the bullet causes the ice to begin to crack. The monk then fires several shots, extending the crack until Dracula is isolated on a block of ice. As Charles climbs to safety, the Prince of Darkness slips under the water and is encased in a frozen natural tomb. Whereas Van Helsing earns his victories in *Horror of Dracula* and *The Brides of Dracula*, the hunters in *Dracula, Prince of Darkness* are almost granted a reprieve, saved for the time being by an accident of nature; no longer is it possible for the living to be saved and protected by the advice and the action of a single man.

If *The Brides of Dracula* focuses on the bravery and determination of Van Helsing and on this solitary vampire hunter's ability to rely on the tradition of cross and stake and to depart—when necessary—from prescribed ritual, *Dracula, Prince of Darkness* offers two hunters (again, the familiar combination of a young man and an older guide) and insists, through Father Sandor, upon strict adherence to ritual, while also demonstrating how ritual can become the murderous tool of superstitious ignorance or the means of resurrecting evil. What remains basically constant in Fisher's vampire films is the presentation of the vampire's female victims (particularly during those scenes when they are attacked/seduced) and of Dracula himself. Count Dracula changes little from *Horror of Dracula* to *Dracula, Prince of Darkness*. Like his gestures and physical appearance, his lust for blood and his egotistical desire to dominate and wreak horrible vengeance on those humans who have challenged him remains the same. This Dracula does not so much invade the modern world searching for brides or converts to a new order of beings as he makes forays into surrounding villages, towns, and monasteries, then retreats back to his castle. Unlike Stoker's King-Vampire, for Hammer's Dracula, immortality is but the endless repetition of a single story; all his energy and attention are directed toward the satisfaction of uncomplicated desires and the victimization of humans who venture—like poachers, uninvited guests, or armed invaders—too close to Castle Dracula. Ironically, however, this Prince of Darkness is often shown fleeing or cowering in the face of the cross-bearing living, and from *The Brides of Dracula* on, Hammer's vampire films emphasize that Dracula absolutely requires not just human blood, but human servants. Through human evil and man's selfish desires for power and immortality, the living bring Dracula to life; through man's weakness and servility, human beings become Dracula's servants.

Whatever variation there is in Hammer's Dracula films derives primarily from the presentation of the living—those human beings who work for or against the vampire. In Freddie Francis's *Dracula Has Risen from the Grave*, for example, a few drops of blood from a cowardly, doubt-ridden priest revive Dracula, and the priest becomes the vampire's servant, a go-between who provides Dracula with access to the victims he desires. The possibility that this priest merely shifts his allegiance from one master to another, from an invisible, perhaps even nonexistent God to the commanding Prince of Darkness, is very clearly suggested here, although this film is ultimately no more critical in its presentation of Christianity than are Fisher's vampire films with their many images of the cross as man's best weapon.

Just as Fisher offers contrary views of ritual without ever exploring the paradoxes and the questions introduced about violence and ceremony in *Dracula, Prince of Darkness*, Francis pairs his weak, dangerous priest with an unswervingly dedicated Monsignor, obviously the good Christian, the spiritual brother of Father Sandor. Monsignor Muller, older and less physically fit than Sandor, is surely no match for Dracula in hand-to-hand combat, as Van Helsing was in *Horror of Dracula*. The Monsignor's real flaw, however, may be that he is too confident. "There is nothing to fear," he tells the standard collection of terrified villagers, who will not venture out of the local tavern for fear of bothering Count Dracula. So with a large gold cross strapped to his back, the Monsignor ascends through mist-covered, treacherous, rocky terrain toward Castle Dracula, where he seals the door with his cross and ends the villagers' fears. Or so he erroneously assumes, for while the Monsignor reads the Latin service of exorcism at the door of the castle, Dracula is revived by the taste of blood from the terrified priest who has refused to complete the journey to the vampire's lair with his superior. Wearied, but confident that "the evil is destroyed forever," Monsignor Muller returns to his home in the city, where he lives with the widow of his brother and her beautiful daughter, Maria. It is this household, and Maria in particular, who becomes Dracula's target, when the vampire obsessively seeks revenge.

In the comfort and familiarity of his own home, a full day's ride from Castle Dracula, the only threat Muller perceives is from Maria's suitor, Paul, a handsome student who has the nerve and youthful presumptuousness to disrupt his girlfriend's birthday party by declaring that he is an atheist. Paul can be barred from the house, but Dracula easily enters the French doors in Maria's bedroom. Her uncle recognizes the cause of Maria's strange illness and is able to save his niece from a second attack by driving the vampire off with a crucifix. However, when the Monsignor attempts to hunt down the vampire, Muller is knocked unconscious by the faithless priest, who now is Dracula's whimpering lackey. Bedridden and incapable of protecting his own niece, the Monsignor must call on Paul to continue the battle against the vampire. (As might be expected, given the role of women in Hammer's earlier vampire films, Maria's mother is not even told the truth about her daughter's condition, much less enlisted as a vampire hunter.) The gap between age and youth is wider in *Dracula Has Risen from the Grave* than in Hammer's previous vampire films, for Paul and the Monsignor are philosophical antagonists, as well as rivals for Maria's affection. Thus the transference of responsibility and control from the celibate, wounded old cleric to the sexually active, energetic, independent young student seems to signal a reversal of the tradition fostered by *Dracula: The Vampire Play* and Browning's *Dracula*, and to provide an ideal scenario for youthful audiences of the late 1960s.

Paul, however, is not Peter Cushing's Van Helsing, and the concluding sequences of *Dracula Has Risen from the Grave* catalogue the limitations and weaknesses of this young hero. To translate the Latin book (presumably containing information about the undead) that the Monsignor has given him, Paul enlists the aid of Dracula's servant, who still wears his clerical collar. Thus the unschooled young man inadvertently places Maria in further jeopardy, and he is unable to rectify the situation. Finding Dracula helpless in his coffin, Paul thrusts a stake deep into the heart of the beast, but since the young free-thinker cannot bring himself to recite a prayer to finalize the ritual of transfixion, Dracula is able to pull the stake out of his chest and escape. Whether or not Francis and screenwriter Anthony Hinds (writing under the name John Elder) "cheat" in this sequence by altering the rules of the game to allow for a surprising plot reversal, the implications of Paul's failure are immediately clear: to the courage and physical strength necessary to drive in a stake must be added faith and the adherence to Christian ritual that the pronouncement of a prayer entails. Having now bested both Maria's uncle and her lover, Dracula leaves the city with the entranced young woman. "My revenge is complete," he announces solemnly.

Like the men in Hammer's earlier Dracula films, Paul must leave civilization, travel through the uninhabited natural green world, and enter Dracula's domain in hopes of rescuing the stolen woman and administering retributive justice to the apparently triumphant vampire. The young man journeys alone, without an older guide like Father Sandor and without the experience and skills of Van Helsing. Paul arrives at Castle Dracula just after the Count has ordered Maria to remove the large gold cross that her uncle has used to bar the castle's entrance in the beginning of the film. Maria, now no more than a puppet, throws the cross down into the barren hillside below the castle. Unarmed, Paul attacks Dracula, and in their struggle both the vampire and the hunter fall over the castle's restraining wall. Even more than in *Dracula, Prince of Darkness*, luck or fate or Christian providence provides a just dispensation: Paul is physically and spiritually saved when natural foliage breaks his fall, and he climbs back to safety; Dracula is impaled on the Monsignor's cross, which glows as if infused with a supernatural light and attracts the vampire the way lightning is attracted to a lightning rod. Maria, like Mina Seward in Browning's *Dracula* and any number of similar victims, comes to herself and stands with Paul, looking down at the writhing fiend. Dracula is not destroyed, however, until a prayer is uttered, a benediction that transforms a gruesome accident into an act of cosmic justice. Before collapsing, the traitorous, weak-willed priest delivers the Latin prayer as he kneels facing the heavens, thereby acknowledging the only true Master. Paul, too, has learned his lesson. He crosses himself in a gesture that signifies both his newfound faith and his acceptance of the Monsignor's world, the world of the Father. Now Paul is an acceptable suitor for Maria, and the two young people embrace. In *Dracula Has Risen from the Grave*, as much as in Stoker's novel, a successful bout with the Prince of Darkness can only teach the young how much they have to learn from their elders and strengthen and justify the hunters' faith and their acceptance of "superstitious," ritualistic Christianity.

This message is revised, however, in Peter Sasdy's *Taste the Blood of Dracula* (released in England in 1969, in America in 1970), the first Hammer film to bring the Count to England, and, aside from *Horror of Dracula*, the most interesting of Hammer's Dracula series. As in *Dracula Has Risen from the Grave*, in Sasdy's film, Count Dracula's primary desire after he has been resurrected through a blood ritual is to seek revenge against certain specific human beings. The young women who come under his spell and are employed in gaining this revenge are discarded as soon as their usefulness ends, no matter how much these living or undead minions may worship Dracula. For the first time in Hammer's series, however, the undead master is not opposed by a living master, a professional vampire hunter or an armed monk or a brave Monsignor. The young people in *Taste the Blood of*

Dracula must fend for themselves; in fact, they must struggle against their elders and live, quite literally, burdened with the sins of their fathers. These fathers are upper-middle-class Victorian paterfamilias, shown for the first time in the film with their families outside a church after Sunday service. Yet that evening the three pious and upright citizens leave their homes, under the guise of doing charity work, and make their monthly trek to a bordello hidden in London's slums, where they seek out pleasure with prostitutes who are the same age as the men's own children. Sasdy and screenwriter Anthony Hinds (again writing under the name John Elder), of course, did not invent the notion that the male ruling class in late Victorian England was repressed, repressive, and thoroughly hypocritical in its attitude toward sex and the family structure. A similar idea—though never offered explicitly as a critique—is suggested in Le Fanu's *Carmilla* and Stoker's *Dracula*. Thus *Taste the Blood of Dracula*, for all its topical, late 1960s mistrust of adults, is the heir to the nineteenth-century British vampire story, which often focuses not only on sexuality, but also on the patriarchal family and the relationship between children and their real, surrogate, or "primal" fathers.[8]

In Sasdy's film Count Dracula is reborn because of these well-to-do Victorian hedonists, who take the place of the foolish tourists and cowardly priests in Hammer's earlier Dracula films. Having explored all available options in their search for "new experiences," the three men in *Taste the Blood of Dracula* enlist the aid of a guide, Lord Courtley, a young Byronic profligate who was disowned by his father for practicing Satanism. Ironically, the middle-aged bourgeois fathers deliver themselves and their money over to a thoroughly corrupt young aristocrat, and this alliance of new money and old decadence looses the Prince of Darkness on the world. The three men, seeking novel, forbidden, sacrilegious pleasure, follow Courtley's map and journey away from the city to a deserted Gothic church, in which Courtley is to perform an elaborate ceremony involving sacred objects (the dried blood, cape, ring, and clasp of Dracula) purchased with the men's thousand guineas. Even more than in *Dracula, Prince of Darkness*, in Sasdy's vampire film, ritual—with its incantory language, formalized gestures, symbolic objects, and necessary bloodletting—becomes associated with evil and the dangers of subservience to an undead master. Courtley mingles his blood with the powdered blood of Dracula and orders the three men to drink the seething mixture, but at the last minute the men refuse to taste the revivified blood of Dracula. As if receiving the sacrament, Courtley drinks, then collapses to the floor. As he gags in a convulsive fit, the other thrill-seekers kick and stab him to death, then flee in terror from the church. Murder is apparently the most exotic pleasure. Unbeknownst to the men, however, the ritual of resurrection succeeds, for Dracula—the aristocrat *par excellence*—emerges from Courtley's decayed corpse and vows to repay the middle-class patriarchs who have destroyed his servant.

The children of these hypocritical men serve as the instruments for the vampire's revenge, so that *Taste the Blood of Dracula* becomes a story about patricide and the violent conflict between the three fathers and their children, who are just maturing into adulthood and independence. This conflict is most extreme in the Hargood family. Mrs. Hargood has been bullied into total, submissive resignation by her husband, William, who is appreciably older than his wife. Even after his death, she is incapable of participating in life or shedding her weepy pessimism. Alice Hargood, another of Hammer's basically interchangeable young women, resists her father's repressive tyranny, for she is not, as he believes, a flirtatious "harlot." In a scenario worthy of the racy, sprawling, family melodramas of the 1950s, Hargood seeks to punish Alice for being a "sexually mature woman" and to satisfy his own frustrated, unacknowledged desires by entering her bedroom and whipping her. Alice climbs out her bedroom window to escape her drunken father, and—in an ironic reversal of traditional vampire film conventions—in the garden below her bedroom Dracula waits, a father/lover whom she cannot disobey. Just as Hargood has prevented Alice from meeting her young suitor, he now interrupts the vampire's embrace of his daughter. Under Dracula's power, but obviously fulfilling her own wishes as well, Alice murders her father, then leaves/elopes with the vampire. Hargood's accessories in the murder of Courtley meet similar fates—one of the men is even transfixed by his daughter, now become a laughing vampire. In each case the father dies alone, helpless, and with open eyes, fully aware that he is the victim of his own child, who now is governed and possessed by the aristocratic vampire the pleasure-seeking fathers themselves helped to resurrect. With Dracula directing the action, the lives and deaths of these men become ironic, blackly comic cautionary tales.

Since the police investigation of these deaths and of Alice's disappearance is "worse than useless," and since there are no adults to whom to turn for guidance and assistance, one single young man, Alice's boyfriend, Paul Paxton, takes on the responsibility of "doing something." Before Dracula's first attack, Paul and his friends are the complete opposite of their fathers. Sasdy films the young adults outside in natural settings where they ride horses, discuss parties, and exchange innocent kisses; in contrast, he shows the fathers isolated in elegantly furnished studies or together in crowded or ominously dark interiors as they pursue "new experiences" or attempt to cope with their guilty remorse. Far from being a rebel or a wild hedonist, Paul—like the other young people of his social class—lives for romantic love, dreams of marriage, and even hopes to start his own business. Upon such conventional aspirations the bourgeois world depends; nonconformity and egotistical individuality are left to the decadent and doomed Lord Courtley. And, appropriately enough, Courtley's satanic rite is answered by Paul's Christian ritual at the end of the film, a ritual that rids the world—yet again—of Count Dracula.

With knowledge gained from a book on vampires, knowledge available only in a sacred text that—like Hammer's vampire films—perpetuates tradition, Paul arms himself and travels over the same path in the daytime that the fathers had taken at night, journeying outside the city to the deserted church where Dracula sleeps with Alice draped atop his coffin, still waiting for the kiss that will transform her into a vampire. As in all of Hammer's previous Dracula films, the king of the undead is not destroyed by a stake, but by a courageous human being and by Christian talismans. Since Paul is not the young atheist hero of *Dracula Has Risen from the Grave*, he needs no assistance. Finally, a young man can alone defeat the vampire who has stolen his beloved. In the end Paul becomes more the priest than the hunter. He bars the door to the church with a cross, substitutes white candles and white altar cloth for Courtley's black mass paraphernalia, then recites a Latin prayer. Trapped inside the church, Dracula struggles like a cornered animal, until he is burned by the sunlight shining through a scarlet, stained-glass cross. Before he plunges from the choir loft onto the altar and disintegrates, Dracula sees this vacant, ominously dark building once again become a candle-lit, living church, filled with the icons of Christianity and the echoes of Latin prayers. (A series of brief, wide-angle images with the camera swirling as if in vertigo nicely approximates Count Dracula's point of view before his fall—allowing us for a moment to share the vampire's frenzied terror.) Unlike the fathers who use church-going to mask their sinful desires and who commit murder and sacrilege in the deserted church, Paul vanquishes the vampire and rescues Alice by bringing the church to life again. Outside the building, free at last from the interference of their elders (including Dracula), Paul and Alice stand arm-in-arm, smile in triumph, and move away.

Because Jess Franco's *El Conde Dracula* (1970) features Christopher Lee as Count Dracula, this Spanish/Italian/West German/English co-production begs comparison with the series of Hammer films I have discussed, which also star Lee as the Count. Like many other filmmakers of the period, Franco and producer Harry Alan Towers exploited the popularity of Hammer's Dracula series; what makes *El Conde Dracula* noteworthy, however, is that Franco and Towers sought to go Hammer one better not by adding more explicit sex and violence, but by remaining "faithful" to Stoker's novel. Hence *El Conde Dracula* was released in its English language version as both *Count Dracula* and *Bram Stoker's Count Dracula*, and the film's opening credits conclude with these words: "Over fifty years ago, Bram Stoker wrote the greatest of all horror stories. Now for the first time we retell exactly as he wrote one of the first and still the best tales of the macabre." According to Barrie Pattison, Franco "claimed that before shooting each day they had checked the novel for accuracy"[9]—such checking apparently designed to ensure that this latest version of *Dracula* be more "accurate" than the films of Tod Browning and Terence Fisher. For example, unlike all previous retellings of *Dracula*, in *El Conde Dracula*, as in Stoker's novel, the vampire's attacks on Mina and Lucy are framed by two journeys to Transylvania; yet even with such similarities in narrative structure, Franco's film without question tells a very different story and offers very different ideological implications than Stoker's *Dracula*.

El Conde Dracula opens in Transylvania, 1897, with Jonathan Harker traveling by train and then by mysterious coach through a dense, moonlit forest to Castle Dracula. After his first conversation with his aloof, formal host, Jonathan falls asleep only to find himself on the floor of a large, barren room, as three female vampires prepare to inflict their fatal kisses upon him. Dracula calls his undead minions off, declaring, "This man is mine!" Jonathan then awakens in his locked bedroom, as if from a nightmare, discovers two suspicious wounds on his neck, and escapes through a window. Exploring the castle, he comes

Count Dracula (Christopher Lee) slips into an icy tomb in *Dracula, Prince of Darkness* (1965), as the living—relying more on luck than on skill, courage, or faith—are saved for the time being by an accident of nature.

The aristocratic vampire (Christopher Lee) challenges the naive, middle-class tourist in *Dracula, Prince of Darkness* (1965) with the female onlookers as the prize. (Museum of Modern Art/Film Stills Archive)

Safe for the time being in their Victorian parlor, Arthur (Michael Gough) and Mina (Melissa Stribling) Holmwood, whose easily victimized, upper-middle-class family is the target of the vampire's attack, get advice from Van Helsing (Peter Cushing) in *Horror of Dracula* (1958). (Museum of Modern Art/Film Stills Archive)

With no wise guide or authoritarian father figure accompanying them, the young heroes of *El Conde Dracula* prepare to gain revenge and freedom by destroying Count Dracula. (Museum of Modern Art/Film Stills Archive)

Having been reborn into a world of abandoned churches and corrupt patriarchs, Count Dracula (Christopher Lee) in *Taste the Blood of Dracula* (1970) prepares to seek two more innocent victims. (Museum of Modern Art/Film Stills Archive)

Armed with a cross, Paul becomes more the priest than the hunter as he recaptures his beloved from the vampire in *Taste the Blood of Dracula* (1970). No fatherly figure of authority need assist the young hero.

Christopher Lee as Hammer Films' Count Dracula, an energetic aristocrat whose animal instincts cannot be controlled.

upon a massive stone sarcophagus containing Dracula. The young man flees in terror, leaping out of the castle from a second-story window.

Abruptly, Franco cuts to Professor Van Helsing's "private clinic" near London, where Jonathan is a delirious patient attended by Dr. Seward, a middle-aged man in Van Helsing's employ. In a padded cell Renfield, another patient, becomes increasingly obsessed with an unoccupied estate adjacent to the clinic. Jonathan's fiancée, Mina Murray, and her friend, Lucy Westenra, arrive and are given rooms in the clinic. Jonathan soon returns to mental health, but Lucy rises from sleep as if in a trance and leaves the building, drawn toward the neighboring house where she ends up in the arms of Count Dracula, new tenant of the estate. Seward diagnoses Lucy as "seriously ill," and her young fiancé, Quincey Morris, arrives posthaste. A transfusion of Quincey's blood revives Lucy, but after two more attacks/trysts in her bedroom, she dies. Before Lucy's funeral, Van Helsing informs Jonathan, Quincey, Seward, and Mina about the habits and the dangers posed by vampires, and by Dracula in particular. The undead Lucy entices a young girl into the forest, and, when the girl's corpse is discovered, Van Helsing, accompanied by Quincey and Jonathan, enters Lucy's tomb and drives a stake through her body, after which Quincey, following Van Helsing's commands, beheads his fiancée with a shovel.

In an attempt to destroy Dracula, Quincey, Jonathan, and Seward travel to the estate, where they encounter a menagerie of stuffed animals that appear to come to life under Dracula's command. Brandishing a cross that Van Helsing has given him, Jonathan repulses the vampire; at the same time, Renfield—who has tried to strangle Mina—lapses into catatonic silence. While the young men and Van Helsing (who is now restricted to a wheelchair because of a stroke) seek assistance from the British "Home Secretary," Dracula lures Mina to a concert hall and attacks her in a scene that probably has its source in Browning's *Dracula*. The Count then surreptitiously secures passage back to Transylvania. With his dying breath, Renfield whispers "Varna," and Quincey and Jonathan leave for Castle Dracula with hopes of arriving there before Dracula returns. Before he departs, Dracula enters the clinic in search of Mina, but Van Helsing protects the defenseless young woman by burning a cross on the carpet of his study with a red-hot poker. At Castle Dracula Jonathan and Quincey transfix the three female vampires and then rout the gypsies who are transporting the sleeping vampire. The young men set fire to their antagonist and toss the burning shipping crate into the rocks below the castle.

What this brief summary of *El Conde Dracula* does not indicate is that the film is, in Christopher Lee's words, "a disappointment because it was done cheaply, without due attention to script, production or anything else."[10] Franco's film demonstrates none of the flair and ingenuity of Badham's *Dracula* and none of the unpretentious craft of Fisher's vampire films. Even Browning's oft-criticized 1931 film benefits from being contrasted to *El Conde Dracula*, which is a representative example of low-budget, non-American, horror/exploitation movies of the late 1960s through the mid-1970s, the period roughly between *Night of the Living Dead* (1968) and *Halloween* (1978). Problems with sound synchronization, dubbed dialogue, and inappropriate locations (palm trees dot the grounds of Van Helsing's English clinic) often turn this film and others like it into unintentionally humorous camp. Franco's numbingly repetitive style is equally typical: his penchant for rack-focus establishing shots (which control our sight by shifts in focus from foreground to background and vice versa), zoom-ins that are used to rivet our attention to every significant detail (neck wounds, crosses, mysterious glances, expressions of fear or pleasure, and so on); zoom-outs to begin sequences; wide-angle shots used to make ordinary sets appear distorted and extraordinary; and predictable, predictive music and sound effects that announce and underline every image and action that is even remotely dramatic and suspenseful. Franco's style depends on techniques associated with television commercials, and, though *El Conde Dracula* lacks the sophisticated sense of visual design, the seamless continuity, and the "invisible" editing of the best television commercials, the film is out to marshal our emotions, to relieve us of the responsibility of making choices, and to limit our vision as much as any imaginative advertising campaign.

The story that Franco visualizes in this style is hardly the "exact" retelling of Stoker's *Dracula* that the prologue promises. No film adaptation of a novel can "exactly retell" its literary source, any more than written metaphors and verbal description can be translated "exactly" into moving images. My interest, to repeat an earlier disclaimer, is not in how and to what degree a novel can be "exactly retold" as a film or play or comic book. Nor am I interested in contrasting certain general properties of these different media. I assume that there are no "exact" retellings, and that alterations, changes, variations—whether intentional or accidental, whether dictated by aesthetic, economic, cultural, or ideological factors—are inevitable, and that such changes attract and merit our attention. Since movies and novels are not oral literature or one-of-a-kind performances, the interplay of convention and innovation in the retellings of Stoker's *Dracula* that I have been considering can and should send us back with the benefit of hindsight for re-readings and re-visions. Just as my viewing of *El Conde Dracula* is influenced by my familiarity with earlier vampire stories, so Franco's film in turn influences my re-reading of Stoker's novel and my re-viewing of Browning's film. Therefore, regardless of its obvious aesthetic failings, *El Conde Dracula* still merits attention as a retelling of *Dracula*, for Franco demonstrates certain possibilities—paradigmatic choices—in the story of the living and the undead that were not pursued by Stoker, Deane and Balderston, or the filmmakers I have discussed. *El Conde Dracula*, as much as *Dracula: The Vampire Play* or Badham's *Dracula*, transforms the genre's available options and reveals alternate provisions and choices that open up the possibility for yet other choices in the retelling of *Dracula*.

In particular, Franco's film highlights by way of contrast the most significant aspects of Hammer's stories of the living and the undead. Like the casting of Christopher Lee as Count Dracula, the delineation of the two young female victims and their heroic lovers in *El Conde Dracula* explicitly evokes the world of Hammer's Dracula films. Like their counterparts in *Dracula Has Risen from the Grave* or *Taste the Blood of Dracula*, all four of these characters in Franco's film wear similarly fashionable clothes and are nondescriptly attractive. In *El Conde Dracula* there is finally little, if any, difference between dark-haired Lucy and fair-haired Mina, or between Jonathan (a solicitor who is Mina's fiancé) and Quincey (a baron who is Lucy's fiancé). No scenes in the film emphasize the special importance of either Lucy or Mina or demonstrate the self-sacrificing love of Quincey and Jonathan for their fiancées. Even though Jonathan is much more prominent in the film than Quincey, these two men, like Lucy and Mina, are interchangeable: Jonathan and Quincey are a bit inexperienced, but ready and willing to take action; Mina and Lucy are pretty, weak, and easily victimized. Most important, all four of these characters are young adults, and their youth is a characteristic more significant in *El Conde Dracula* than any individualizing traits like proper names or unique physiognomy. Class, spiritual status, occupation, national origin, personal idiosyncrasies—all these defining characteristics are irrelevant or are at best very secondary compared to the age of the young victims and hunters, and so the terms of the confrontation in the film are exceedingly simple and clear.

Threatening the young people is Dracula, who, like Stoker's character, is initially gray-haired, but becomes more youthful with each infusion of young blood. Franco, as David Pirie notes, "presents his Dracula with an almost funereal dullness, abandoning all the captivating energy and intelligence described in the novel" (and depicted, we may add, in a film like *Horror of Dracula*).[11] In Castle Dracula, more like a vacant, inhospitable warehouse than the home of an aristocrat, Dracula only comes to life when he speaks of his family's ancient tradition of battlefield bravery. In his English estate the King-Vampire is surrounded by a host of stuffed predatory animals (fish and birds as well as mammals) that seem to move at his command. Far from the grand egotist, who seeks to establish a new order, or the seductively domineering foreigner, who can evoke desire as well as terror, Dracula in *El Conde Dracula* most often appears as an aged, anachronistic warrior, relying on tricks of suggestion and transformation in an attempt to recapture his youth. He is a fit monster for a world in which youth, rather than spiritual salvation or power or even immortality per se is the primary value. Appropriately, the vampire's attempt to destroy and thus usurp the vitality of youth fails when Quincey and Jonathan set fire to Dracula, who then rapidly ages, burned into impotent old age through the efforts of the young men.

Noticeably absent from this final struggle between the living and the undead is Professor Van Helsing, who has a very different role in Franco's film than in other versions of *Dracula*. Rather than Stoker's wise, pious, fatherly guide or Fisher's ingenious man of action, Van Helsing in *El Conde Dracula* is a gray-haired, late middle-aged Englishman who runs a private clinic. He does not practice medicine (Seward, dressed in a white labcoat, checks pulses and handles blood transfusions), but instead he observes Jonathan and his other patients, presumably in hopes of furthering his lifelong "study of what some people call the black arts." Because of his knowledge of the occult, Van Helsing can identify the telltale signs of the vampire's presence and inform the young people about Dracula's strengths and weaknesses. Similarly, the only crosses in the film are the ones that Van Helsing arms Jonathan and Quincey with before their first confrontation with Dracula, and the cross the Professor himself burns into the carpet in his study, which causes the vampire to flee and thereby protects Mina. Knowledge and the access to required objects, then, are Van Helsing's particular attributes, coupled with a penchant for giving orders and for being much more concerned with the black arts (as described in old books and ancient legends) than with the young victims under his care.

All the Van Helsings I have discussed share at least one characteristic with their undead antagonists—strength of will, foreign origin, unwavering commitment, and so on. Only Franco, however, suggests that Van Helsing, with his preoccupation with the occult, may in fact be a threat to the living instead of a paternalistic savior. "You know so much about the black arts," Quincey says to the Professor, "suppose you too were Dracula's servant?" Hence Franco's ominous zoom-ins to the Professor's stern, knowing expression, his editing that emphasizes the physical resemblence between Dracula and Van Helsing, and even his inclusion of a suspicious, lower-class attendant who dutifully carries out Van Helsing's orders. All these obtrusive, cliched details lead us, like Quincey, to question Van Helsing's motives, until finally the Professor proves his allegiance by hammering a stake into Lucy's heart. (Given *El Conde Dracula*'s emphasis on the struggle between age and youth, Van Helsing's destruction of Lucy is at once a justifiable act that protects the world and a victory of age over youth.) Having demonstrated the correct procedure for disposing of vampires, Van Helsing retreats into his study and returns to his reading while Jonathan and Quincey seek out Dracula.

The young men must leave the figure of authority behind once they have learned his rather simple lessons, but not before Quincey and Jonathan attend a meeting Van Helsing has arranged with the Home Secretary, who promises government assistance in the hunting of Dracula. This sequence, which is the most immediately recognizable of Franco's interpolations in his "exact" retelling of Stoker's *Dracula*, also includes Van Helsing, now confined to a wheelchair because of a stroke that has left his legs "a little uncertain," he admits, but his "intellect" unimpaired. This audience with the Home Secretary and Van Helsing only hinders the young men's efforts, for, while Quincey and Jonathan are occupied with the promises and assurances of their elders, Dracula lures the unprotected Mina into a trap and then easily escapes from England. The adult establishment with its socially sanctioned defenders is of no help whatsoever; working through the system, the young men lose time and almost lose Mina. In this regard, *El*

Conde Dracula has less in common with Stoker's novel than with explicitly topical youth films and social problem melodramas of the late 1960s set in a campus or ghetto environment.

Once they discover Dracula's destination, Jonathan and Quincey immediately depart England for Transylvania, leaving Mina, who is now a semiconscious invalid, with the immobile Van Helsing. As so often in the film, Van Helsing turns to his books. While he reads, Dracula emerges from the shadows of the study, intent on carrying off his young victim. "You have learned much. You can do nothing," the vampire mockingly declares to Van Helsing. But Dracula is wrong. Even if he cannot end Dracula's existence, Van Helsing can forge a cross of fire that temporarily protects Mina and forces the vampire to flee. However, the task of actually destroying the now sleekly black-haired, falsely youthful King-Vampire falls to the two young men, who leave Van Helsing and Mina far behind.

To emphasize a distinction that is readily apparent, Franco cuts back to England for a brief scene after Jonathan and Quincey have dispatched the three female vampires in Castle Dracula. Mina and Van Helsing wait for news in the study: "We can only pray," the Professor affirms as he reaches for yet another old leather-bound volume. Meanwhile, atop the imposing walls of Castle Dracula, the two young men pause only long enough to let a procession of gypsies approach, before routing Dracula's attendants and setting fire to the vampire. Books and prayers—and crosses and stakes as well—finally have no place in the realm of violent action. In order to rid the world of Dracula, the young hunters rid themselves of the defenseless woman and the suddenly pious, crippled old man.

Interestingly, a similar situation occurs in Roy Ward Baker's *Scars of Dracula*, a Hammer film released in England in 1970, the same year as *El Conde Dracula*. Simon Carlson, the young vampire hunter in *Scars of Dracula*, receives "guidance" from a frail, white-haired priest, whose village has long suffered under Dracula's dominion. But when Simon embarks on foot for Castle Dracula, the elderly priest returns to his church where he attempts—unsuccessfully, it turns out—to protect Sarah, Simon's girlfriend and Dracula's intended victim. From this point, however, *Scars of Dracula* differs substantially from *El Conde Dracula*. In the final confrontation in Baker's film, Simon and Sarah, with no means of defense, are saved from Dracula's wrath when a bolt of lightning strikes the vampire, who bursts into flames and tumbles over the side of Castle Dracula down a steep precipice. In keeping with the conventions of earlier Hammer vampire films, Simon and Sarah then embrace. With the destruction of the vampire, the couple is again reunited and safe.

The final image of *El Conde Dracula,* which has no direct source in Stoker's novel, can be taken as a commentary on the endings of Hammer's vampire films, with their emphasis on the young romantic couple. In *El Conde Dracula* the slaying of the vampire is most definitely not an accident or an act of nature or a just punishment sent down from the heavens; it is a human action that seems no more difficult than the "formal proceedings" that bring about the end of Carmilla in Le Fanu's story. Yet, whereas Carmilla's death is an affirmation of the patriarchal ruling class, the world of fathers, in *El Conde Dracula* the destruction of Dracula brings forth no regeneration of the status quo or long-awaited marriage or family reunion or communal thanksgiving. In the final image of the film, Jonathan and Quincey, together atop Castle Dracula, look down at the funeral pyre that consumes their antagonist. Once these victorious young men have ventured into the world, earned their independence by taking risks, been initiated into a life of action, and settled their personal debts with Dracula, why should they return to passivity, piety, and the narrow confines of Van Helsing's study? Franco's protagonists may look like typical Hammer young adults, but they share little with the chastened husbands and Christian heroes of *Dracula, Prince of Darkness, Dracula Has Risen from the Grave*, and *Taste the Blood of Dracula*. Released roughly the same time as *Easy Rider* (1969), *El Conde Dracula* is the vampire film ultimately become in an odd fashion adjacent to the "buddy movie," a subgenre that shares Franco's assumptions about freedom, action, age, and gender.

Set against the unequivocal triumph of Jonathan and Quincey in *El Conde Dracula*—their destruction of the aged usurper of youth and their independence from Van Helsing—the particular ideological emphases of the Hammer films I have discussed become even more apparent. Hammer's Dracula films all conclude with the juxtaposition of two images: first, the couple—from the Holmwoods in *Horror of Dracula* to Paul and Alice in *Taste the Blood of Dracula*—then a shot of, for example, an empty ring or a bloodstained cross, which signifies the absence, if not the absolute destruction, of Dracula. Though the survivors become progressively younger in each film in this series, the image of the couple remains strikingly constant, with the dependent woman once again under the protective embrace of the man who has rescued her from her own desires for the vampire, as well as from Dracula's unclean violation. Since in each case the couple has embraced in a similar fashion earlier in the film, this image indicates both the restoration of normality and the distance the couple has traveled before they achieve their reunion. Like the image of a tree-lined residential street with smiling children at play in a World War II documentary, the final shot in these films of the couple reunited in the natural world, outside of the vampire's domain, is an image of why we fight and what rewards we can expect for our sacrifices. It is also, needless to say, an exceedingly safe image that underlines and perpetuates bourgeois society's all-important reliance on the discrimination between sexual roles and on monogamous, heterosexual relationships. If the romantic couple comes to inherit the earth in *Dracula Has Risen from the Grave* or *Scars of Dracula*, the young lovers only purify society, they do not fundamentally alter it any more than does Van Helsing in *Horror of Dracula*. By *Taste the Blood of Dracula*, only the young couple remains, with no third party like Van Helsing or Father Sandor present, and the final image of this film suggests even more than the previous Hammer Dracula films that the hunter must prove himself worthy of his bride by recapturing her, by successfully completing the romantic quest—the same quest that Badham so thoroughly undercuts in his 1979 adaptation of *Dracula*.

Yet like Badham, and Browning and Deane and Balderston as well, Hammer's directors forego Stoker's emphasis on the formation of a new community free of skepticism and selfishness. (Franco's pair of victorious young men are also far from the moral community that in *Dracula* is built around both a woman and a wise elder.) However, Hammer's Dracula films are not—like the three versions of *Dracula* I discussed in chapter 3—concerned with the relationship between vampirism and madness, nor with the insufficiencies of modern science, particularly as practiced by Dr. Seward. For example, Renfield appears only in *Dracula, Prince of Darkness*, and then only as a minor, almost comic, character. Once again, *El Conde Dracula* offers a telling contrast, for in Franco's film, Renfield—described by Van Helsing as a man driven mad because he witnessed his daughter become the victim of a vampire in Transylvania—plays an essential role. As in Browning's *Dracula*, violent, uncontrollable madness in *El Conde Dracula* is attributed to evil forces that reside outside of England, and the sole cure for this madness is death. Fisher, Francis, and Sasdy focus instead on the role of ritual, faith, and the forces of nature in the confrontation between the living and the undead. But perhaps most important, the destruction of Count Dracula in Hammer's films always involves the supernatural or at least the possibility that a divine force much greater than man is somehow operating through or with the natural phenomena and human actions that destroy the king of the undead. Even as they vary certain conventions of the genre, these texts—again, quite unlike *El Conde Dracula*—reaffirm a set of conservative, traditional beliefs and modes of action that provide the only meaning and the only protection for man and that allow for the realization of bourgeois romance and marriage.

At the same time that they insist that the living must reestablish their connection with God through the affirmation of faith and the enactment of ritual, Hammer's vampire films place Dracula more in the natural than the supernatural world. Here the monster is not able to magically transform himself into wolf or bat or mist. What Fisher, Francis, and Sasdy make us see is both Dracula's extremely human preoccupation with poetically just vengeance and the suddenness with which the vampire's animal instincts take over. And, after *Horror of Dracula*, these films place great emphasis on the resurrection of the Prince of Darkness. In Hammer films the resurrection of Dracula is not only a major narrative event (actually it is the beginning of the real story) but also a visual tour de force, like the birth of Frankenstein's creature or the transformation of man into wolf in werewolf movies. Dracula rises from the grave into the world of the living; the vampire is dependent on this world, obsessed by it, superior to it, yet in the end destroyed by it. Lest we perhaps forget, in the Hammer films that announce in their very titles the prominence of Dracula, the Count's rebirth and true death remind us how important the living are—the villagers who prefer terror and perpetual watchfulness to dangerous quests; the fiancées and wives who lose their ability to resist after their eyes lock into the gaze of the vampire; the dedicated underlings and weak-willed lackeys who serve the forces of darkness; the satisfied, comfortable, ordinary men who must be reeducated and armed; the priests who must become hunters; and the hunters who become priests who become husbands.

NOTES

1. According to Terence Fisher, director of *Horror of Dracula* as well as many other Hammer productions, including *The Curse of Frankenstein* (1956) and *The Mummy* (1959), "We weren't influenced at all by the old Universal horror films when we started ours. I didn't screen them or refer to them at all. I was uninterested in them. I started from scratch. You can't go back and *remake* a film; you can remake a subject but that's different" (quoted in John Brosnan, *The Horror People* [New York: New American Library, 1977], p. 113). Cf. Andrew Tudor's conclusion that "the crystallised rules of horror are very straightforward . . . the boom years of Universal Studios do most to define the genre." Tudor assumes that Universal's "*Dracula* and *Frankenstein* are the defining movies of the classic horror film" (*Image and Influence: Studies in the Sociology of Film* [New York: St. Martin's Press, 1975], pp. 203, 205). For an interesting personal commentary on the difference between Universal and Hammer horror films, see Harry Ringel, "A Hank of Hair and a Piece of Bone," *Film Journal* 2, no. 4 (1975), 14–18.

2. David Pirie emphasizes Sangster's important role in making what Pirie calls certain "sad but forgivable changes" in "the novel's narrative" (*A Heritage of Horror: The English Gothic Cinema, 1946–1972* [New York: Avon, 1974], p. 87). For the sake of convenience and textual conformity, I refer to *Horror of Dracula* as Fisher's film.

3. C. F. Bentley, "The Monster in the Bedroom: Sexual Symbolism in Bram Stoker's *Dracula*," *Literature and Psychology* 22 (1972), 28.

4. The bedridden Lucy's appearance before Dracula's arrival so closely resembles Dorothy's in *The Wizard of Oz* (1939) that this scene in *Horror of Dracula* might well be an allusion to Victor Fleming's film, another story that tells of the vulnerability as well as the importance of "home" and the family.

5. Pirie describes the two antagonists in this fashion: "Dracula has at last returned to the tradition in which he was created—the tradition of English (as opposed to European) Gothic; the villain again becomes what he was always meant to be, the charming, intelligent and irresistible host . . . at the same time the hero, Van Helsing (played so superbly by Peter Cushing), takes up the familiar stance of the Renaissance mastermind, and represents for a fleeting and nostalgic moment the union of scientific exploration with religion" (*Heritage of Horror*, p. 87).

6. For more information on Hammer, see ibid., pp. 22–49; James Ursini and Alain Silver, *The Vampire Film* (New York: A. S. Barnes, 1975), pp. 79–86, 97–112, 124–33; and S. S. Prawer, *Caligari's Children: The Film as Tale of Terror* (New York: Oxford University Press, 1980), pp. 240–69. In this chapter I will be concerned only with Hammer's series of Dracula films from *Horror of Dracula* to *Taste the Blood of Dracula*, since these films form a coherent body of material and a context for all later vampire films. Hammer also released several other vampire movies, including a series of films loosely adapted from *Carmilla* (for example, *The Vampire Lovers* [1970]), and "original" works like *Kiss of the Vampire* (1962) and *Vampire Circus* (1971). I have chosen to focus

on those Hammer films released before 1970 that identify themselves as part of the *Dracula* tradition.

7. Pirie, *Heritage of Horror*, pp. 90–91.

8. See ibid., pp. 94–97.

9. Barrie Pattison, *The Seal of Dracula* (New York: Bounty Books, 1975), p. 86.

10. Quoted in Brosnan, *Horror People*, p. 172.

11. David Pirie, *Vampire Cinema* (London: Hamlyn, 1977), p. 154.

CHAPTER

5

Dracula (1973) and *Count Dracula* (1977)

BETWEEN THE RELEASE of Jess Franco's *El Conde Dracula* and John Badham's *Dracula* come the other two film versions of Stoker's novel that appeared during the 1970s, Dan Curtis's *Dracula* (1973) and Philip Saville's *Count Dracula* (1977), both of which were originally produced for television. Neither Curtis nor Saville rely on *Dracula: The Vampire Play* as a source, and their adaptations of *Dracula* are less dependent on the Hammer tradition than is Franco's film. Like Saville, Curtis and screenwriter Richard Matheson (whose novel, *I Am Legend*, I will consider in chapter 7) return directly to Stoker's novel for dialogue, details of characterization, and narrative structure. Curtis's film is even announced during the opening credits as "Bram Stoker's *Dracula*." While Franco identifies his *El Conde Dracula* as *Dracula* "exactly retold," Saville and Curtis seem to be not quite so naive about the status of retelling. Their films, I believe, are coherent, internally consistent interpretations of Dracula the King-Vampire and of Stoker's novel. Of course, all adaptations are to some degree interpretations, in the various common meanings of this word; retellings *are* translations, explanations, and performances of what has been previously told. Judging from their films and regardless of their degree of aesthetic success and intellectual insight, Curtis and Saville realize that adaptors are inevitably interpreters and ideally also conjurors who bring the dead not just back from the grave, but forward to a new life. A close examination of these two 1970s versions of *Dracula* makes particularly clear just how different and in many respects antithetical two retellings of the same novel can be, even though both texts were produced for television and both are clearly set apart from the Hamilton Deane and John L. Balderston tradition as well as the Hammer tradition.

The focus of Curtis's *Dracula* is made explicit at the end of the film after the vampire has been destroyed. Sounds of men chanting "Dracula! Dracula!" and of battlefield noise mingle with music fit for a military funeral, and the camera moves past Dracula's corpse, not to follow the victorious living, but to gaze once more up toward a large painting that earlier caught the attention of Jonathan Harker, then of Van Helsing. The painting depicts Vlad Tepes—the same man we have come to know as Dracula in the film—in full battle regalia, mounted on a rearing steed, as if frozen in the moment of his triumph. Superimposed over the painting, the following words appear in red letters: "In the 15th Century in the area of Hungary known as Transylvania, there lived a nobleman so fierce in battle that his troops gave him the name, Dracula, which means 'devil.' Soldier, statesman, alchemist, and warrior, so powerful a man was he that it was claimed he succeeded in overcoming even physical death. To this day it has yet to be disproven."

These words corroborate what the painting implies, that Count Dracula was a real historical personage, a nobleman and warrior, fierce and powerful, much as he is described in Raymond T. McNally and Radu Florescu's *In Search of Dracula: A True History of Dracula and Vampire Legends* (1972), a popular book that likely influenced Curtis and Matheson.[1] Whatever crimes he may have committed, this Dracula is the Prince of Wallachia (as the brass plate on the painting informs us), not the Prince of Darkness. His fierce bloodthirstiness notwithstanding, this Dracula is a human being: his death is precisely that, a death, and not a magical disintegration; his private domain is no dank crypt, but an upstairs room that contains, in addition to his portrait and red satin-lined coffin, a music box, books, and suits of armor. Similarly, Carfax Estate in this *Dracula* is far more habitable and ordinary than, for example, the abbey in Tod Browning's film. Unlike Stoker's King-Vampire, this nobleman has not fully accepted that "the warlike days are over . . . the glories of the great races are as a tale that is told" (D, 39). After 400 years Dracula in Curtis's film remains the Warrior-Prince, a fact emphasized in the first sequence of the film before Jonathan Harker is introduced. Like Vlad Tepes in the painting, Castle Dracula in the opening shot of the film looms high above the lakes and surrounding forest, as we hear a chorus of wolves, which then run in a pack to the castle, following the vampire's unspoken orders. As later in England when he will send a wolf crashing through Lucy's bedroom window, Dracula does not become a wolf; he commands wolves. In our first sight of the vampire, Dracula quickly strides down a flight of stairs past the camera, moving in a manner that is exactly opposite the languid movements of Bela Lugosi in Browning's *Dracula*. Curtis's Dracula warrants respect, even if he now holds dominion only over the wolves, the three female vampires in Castle Dracula, eventually Lucy and Mina in England, and at times the camera, which stares up at his portrait in a sort of homage to the glories of the past. By emphasizing that Dracula is a Warrior-Prince from the "warlike days," Curtis begins to explore how *Dracula* is a story of anachronism, of the relationship between the past and the present, and of the price paid for living beyond one's own lifetime.

Even though Curtis never reveals how Vlad Tepes managed to overcome physical death, *Dracula* (1973) does explain and therefore to some degree demystify the vampire—such, I take it, is one effect of the thumbnail biography that identifies Dracula as a real person. The portrait that hangs in Castle Dracula, however, includes one other piece of explanatory information. From astride his horse, Dracula cranes his neck to look back toward a woman in the left corner of the painting. The woman, we discover through two subjective sequences, was Vlad's beloved, and in undeath as in life Dracula seeks her out. His love for her motivates him, makes him explicable by our standards, and thereby makes him human. For example, soon after Jonathan's arrival at Castle Dracula, his host notices a photograph the young man carries of himself and Mina and their friends, Lucy Westenra and Arthur Holmwood. (The small, portable photograph is a simple, balanced composition with all four people of equal proportion, even though the men stand behind the seated women. This snapshot portrait is a fit image of the way the modern world, particularly these young men, sees itself. In contrast, Vlad Tepes completely dominates the fifteenth-century painting in which he appears as a figure of action larger than life, surely larger than his diminutive beloved.) For a moment, Dracula is rendered speechless as he stares at the photograph, for Lucy is the perfect twin of the woman in the painting. A simple, tinkling music box theme accompanies his reverie, as it will later accompany a brief sequence in which Dracula remembers or imagines embracing his wife while both were still alive. Dracula's reverie, framed by out-of-focus dissolves, is trite and sentimental, with his beloved running in slow motion to meet him in a green, sunlit field, where they smile and embrace. This cliched romanticism, like Dracula's obsession with Lucy Westenra, is yet another sign of the vampire's proximity to the world of men. (A comparable image of romantic love occurs later in the film when Arthur rows his recuperating fiancée on a shimmering, picturesque stream.)

Because Lucy Westenra is the woman in the painting as surely as Dracula is Vlad Tepes, the vampire journeys to England to recover his past by recovering his bride. Having once lost his wife to armed invaders (as another flashback reveals), when Lucy is destroyed by Van Helsing, Dracula's rage knows no bounds, and in revenge he forces Mina to drink his blood while Van Helsing and Arthur helplessly watch. However animalistic his guttural snarls and howls of anger, Dracula's motives in Curtis's film—the obsessions that lead to his destruction—are the same motives that transform all the Jonathan Harkers I have discussed from fiancés into hunters: for these characters, love and desire and revenge make insignificant almost everything else in the world besides the quest.[2]

Curtis's identification of Count Dracula as Vlad Tepes and, more important, the human motives ascribed to the vampire in this version of *Dracula* work to make Dracula a more explicable, and hence a more human and more realistic figure—a villain, we might say, instead of a monster, perhaps even a monomaniac instead of a villain.[3] Dracula's humanity or lack of humanity, his villainy or monstrousness, are defined in the context of the human beings who become his victims or his opponents. Lucy Westenra, for example, is from the first a completely innocent victim, singled out as the object of Dracula's desire only because she resembles a long-dead woman. After each of the vampire's attacks, Lucy becomes more anguished and more lifeless, until her body is discovered by her fiancé sprawled against a tree outside her home, crumpled and used up, with her cheeks tearstained and her open eyes glazed like a doll's. Yet during Lucy's nighttime rendezvous with the vampire, she obviously enjoys Dracula's caress, and, when she leaves her tomb to tempt Arthur, Lucy shows a vitality that she never exhibits in life. As so often in stories of the living and the undead, the pleasure and the new life given by the vampire are at the same time pain and death. Curtis deepens this ambivalence because Lucy is not merely a source of sustenance or physical pleasure for Dracula. In his fashion he loves Lucy and has risked a journey into the modern world in hopes of taking her as his partner for all eternity. Mina, on the other hand, is only a pawn through whom Dracula will vent his rage and achieve his revenge against Van Helsing, Lucy's destroyer and savior.

If Arthur and Van Helsing are not able to save Mina, she is destined to become the vampire's "slave" (not his bride or partner), a sister to the undead women in Castle Dracula, who, ironically enough, feast on Mina's fiancé, Jonathan Harker. Like Franco and Stoker, Curtis allots a substantial portion of his *Dracula* to Jonathan's journey through Transylvania and his experiences in Castle Dracula. (Curtis also nicely suggests how Jonathan's journey is very much a matter of being transported, all according to Dracula's systematic plan.) However, more than his counterpart in *El Conde Dracula*, who disregards a series of unambiguous warnings, Jonathan in *Dracula* (1973) is not so much stupid and foolhardy as merely unprepared and understandably willing to cater to the wishes of his aristocratic client. That Jonathan's attempt to conduct real estate business with the Count seems so shortsighted as to almost constitute a crime is an irony that comes from our hindsight and our familiarity with the story of Dracula.

With Jonathan we journey to Castle Dracula, and meet Count Dracula, who first appears as a somewhat eccentric host and then as a vampire. (*Nosferatu* and *Nosferatu the Vampyre*, which I will examine in the next chapter, offer the most interesting treatments of this journey and this introduction.) When his suspicions are raised by Dracula's curt orders—the commands of a prince—and by the locked doors that trap him inside a room that is the epitome of a tastefully decorated Victorian drawing room, without cobwebs or shadowy recesses, Jonathan discovers a passageway hidden behind a tapestry and so explores the castle. The drawing room, it turns out, is only a nineteenth-century facade, like the Count's gracious demeanor; Dracula's true residence is the private room I described earlier, the room containing an elegant black coffin, suits of armor, a music box, and the painting of Vlad Tepes and his wife. Dracula protects Jonathan from the hissing, ravenous vampire women who suddenly appear in this room, but, once the young man has entered Dracula's inner sanctum, his fate is sealed. In the crypt area below the castle that served as Vlad Tepes's torture chamber, Jonathan fails in his attempt to behead the sleeping vampire and is knocked unconscious by one of the gypsies who is loading the boxes of Transylvanian earth that are to be transported to England. Jonathan awakens long enough to see the undead women pounce on him. Unlike his counterpart in Stoker's novel, he gets no second chance to take revenge upon the Count or to purge his "brain fever" through violent action. Later, when Arthur and Van Helsing journey to the castle, Jonathan—now a hungry vampire—attacks the men and is knocked by Arthur into a pit full of sharpened upright stakes. The nineteenth-century solicitor who unknowingly ventured into the past is impaled like a fifteenth-century victim of Vlad Tepes (who was known not only as "Dracula," but also as "Vlad the Impaler.")[4]

Arthur Holmwood, Lucy's fiancé, fares little better than his friend Jonathan, even though Arthur has the advantage of first confronting the vampire in a familiar English environment. Like the young suitors in Hammer's Dracula films, Arthur has good intentions, but he still loses his beloved and is obviously no match for Dracula. In Curtis's *Dracula* the vampire knows exactly what he wants and how to achieve his desires, while Arthur is not able even to console Lucy after her "terrible nightmares" of "something sweet and yet so bitter." The Count issues commands; Arthur asks questions, especially of Van Helsing. (Long after he has been tempted by the undead Lucy, Arthur still asks, "What are they?" as Van Helsing opens the coffins of the vampire women in Castle Dracula.) Without Van Helsing's supervision and leadership, Arthur fails, much as Jonathan fails to survive in Castle Dracula. Dozing off when it is his turn to stand watch, Arthur allows Lucy the opportunity to escape from her bedroom and join the vampire under the moonlight. Seeing his lover at the window the night after her funeral, Arthur allows Lucy inside the house and succumbs to her kisses and whispered vows of eternal love. Here he is saved by Van Helsing, the stern, fatherly figure who prevents the vampire's corrupt, infected kiss, regardless of how much the young man desires Lucy.

A sequence that comes before Lucy's death, however, offers the best picture of Arthur's strengths and weaknesses: because of Van Helsing's precautions, Lucy is recovering, and the Doctor leaves her in Arthur's care with strict instructions to "continue every safeguard." Dressed in formal attire and armed with a revolver, Arthur sits up with Mrs. Westenra watching over her sleeping daughter. When Dracula sends a wolf crashing through the window into the room, Mrs. Westenra faints (parents yet again are no help). Arthur wrestles with the wolf, finally shoots it, then passes out. Lucy awakens, like Sleeping Beauty called by her Prince, and leaves the house alive for the last time. Arthur fights with and is wounded by a ferocious wolf, yet he still cannot protect Lucy. Since he does not fail for a lack of courage or of love for his fiancée, the sequence suggests that he fails because of a lack of knowledge and assistance. The revolver that Arthur so confidently reveals to Mrs. Westenra betrays his ignorance of the rules of this game, for no modern weapon can destroy this centuries-old undead warrior. Van Helsing could have told Arthur this simple fact and could have protected Lucy while the young man fought with the wolf, but Van Helsing is absent.

In all the adaptations of Stoker's novel that I have considered, Van Helsing's presence is essential, even when he is ultimately left behind as in Franco's *El Conde Dracula* or killed as in Badham's *Dracula.* If the vampire is contrasted with the young man (or men) as they struggle for possession of the same women—contrasted in motives, methods, and in the value they place on these women—the contrast between Count Dracula and Professor or Doctor Van Helsing is of at least equal thematic and ideological importance in stories of the living and the undead. In Curtis's film, Van Helsing—a "dear friend of Arthur's family"—has no fiancée and no wife, and no desire for one. He is a doctor who, as he puts it, "accepts what is," not a professor and surely not a student of the black arts or a full-time vampire hunter. Neither is he an elderly, eccentric foreigner, but rather an energetic, businesslike, middle-aged Englishman, almost the quintessential ruddy, controlled, stiff-upper-lipped British professional. (This impression is due to a great extent to Nigel Davenport's performance as Van Helsing, which is as understated as Jack Palance's Dracula is intentionally overstated.) While Dracula hisses with hungry desire and howls with rage when his plans are foiled, Van Helsing shows no such emotion. Even when he drives a stake into Lucy's heart, the Doctor registers no fear and no satisfaction. (Arthur, in contrast, turns away, unable to witness the transfixion.) Van Helsing successfully wields the cross without insisting on his piety or demonstrating any deep Christian faith and without seeing himself as a holy crusader. And for him, destroying the undead with a stake is less a ritual (or a rite of passage or a baptism in blood) than a necessary task that is not discussed or verbally justified, but merely carried out as quickly and efficiently as possible.

It is this particular Van Helsing who—with Arthur's sometimes helpful assistance—forces the invading foreigner out of England, then ends the reign of the Prince of Wallachia. Like the vampire hunters in Stoker's novel, Van Helsing and Arthur in Curtis's *Dracula* retrace, with greater urgency and knowledge than Jonathan Harker, the journey with which the story has begun. Before facing Dracula, these two Englishmen must pass through the horrors of the crypt beneath Castle Dracula: the three vampire women asleep in their coffins, the ancient torture machines of Vlad the Impaler, and the sudden attack by the undead Jonathan, who is prevented from biting Van Helsing by Arthur's intervention (proving again that even the most capable of the living needs life-saving assistance). Having destroyed these lesser vampires, Van Helsing and Arthur enter the Count's private room, which Dracula himself calls his "domain." As in all the works I have discussed, the precise sequence of events in the final confrontation merits close attention in Curtis's *Dracula*, for these events determine not just who will survive, but how and why the fittest survive.

While the two hunters look up toward the portrait of Vlad Tepes and note the "incredible" resemblence between Lucy and the young woman in the painting, Dracula enters the room and moves slowly forward for the kill. Arthur has learned his lessons well; he wards off the vampire with a large silver cross, until Dracula is able to overturn a library table and knock the cross from the young man's hand, then to fling Van Helsing into a suit of armor that crashes to the ground. As powerful as the cross is as a protective, defensive weapon, it still must be held in human hands, and thus it can be dropped or misplaced. (Francis's *Dracula Has Risen from the Grave*, in which Dracula is impaled on a gold cross that has fallen out of human hands, is a noteworthy reversal of this generic assumption.) And the possession of this sacred object, like the possession of Christian faith, does not by itself guarantee man's survival. For example, the cross that the dead captain of the beached *Demeter* holds in his locked grasp early in the films of Curtis and Badham may save the captain's soul, but it has not saved his life. After Arthur loses his cross (in which he has put all his confidence), he reaches to recover it, and Dracula is upon him.

Now Van Helsing must be the lifesaver and the aggressor. Very much like his counterpart in Fisher's *Horror of Dracula* (Nigel Davenport's British Van Helsing seems at times to be modeled on Peter Cushing's vampire hunter in the 1958 Hammer film), Van Helsing's function is to let in the sunlight by pulling down heavy curtains that have excluded the natural world from Castle Dracula. The vampire is dazed and immediately weakened by the light; he staggers in operatic death throes as the two men trap him in his own domain—now reclaimed by the living and illuminated by the intense white light of the sun. This Dracula does not disintegrate or suddenly age and decay like the vampires in *Horror of Dracula* or *El Conde Dracula*. In his death Curtis's

Dracula proves to be more human than ever. The Warrior-Prince is, after all, suffering the fate that all men—Yoricks as well as Hamlets—must suffer. Death does not bring this Dracula a "look of peace," such as Mina sees for an instant on the Count's face in Stoker's novel. In Curtis's film the vampire leans against the table he earlier overturned, which now stands upright on its side. He turns to face the sun, and Van Helsing moves inexorably forward armed with a pike and backlit by the sunlight (so that he seems to emerge from the midst of the sunlight).

In stories of the living and the undead, weapons are never only "instruments of offensive or defensive combat," never merely "something to fight with" (to cite two common definitions), any more than they are in westerns like *Shane* or *The Wild Bunch*. When Van Helsing arms himself with a pike, taken from the smashed suit of armor, we know that he has not chosen a wooden stake, a Kukri knife, a torch, or a grappling hook. Using the Prince of Wallachia's own weapon, Van Helsing thrusts the pike through Dracula's chest, pinning him to the table like a prized kill of the hunt, impaling him like a victim of Vlad Tepes, transfixing him as befits a vampire. In an isolated castle, using a medieval weapon, facing a fifteenth-century tyrant, the modern man rids the world of this undead interloper from the past. With no prayers—after all, this has been man's triumph, not God's—Van Helsing and Arthur matter-of-factly walk away from Dracula's corpse and move out of the image, leaving behind a still-life tableau of a dead past. No more vampires enliven the room. "I never heard you come in. Who are you?" Jonathan in the beginning of the film asked of the vampire wommen, who appeared while the young man was casually perusing the fifteenth-century portrait as if he were in a museum. At the end, after the hunters exit, the camera moves past Dracula to gaze again at the painting. Now the world is safe, the past is only knowable through paintings, artifacts, and words ("In the 15th Century in the area of Hungary known as Transylvania there lived a nobleman . . ."); we will not encounter it, as Jonathan, Lucy, and Mina have, in the flesh.

Curtis's *Dracula* is a made-for-television movie, a type of narrative whose widely used name acknowledges that this hybrid form is somehow different from either a theatrical feature film or a television miniseries or special. Curtis, in fact, is probably the master of the made-for-television horror film, for in addition to *Dracula*, he has directed *The Night Strangler* (1973), *The Norliss Tapes* (1973), and *Scream of the*

Wolf (1974) and produced, among other movies, *The Night Stalker* (1972), one of the most popular of all made-for-television movies. (Before *Dracula*, Curtis also produced *Dark Shadows*, a daytime soap opera horror series for ABC from 1966–71, and then directed two feature films based on this series and its vampire character, Barnaby Collins.) His film version of *Dracula*, however, was not made with only the particular requirements of American commercial television in mind, for the film was released theatrically outside of the United States.[5] In retelling Stoker's novel as a made-for-television movie Curtis was required to work within a basically inflexible format that demanded a length of approximately 90–100 minutes, a narrative structure that could accommodate a series of commercial interruptions, and a strict censorship of, for example, certain acts of graphic violence that might very well be allowed in a PG-rated (and definitely in an R-rated) theatrical film. Such demands necessarily affect the process of adaptation. For example, commercial breaks in *Dracula* (1973) often serve to bridge temporal ellipses, and even to protract and emphasize a particularly disconcerting or suspenseful moment—such as when Lucy describes her nightmares to her bewildered fiancé or when Arthur and Van Helsing are about to enter Dracula's domain.

If "intimacy" and an emphasis on "faces, reactions, explorations of emotions registered by human beings" are, as Horace Newcomb argues, the basis of a "television aesthetic,"[6] then Curtis's *Dracula*, with its reliance on physical action, movement, and locations outside a soundstage, is more a film designed for the big screen rather than the small screen. On the other hand, Curtis does fashion Stoker's novel into a more circumscribed and more intimate story of the living and the undead, but then so, too, do Deane and Balderston and Browning. Perhaps what *Dracula* (1973) most obviously shares with made-for-television movies—and with Franco's *El Conde Dracula* as well—is an overreliance on what Fisher, after seeing the film, called "all this horrible bloody business with the zoom lens."[7] Of course, a zoom is not inherently any more or less aesthetically valid than a hand-held moving camera or a tracking shot—witness, for example, Nicolas Roeg's masterful use of the zoom in *Walkabout* (1971) and *"Don't Look Now"* (1974).[8] However, for Franco and to a lesser degree for Curtis, the zoom is an obtrusive means of guiding the viewer's attention and imposing heightened significance, more exclamatory than any exclamation point could ever be. The story of Dracula in Stoker's novel, as I noted in chapter 2, is told by a series of first-person narrators; each perspective is limited and therefore vulnerable, and so the living must collate their separate stories into a collective narrative. The use of the zoom lens in *El Conde Dracula* and *Dracula* (1973), however, often suggests that the camera embodies an informed, intrusive, controlling narrator, superior to both the living and the undead (and to the viewer as well). Ironically, this sense of the camera as an almost omniscient force occurs in two 1970s vampire films, in which the living do not rely on faith or divine intervention in order to triumph over the undead.

Philip Saville also uses the zoom lens repeatedly in *Count Dracula* (1977), but for Saville the zoom is one of several means of entering and exploring the space before the camera; emphasis and exclamation in this version of *Dracula* most often become the responsibility of the actors or the product of editing. *Count Dracula* looks so different from Curtis's *Dracula* because this BBC/American public television co-production is often filmed in a "live-on-tape" format that is intended exclusively for television showings, not for theatrical release. Like most of the programs in the *Masterpiece Theater/Great Performances* tradition of serial video drama, which was perhaps the most popular and well-received contribution of public television during the 1970s, *Count Dracula* has certain basic differences from the standard made-for-television commercial network movie: it is composed of several parts or episodes, each uninterrupted by commercials (in the case of Saville's film, three parts, each approximately 45 minutes, thus making *Count Dracula* the longest adaptation of Stoker's novel); it relies heavily on interior sets that look very much like elaborately detailed stage sets, befitting the emphasis on bravura performances (*Great Performances*) and on ensemble acting, usually by British actors trained on the stage who differ as much from the stars of American network television as from the American actors featured in films like *The Godfather* or *Badlands*; and it presents itself as an adaptation of literature (or a dramatization of history) that demonstrates a serious respect for its source, a preference for adult themes and situations, and a great dependence on the word (these works are *Masterpieces*, and they are *Theater*). Each of these factors influences Saville's transformation of *Dracula* into *Count Dracula*, "A Gothic Romance based on Bram Stoker's *Dracula*."

Like Curtis's film, *Count Dracula* begins with and places much emphasis on Jonathan Harker's solitary journey into a strange land and his nightmarish experience of being transported, isolated, and imprisoned.[9] In Curtis's *Dracula*, we can only gauge Jonathan's character (his modern beliefs, his personal aspirations) by noting the obvious differences between this traveler and the Transylvanians he encounters and by witnessing his discomfort turn to panic. Stoker, using first-person narration, presents this entire episode as Jonathan experiences it, or rather, as Jonathan records it in his journal. From these entries, we learn something about Mina and a great deal about Jonathan, but since he is not writing a novel, a history, or an autobiography, Jonathan does not explicitly describe in detail the world he has left behind—the world, that is, of Mina and of late nineteenth-century England. Saville forces us to see both Transylvania and England and to contrast these two environments by cutting back at several points from Jonathan's adventures in the East to what is presumably the contemporaneous situation in England.

Count Dracula, in fact, begins in England, with a pre-credit prologue that has no source in the novel: standing in a bright, lushly green natural setting (more like a park than a forest or a garden), Jonathan bids good-bye to Mina before he departs for Transylvania, as Lucy and Mrs. Westenra watch (here Lucy and Mina are both daughters of Mrs. Westenra). The young lovers kiss, then Jonathan waves to the three women as his carriage drives off. The boyish solicitor leaves the all-female Westenra household—a matriarchal enclave that will be invaded and utterly destroyed in the course of the story—to journey to Castle Dracula, where there are also three females, the undead daughters/brides of a single vampire king. Once Jonathan has begun to understand the true nature of his host and to question his own sanity, Saville returns to the Westenra house, where the sisters in white nightdresses lie in bed together and laugh like little children, then are served hot chocolate by their mother. The brief sequence offers an image of security and juvenile carelessness from which Jonathan has now been permanently excluded, though Mina's concern about Jonathan's overlong absence has begun to isolate her from the child's world as well. By juxtaposing the two domains, Saville also emphasizes how the vampire women who laugh and caress Jonathan in the forbidden room of Castle Dracula are in many ways the sisters of Lucy and Mina—young and pretty, but also active and sexually experienced. Before the three vampires, Jonathan can close his eyes and become both a child passively given over to the hands of women and also a young man about to lose blood and sexual innocence. Later in the film this particular scene will be ironically transposed into different keys: Jonathan will marry Mina, but Dracula will become her partner in the marriage bed (just as the young man had almost become the partner of the vampire's brides); and the three female vampires will beckon Mina to leave Van Helsing—her surrogate father—and join them as their "sister" (much as they beckoned Jonathan, after he had left the Westenra sisters behind in England).

In one final interpolation before Jonathan escapes from the castle, Saville cuts not to the Westenra household, but to Seward's asylum, where Renfield is imprisoned. This contrast, like the others, is ironic and significant. Jonathan, who wonders if he is "mad," is imprisoned by Dracula, apparently as part of some far-reaching plot that involves Lucy and Mina. At the same time Renfield, who eats insects and raves like a "madman," is locked up under Seward's protective care, but is awaiting the arrival of the "Master." Unlike Jonathan, Renfield will not escape or be "cured." He will die attempting to save Mina's soul, while Jonathan remains asleep as his wife tastes the blood of Dracula.

By adding a prologue and altering the order in which the events in the first chapters of Stoker's *Dracula* are presented, Saville directs our attention to certain themes (desire and madness, for example), indicates Jonathan's distance from a world that is familiar and comforting, and emphasizes the young man's isolation and vulnerability in Castle Dracula. It is appropriate, therefore, that the prologue depicts a scene of departure. When Jonathan comes back to this house with Mina as his wife, both Mrs. Westenra and Lucy will be dead. In the prologue Jonathan is taking leave of a secure child's world, an Eden of sorts, verdant and peaceful, that Saville associates with an all-female family. In Part II of *Count Dracula*, beginning with the vampire's attacks on Lucy, the Westenra household is taken over by men, so that when Jonathan returns from his ill-fated journey, he soon joins an all-male group that has formed to combat the vampire.

Unlike all of the other retellings of *Dracula* I have discussed, *Count Dracula* shares with Stoker's novel an interest in the way the living must unite under the leadership of Van Helsing in order to rid the world of Dracula. Saville and screenwriter Gerald Savory drop the Arthur Holmwood character, but retain the American Quincey Morris, here Lucy's fiancé (she chooses Arthur in the novel), and John Seward, the head of Purfleet Asylum, who is equally devoted to Lucy. These men are by no means inexperienced adolescents, but rather young adults with positions of social responsibility (Quincey is associated with the American embassy in London) and with the benefits of worldly success. Yet Quincey can no more protect Lucy or cheer her up than Seward can diagnose or cure her. As in the novel, Seward calls in Van Helsing, his friend and teacher, for a specialist's opinion.

Saville turns to Stoker, not to *Dracula: The Vampire Play* or *Horror of Dracula*, for his characterization of the Professor. The difference between this elderly, eccentric, devoutly Christian foreigner and, for example, the English Van Helsing in Curtis's *Dracula* suggests again the range of variation from one adaptation of Stoker's novel to the next. In *Count Dracula*, as in all these retellings of *Dracula*, Van Helsing provides information—a diagnosis, a prescription, and ultimately a cure for Lucy. More important than any specific information, however, is the Professor's willingness to accept the reality of evil and hence the existence of monsters. This ability governs all of Van Helsing's actions and distinguishes him from the younger men. "I sense something evil, and I must try everything to combat it," Van Helsing tells Seward, "I believe there is a monster in our midst." For Van Helsing, life is more than merely material phenomena; survival requires trusting in what can only be sensed, the ability to believe without actually seeing, i.e., faith. What the men learn from Van Helsing is not only that evil exists but also that man has a duty to combat it, for, as the Professor realizes, "evil will not disappear simply because we disapprove of it."

While Van Helsing can seal Lucy's room with garlic, he cannot protect Lucy from the well-intentioned but fatal ministration of her own mother, who dies much as in Stoker's novel, allowing Dracula to take her place in bed next to Lucy. (The vampire has already substituted for Quincey in Lucy's "dreams" and later will substitute for Jonathan in the Harker's double bed.) The sequence of events in *Count Dracula* from Lucy's illness to her true death runs parallel to chapters 8–16 of Stoker's novel, although Saville omits certain details in Lucy's story, most notably the series of blood transfusions that revivify Lucy and wed her to Van Helsing and her suitors. In both works Lucy's death and her undead resurrection are what bring the younger men to accept Van Helsing's authority, even though the Professor leads them into the night to do "terrible things." What Van Helsing calls the "exorcism" of the vampiric Lucy closely follows Seward's account of the scene in *Dracula*,[10] and once again it should be noted how vastly different the presentation of this pivotal event is in the various retellings of Stoker's novel—from being an offstage action that is merely reported in *Dracula: The Vampire Play* to being an unpleasant but necessary task carried out in a matter-of-fact fashion by the unflinching Englishman in the films of Fisher and Curtis.

Count Dracula, of all the film versions of *Dracula*, offers the most graphic treatment of this scene. Lucy's blood spurts when she is transfixed, and she reaches upward in shocked recognition of her fate (a sight probably as surprising to viewers used to public television video drama as it is to Quincey, Lucy's fiancé). As conducted by Van Helsing, this piece of wild work is strictly ritualistic: completely secure in his knowledge and faith, Van Helsing proceeds step by step, using the occasion to teach the young men a lesson about true death and God's mercy. Thus he allows Quincey to be tempted by his undead fiancée, then protects the American with a small silver crucifix, the sight of which transforms Lucy into a hissing animal. Inside the tomb, Van Helsing removes all the necessary tools from his bag, positions the stake over Lucy's heart, and hands Quincey the hammer. As Seward watches and Quincey strikes the blows, Van Helsing reads the Latin Prayer for the Dead, then completes the ritual himself by filling Lucy's mouth with garlic flowers and cutting off her head with what looks to be a surgical knife. Unlike the transfixion, the actual decapitation is not shown, only implied by Van Helsing's actions and by the soundtrack; then Saville abruptly cuts to a close-up of the silver crucifix, now lying on a table. This transition, which has no direct source or analogue in Stoker's novel, is essential in *Count Dracula*, for it reaffirms that Van Helsing is entirely correct in believing that transfixion and desecration are redemptive acts, acts of mercy. The crucifixion of Christ defines the nature and the value of suffering, such as the vampire hunters, in their fashion, have and will continue to undergo, just as Christ's resurrection represents the triumph over death that is so blasphemously parodied in the vampire's undead existence.

To emphasize the role of the crucifix, literally its place in this world, Saville slowly zooms-out from this sacred object to an overhead shot of the table on which it rests, around which sit Van Helsing, Seward, Quincey, Jonathan, and Mina. All now have "no doubt," as Van Helsing puts it, that the vampire is indeed in England; all pledge their full effort to "fight" the "terrible and mysterious enemy." At this point Saville inserts another brief close-up of the crucifix, then returns to the overhead angle as the hunters all rise and join hands, forming a circle around the table and thus around the crucifix. Such is the nature of the community in Saville's *Count Dracula*, a community that makes its appearance after, and is the product of, a violent ritual, that gathers around the cross and in opposition to the monstrous evil, and that assumes the shape of a circle with each member linked in mutual interdependence. Like the community united during a state of war that Robert A. Nisbet discusses in *The Quest for Community* (1953), the vampire hunters in Saville's *Count Dracula*, as in Stoker's novel, collectively gain what Nisbet calls "the attributes of moral community—a sense of identification, of security, and of membership," as well as "the intoxicating atmosphere of spiritual unity that arises out of the common consciousness of participating in a moral crusade," a crusade mobilized not merely against an enemy, but against a "symbol of total evil."[11]

With the best of intentions, however, the men break the circle by excluding Mina for her own safety, for "she is too precious," as Van Helsing tells his allies (affirming once again Mina's role as a rare, valuable object, the prize for which Dracula and the men struggle). Any individual who is not in the community is vulnerable—even if he is locked in protective custody like Renfield or if she is sleeping next to her husband like Mina. And once Mina's blood mingles with the vampire's, the men must become more than detectives who track down Dracula's hideouts and priests who "sterilize" the vampire's boxes of earth with consecrated host. All the community, now including Mina, must become armed hunters who track the beast and dare not allow it to escape.

The concluding sequences of *Count Dracula* continue to run parallel to Stoker's *Dracula*, as Saville—unlike Franco or Curtis, whose films also conclude with the hunters' successful destruction of Dracula and his brides—seems intent on retaining certain of Stoker's thematic as well as narrative emphases. Yet the hunters in *Count Dracula* do not have to endure snowstorms or fear packs of wolves, since the green, pastoral countryside of Transylvania looks neither foreign nor threatening. By placing the final journey in this familiar environment, Saville, it seems to me, lessens the nightmarish, fantastic quality of the dangerous quest that ends *Dracula*. In this film three separate tasks must be completed by the hunters, who split up into two groups, the younger men on horseback, Van Helsing and Mina in a wagon. First, Van Helsing must protect Mina from the three vampire women, who seem to materialize out of the forest at night calling for their "sweet sister," and he also must protect Mina from her own awareness that "I too am their sister." With pieces of the host, Van Helsing creates a circle around Mina (she takes the place of the crucifix in the earlier circle), an area of safe, sanctified ground; using Christian objects, he transforms nature into culture, the profane into the sacred, which is pictured as being circular, much like the image of the moral community after the true death of Lucy. Van Helsing's additional work, as he tells Mina the next morning, is at Castle Dracula, where he enters the crypt and methodically drives stakes into the undead women. While carrying out this task, he is not tempted as is his counterpart in the novel, and the Professor by himself succeeds where Jonathan alone had failed.

Before all the hunters can be reunited in victory, however, they must defeat the armed gypsies, who are transporting Count Dracula's shipping crate (that serves as his coffin) back to Castle Dracula. Mina and Van Helsing, with loaded carbines, look down from a hilltop as the three horsemen pursue the gypsies. The actual skirmish begins when Seward fires his rifle, wounding one of the gypsies. Several details stand out in the series of brief images that compose this sequence: Quincey, always the American, is wounded, yet still manages—like a gunfighter—to kill one of the gypsies with a quick shot from his revolver; Jonathan, after beating off one foe with a riflebutt, is himself then overpowered, only to be saved at the last instant when Mina kills the attacker with a single perfect long-range shot (proving again her worth and necessary role as part of this community); and when the sole surviving gypsy escapes with the wagon bearing the sleeping vampire, the only person in a position to stop him is Van Helsing, who fires twice and misses (proving that even the Professor is fallible and cannot single-handedly triumph over the King-Vampire). In a more general and more significant sense, this sequence demonstrates how thoroughly the solictor, the alienist, and the dewy-eyed fiancé have adapted to their new role as hunters, and how much they have accepted that they must kill to achieve the end they desire—kill the living as well as the undead. Seward, for example, shouts no warning before he opens fire, and the entire attack is pictured as an ambush (which is always a legitimate military strategy if conducted by our side, a murderous, cowardly trick if conducted by the enemy).

The surviving gypsy reaches the courtyard of Castle Dracula but is prevented from closing the gates by Quincey, who collapses because of his chest wound. Seward and Jonathan help pry the lid off the shipping crate, and at the last instant before sunset Van Helsing plunges a stake into Dracula's heart. With all of Saville's reliance on the details of Stoker's *Dracula* (as, for example, in the destruction of Lucy), this final substitution of Van Helsing for the younger men who slay the vampire in the novel particularly stands out. The change cannot be attributed to budgetary limitations or censorship codes, and it has nothing to do with the differences between literature and film as two narrative media. By allowing Van Helsing to transfix the King-Vampire, Saville allies his retelling with *Dracula: The Vampire Play* and Browning's *Dracula*—works in which the living survive because the wise, elderly guide wields his stake in accordance with tradition. In Stoker's novel—like *El Conde Dracula* and, to some extent, Badham's *Dracula* in this regard—tradition is successfully violated and transcended by the young men, who come of age by killing the King-Vampire. If Van Helsing in *Count Dracula* seems somehow to be the "logical" choice as Dracula's slayer, I think it is because one hunter seems to us much preferable and much safer than two. This is especially true when, first, the two are young men fired by revenge and the one is a pious, wise, white-haired, doctor-priest-father-teacher, who is immune to sexual desire; second, when the violence committed by this man can be understood and justified as ritual (Van Helsing kills no one with his carbine); and third, when we nostalgically wish for a world made safe by a just yet powerful figure of authority who acts in full accordance with a still vital, still effective body of traditions.

Once Van Helsing has driven the stake into the vampire, smoke spews out of the shipping crate, causing a whirlwind in the courtyard that forces the living away from the wagon. After the air clears, Van Helsing crosses himself, looks in the crate, and pronounces: "Dust to dust, ashes to ashes." All that remains of Count Dracula is his smoldering black tunic through which the stake has been driven. No rosy beams suddenly illuminate the scene, as they do in the novel, yet Mina's scar has disappeared. A slow dissolve links the image of the stake and Dracula's empty tunic with Saville's final image of the living: in the sunlight, outside the walls of the castle, the survivors are gathered. Quincey leans against a tree, while Jonathan, Mina, Seward, and Van Helsing all stand with heads bowed, as the Professor prays: "Thank you, God, for protecting us and for all your mercies and for choosing us to be your instruments for good." (In Stoker's novel, Van Helsing does not at the end assume the role of the priest; instead, Quincey offers a brief prayer of thanksgiving before he dies.)

The living have witnessed and endured much suffering and have survived. They remain in communion at the end—their victory commemorated in this final group portrait, which is best appreciated as a contrast to *Count Dracula*'s opening image of the Westenra household before Jonathan's departure for Transylvania. If Jonathan and Mina have traveled far from the confines of her mother's home, the route that the Harkers and their fellow survivors have taken is indicated by the slow dissolve that Saville uses to move from Castle Dracula to the final image of the living. The pious, thankful community visually emerges out of Dracula's smoldering, empty coffin. The moral community is formed because of the King-Vampire and eventually obliterates him, replacing his darkness and obscuring smoke with its sunlight, substituting what I have called a group portrait for a tight close-up. Since the stake is so prominent in the first of the two images in this dissolve, the transition also reminds us that the stake is at the heart of the moral community, that victory and communal worship are made possible by ritualistic violence and by Van Helsing's knowledge of and allegiance to tradition.

What this dissolve at the end of *Count Dracula* so effectively demonstrates is that the living must be understood in contrast to the undead, just as the vampire women in Castle Dracula must be understood in contrast to Mina (hence one ultimate danger in the film is that Mina may indeed become the "sister" of these creatures). Since I have insisted that *Count Dracula*—more than any other retelling of *Dracula*—retains Stoker's interest in the nature of and the necessity for a community of the living, it is noteworthy that the presentation of the King-Vampire in Saville's film differs as much from Stoker's *Dracula* as it does from Browning's *Dracula*. On the one hand, Saville's aristocratic vampire is affable, urbane, and wryly ironic, very much like the vampire hero of the Fred Saberhagen novels I mentioned at the beginning of chapter 3. For example, when Jonathan is amazed that his shaving mirror in Castle Dracula does not reflect his host, Dracula remarks with a smile that "the trouble with mirrors is that they don't reflect quite enough," and then with no further explanation casually drops the looking glass out the window. By casting Louis Jourdan as the Count, Saville immediately provides Dracula with a suave, continental manner that has been associated with Jourdan from *Letter from an Unknown Woman* (1948) and *Gigi* (1958) through all the rather limited and stereotyped roles in his career. Jourdan never seems as menacing and physically powerful as Christopher Lee, as foreign as Bela Lugosi, or as potentially unstable as Jack Palance. Frank Langella in Badham's *Dracula* provides the performance that is perhaps most similar to Jourdan's, for both films portray Count Dracula as an aristocratic lover rather than a princely warrior or a satanic villain.

In these two films of the late 1970s, Dracula's attacks are quite obviously pleasurable sexual experiences for his victims, who always make gestures of compliance and moan with ecstasy at the experienced touch of the Count. (The attacks, in other words, are not rapes.) Often visualized in silhouette images, slow motion, superimpositions, or "unnatural" color images, these passionate encounters annihilate time and identity and transform the victim's bedroom into a private realm quite distinct from ordinary life. (Saville uses the same visual effects when Jonathan succumbs to the temptation of the three brides in Castle Dracula.) In Badham's film the vampire's embrace promises to elevate Lucy into a queen who will not be bound by the strictures of the decaying modern world. Dracula in Saville's film similarly offers his victims a union beyond anything Quincey or Jonathan, who are so often absent, can provide. The sleepwalking Lucy in *Count Dracula* chooses Dracula of all her suitors, as one striking image suggests: after Van Helsing has given her a sleeping draught, Lucy glances once more before she falls asleep at the concerned men around her, who look to her eyes hazy and out of focus. Then behind the men Dracula appears, a clear and sharp figment of Lucy's imagination, a figure she sees as the censorious barriers of waking consciousness are removed.

Mingling their blood, the vampire and his brides/daughters share a bond closer than any human marriage. "Vampires are nourishment to one another," Saville's Dracula declares, "beautiful, fundamental nourishment"—a sentiment not shared by Stoker's supremely egotistical King-Vampire, who mocks Mina as he places his "foul, awful, sneering mouth" on her throat (D, 293) or by Dracula in Hammer films, who has only snarling disdain for his brides. Thus, against the community presided over by Van Helsing, the vampire offers another type of interdependence, which is based on physical pleasure rather than on spiritual values and on a common evil opponent. When Dracula actually confronts his pursuers in *Count Dracula*, he even delivers an apologia for his kind, who merely attempt to survive and have no interest in questions of good and evil and no desire to "capture souls," only blood. Vampires, Dracula tells the men as a cruciform reflection of light strikes his face without blinding or disabling him, need no cross ("an instrument of torture and humiliation," the Count reminds the hunters) as a talisman, but like Christians, the undead too "must recruit disciples."[12] From Van Helsing's viewpoint, the community that gathers around the crucifix in *Count Dracula* defines itself in opposition to evil; Saville suggests how the opposition between the living and the undead might well be between two different types of nourishment and two different conceptions of what constitutes survival.

For all of the vampire's articulate logic in *Count Dracula* and the communion he offers of "beautiful, fundamental nourishment," Saville continually reminds us that blood is indeed the life for the undead—glistening on the vampire's mouth following every embrace and staining the faces of Lucy and Dracula's other brides after they feed. So, too, the Count's urbanity and ironic wit are balanced by his shapeshifting ability to become a wolf, a bat, or a cloud of mist. The most interesting way we see Dracula, however, is in a close-up that Saville inserts at several points in the film. This shot first appears after Jonathan accidentally cuts himself while shaving. As if in response to the sight of blood, the vampire's face fills the frame in a black-and-white negative image, his eyes open, staring straight forward and highlighted, like his mouth, in luminous red. Suddenly, momentarily, it seems as if Dracula's veneer has been stripped away, leaving only his predatory hunger. This negative image, which also appears during Dracula's passionate meetings with Lucy, pictures the vampire as a wolf, ready to feed. It also removes Dracula from our world, suggesting that he is "negative," antithetical to the "positive" moral community of the living. Since *Count Dracula* is generally filmed in an uninteresting *Masterpiece Theater* style—with a limited number of camera set-ups predictably employed in the interior dialogue scenes and an obtrusive use of mood music—these negative images very much stand out, implying, as I noted in my discussion of *Dracula: The Vampire Play*, how the vampire's presence ruptures the "realistic" (conventional, illusionary) manner in which we see Van Helsing, Mina, and their compatriots.

In addition to emphasizing the vampire's hunger, animality, and opposition to the living, this negative image of the vampire's face also suggests Dracula's omniscience as he intently stares forward with open red eyes. Thus this image appears immediately after Renfield asks: "Master, are you coming soon?" And Saville's juxtaposition of question and visual response implies that the Count, who has not yet departed for England, sees and hears his servant, just as he seems to watch Lucy as she sleepwalks to the graveyard at Whitby. Having focused and amplified the significance of this image by repeating it at key points throughout the film, Saville returns to the negative black-

and-white image of the vampire at the end of *Count Dracula*. Following the dissolve I described earlier, which moves from the stake (and thus the destruction and the absence of the undead) to the hunters offering thanksgiving to God, one final dissolve remains, one last replacement to end the film.[13]

From the moral community, united in prayer, Saville dissolves to the negative image of Dracula, in an even tighter close-up than earlier in the film, so that only the bottom half of the vampire's face is visible. Dracula's red-tinted mouth moves in slow motion as the credits begin to roll over this image. While the credits continue, the camera pans very slowly from Dracula's mouth to his eyes, then moves in to single out one open eye before the film ends with a fade-out. In one sense, this concluding shot links *Count Dracula* to the tradition of nineteenth- and twentieth-century vampire stories, from John Polidori's *The Vampyre* with Lord Ruthven's "dead grey eye," through Stoker's insistence on the power of Dracula's hypnotic gaze, to the many interpolated close-ups of Bela Lugosi's squinting stare in Browning's *Dracula*, to the detail shots of Christopher Lee's all-red or bloodshot eyes in Hammer's vampire films. Saville expands on these previous works, in which the vampire is a mesmerist or a red-eyed animal, by raising the possibility that Dracula in his waking moments is omniscient; all of human life, including the viewer, comes under his gaze.

To assert, as I have done, that this final image of Dracula replaces an image of the moral community is to imply that in *Count Dracula* the vampire triumphs over the living. The contrast between these concluding images could hardly be more complete: in natural light, the living silently stand in a medium long shot with their heads bowed, arranged in a sort of group portrait; in unnatural light and color Dracula appears in a tight close-up, his eyes open, his mouth moving, speaking words we cannot hear, and confronting us with an unblinking, unrepentant stare. No living person in the film ever dominates the frame in this manner. Mina and Van Helsing and their allies are always situated within the world; only Dracula can abolish the world, filling our field of vision with his individual presence—a moving presence quite unlike the painted image of Vlad Tepes that ends Curtis's *Dracula*. The living believe that they and God and good have triumphed. We alone know that the vampire has survived, although perhaps we can try to dismiss this image as merely background for the final credits and therefore not proof of anything. (I assume that the credit sequences in a film should always be understood as part of the film's narrative.)

By complicating the end of his film, imbuing it with irony and ambiguity, Saville makes his "Gothic Romance based on Bram Stoker's *Dracula*" into a more open-ended story than any other retelling of the novel, except Badham's 1979 film. What makes *Count Dracula* such an interesting work is that in many ways it is the most traditional of all the adaptations of *Dracula*, in that it shares Stoker's emphasis on the importance of faith, ritual, and the moral community, while ultimately Saville challenges these same values and overturns tradition with his open ending and with his presentation of the vampire.[14]

Count Dracula's affinity with *Dracula* seems to be reflective of the BBC/PBS attitude toward adaptation, in which the literary text is "faithfully," if tediously, dramatized into a series of conversation scenes, and thereby transformed into a talky, visually uninteresting period piece. Dracula, through his promise of escape and through the way he is often presented in unrealistic video images, subverts the *Masterpiece Theater* atmosphere, much as Saville could be said to subvert Stoker's *Dracula* with his conclusion, an open ending that links *Count Dracula* with Badham's *Dracula* and other horror stories of the late 1970s.

Looking backward from the questions that end Badham's *Dracula* and Saville's *Count Dracula*, through Hammer's ongoing Dracula saga in the 1960s and Deane and Balderston's epilogue to *Dracula: The Vampire Play*, finally to Stoker's novel where the birth of Quincey Harker closes off the story that began with his father's business trip to Castle Dracula, one line of development can be identified in the works considered in the last three chapters—a movement from Stoker's closed ending to a progressively more open ending, from resolution and much-deserved reward to ambiguity and exhaustion or false security. Saville and Badham, from this perspective, could be said to have brought *Dracula* into the contemporary world of horror, which has found a variety of terrifying ways to prevent closure, so that openness itself becomes the norm (a point made evident, for example, in the sequels to *Halloween* [1978] and *Friday the 13th* [1980] and also in the closed-ended *Alien* [1979], which plays on our expectation that something will undercut and subvert Ripley's final triumph over the monster). Yet the open ending is not the product of the 1970s or of the twentieth century. Universal proved during the late 1930s and 1940s that every horror movie can have a sequel; Laura still recalls and fantasizes about the vampire's embrace in the final paragraph of *Carmilla*

(1871); Lord Ruthven disappears unpunished at the end of *The Vampyre* (1819); and folktales about vampires and other monsters suggest that storytellers have always had the option of ending with the unresolved and the unresolvable, as well as with the outright victory of the monster. We might say that there have been open-ended horror stories for as long as man has had nightmares. In addition, to chart a simple linear development from closed to open endings in the retelling of *Dracula*, we must ignore the films of Browning, Fisher, Curtis, and Franco. These four films are not merely exceptions to some general rule; they are proof that there is no general development from closed to open endings. What the works I have discussed in this chapter begin to make clear, then, is that open and closed endings are always available options, but that one type of ending may become the preferred and, therefore, the expected choice in a given period.

Similarly, these adaptations of *Dracula* offer different notions of what constitutes evil, the monstrous, and the unnatural, as well as diverse images of the relationship between the living and the undead, men and women, and the young and the old. Though certain connections between these works are apparent—in, for example, the manner in which the elderly, authoritarian Van Helsing becomes altered in the films from *Horror of Dracula* on—again no simple, easily charted line of progress or deterioration, no developing post-Victorian change of attitude can be identified that accounts for all or even most of these retellings. At best, as our familiarity with the story increases, we can identify certain themes, questions, problems, oppositions, relationships, situations, and dilemmas that the story of the living and the undead—and particularly of Dracula, Jonathan Harker, Van Helsing, and Mina et al.—seems well suited to explore, then allow the films themselves to teach us about these topics and perhaps about the nature of adaptation and genre in popular art as well.

Passing from Stoker's novel to Deane and Balderston's play to Browning's film inevitably brings to mind the differences among novel, theater, and film, or, more accurately, among the late nineteenth-century popular novel, the realistic commercial theater of the 1920s, and the early Hollywood sound film. As commercial enterprises, the adaptations I have discussed are all products to some degree of different technological, aesthetic, and economic environments. Studying these retellings may reaffirm our prejudices for or against the movies and may even reveal something about the nature of the cinematic as opposed to the literary. But, more important, such a study breaks down the sort of reductive biases that encourage generalizing about the horror film or Hollywood movies or twentieth-century popular culture. Even the degree to which these retellings are determined by a range of different external environmental factors is varied enough to preclude any precise generalizations. While Browning's *Dracula*, for example, is affected by censorship codes and the technological state of filmmaking apparatus, Saville's *Count Dracula* is strictly bound to the specific narrative and dramatic format of noncommercial video serial drama. And while all these works are in some fashion cultural documents, reflecting and embodying changing attitudes, values, and assumptions and tapping widely held fears and aspirations, the angle of reflection and the culture that is documented vary dramatically. *El Conde Dracula* and *Taste the Blood of Dracula*, for example, in different ways seem designed to endorse the self-confidence as well as articulate the misgivings of a youthful, late-1960s audience. *Dracula: The Vampire Play* and Browning's *Dracula*, on the other hand, seem to reaffirm without being aware of it certain images of women as victims and objects of desire.

To say that there are no broad, all-encompassing generalizations to be drawn about the relationship of all these retellings to Stoker's *Dracula*, about the changes in the story of Dracula from 1897 to 1979, about the connection between these works and the culture and specific environments from which they emerge, and about the adaptation of a novel into a play or a movie or a television program is not to deny the importance of these topics. Indeed, I have attempted to explore precisely these topics. What I seek to deny or to forestall is the appealingly safe, critical recourse to oversimplification. My conclusions about these works *are* my analyses of these works, in which the play of tradition and variation is the primary concern. For in this play the reworking of the source takes place, and a different, yet related story emerges, as different and even ideologically and formally antithetical as Curtis's *Dracula*, for instance, is in many ways to *Count Dracula*, or as *Dracula: The Vampire Play* is to *El Conde Dracula*.

Even if these works do not technically constitute a genre in and of themselves, the retellings of *Dracula* demonstrate several important points that I think are applicable to most popular genres, subgenres, cycles, or formulas. Not only a revisionist work like Badham's *Dracula*, but each new version of Stoker's novel inevitably affects our rereading or reviewing of its predecessors. Just as we cannot ignore that Browning's *Dracula* was produced and released in 1931, so once we become familiar with other versions of *Dracula*, we cannot experience or analyze Browning's film apart from the ahistorical context of these later versions (which is not to deny the significance of other contexts, such as the films of Bela Lugosi or Tod Browning, the rest of Universal's series of horror films, other film adaptations of stage productions in the early 1930s, and so on). In fact, the ideological assumptions, the values, and attitudes expressed in Browning's *Dracula*—many of the elements that could be said to mark the film as a product of Hollywood in the early 1930s or as a particular type of entertaining, escapist response to the Depression—become most evident when the film is seen and examined in the context of other retellings of Stoker's novel. As I noted earlier, *El Conde Dracula* may have little in common with earlier versions of *Dracula*, but Franco's film, like every retelling of the novel, reveals new ways in which the story can be told, new emphases, additional options and choices, details and events whose potential for significance suddenly becomes apparent. Such, I take it, is one of the pleasures of getting to know any popular genre and one of the bases for analyzing a popular genre. I hope that I have been able to some extent to suggest the way I was educated by these films in the importance of variation and detail, in assessing the new in the context of the old, and in rethinking the old in the light of the new. As retold in the twentieth century, *Dracula* becomes a group of stories all concerned with violence, violation, and the how and why of survival, with the sacred and the secular, with wisdom and action, and with the other thematic concerns I have dwelt on in this chapter. But to achieve any more than a superficial familiarity with the oft-told story of Dracula, we must pay attention to what each individual retelling suggests about such topics and to the particular story that each tells of the confrontation between the living and the undead. As Van Helsing realizes and Jonathan Harker must learn, weapons are necessary if the living are to survive this confrontation, but a shovel is not a revolver is not a torch is not a pike is not a candlestick cross is not a sharpened, charred stake.

NOTES

1. McNally and Florescu's nonfiction book was adapted in 1971 by Calvin Floyd and Tony Forsberg as *In Search of Dracula*, an amateurish collection of travelogue sequences in Romania, recreated historical incidents, and clips from previous vampire films, with Christopher Lee as narrator and also per-

forming as Stoker's Dracula and Vlad Tepes. Interestingly, when Lee summarizes the plot of Stoker's novel in *In Search of Dracula*, he declares that the novel ends when Count Dracula is "caught by the hero, Jonathan Harker, and the vampire expert, Professor Van Helsing." Thus does the "original" story get misremembered and misreported in accordance with later retellings; Lee's summary fits only Curtis's *Dracula*.

2. Curtis's attempt to humanize Dracula depends to a great extent on Jack Palance's performance as the Count. Palance is not by any means a major Hollywood star, but he does have an identifiable persona that is based on what David Thomson calls a "unique note of repressed hysteria" (*A Biographical Dictionary of Film* [New York: William Morrow, 1976], p. 427). *Dracula* (1973), in fact, emphasizes the same characteristics that are found in Palance's most impressive roles, in *Shane* (1953), for example, and *Attack!* (1956)—"repressed hysteria," and also egotism, rage, and the potential for brutal violence.

3. I would not suggest, however, that Curtis's Dracula is a victim of "existential anguish," as do James Ursini and Alain Silver (*The Vampire Film* [New York: A. S. Barnes, 1975], p. 88), who offer the most detailed treatment of *Dracula* (1973).

4. Later in Curtis's *Dracula*, Van Helsing will draw Arthur's attention to a torture device in Castle Dracula known as an "iron maiden," a spiked casket formed in the shape of a woman. This object is not mentioned in Stoker's novel, but perhaps Curtis and Matheson include it in *Dracula* (1973) as an allusion to *The Squaw*, a story of crime and punishment found in Stoker's *Dracula's Guest* in which the Iron Maiden of Nuremberg is the principal prop.

5. I have not been able to determine if the television version of *Dracula* (1973) is identical to the theatrical version, though in a comparable case—Steven Spielberg's *Duel* (1971)—the theatrical print is almost twenty minutes longer than the original telecast.

6. Horace Newcomb, "Toward a Television Aesthetic," in *Television: The Critical View*, ed. Horace Newcomb (New York: Oxford University Press, 1976), p. 275.

7. Quoted in John Brosnan, *The Horror People* (New York: New American Library, 1977), p. 114.

8. One of the most informative and well-reasoned essays on the zoom is John Belton and Lyle Tector, "The Bionic Eye: Aesthetics of the Zoom," *Film Comment* 16 (Sept.-Oct. 1980), 11–17.

9. Among the unique adaptations of Stoker's *Dracula* is a children's book entitled, *Paint Me the Story of Dracula* (New York: Grosset and Dunlap, 1976), which comes complete with watercolors and illustrations to be painted. As "Retold by Dennis Green from the novel by Bram Stoker," this *Dracula* focuses exclusively on the adventures of Jonathan Harker: his departure from England on a business trip for his employer; his journey to Castle Dracula, complete with wolves, mysterious warnings, and forbidding darkness; his odd, elderly host and his "strange dream" of the "beautiful," yet "cruel" vampire women; and his realization that Dracula is a vampire who lives in a world of "decay," feeds his brides young children of the local peasants, and plans to

"take his horror to England." However, this retelling includes Jonathan's solitary, courageous destruction of the vampire with a sword (because no stake is available). The story ends with Jonathan's mind "full of blood and horror," as he decides to keep the entire episode a secret when he returns to England, for fear that no one would believe him. Even more than the comic book version of *Dracula*, Green's book is addressed to a specific audience, and it raises some interesting questions about how Jonathan Harker's adventures in Transylvania are tied to certain basic childhood situations and dilemmas—for example, of being given responsibility, then being manipulated by adults; and of being isolated, tempted by the dreamlike pleasures of passivity, then being forced to survive by means of independent, aggressive action. In this children's book Jonathan can get no help from a father figure, yet while he is able to triumph because of his own bravery and ingenuity (replacing a wooden stake with a sword), Jonathan is still alone and burdened at the end of the story with the secret knowledge of "blood and horror"—burdened, presumably, by what he has done as well as what he has seen or dreamed. This open ending, I find, captures a fundamental psychological truth about the consequences of actions and experiences that Stoker's *Dracula* does not acknowledge.

10. Van Helsing's description of this procedure as an "exorcism" inevitably calls to mind *The Exorcist*, which in both novel and film is a major reference point for the horror story of the past ten years and is, like *Count Dracula*, a work much concerned with the nature and role of ritual and faith. Lucy Westenra's rapid transformation, as she lies in her own bed, from a sick young woman to a sexually mature adult to a snarling, hissing fiend is reminiscent of Regan McNeil's transformation through similar stages in *The Exorcist*, though Regan does not become the seductive temptress until the end of *Exorcist II: The Heretic* (1977).

11. Robert A. Nisbet, *The Quest for Community* (1953; rpt. New York: Oxford University Press, 1973), pp. 43, 39.

12. Saville's Dracula implies that vampires are not a different race from the Europeans, but actually a different species (although the vampires in *Count Dracula* do not seem to have the potential to breed with one another). With varying degrees of success and sophistication, this idea has also been explored in several contemporary novels, including Anne Rice's *Interview with the Vampire* (1976), Suzy McKee Charnas's *The Vampire Tapestry* (1980), Jan Jennings's *Vampyr* (1981), and Whitley Strieber's *The Hunger* (1982).

13. As Saville demonstrates in *Count Dracula*, a dissolve, unlike a fade-out/fade-in or a straight cut, can draw attention not only to the transition from A to B and the superimposition of A on B, but also the replacement of A by B.

14. A comic book adaptation of *Dracula*, published by Ballantine Books in 1966, includes even more of Stoker's episodes and specific events than does *Count Dracula*, although both of these retellings stand alone in their emphasis on the formation of a community to defeat the vampire. This comic book *Dracula*, with illustrations by Alden McWilliams and text by Otto Binder and Craig Tennis, is an excellent example of the storytelling possibilities of this mixed form: its written text, including third-person narration, interior monologue, and conversation, is combined in a number of different ways with illustrations

that make impressive use of shifting angle and perspective, variable frame size, and linear continuity. This comic book does allow Quincey and Jonathan to destroy the King-Vampire with their knives, an action that concludes the hunt, which is here a quasi-military operation directed by Van Helsing (who closely resembles in physical appearance Edward Van Sloan, the actor who played Van Helsing in *Dracula: The Vampire Play* and Browning's *Dracula*). What is generally omitted in this retelling is the social and spiritual context Stoker insists upon. No silver crucifix or prayers of thanksgiving unite this group, who are last seen standing over the dust of their nemesis, as Van Helsing declares: "Now it is over . . . Dracula is no more"—a neat, uncomplicated closed ending to a tale of action and adventure.

PART THREE

The Sacrifice of the Pure-Hearted Seer

You must picture the consternation of our little town, hitherto so tranquil, and now, out of the blue, shaken to its core, like a quite healthy man who all of a sudden feels his temperature shoot up and the blood seething like wildfire in his veins.

Albert Camus
The Plague

Lucy Harker: I see something horrible.
Nosferatu the Vampyre

CHAPTER

6

Nosferatu, A Symphony of Horror and *Nosferatu the Vampyre*

TWO MAJOR FILMS, arguably the most interesting and accomplished cinematic retellings of Stoker's *Dracula*, are noticeably absent from my survey in the previous three chapters: F. W. Murnau's *Nosferatu, Eine Symphonie des Grauens* (*Nosferatu, A Symphony of Horror* [1922], hereafter referred to as *Nosferatu*) and Werner Herzog's *Nosferatu, Phantom der Nacht* (*Nosferatu, Phantom of the Night* [1979], hereafter referred to as *Nosferatu the Vampyre*, the title used in its American release). Because Prana films, the company that produced *Nosferatu*, did not purchase the screen rights to Stoker's *Dracula*, Murnau and screenwriter Henrik Galeen—at least in part to circumvent potential legal problems—changed the names of the principal characters, developed a new set of physical characteristics for the vampire, and shifted the story from England in the late nineteenth century to Bremen in 1838. Yet in the original opening credits, *Nosferatu* is identified as being "based on the novel *Dracula* by Bram Stoker and freely adapted by Henrik Galeen."[1] *Nosferatu the Vampyre*, which Herzog calls not simply a "remake" but an "absolutely new version" of Murnau's *Nosferatu*,[2] is identified in Hans Helmut Prinzler's authoritative filmography of Herzog as "nach Motiven des Films *Nosferatu, Eine Symphonie des Grauens* von Friedrich Wilhelm Murnau und des Romans *Dracula* von Bram Stoker."[3] Because of the unique relationship between these two remarkable German films and these two widely acclaimed filmmakers, as well as the fact that these films are vastly different from other adaptations of *Dracula*, indeed, from all other vampire films, *Nosferatu* and *Nosferatu the Vampyre* deserve separate, extended consideration.

Murnau's *Nosferatu*, one of the acknowledged masterworks of the German silent cinema, has a much more commonly accepted place in the history of film than does Jess Franco's *El Conde Dracula* or even Tod Browning's *Dracula* and Terence Fisher's *Horror of Dracula*. It is in the context of German expressionist film in the 1920s that Lotte H. Eisner, for example, praises *Nosferatu*'s "overwhelming and poignant images," and Siegfried Kracauer in *From Caligari to Hitler* assesses the nature and the appeal of "absolute authority" in Murnau's film.[4] *Nosferatu* is also recognized as being probably the first vampire film, and its historical importance has been duly acknowledged by all historians of this genre and of the horror film in general, even when these writers, like Carlos Clarens in *An Illustrated History of the Horror Film*, find Murnau's film to be "crude, unsubtle, and illogical."[5] However, only a few discussions of the film, most notably Gilberto Perez Guillermo's 1967 *Sight and Sound* article and Robin Wood's perceptive essay in *Film Comment* on *Nosferatu* as a version of the "descent myth," explore in any detail the relationship between the living and the undead in Murnau's film. Even fewer critics compare *Nosferatu* with Stoker's *Dracula*.[6] These relationships will be a primary concern in my examination of *Nosferatu* as a retelling of *Dracula* that discovers and explores certain significant narrative and thematic possibilities of the vampire story, certain options not taken up by Stoker, for example, or Browning. In turn, Murnau's account of the confrontation between the solitary vampire and the various inhabitants of bourgeois civilization provides the most important context for Herzog's *Nosferatu the Vampyre*, which continues the process of discovery, exploration, and revisioning.[7]

There are two Bremens in *Nosferatu*: the familiar, easily traversed town that Jonathan Harker leaves when he embarks on his business trip to Castle Dracula, and the larger, more complex, and eminently vulnerable city that the vampire and his rats journey to and infect. In his story of the encounter of Nosferatu with the citizens of Bremen, Murnau demonstrates first, in the opening sequence of the film, the fragility and superficiality of Jonathan and the world he believes he inhabits, and then during the second half of the film, the inherent flaws and near-fatal weakness of bourgeois civilization in the face of the threat posed by the vampire.

Like Philip Saville's *Count Dracula*, Murnau's *Nosferatu* begins with a departure, so that we receive a clear picture of the world Jonathan takes leave of, a world he thinks is his. After a brief, high-angle, postcardlike image of the city's rooftops, Jonathan is introduced as he preens in front of a mirror. He smiles with trouble-free satisfaction, pleased with what he sees, but the remainder of this opening sequence suggests how little Jonathan does or can see. In his boyish, buoyant desire to get to work, Jonathan is blind to his wife's pensiveness and her seemingly exaggerated grief at his departure, and also to his employer's exceedingly odd appearance and suspicious behavior—all details that the camera singles out for us in iris-masked close-ups. What Jonathan does see is domestic bliss. Nina, his wife, plays with a kitten, as sunlight streams in through an open window, which connects the small, thriving flower garden outside with the unpretentious, comfortably furnished parlor that is complete with print wallpaper and framed portraits. Like a suitor, Jonathan presents Nina with a bouquet of flowers he has cut from the garden, and the young couple embrace before he leaves for work. This scene is less like the sentimental image of the working-class home in, for example, the "modern" story of D. W. Griffith's *Intolerance* (1916), than like an equally fanciful image of the bourgeois home as a comfortable, private domain contiguous with domesticated, ornamental nature—a modern Garden of Eden, in which the man goes and does, while the woman entertains herself with idle childish diversions or passes the time with needlepoint before her husband reappears from his sojourn in the public world of commerce.[8] When Jonathan returns from work, Nina will be sewing, seated in the same room as when he left the house; her reassuring predictability is his delight.

For Jonathan it is a brief walk down a quiet lane from his home to his place of work, where he wears the same smile as he does when looking at himself in the mirror or presenting Nina with a bouquet. All is right in Jonathan's world, and the young man immediately agrees to travel to Transylvania at his employer's request, for the trip offers "a good opportunity," presumably to earn money and gain advancement. What complicates the situation—though not for Jonathan—is that Jonathan's employer is the "Real Estate Agent Renfield," a "strange man," as a title declares, whose stylized, exaggerated make-up and physical mannerisms cause him to resemble certain figures in *The Cabinet of Dr. Caligari* (1919). Renfield studies a letter from Dracula written in cryptic hieroglyphs and maniacally laughs with pleasure at the prospect of the trip costing his young employee "pain or even a little blood." This "strange man" who controls Jonathan's life and handles the buying and selling of private property is as much a part of Bremen as are the Harkers.

And so, too, is the dwelling that Renfield proposes to sell to the aristocratic vampire, a six-story building, one of a connected series of what look to be deserted warehouses or factories. This unmistakably urban building has no private garden, but only rows of boarded-up or empty window openings in its facade. As Robin Wood notes, this building faces the Harkers' house like "a mirror in which there is as yet no clearly defined reflection."[9] It also faces Renfield's office, suggesting again the proximity of these three very different buildings. Unlike Carfax Abbey in the vampire films of Badham or Browning, Nosferatu's future home is inside the city limits. Within Bremen there is darkness sufficient for the vampire, who will not need to seek out a cellar or ancient crypt. Jonathan, however, sees only the bright sunlight and pays little heed either to the building he is to sell or to Nina's deep concern as he departs.

To reach the "Land of Phantoms" and Castle Dracula, Jonathan leaves Bremen on horseback, passes through a natural environment that is uncultivated and expansive, in contrast to the Harker's enclosed garden, and then stays at a rural inn, where the local peasants are terrified at his mention of Castle Dracula. The inn, like the vampire's castle, serves as one antithesis to Bremen, for the peasants in their folk costumes embody a rural, premodern mode of living (much more than do the villagers in Hammer's films, for example). Almost all of the peasants are older than Jonathan and are pictured as part of a group, as in, for example, a shot of four women who huddle together in fear of "evil spirits." When one of these women crosses herself, the peasants' belief in superstition becomes linked to their Christian faith. Fear, faith, and superstition are foreign to Bremen—at least the Bremen we have thus far seen, Jonathan's Bremen. Jonathan's response is to laugh at the frightened peasants in the inn, then at *The Book of Vampires*, a small, old volume he discovers in his room like a Gideon's Bible, and finally at the coachmen who refuse to carry him into the Land of Phantoms at night. Jonathan's laughter seems to be a matter of smug condescension and stupidity rather than an outright attempt at ridicule, for he has laughed at Nina in much the same way. Whether or not Murnau desired Gustav Von Wagenheim to portray Jonathan in the manner he does, the effect of Von Wagenheim's performance is to render the young traveler a shortsighted, foolish egotist (recall that he is preening himself in front of a mirror the first time we see him), much different from Stoker's young solicitor, who is to some degree the best that Victorian England has to offer.

On foot, Jonathan crosses a bridge to enter the Land of Phantoms, and soon he will cross the threshold of Castle Dracula when a massive door swings open before him. By crossing bridges and thresholds Jonathan takes steps that are quintessential in many journeys of exploration and discovery, although he has no desire either to explore or discover (he will be forced to do both), merely to get the Count's signature on a contract. The Phantom in this land is Nosferatu, who arrives by coach in fast-motion, transports Jonathan through a forest of white trees in a brief negative image, and later materializes out of the black darkness in his castle—all images that associate the vampire with the supernatural and with the antinatural, and also with uniquely cinematic techniques. Yet the castle itself, for all of Murnau's so-called expressionism, is neither a nightmarish labyrinth nor a storybook Gothic *Schloss*, but rather a "real" location overlooking acres of forestland. The exterior night scenes in *Nosferatu* are all brightly illuminated, allowing us to see the castle clearly, without the interference of mist and shadow, and without the aura of moonlight. The castle exists as surely as does the rural inn or the Harkers' home in Bremen.[10]

From a distance, Castle Dracula's one anomalous feature is a large tower that seems to grow out of a rocky promontory, protruding more like a gnarled tree trunk than a handmade structure. This tower is the first part of the castle that Jonathan (and the viewer) sees, and it will become the young man's prison and thus a point of comparison with the many later images of confinement and imprisonment in Bremen. In the castle Jonathan, unlike his counterpart in Stoker's novel, hears no oratorical history of the Dracula family's military prowess as a "conquering race," and he meets no tempting vampire women. Only Nosferatu is there, emerging through a low archway out of pitch black darkness to greet his visitor. The principal elements of this particular image will be repeated in various ways throughout *Nosferatu*: the vampire will emerge in a similar fashion before he enters Jonathan's bedroom in the castle; the darkness of this tunnel/cave recalls the empty black openings in the house the vampire will inhabit in Bremen and foreshadows the darkness of the *Demeter*'s hold, from which Nosferatu and his rats will emerge; and the arch, in Wood's words, "is a visual leitmotif in the film. Murnau uses it particularly to characterize the vampire as a repressed force" and "to link Nosferatu with Jonathan," who also is often framed by "arch-shapes."[11]

Even after the disconcerting experiences of his first night in the castle, Jonathan is able to dismiss with a laugh the two wounds on his neck and the odd manners of his host. As in Bremen, Jonathan cannot see what is obvious, and his failure in Castle Dracula will prove to be the opposite of Nina's later success in Bremen. When it is too late to do any good, Jonathan reads *The Book of Vampires*, then begins to explore the castle. In *Nosferatu*, opening a door or window is an action as dangerous as it is necessary; it is an action that creates the possibility for both exit and entrance, for seeing and being seen, for letting in the sunlight and letting in infection and darkness. Once Jonathan barely cracks open his bedroom door, for example, the vampire seems to come to life and cannot be excluded from the room. Faced with this horrible prospect, Jonathan cowers under the bedcovers like a terrified child, which in his naiveté he is and has always been. When he awakens the next morning, Jonathan moves through a series of arched doorways until at last he sees the vampire in his coffin, but the young man can only crawl away in fear. Unlike Stoker's solicitor, Jonathan in *Nosferatu* does not and apparently cannot even attempt to destroy the monster. After Jonathan returns to Bremen, he still does not become a hunter, and thus he has no opportunity to purge his fear and hatred, to gain revenge, and to regenerate himself through violence.

Jonathan escapes from the castle after the vampire has departed, is injured in his fall from the window and carried to a hospital by peasants, and is nursed back to health by a nun. Sensing the danger posed by the vampire, Jonathan rushes toward Bremen, but he never truly recovers from his experience at Castle Dracula and, in particular, from his look at Nosferatu asleep in a rotting coffin—a sight that casts doubt on all that Jonathan believes. The young man has helped provide the vampire with a haven in Bremen and, more ominously, has inadvertently let Nosferatu see a portrait of Nina, whose "splendid throat" is now the vampire's target. Thus Jonathan, who has already lost blood and his smile of self-satisfaction, now stands to lose Nina and the world he seemed so fully in possession of in the beginning of the film.

Jonathan's story up to his escape from Castle Dracula—up to the end of what is identified as Act II in Murnau's script—shares certain details with the opening section of Stoker's *Dracula*, but the remainder of *Nosferatu*, aside from the action on board the *Demeter*, has very little in common with the novel or with the retellings of *Dracula* I have discussed thus far. The vampire's journey to Bremen begins the second half of the film and serves as a transition from Jonathan and his naive conception of the good life to Nina and a more sombre, pessimistic, and critical view of life in Bremen. To insist that the undead must be understood in the context of the living, Murnau cuts between the vampire's sea voyage on the *Demeter*, Jonathan's recovery and his journey home, and three inhabitants of Bremen, who introduce us to three entirely different sectors of their native environment: Dr. Van Helsing, lecturing to a group of students; Renfield, now imprisoned in what seems to be a lunatic asylum; and Nina, waiting alone for Jonathan's return. The scenes on board the *Demeter* show Nosferatu's easy victory over the armed seamen who attempt to face the mysterious foe they are transporting. The vampire quite literally scares two of the men to death when he magically appears, then disappears, and when he rises stiff and erect from his coffin. The captain, who ties himself to the wheel as Nosferatu emerges from the hold, ends up dead as in Stoker's novel, Curtis's *Dracula*, and Badham's *Dracula*; his punctured throat is a detail we see in almost a clinical close-up, a piece of evidence that underlines the captain's significance as a victim and as a figure of authority who fails, in contrast to those people in each of these works who will succeed after the unmanned ship reaches its destination.

While the *Demeter*, powered by the vampire, cuts through the open sea, making unimpeded progress, Jonathan, though still shaken, begins his arduous trek home—as if the young man will be a factor in the coming confrontation between the living and the undead, as if Jonathan is racing his antagonist to Bremen, with Nina as the prize for the winner. In Bremen Nina and Renfield both await the arrival of these travelers, while Van Helsing lectures to a group of attentive young men about carnivorous plants and polyps, which he describes as "vampires." The actual close-up footage of these two natural phenomena in action depicts an aspect of nature far removed from the Professor's pedantic posturing and the small, well-furnished room in which he delivers this lecture. For Van Helsing, vampirism is only one term in a metaphor that we realize is inaccurate, a metaphor that also situates the vampire as part of the natural world, although Nosferatu's ontological status as a natural or a supernatural being and his identity as a form of man or animal or monstrous Other remains ambiguous throughout the film. Bremen, it turns out, has no priests, theologians, or students of the occult, so Van Helsing is therefore the only figure who is concerned with "secrets" and "strange correspondences" (these topics are the subject of his course, as a title informs us). Yet the "scientific" knowledge Van Helsing teaches with such certainty has no practical value. (In the original script, Van Helsing is described as a "Paracelsian," but the film never suggests that his scientific research extends into the occult or borrows from the principles of magic and alchemy.) This aged figure of authority does not lead his students into battle against the vampire. As the conclusion of *Nosferatu* so strikingly demonstrates, Van Helsing does not and apparently cannot *do* anything.

Murnau contrasts science, in the person of Van Helsing, with the vampire, on the one hand, and with medicine, in the person of a middle-aged Bremen doctor, on the other. As Nosferatu approaches by sea, more elements of the bourgeois world are revealed—first Van Helsing's classroom, then the asylum in which Renfield, who has "lost his reason," is imprisoned in a solitary confinement cell. While science explains "secrets," madness is imprisoned with no pretense of being "cured" and is thereby removed from society, hidden from view and treated as a crime, without ever being acknowledged as such. The doctor, who can only watch as Renfield is tied up, is more confident when he diagnoses Nina's illness, after she rises from her bed in a "somnambulistic dream" and walks out into the moonlight (she is staying at the home of her friends, the Westenras, while Jonathan is away). Murnau's editing suggests that this trancelike movement is occasioned by Nosferatu's approach toward Jonathan's bedroom in Castle Dracula. As the doctor and Nina's concerned friends watch, Nina throws out her arms and calls for Jonathan, and the vampire lifts his head in a matched response. While Seward in Stoker's *Dracula* mistakenly diagnoses Lucy Westenra's illness as some type of anemia, the doctor's error in *Nosferatu* is to dismiss Nina's "somnambulistic dream" and her telepathic awareness of Jonathan's predicament as the symptoms of some physiological illness. Nina's dreamlife, her psychic/spiritual/paranormal power of perception, her awareness of the vampire, and even her love for Jonathan make this young woman almost as much an alien in Bremen as Renfield, though both of these patients are native inhabitants of the bourgeois city—citizens who are labeled "mad" or "ill."

Nina's dreams continue, and she again moves to the balcony outside the room in which she sleeps. Still in a trance, with arms outstretched toward the sky, Nina tells her friend: "He is coming." Since this action is preceded by an image of the *Demeter*'s prow thrusting through the water, Murnau suggests that Nina senses and responds to the vampire's approach, just as Nosferatu had earlier "reacted" to Nina's call of warning to Jonathan. In this manner, Nina is again linked to Renfield, who also realizes that "the Master is coming!" But while Renfield remains locked up until he kills a guard and escapes after his Master's arrival, Nina chooses isolation and waits at the seashore for her husband's return. (Since Jonathan is traveling by land, and Nosferatu by sea, Murnau again hints that Nina in some fashion realizes that the vampire, not Jonathan, will soon share her marriage bed.) After the sequences in Bremen and Castle Dracula, which are almost always characterized by internal framing devices (notably arches) and by a sense of constriction and enclosure, the images of Nina seated on a bench at the shore seem remarkably open. Sky, sand, and sea all extend beyond the frame, and the waves and wind bring motion into the tableau. But Nina remains still, surrounded by crosses (presumably grave markers) that protrude at odd angles from the sand, like driftwood that has been arranged to resemble a cluster of dead trees. The crosses "associate" Nina "with Christian redemption and death," as Wood concludes;[12] they also contrast with the crosses that Jonathan sees on his journey, which signify the vital faith of the peasants and the nun. Up to this point in the film, that is, before the vampire's arrival, Bremen contains no crosses, no religion to accompany its commerce, science, and medicine. This secular world would seem to have no need for the cross. The seaside cemetery has become a sort of picturesque ruin, deserted except for Nina, who is "ill" and has dissociated herself from Bremen.

In Stoker's novel Dracula's arrival in England is heralded by a tempestuous storm, which allows the vampire to disembark from the wrecked *Demeter* without attracting undue attention, and which provides a natural fanfare fit for a king. In *Nosferatu* the *Demeter* glides into the still water of Bremen's harbor, and the vampire carries his coffin through the streets, meeting no one along the way. Again, the "night" looks as bright as an overcast day, emphasizing—intentionally or unintentionally—the dreamlike emptiness of the city. Murnau's deep-focus long shots in this sequence show a vacant world,[13] a ghost town in which the vampire can move freely, passing under and alongside archways that are strikingly similar to those in Castle Dracula. This path takes him to the deserted building across from the Harkers' home. The people of Bremen—except for Nina who runs out into the street to embrace Jonathan when he returns from his journey this same night—remain inside their houses during the hours of darkness, and their undefended city will make an excellent hunting ground for the vampire. Holding a coffin under one arm, Nosferatu disappears as he moves through the arched wooden door of his new home. Before our eyes, he blends completely into this environment, so much so that he remains invisible until the end of the film when Nina calls him forth.

Accompanying the vampire to Bremen in the hold of the *Demeter* are the rats that swarm out of Nosferatu's extra coffins when these boxes of earth are opened by dockworkers and frightened seamen. A single rat seen in close-up contributes to the eerie, decadent ambience of Castle Dracula in Browning's *Dracula* and is an important detail in the dank, deserted tunnel where the undead Mina reunites with her Papa in Badham's *Dracula*. Stoker, of course, had no trouble with the practical logistics of filmmaking; he could just as easily include an army of vermin in his novel as one or two rats, and so he does when Van Helsing and the young men attempt to purify Carfax Abbey. The foul, decrepit chapel became "alive with rats," Stoker's Jonathan writes, "they seemed to swarm over the place all at once, till the lamplight, shining on their moving dark bodies and glittering, baleful eyes, made the place look like a bank of earth set with fireflies . . . the rats were multiplying in thousands" (D, 258). As preternatural and nightmarish as this scene seems, these rats are indeed ordinary creatures, for they are routed by Arthur Holmwood's terriers (another of the aristocrat's contributions to the success of the hunt). The episode demonstrates, in Van Helsing's words, the King-Vampire's "power over the brute world" (D, 259). Like Dracula's shapeshifting transformations to mist or bat, this power overturns whatever natural order might exist. It is, however, a power that the living in Stoker's novel can overcome.

The rats that stream out of the dark hold of the *Demeter* after Nosferatu arrives in Bremen are not a vicious army willed into action by a superior being. These rats do not so much follow the vampire or do his bidding as accompany him to a new, hospitable environment. Most important, however, is the fact that Murnau and Galeen make Nosferatu's rats the bearers of the plague, thereby linking the vampire and the plague as both simultaneously invade the bourgeois world. This association has no precedent in Stoker's *Dracula* or any pre-1922 vampire stories I am familiar with, and it is only rarely suggested in the vast amount of material summarized by Montague Summers in *The Vampire: His Kith and Kin* and *The Vampire in Europe*. Yet the connection between the vampire and the plague is in one sense eminently appropriate, since the vampire can be seen as the carrier of a communicable disease, which he transmits to his victims, who in turn seek out new victims. (Conversely, the narrator of Daniel Defoe's *A Journal of the Plague Year* [1721] bemoans a "seeming propensity or a wicked inclination in those that were infected to infect others," as if to suggest that the plague brings forth man's basest and most villainous instincts.[14]) In this manner, the "horrible pollution" spreads, and for Summers, "this is perhaps, and with good reason, the most dreaded quality of the vampire, and examples thereof occur again and again in legend and history."[15]

In *Nosferatu*, however, the vampire does not create new undead creatures. For Murnau, vampirism is not a plague, which is here an epidemic disease borne by rats, although the vampire is intimately linked to the plague as the conclusion of the film makes clear. The more disturbing implications of Murnau's association of epidemic disease with the undead are explored not only in Herzog's *Nosferatu the Vampyre*, but also in Richard Matheson's *I Am Legend* and George Romero's *Night of the Living Dead* and *Dawn of the Dead*. This influence alone would guarantee Murnau's *Nosferatu* an important place in the development of the horror story in the twentieth century.

Once he has visually established a connection between the vampire and the plague—including giving Nosferatu two thin front teeth that protrude like the teeth of a rat—Murnau chooses to leave the exact nature of the link unexplained, although a newspaper account declares that the victims of the "mysterious epidemic" have "two bloody marks" on their necks. (Similarly, we do not know if any of the *Demeter*'s crewmen died after being infected by the rats onboard the ship, nor do we know if any citizens of Bremen died after being bitten by the vampire.) Soon after the arrival of the *Demeter*, both Nosferatu and the rats disappear like phantoms into the darkness of Bremen. Murnau focuses only on the effects of the vampire's presence in the city, and in so doing tells a very different story than do Hamilton Deane and John L. Balderston, for example, who adapt *Dracula* into a drawing-room mystery involving only a handful of people in an isolated, contained environment. In contrast, Nina and Jonathan's fate in *Nosferatu* cannot be separated from the fate of the society they inhabit. At least as much as Stoker's novel, Murnau's vampire film is about the relationship between the public and the private, between civic responsibility and personal motives, such as the desire for love or vengeance. In Stoker's *Dracula* these realms are separate, but man can perform heroic acts that satisfy and benefit both the private and the public. The destruction of Count Dracula is absolutely necessary, Stoker's Van Helsing tells Mina, "For your sake in the first, and then for the sake of humanity" (D, 324). These hunters will risk all "for the safety of one we love—for the good of mankind, and for the honour and glory of God" (D, 326).

Only after the *Demeter*'s arrival does the public, civic aspect of Bremen appear, an aspect that is not a part of the simple, sunlit, congenial world Jonathan sees in the beginning of the film, which does not and need not include doctors, professors, pallbearers, or government officials. As I have suggested throughout this discussion, *Nosferatu* is organized so that we see more of and learn more about Bremen as the film progresses, as if the city is forced to reveal its true identity under the pressure of the vampire, somewhat like Jonathan in Stoker's novel reveals his repressed desires when he is in the company of the vampire women in Castle Dracula. For example, the task of examining the *Demeter* falls to Jonathan's friend Westenra and several other well-dressed men (presumably customs officials) who are mystified by the situation and carry the dead captain and his log off the ship. The official investigation continues in a spacious meeting room (identified in the original script as the Port Authority Building), where a larger group of men are gathered as Westenra reads the log, and the same doctor who treated Lucy and Renfield examines the corpse. These men, it would seem, are the monied ruling class in Bremen, who are guided in their decisions by the doctor—not by Van Helsing, who does not traffic in practical diagnoses and prescriptions. After Westenra reads the entry in which the captain records his fears about carrying the plague on board the *Demeter*, the doctor warns the men to "stay in your houses!" Because Murnau uses a high-angle long shot when the men quickly disperse and exit the building, the scene emphasizes the abrupt disbanding of this assembly (like rats leaving the proverbial ship). Neither this collection of affluent citizens, nor any group, for that matter, will be capable of protecting Bremen. Ironically, the same port that is the basis of Bremen's economy (the meeting hall is adorned with a large painting of a ship at sea and a model of a ship prominently rests atop a table) allows Nosferatu and the plague easy access to the city.

The doctor's command is a defensive measure that proves as unsuccessful as Nina's plea early in the film that Jonathan not travel to Transylvania. From the meeting hall, now containing only the captain's corpse, Murnau cuts immediately to a long shot looking down on an empty, narrow city street with buildings visible on both sides of the frame; one lone figure in the distance moves toward the camera, then delivers an official message: "Because of the rapid spread of the plague, the mayor of the city of Bremen has commanded that no more sick can be brought to the hospital." A series of reaction shots show both young and old people shutting their windows, further closing themselves in. These actions make each house a potential tomb and ensure that each family is destined to live or die as a unit in private.[16] As the plague infests the city, Bremen appears more confined, restricting, almost claustrophobic, even more "modern" in the sense that its people are isolated, trapped, and afraid in an impersonal urban environment—the opposite of Jonathan's confidence and comfort in the beginning of *Nosferatu* and the opposite also of those values and benefits that membership in a community is often said to provide.

The effects of the mayor's policy are shown in the next brief sequence, as a single elderly man in a black suit and top hat walks from house to house on an empty street, marking crosses on the doors of infected households. At one door he pauses only long enough to allow four pallbearers to carry a coffin out into the sunlit street and past the camera. All seen primarily in long shots so that they remain anonymous and distant in an otherwise motionless tableau, all dressed alike and similarly stiff and careful in their movements, these men are the last vestiges of civic authority, which attempts to maintain a semblance of order as the city dies and which never realizes that a vampire lurks in its midst. That Murnau is able to depict the infestation of Bremen in three brief sequences (the shots of the cross marker are not introduced or otherwise "placed" by any explanatory title) emphasizes not only the rapid spread of the plague, but also the complete vulnerability and defenselessness of the city. Bremen can only identify and carry off its dead; it can do nothing to protect the living.

Inside one of the closed, now completely private houses, Nina cannot resist her desire to read *The Book of Vampires*, which informs her of the sole way the living can be protected: "only a woman is able to break the terrible spell—a woman pure of heart must offer herself to Nosferatu. The woman must remain at the side of Nosferatu until the crow of the rooster heralds the break of day." When Jonathan enters the room, he snatches the book away, as if to remind Nina that ignorance can be bliss and knowledge can be fatal. But he cannot comfort his wife or dispel her fears about the ominous, decrepit building,

Nosferatu's dwelling, which she sees from her bedroom window "each night, the face of my . . ." [*sic*].

Lotte Eisner translates this title as: "This is how I see it—every evening . . .!!!" and in Roger Manvell's edition of the screenplay this title appears as: "Look! Every night, in front of me . . ." [*sic*]. The first of these titles makes more obvious what is left ambiguous in the other versions, i.e., the possibility that from her window Nina sees Nosferatu every night and not merely the abandoned building, which is what we see immediately before this title appears. If Nina does see the vampire every night, then she has access to what remains hidden even from the camera, not to mention Bremen's other citizens. Besides Renfield, no one else in Bremen except the Harkers knows the truth. Jonathan makes no effort to reclaim his world. He would do nothing save follow official orders, deny Nina access to *The Book of Vampires*, and bury his head in a pillow like a frustrated, frightened child. Nina has been set apart from Bremen throughout the film, literally when she sleepwalks out of the Westenras' home and when she waits in self-imposed isolation at the seashore, but also set apart because of her fears, nightmares, premonitions, and telepathic powers—all symptoms of what the doctor diagnoses as an "unknown disease." Yet Nina is the one who will sacrifice herself for Bremen, following the ritual laid down in the ancient book (no wise, elderly man will guide her), a relic from the superstitious, premodern land of the peasants that proves the importance of written language as a means of preserving tradition.

But why does Nina assume this responsibility? The hunters' motives in Stoker's novel are clearly enunciated, and we know the personal reasons why Jonathan and Van Helsing in Badham's *Dracula*, for example, risk their lives and souls to challenge the vampire. Nina's act, too, is a personal gesture, motivated by her love for Jonathan. "Ich Liebe Dich" she embroiders on a sampler before she makes her final decision. Wood suggests that Nina also "secretly and ashamedly *desires* the vampire,"[17] although it is difficult to read "desire" into Nina's terror and anguish, particularly in light of the much more overt desire shown by young women in later versions of *Dracula*. It seems more likely that Nina knows that her nightmare will end only if she confronts the creature who haunts her sleep and her vision, only if she offers the vampire her "pure" heart.

In addition to her personal motives, Nina acts because she sees, as we see, the effect of Nosferatu's presence on Bremen. Murnau's use of windows underlines this point. In the beginning of *Nosferatu*, Nina stands at an open window that overlooks a private flower garden. This view no longer appears at the end of the film, and in its stead, two other vantage points in the Harkers' home are revealed: one, in the bedroom, that opens onto the vampire's dwelling amid a row of deserted buildings; another, apparently in a parlor, that overlooks a narrow city street, lined on both sides with a connected series of multistory apartment houses. Jonathan turns away from these windows, but through them Nina sees the cause of the plague and its effects. Directly before she opens *The Book of Vampires* for the second time, Nina stares down at the street, which is empty save for a procession of coffins being slowly borne in single file. We see a shot of Nina standing near the parlor window as she looks out, then Murnau allows us to share her point of view. Part of the window frame is visible in this subjective image, creating an even more complete sense of enclosure, emphasized also by a slight oval mask around the image, and reminding us of the barrier between Nina and the public world outside her home. Later, at night, she opens the bedroom window, beckoning the vampire to enter her bedroom, in order to stop the weary procession of coffins. Her sacrifice is at once a personal and a civic action; no other solution will suffice, for the ritual must be followed to the letter, even though Nina has no guarantee it will be successful.

However, before Nina offers herself to Nosferatu, Murnau inserts one last glimpse of Bremen in a sequence that seems at first glance an anticlimactic digression. After detailing the emptiness and death that overtake the city, and the slow-moving, anonymous pallbearers who are the last vestige of life outside Nina's window, Murnau suddenly cuts to closer shots of other citizens, haggard old women and young men who are obviously not of the mercantile class. These people are gathered outside a building, discussing Renfield's escape from the asylum after he murdered a guard. When the madman himself appears, running down an alleyway, the people pursue him, joined by many others who almost magically stream out of doorways and take up the hunt, disregarding official orders and personal safety, disregarding the plague. "Any community that has fallen prey to violence or has been stricken by some overwhelming catastrophe," René Girard writes in *Violence and the Sacred*, "hurls itself blindly into the search for a scapegoat."[18] The fear, hatred, and repressed energy of Bremen is at last released and focused on Renfield, a perfect scapegoat since he is now "crazier" and more alien than ever, laughing from a rooftop perch as he is pelted with stones and swinging to the ground like a chimpanzee. In pursuit of Renfield, the mob of men, women, and children rush through Bremen's narrow streets and emerge onto a country road outside the city's limits. The madman eludes them, but the people run across an open field and appear as backlit silhouettes as they tear apart a scarecrow in an irrational dance of destruction and impotent rage.[19] A cut back in the middle of this sequence to Nina alone in her bedroom emphasizes the contrast between the pure-hearted woman's individual, solitary decision and the mob's frantic, futile burst of anarchic, violent energy. Both of these alternatives, it should be noted, differ completely from the moral community of vampire hunters in Stoker's *Dracula*, and both the mob and Nina defy official orders designed to ensure public health and safety in Bremen. As the citizens run across the field and out of the frame of the image, Murnau cuts to Nosferatu, who stands behind the frame of a broken window, grasping the bars and staring forward, awaiting Nina's call. The mob of citizens is no more successful in breaking the "terrible spell" or in relieving the "mental terror" that is strangling Bremen than are the city fathers or the doctor.

The concluding sequence of *Nosferatu*, in which the vampire is destroyed, draws together and elaborates upon several situations and thematic motifs that Murnau has used throughout the film. The sequence begins with Nina, dressed in a white nightgown, suddenly waking up in her bedroom, similar to her earlier awakening when Nosferatu was about to attack Jonathan. As before, Nina dreams of the vampire, and her horror and nightmare awareness are Bremen's salvation. While Jonathan soundly sleeps in a chair beside her bed, Nina is awake and alone, and her gestures, exaggerated even by silent film standards of acting,[20] suggest that she fully realizes the import of her solitary, individual decision to throw open her bedroom window and thereby free Nosferatu to move out from behind the bars of the dark cage in which he is trapped. By opening the window, Nina violates official orders and signals her willingness to allow the outside world into her private domain, rather than merely to watch the street from a safe enclosure or to turn—like Jonathan—completely away from what is outside. Nina is thus consistently associated with the act of opening—the window, *The Book of Vampires*, her eyes when she awakens—a type of action that contrasts with the act of closing in, hiding one's eyes, not daring to look, and seeking refuge in confinement.

Unlike the sacrificial victims in the regeneration rituals of the Aztecs and other "primitive" cultures, victims who participate in an elaborate communal ceremony,[21] Nina herself elects to follow the instructions of *The Book of Vampires*. She is thus more alone and isolated in her decision than are the hunters in *Dracula*, who look to each other for mutual support and who, with Lucy's "true death," see conclusive proof that the ritual is successful. When Nina awakens Jonathan and sends him to get Van Helsing, it is not clear whether she actually expects the Professor to help or whether she is removing her husband so that the vampire can occupy her bed in accordance with the ritual. What is immediately clear, however, is that Nina is terrified as the vampire approaches. She cringes in pain as the elongated shadow of Nosferatu's clawlike hand crawls up her body and forms a fist around her heart. Nina is not willingly seduced, she is violated, raped. Her corpselike passivity as the vampire feeds on her signifies acquiescence, not pleasure.

Nina's immobility contrasts completely with the other action occurring simultaneously in Bremen: the doctor is called to check on Renfield in the asylum, and Jonathan attempts to shake Van Helsing out of a deep sleep. Murnau inserts these two brief scenes, then cuts back to Nosferatu with his head bent over Nina's neck to underscore the difference between Nina's passive sacrifice and the men's futile, meaningless activity. There is no wild work to be done in *Nosferatu*; a single willing victim is required, not a group of armed hunters. Before Jonathan is able to return home with the Professor, Nina satisfies the conditions set forth in *The Book of Vampires*. By opening her window, she allows not only the vampire, but also the purifying morning sunlight to enter her bedroom. Day breaks and Nosferatu has a final moment to realize his plight before he disintegrates in the sunlight that streams in through the open window—recalling, by way of contrast, the sunlight shining through a different window in the first image of Nina in the film. If this final sequence does offer a "pathetic sudden revelation of the vampire's essential helplessness," as Jack Kerouac argues,[22] it is because, I think, Nina's offer of a "pure" heart humanizes Nosferatu. She evokes his desire and reveals his weakness, and Murnau visually represents this process by reducing Nosferatu's dominant stature, until we see his death in an eye-level medium shot quite unlike the many low-angle shots of the vampire earlier in the film.

Murnau then cuts to Renfield securely bound in his prison cell (though it never is revealed how the madman was recaptured). "The Master is dead," Renfield immediately realizes, and his head slumps forward to his chest. It does not matter whether Renfield actually dies along with his Master; all that is important for Bremen is that the insane real estate agent has been rendered harmless, not because of the ropes that bind him, but because Nina has broken Nosferatu's spell and thereby drained Renfield's maniacal, villainous energy as well. Thus, appropriately, the next shot returns us to Nina, whose eyes open directly after Renfield's close, and the young woman looks around her sunlit bedroom, aware of the vampire's absence. She reaches out for her husband and calls his name, as she had awakened the previous night and called Nosferatu. In the street Jonathan and Van Helsing approach the Harkers' home, and all the clues point toward a reunion of the Harkers in the new dawn that will climax an eminently happy resolution.

German film historian Lotte Eisner, in fact, describes just such an ending that appeared in a 1930 bowdlerized version of *Nosferatu* entitled *Die Zwoelfte Stunde (The Twelfth Hour).*[23] This film concluded with a final image of the Harkers again living in simple happiness. Murnau's "symphony of horror," however, insists that health and well-being have their price. Jonathan rushes into the bedroom and embraces Nina for an instant before she suddenly goes limp and dies in his arms. Murnau then cuts to a shot looking into the bedroom through a doorway, as Van Helsing peers in on Jonathan, who lies on the bed holding Nina's corpse. Once again, the frame-within-the-frame creates a sense of restriction and confinement. This tableau signifies, in Guillermo's words, the "irreducible triumph of death,"[24] and much more as well, including, for example, Jonathan's inability to prevent his wife's sacrifice, to protect her, or to save her by his love. Van Helsing, the onlooker, appears even more ineffectual and incapable of helping Nina (or Bremen for that matter); he can only witness her death from outside the bedroom, the private area where the fate of Bremen was decided. The most important "secrets" still remain outside the Professor's purview. Ironically, Jonathan's business trip to Transylvania and his departure from home in the opening of *Nosferatu* have led inevitably to this domestic tragedy. Indeed, only in this final image of the Harkers, after Nina has sacrificed her "pure" heart to the vampire, do Jonathan and his wife share the same bed—their marriage ends before it can truly begin.

The price the Harkers must pay, the personal suffering memorialized in the last image of the bedroom—a private place from which we are finally excluded—yields public benefits, for as a title informs us: "And at that moment, as if by a miracle, the sick stopped dying, and the oppressing shadow of the vampire disappeared in the morning sun." "*That* moment" is as much the moment of Nina's death as of Nosferatu's disintegration; it is the moment when the ritual cure is completed, and the society—not the savior—reaps the benefits. We do not actually see Bremen's miraculous recovery, and Guillermo convincingly argues that the light of the morning sun could do nothing to dispel "the absolute barrenness, the inescapable hostility of that outside world."[25] Nina's sacrifice does not restore the comfortable Eden that Jonathan thinks he inhabits in the beginning of the film. We do not know exactly what *is* salvaged or restored, only that the plague has ended. The final image of the film is a long shot looking up toward the ruins of what seems to be Castle Dracula. The effect of Nina's action apparently extends even into the Land of Phantoms, for the tower that Jonathan sees as he first approaches the castle has at last been leveled.[26] We are left not with the restoration or the triumph of the living, but with ruins, a synecdoche for the vampire's absence.

Nosferatu has been destroyed, Renfield is no longer a menace, the plague has ended, and Castle Dracula is in ruins—the threat in all its manifestations has been vanquished, and Bremen is safe and healthy through no effort of its own. Such is the stuff closed endings are made of. The final title of the film that I quoted earlier should remind us that *Nosferatu* has been "narrated" from the "diary of Johann Cavallius, able historian of the city of Bremen." (In the print I have studied, the first image of *Nosferatu* is an old book that opens to begin the film.) This story of the "terrible epidemic" in 1838 has long since ended, and any mystery about it has been understood by the omniscient historian/narrator who addresses us in the titles at several points in the film. This narrator, following Cavallius, is satisfied to have discerned the "origin" (beginning) and "climax" (end) of the epidemic in the "innocent figures of Jonathan Harker and his young wife, Nina." The narrator's account ends with Bremen miraculously freed from the shadow of the plague and from foreign predatory evil and native homicidal madness as well. A similarly closed story is told by the pious, sensible saddler who narrates Defoe's *A Journal of the Plague Year*, but the saddler sees in the end of London's epidemic a manifestation of God's power and mercy: "Nothing but the immediate finger of God, nothing but omnipotent power, could have done it. The contagion despised all medicine; death raged in every corner." And after "men everywhere began to despair . . . it pleased God, with a most agreeable surprize, to cause the fury of it to abate."[27]

What troubles the saddler is that men soon forgot God's "works" after He "disarmed this enemy"; so, in effect, London at the end of *A Journal of the Plague Year* is moving toward another terrifying dispensation of God's wrath.[28] The conclusion of *Nosferatu*, however, is marked by neither the prospect of a new epidemic sent forth by an angry God nor the realization, such as Doctor Rieux makes at the end of Albert Camus's *The Plague*, "that the plague bacillus never dies or disappears for good . . . perhaps the day would come when, for the bane and the enlightening of men, it would rouse up its rats again and send them forth to die in a happy city."[29] What complicates the resolution of Murnau's film is not the persistence of the threat, but the final fate of Jonathan and Nina. Her death and his grief remind us that the public and the private, the city and the home, are two different realms and that the return of civic well-being—deemed a "miracle"—is, in fact, the product of private suffering. The inclusion of the elderly Van Helsing in the final image of the Harkers reaffirms the sense that it is the young in *Nosferatu* who are sacrificed to save what is deemed most valuable and necessary. This situation, we should note, is exactly the reverse of the ending of Browning's *Dracula*, the next film version of Stoker's novel to appear after *Nosferatu*.

Is Bremen worth the sacrifice of Nina, whose dreams and fears as well as her love make her irreplaceable? (Herzog in *Nosferatu the Vampyre* will pose this question much more directly. His film, in fact, taught me to see the importance of this question in Murnau's *Nosferatu*.) The hunters in Stoker's novel are rewarded for having shed "tears and blood" (D, 303). Quincey's death *is* justified, for he has helped save Mina and all of humankind, and he dies seeing his earthly reward and foreseeing a heavenly reward, if only in the peace of "true death." Nina receives no earthly comfort or spiritual revelation and no promise of heavenly reward—her death seems almost as surprising to her as it is to Jonathan, since *The Book of Vampires* does not explain that the woman pure of heart will die along with the creature she destroys.[30] If, as I have suggested throughout this study, in stories of the confrontation between the living and the undead the fittest survive, then these stories are about how we define and characterize fitness. Murnau's *Nosferatu* proves that the fittest—Bremen in this case—need not be the most morally and spiritually deserving.

Before we see the living or the undead in *Nosferatu the Vampyre*, we see the dead—not as cadavers in a morgue or skeletons in a Gothic tableau, but as mummies caught forever at the instant of death. The

The vampire (Max Schreck)—predatory, awkwardly rigid, phallic-shaped—journeys to the bourgeois world in F. W. Murnau's *Nosferatu, A Symphony of Horror* (1922). The low-angle camera set-up suggests Nosferatu's dominant stature in relation to the helpless crew of the ship. (Museum of Modern Art/Film Stills Archive)

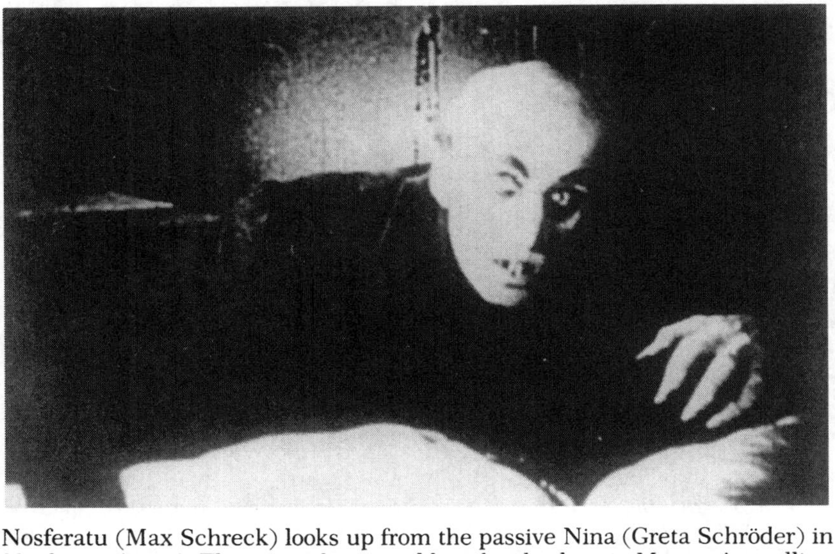

Nosferatu (Max Schreck) looks up from the passive Nina (Greta Schröder) in *Nosferatu* (1922). There is no heroic wild work to be done in Murnau's retelling of Stoker's *Dracula*; a single, willing, sacrificial female victim is required, not a group of armed hunters. (Museum of Modern Art/Film Stills Archive)

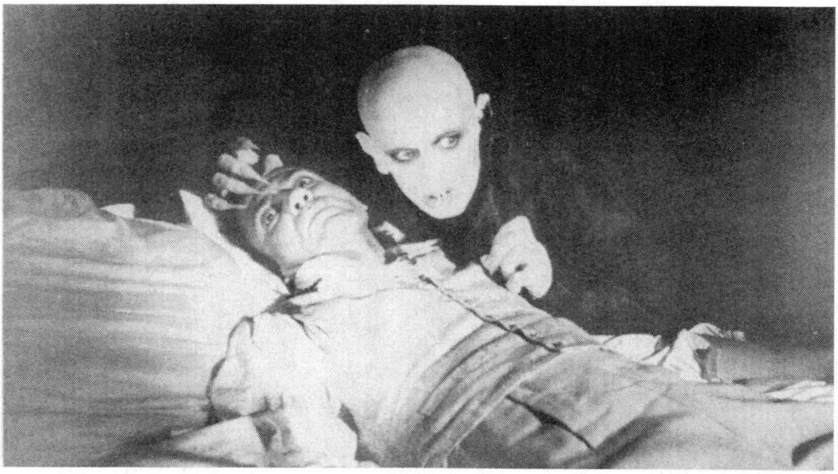

Nosferatu (Klaus Kinski) lifts his head from the neck of Jonathan Harker (Bruno Ganz) in Werner Herzog's *Nosferatu the Vampyre* (1979), as if the vampire feels the strength of Lucy Harker's fear and love in a way that Jonathan never does.

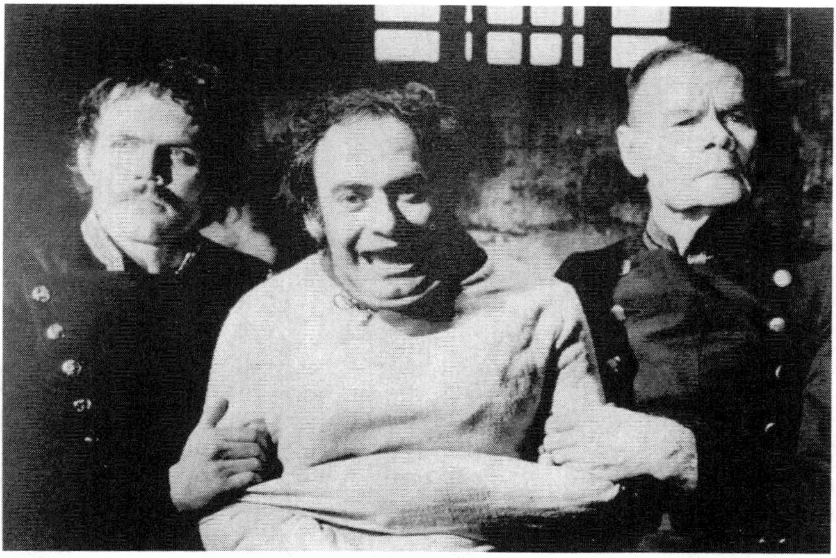

Baffled by Renfield's "wandering" mind, Van Helsing has the madman locked up in *Nosferatu the Vampyre* (1979). The camera pauses before this image of Renfield (Roland Topor) restrained by two attendants, a scene that resembles a parody of an allegorical painting about lunacy under institutional care. Very few sights in Transylvania can match the strangeness and absurdity of this slice of Wismar's life.

To the accompaniment of *Das Rheingold*, the rats in *Nosferatu the Vampyre* (1979) enter the quaint, clean, bourgeois city en masse, and Wismar lies before them unprotected and ready to be overrun.

From high above the townsquare in *Nosferatu the Vampyre* (1979), the camera sees Wismar's men engaged in a communal ritual that seems to embody order, dignity, and stoical acceptance of death. When seen from ground level, however, this ritual is revealed to be a meaningless gesture, the last recourse of a male ruling class that can neither protect the living nor bury the dead.

Dressed all in black, surrounded by darkness as he reflects on time and death, Nosferatu (Klaus Kinski) in Herzog's film appears as a disembodied head—more pathetic and alone than monstrous or threatening or aristocratically domineering.

Immediately before Nosferatu's arrival Lucy (Isabelle Adjani) in *Nosferatu the Vampyre* (1979) is in danger of succumbing to the stasis of Wismar and becoming a still life. She is inside a building, enclosed by glass that is rippled and pocked with impurities, framed by curtains and bars. Apparently a mechanical gaze has replaced her visionary ability to see.

Blinded by the rosy beams of the morning sun, Nosferatu (Klaus Kinski) in Herzog's film wheezes as if all the life is being sucked out of him. Nosferatu—ripped by pain, his centuries of futility over—becomes fully human as a result of Lucy's sacrifice.

dead are together in a cave—a gruesome parody of the individual grave—that has no beginning or end, entrance or exit, although there is light sufficient for us to see the erect bodies of men, women, and children that form a line along one wall, as if they have been propped up for display.[31] At first, Herzog cuts from one shot to the next, from a group of four bodies, including a child wearing a bonnet, to a face seen in close-up. The droning, repetitive sound of a slow chant (performed by voices, organ, and gong) seems almost to surround the bodies and fill the cave with a never-ending, melodyless hymn.[32] The editing of the images is not quite in synchronization with the hypnotizing cadence of this music, and neither is the camera when it begins its hand-held movement inside the cave. Without settling into the rhythms of the music, the camera explores this world of the dead by tilting down, for example, from the head to the spindly legs and old-fashioned, now pathetically incongruous short boots worn by one of the mummies. Faces, however, are what most attract the camera, and rightfully so, for it is in their faces that these victims preserve their individuality and humanity. Each face is unique in physiognomy and in the way that the eyes are absent and the mouth and expression register terror or acquiescence or nonawareness. After several images the full German title of the film appears (*Nosferatu, Phantom der Nacht* [1979]) superimposed over a face contracted and strained in a silent scream, as if this mummy is warning us of the phantom of the night. Yet finally it is death and not the vampire that these dead speak of—death that is not peaceful (and can be terrifying and agonizing), that cuts life short, and that arrives and presents itself differently to every human being. The camera moves to another face, then another, pausing once again in a gesture of interrogation and curiosity as it peers at the empty eye sockets and open mouth of a man who has seen what the camera cannot see. The row of mummies has no end; the camera does not search for a way out of the cave, if indeed there is an exit.

With an abrupt cut, Herzog removes us from the underworld, replacing the cave with a shimmering, hazy blue expanse of what is presumably moonlight through which a bat flies in extreme slow-motion without a point of origin or destination.[33] This image unites the natural and the supernatural, and through slow-motion it extends the limits of what can be seen. Like the mummies, the bat suddenly appears; it is not merely another detail in a descriptive sequence. The mummies are dead, enclosed in a cave. The bat is alive and alone, with no limits to its motion, although Herzog's use of slow-motion suggests that the blue atmosphere itself is heavy and resistant to the bat's graceful flight. In the cave a steady pulse, like an electronic heartbeat, mingles with the droning music. When the bat appears, this pulse is replaced by the whooshing sound of the wind. The chant of the dead, however, continues during the bat's flight, linking the cave and the blue moonlight, the mummies and the bat, together into one sequence that ends when Lucy Harker's scream silences the circling sound.

From the bat flying in the field of blue light, Herzog cuts to Lucy asleep in bed. With a scream, she snaps awake and sits up, her eyes wide open in terror. Like certain of the mummies, she stares toward the camera. Near her open window what seems to be a "real" bat emerges from the curtains and flies off. Jonathan, also dressed in white nightclothes, leaves his twin bed and comforts Lucy, assuring her that "it's all right." "I see something horrible," Lucy says, then clings to her husband as both lie down together in her bed—as if to suggest that *Nosferatu the Vampyre* will in some respect begin where Murnau's *Nosferatu* ends, with the Harkers together in bed. This bedroom, however, is not bathed in the purifying light of dawn, but in moonlight and deep shadows that contrast with the whiteness of Jonathan and Lucy's nightclothes and of the furniture and bedding as well.

Like the cave of the dead and the bat flying in slow-motion, Lucy's awakening precedes our first sight of Wismar, the city in which the Harkers live in *Nosferatu the Vampyre*. Together, these opening images constitute a prologue that has no source in Murnau's *Nosferatu*. Death (the mummies) and isolation (the bat) are among the most important themes and situations in Herzog's film, and Lucy's awakening, which introduces us to the world of living human beings, will continue throughout the film until her death. This opening, Jacques Petat argues, is also a "reference" to *Nosferatu* in that the mummies are a "metaphor" for Murnau's film, which Herzog will bring to a new life.[34] A more convincing case can be made, I think, that the prologue in *Nosferatu the Vampyre* refers in various ways back to Herzog's own earlier films. For example, the mummies call to mind the half-decayed corpse that hangs in a cannibal village in *Aguirre, The Wrath of God* (1972), a death's-head that the camera pauses to view in much the same way that it views the bodies in the cave of the dead. Florian Fricke's music in *Nosferatu the Vampyre* also recalls the music he composed for *Aguirre*. Extreme slow-motion is associated in both *Nosferatu the Vampyre* and *The Great Ecstasy of the Woodsculptor*

Steiner (1974) with the beauty, mystery, and isolation of flight. These and other self-references (like the casting as the vampire of Klaus Kinski, who played Aguirre and was soon to play Woyzeck and later the lead character in *Fitzcarraldo* for Herzog) provide an important context for *Nosferatu the Vampyre*.[35] Yet finally the introduction to the film is most interesting in what it suggests about Lucy.

Lucy, not her husband as in Murnau's *Nosferatu*, is the first of the living whom we see in Herzog's film. Her scream as she awakens ends the repetitive music and ushers in the "objective" world of synchronous sound and dialogue. Her scream and sudden awakening also suggest that she has had a nightmare, and, since a bat flies out the window of her bedroom directly after her eyes open, one possible conclusion is that the image of the bat flying in slow-motion through the blue moonlight has been part of Lucy's dream, the substance of her nightmare, which is somehow linked to the animal at her window. "I see something horrible," she tells Jonathan, though he sees nothing, and no dream disturbs his sleep. What she "sees" does not disappear like the animal at her window in the light of waking consciousness; "something horrible" is still present for Lucy. Her vision—what and how she sees—is as important in *Nosferatu the Vampyre* as Kaspar Hauser's vision is in Herzog's *Every Man for Himself and God Against All* (1974), although Kaspar's dreams and reveries are clearly announced and identified as such. If the flying bat could be taken to be Lucy's subjective image, why not the cave of the mummies as well, since the same music unites the two sequences before Lucy's awakening? We would then enter the film through Lucy's subjective point of view, her premonitions, fears, and dreams of death and isolation, of an endless cave and thick, almost palpable blue light. Herzog does not unequivocally indicate the origin of these opening images through voice-over narration or visual clues, but by juxtaposing them with Lucy's awakening, he alerts us to possible connections and to Lucy's role as the one who sees, who dreams, and who awakens alone and in terror.

Jonathan is still able to comfort his wife at this point in their relationship; Lucy can cover her eyes in her husband's embrace. By calming her, he ushers in the morning, when the camera—and later Jonathan as well—moves from the Harkers' bedroom to the quaintly beautiful streets of Wismar. The first two images of Wismar show the city in the bright light of early morning with no sign of human life. Seen from two different stationary, eye-level angles, Wismar seems to consist of a series of canals spanned by small stone bridges and of rows of unimposing buildings that line clean, winding streets. The city is a tribute to man's ability to refashion the natural world completely into an urban environment that serves and protects its inhabitants, facilitating city life without trapping people in an ugly, polluted prison. (During the filming of *Nosferatu the Vampyre* in Delft, Herzog told a press conference that he chose the city because "it's so well-ordered, so neat and beautiful, so bourgeois."[36]) Jonathan will later complain about the "canals that circle back on themselves," but in these introductory images of Wismar the water is almost completely still, so that the canals serve only to reflect buildings, bridges, and man's other works. Unlike the waves at the shore or the river in the Carpathian Mountains, in Wismar water and nature in general have no vitality and bring forth no change. The canals are picturesque but stagnant, perhaps picturesque because they are stagnant. The city is perilously close to becoming a still life whose stasis seems almost to freeze the camera into immobility, and the stilling of life will prove to be a constant threat throughout *Nosferatu the Vampyre*. If the canals are to Wismar as blood is to a living body, as Jean Roy suggests,[37] then the city is a corpse and its quaint charm a cosmetic trick.

As in Murnau's *Nosferatu*, in Herzog's film the city is initially associated with Jonathan, most notably when he walks to work in the first sequence after the opening credits end. Bringing life to the empty, still city, Wismar's inhabitants engage in unhurried commerce, conversation, and other everyday activity, all beautifully evoked in a long shot as the camera pans to follow Jonathan as he leaves his home and walks down an uncrowded but busy street next to a canal. (The scene very much calls to mind a nineteenth-century genre painting, as well as Jan Vermeer's *View of Delft* and *Street in Delft*.) The panning movement of the camera emphasizes Jonathan, who stands out also because he walks more stridently than anyone else, moving right to left against the general flow of movement in the image. Apparently for Jonathan time is not to be wasted. At home, Jonathan paused only long enough to give Lucy a quick kiss good-bye before he rushed off like a commuter with a train to catch. Jonathan does not stride with the self-satisfaction and naive optimism of his counterpart in Murnau's film, but he is ambitious, and his employer provides him with a destination "beyond the Carpathian Mountains" in Transylvania. The young man immediately agrees to accept this "mission," regardless of Renfield's cackling laughter when he describes Transylvania as "gloomy yet exciting." Jonathan accepts because only to him can Renfield entrust this important mission and because, Jonathan believes, "it will be good to escape this town for a while." That Wismar will, however, remain Jonathan's home is evident when he declares that he will use the "worthwhile" commission from this business trip to "buy Lucy a nicer house; she deserves better."

Lucy may deserve a "nicer house," but she obviously does not desire this or any other sign of upward social mobility. Lucy desires Jonathan. Like Nina in *Nosferatu*, Lucy remains at home while her husband goes to work; even the kitten she holds as Jonathan rushes off is an allusion to our first sight of Murnau's heroine. With her dark hair and extremely pale skin, Lucy resembles a character in a silent film, particularly when she is dressed in white as in the beginning of the film. Isabelle Adjani's often stylized, broad gestures as Lucy reinforce the connection between Lucy and Nina, both of whom are troubled and unremittingly serious from the outset. Lucy's anxiety and concern about Jonathan seem to be connected to her nightmare. The bright sunlight that illuminates the Harkers' home has not, it seems, been able to dispel whatever "horrible" thing she sees.

Although Herzog often shows Lucy inside the Harkers' small house, she does not come to emblemize the values of domesticity and the home. That is why Jonathan's idea that Lucy would appreciate or covet a "better house" seems so foolish, unless the statement is taken as a transposition of his own aspirations. For Lucy, love is the primary value. "It is because my love is so strong," she tells Jonathan, "that I feel this strange, deadly fear." Lucy makes this confession not in her home or even inside the city but at the shore while she and Jonathan walk arm in arm along the sand with no one else in sight. Before her husband's departure, it is Lucy's idea to go to "the beach where we used to meet," and she will return alone to the shore during Jonathan's long absence. The breaking waves and the open sea and sky that seem to extend into eternity form the milieu in which Lucy can declare her love. Though hardly with the condescension of his counterpart in Murnau's film, Jonathan chooses to disregard his wife's fears and her vague "feeling" that he will be in "danger," just as later he will not heed the gypsies who warn him about the vampire's "phantom castle." He returns Lucy to Wismar and entrusts her to the care of friends to whom he declares that "she is dearer to me than all the world." Although he does not stay with Lucy, Jonathan does carry a small oval portrait of his wife enclosed in a locket—a still-life image the sight of which will send Dracula in search of the living woman and the love she bears, the very woman whom Jonathan has left behind, in what he himself calls his "blindness."

Jonathan disregards Lucy's fears—and hence her love as well—and rides on horseback through a stone arch and over a small bridge that connects Wismar to the expansive, mysterious world outside the city. Jonathan journeys to Castle Dracula; he is not transported. He chooses to leave Wismar (in Stoker's novel, Jonathan is never faced with a comparable choice; Mina has not warned him to forsake his business trip), and his decision seems to be much less a matter of opting for his job and his pocketbook as opposed to his wife's kisses and her vague misgivings than a matter of choosing to let go (quite literally) of Lucy's love and fear so that he can venture alone into a distant land of "wolves, robbers, and ghosts." Given Jonathan's fate in the concluding sequence of *Nosferatu the Vampyre*, we can say that with this decision Jonathan elects to be himself, rather than to be Lucy's husband, the object of her love.

Herzog uses music to differentiate the stages of Jonathan's journey from Wismar to Castle Dracula. As Jonathan leaves Lucy, a light, mantralike theme featuring guitar and percussion begins and continues until Jonathan crosses a wooden bridge in front of an isolated rural inn. Throughout this part of the journey—all in the daylight—Jonathan is on horseback. His movement is never impeded, and the path is easy to follow through rolling green countryside with fir trees covering distant hills. Jonathan has escaped Wismar and is alone. Even when he rides through a small town, where we can hear the sounds of life, no other people appear. As he approaches the inn, which is set off by itself in a lush meadow near the foot of the Carpathians, the voices of gypsies replace the music. Only synchronous sound is used during the scenes at the inn, as if to suggest that this place, with its buzz of human voices and barnyard sounds, is the last unquestionably "real" outpost before Jonathan enters the Land of Phantoms.

As I have noted, Jonathan Harker's brief sojourn at the inn is often a prominent scene in the retellings of *Dracula* (whereas in the novel, Stoker places much more emphasis on the young solicitor's coach rides), because it allows for a direct confrontation between the modern and the primitive, the urban and the rural, the skeptic and the superstitious, the one traveler and the group of local inhabitants—all contrasts that define Jonathan as much as does his response to the warnings he receives. In lieu of the well-meaning provincials in Dan Curtis's *Dracula* or the frightened (and obviously English) villagers in

Fisher's *Horror of Dracula* or the peasant community in Murnau's *Nosferatu*, Herzog offers a band of gypsies, whose language and faces—attracting the camera's gaze as did the faces of the mummies—are unlike anything we have seen or heard in Wismar. The innkeeper, who with his equally frightened wife is fair-skinned and speaks German, warns Jonathan of "evil spirits," and his wife will later enter the guest's room, hang a rosary around Jonathan's neck, cross herself, and hand him a book "about vampires and bloodsuckers, of corpses which devour their own flesh and of the living dead and of werewolves." For this woman, the cross is a protection against a panoply of evil monsters that roam the night. The gypsies, however, offer Jonathan a different warning, which has nothing to do with good or evil per se. Outside the inn at night, the camera scans the faces of the gypsies who are gathered around a campfire, and Jonathan listens as the innkeeper translates the gypsies' strange language: "He says you shouldn't go . . . the light suddenly divides and the land rises to heaven and falls to no one knows where. The gypsies believe there is no castle. It is only in people's imagination. He says it's a ruin, a phantom castle. Whoever ventures too far into the Land of Phantoms is lost."

Jonathan does not laugh at this warning with the amused disdain of a sophisticated modern man or dismiss it as an interesting local legend. He listens intently to the gypsies, and in the morning he sets out for Castle Dracula on foot because he cannot hire a coach to transport him to the Borgo Pass. Jonathan does not disregard or misapprehend the warnings of Lucy, the innkeeper, and the gypsies; he chooses to continue in spite of these warnings, however physically and psychically difficult the journey promises to be. The conclusion of *Nosferatu the Vampyre*, after Jonathan has become the "new" Nosferatu, suggests that at some level Jonathan undertakes this journey of escape knowing that in the Land of Phantoms, when he is free of all human connections, he will discover his own destiny and his true identity.

As Jonathan sets out from the inn on a well-worn path to the Borgo Pass, the droning music that accompanied the opening images of *Nosferatu the Vampyre* begins again, as if the chanting voices come from the mountains to call Jonathan forth. The music links this stage of Jonathan's journey with the cave of the dead and the slow-motion flight of the bat, perhaps signaling that this treacherous path leads him closer toward death and eerie isolation, toward what Lucy sees. Again the camera is often hand-held, moving behind Jonathan and accompanying him into a natural environment (just as it will later follow his exploration of Castle Dracula) that has been reduced to its turbulent, awesome, unmixed elements—rushing water, rocky, mountainous earth, and overcast nighttime sky. In Wismar nature is controlled, made manageable and decorative, and thus stagnant. Jonathan's distance from his home can be measured by the difference between Wismar's still canals and the powerful, unharnessed white water river that cuts its own channel through the Carpathian Mountains.

Only after Jonathan passes alone through the narrow gate between stone mountainside and river, moving forward toward a diffuse aura of blue light (like the sky the bat flies through), and then finds his own way up a hillside where no path exists, does he come within sight of Castle Dracula. At the crest of a hill, Jonathan sits like a solitary pilgrim in contemplation, silhouetted against the evening sky. The camera pans upward, following the direction of his stare. Between two peaks, heavy gray clouds slowly roll, obscuring the moonlight, and Richard Wagner's *Das Rheingold* begins, as if generated by this image of power and motion. Herzog has said that he used *Das Rheingold* in *Nosferatu the Vampyre* not because he sought to allude to the characters or action of Wagner's music-drama, but because "this particular piece of music fits extremely well."[38] Whatever its original context or its particular emotional resonances—the sense of gathering force and almost otherworldly majesty, for example, which surely fits in this context—*Das Rheingold* accrues connotative associations and added significance each time it is repeated in *Nosferatu the Vampyre*, after it announces and accompanies our first glimpse of Castle Dracula. Again suggesting that his film will continue beyond where Murnau's *Nosferatu* concludes, Herzog shows the ruins of Castle Dracula in silhouette in a low-angle long-shot very similar to the final image of Murnau's film. This image holds for several seconds, then fades out, and no reaction shot proves that Jonathan has shared our glimpse of the castle.[39] The young man makes the final part of his journey in a coach that suddenly appears on the road through the pass to carry him to his destination. Again the parallel with Murnau's film is clear, but Herzog does not rely on disruptive fast-motion or negative images to define the Land of Phantoms as Nosferatu's unnatural domain. Whether the Borgo Pass with its ruined castle and beams of blue light is a "real," if sublime and mysterious, natural environment or a phantom land controlled by the vampire or imagined by Jonathan, this realm reminds us of all that has been excluded, repressed, or controlled in Wismar.

Das Rheingold continues until the doors to Castle Dracula swing open as if in response to the young man's unspoken command, and Jonathan confronts his host. With a hat covering his bald head, Nosferatu stands in the doorway and quietly invites Jonathan inside, quite unlike the menacing figure in Murnau's film, who emerges out of a dark archway like an animal attracted to its prey. Jonathan follows the Count through a room suffused with blue light, then into a dark dining area illuminated by the glow of candles and fire light that underscores the differences between Jonathan and the vampire. The blue atmosphere through which the bat flies in slow-motion and the beams of blue light in the Borgo Pass are both now associated with Nosferatu, who will later emerge out of a dark tunnel backlit by a bluish aura to feed on Jonathan. Crossing the threshold of Castle Dracula, whose large arched doors clang shut behind him, the young man enters a domain that "seems sometimes unreal . . . like a dream"—even when daylight clarifies the interior design of the castle and when he can look out the window of his room to the sunlit countryside below. In the daytime the estate is less mysterious and forbidding than hauntingly empty and deceptively easy to see. And as Jonathan moves through the castle in the daytime, tremulous electronic music mingles with the echoing sounds of his footsteps. Much more than Murnau, Herzog leaves open the possibility that the castle may exist "only in people's imagination," as the gypsy tells Jonathan. For example, after Jonathan explores the castle's labyrinth of narrow, smoothly contoured hallways, tests a series of locked doors that prevent his departure, and enters the room that has been specially prepared for him, Herzog inserts another low-angle long shot of the ruins framed against an ever-changing sky (filmed in time-lapse images). Jonathan awakens after his first night in the phantom castle to discover a table laid with dishes of beautifully prepared food and a young child who repeats one melody over and over on his out-of-tune violin. The dark-skinned child, who is as oblivious to Jonathan as Jonathan is to him, seems almost like an emissary from the gypsies, a reminder of warnings unheeded. The sound of the child's violin continues even when we see the long-shot of the ruined phantom castle.

Most disconcerting of all to Jonathan, of course, is his host, who is physically much more similar to Murnau's vampire than to any other incarnation of Count Dracula. Yet Herzog's Nosferatu often has a frailty that Murnau's vampire lacks and a broader range of expression—and therefore of emotion and sentiment—as well. Most important, Count Dracula in *Nosferatu the Vampyre* speaks. Murnau's vampire has three or four lines of dialogue that are presented in titles, but we hear Herzog's vampire speak, slowly, in a quiet voice that contrasts with the guttural, snarling whimpers he makes after he sees the blood on Jonathan's finger. At the sight of blood Nosferatu comes to life as a predator, unable to control his hunger. But he also comes to life later when he sees the portrait of Lucy that Jonathan inadvertently removes from his pocket along with the contract for the house in Wismar. (Jonathan's error here could also be read as an "unconscious" offer of Lucy to the vampire in exchange for the freedom Jonathan ultimately achieves as the new Nosferatu.) The vampire's long, pointed fingernails surround and clutch the portrait. Nosferatu's revitalization at the sight of Lucy suggests less animalistic appetite than the infatuation of the beast with the beauty—an infatuation that traditionally reveals the inner "humanity" of the beast. Nosferatu travels to Wismar not only with Lucy's "lovely throat" in mind, but also with a need to share Lucy's love.

Even though the vampire in *Nosferatu the Vampyre* at times looks like and gestures in an almost identical manner to Murnau's Nosferatu, what sets Herzog's Nosferatu apart from Murnau's is, according to Herzog, that "my vampire plays against his appendages—his long claws, his pointed fangs. He is so suffering, so human, so sad, so desperately longing for love that you don't see the claws and fangs any more."[40] During the scenes at Castle Dracula, this sadness is expressed in and through Nosferatu's language, his confessional yet abstract speech. *Nosferatu the Vampyre* is not the first work to portray the vampire as a figure whose sadness and suffering (especially concerning the pain of immortality and isolation) somehow humanize him. The title character in James Malcolm Rymer's *Varney the Vampyre or, The Feast of Blood* (1847), for example, has a "strange and fearful mixture of good and evil" in his "disposition," and he endures "periods of acute suffering, of intense misery" before his suicidal leap into Mount Vesuvius.[41] James Ursini and Alain Silver in *The Vampire Film* list several movies, including *House of Dracula* (1945) and *The Vampire's Ghost* (1945), that feature a "sympathetic male vampire,"[42] and this tradition persists in contemporary novels like *By Blood Alone* (1979), in which the undead protagonist describes the "unspeakable misery" of his accursed existence to a psychiatrist.[43] At the point in Stoker's novel where Count Dracula tells Jonathan of the Draculas' triumphs during the "warlike days," Herzog's Nosferatu allows his uncomprehending young guest to overhear a philosophical reverie: "I don't attach much importance to sunshine now, or the glittering fountains of youth. I love darkness and shadows where I can be alone with my thoughts. I am a descendant of an old family. Time is an abyss, profound as a thousand nights. Hear the howling outside. Centuries come and go. To be unable to grow old is terrible. Death is not the worst; there are things more horrible. Can you imagine enduring centuries, and each day experiencing the same futilities?" Dressed all in black, surrounded by darkness as he reflects on time and death, Nosferatu appears as a disembodied, chalky white head, just as he does when he listens to the music made by the "children of the night." This image pictures him as more pathetic and alone than monstrous or threatening or aristocratically domineering. It also suggests that Nosferatu is "so sad" because he is "alone with his thoughts," because his head—the source of his thoughts, language, memory—is not connected with his body—his hunger and appetite. He pursues Lucy in hopes of resolving this split and ending the centuries of the "same futilities."

While Jonathan is in Castle Dracula, Herzog cuts back three times to Lucy in Wismar, thereby insisting on Lucy's physical separation from her husband and also indicating how Jonathan's journey to Transylvania has insolubly linked his and Lucy's fate with Nosferatu's. In these scenes Lucy is alone or is in some way set apart from Wismar—like Jonathan in the Carpathian Mountains, like Nosferatu in his castle. For example, after Jonathan lapses into sleep while seated across from the Count during his first night in Castle Dracula, Herzog cuts to Lucy, who suddenly awakens in her bed, as in the beginning of the film. Yet here Lucy does not scream, even though a bat crawls up the curtains next to her open window. In terror she crosses her arms over her chest and leans back into a pool of moonlight. Again, Lucy's awareness—her state of being awake and in fear—is contrasted with Jonathan's sleep. The bat she sees is not literally the vampire, though eventually Nosferatu will also enter Lucy's bedroom, and he will be no less tangible and "natural" than the bat. With Jonathan gone, Lucy has no one on whom to turn for comfort. She is alone in her bed, then alone at the shore the next time we see her. Both of these scenes parallel earlier scenes of Jonathan and Lucy together in *Nosferatu the Vampyre*, and both signify Jonathan's absence and demonstrate how Lucy, in her love and fear, is isolated from the life of Wismar. Whether Jonathan merits her love or not, Lucy lives only to retrace their steps on the beach and then to experience in her dreams Jonathan's plight in Transylvania. Like Nina in Murnau's *Nosferatu*, Lucy in a trance leaves her bedroom in the Westenra house and enters the bluish moonlight, as if she, too, is crossing the threshold of Castle Dracula. Later, when Nosferatu moves toward Jonathan, Lucy in her bed recoils in terror, her eyes wide open with fear, as she clutches her neck and screams out "Jonathan!" In response, Nosferatu lifts his head from Jonathan's reclining body; the vampire feels the strength of Lucy's love and fear in a way that Jonathan never does.

As with Nina in *Nosferatu*, Lucy's sleepwalking and her apparently inexplicable nightmare are diagnosed as symptoms of a physiological ailment. In *Nosferatu the Vampyre*, however, Lucy's physician is Doctor Van Helsing, who is also in charge of the asylum in Wismar and thus is presented as a sort of town doctor and a confident spokesperson for science.[44] Though he does not lecture to attentive students, Van Helsing does have a microscope and other scientific apparatus, including body organs preserved in jars, in his office. Yet he seems completely baffled by Renfield's "wandering" mind and hysterical laughter, and he is equally "mystified" after examining the corpse of the captain of the *Demeter*. Van Helsing has Renfield placed in an "isolation cell," then tied into a straightjacket and restrained by two attendants. The camera pauses before this tableau—the fruit of Van Helsing's labor—as Renfield bounces up and down in his straightjacket, mumbling about the "rustling of sails," while the two uniformed attendants, who look half-blind and feeble-minded, attempt to sit perfectly still and hold the madman's arms. The barred window above and behind these three men reminds us that the guards, like the lunatic, are imprisoned. The scene resembles a parody of an allegorical painting about lunacy under institutional care; very few sights in Transylvania can match the strangeness and absurdity of this slice of Wismar's life. Soon after he is bound, the madman easily escapes, and the plague rages in Wismar regardless of Van Helsing's efforts on behalf of medicine, science, and sanity.

Following Murnau, Herzog establishes a network of correspondences by cutting between the vampire's voyage on the *Demeter*, Jonathan's attempt to return home by land, and various aspects of the bourgeois city. This section of *Nosferatu the Vampyre*, including the scenes involving Renfield and Van Helsing that I have already mentioned, reveals the power of the vampire and the vulnerability of the city even before Nosferatu and the rats complete their journey. On the *Demeter*, for example, we see only the captain as he writes in his log about the "strange presence on board," before tying himself to the wheel. No seamen even attempt to destroy the vampire, who is seen only once, moving across the darkened deck above the camera, which rests inside the hold (a camera set-up that directly alludes to the comparable set-up in *Nosferatu*). While the *Demeter* moves under full sail toward Wismar, Jonathan begins his journey home, for he realizes that "Lucy is in danger. . . . Evil is on the way." Yet Jonathan is seriously ill (in retrospect, it is clear that he has already begun his transformation into a vampire), and he never makes it to a hospital, only to the small hut of some gypsies who cannot understand his frantic warnings. After resisting the efforts of a nun to detain him, Jonathan rides toward Wismar with great urgency, but when he is finally transported to his home—after Nosferatu's arrival in Wismar—Jonathan suffers from delirium and a hypersensitivity to sunlight that Van Helsing erroneously diagnoses as "severe brain fever." By cutting from Van Helsing's feeble attempts to control Renfield to the captain of the *Demeter* and to Jonathan's last-ditch effort to "stop the black coffins!" Herzog emphasizes the failure and inadequacy of male authority figures, above all Van Helsing, who has absolutely no way of understanding and combatting what he and his city will soon face.

In direct contrast to Van Helsing, Lucy seems to sense what the future holds. Like Nina in Murnau's *Nosferatu*, Lucy sits alone and motionless in a small graveyard by the shore, facing away from the crosses and headstones (which are all tilted and askew in the sand, as in *Nosferatu*) and toward the sea. In her isolation and her concern for Jonathan, Lucy comes to this neglected site, with its neglected symbols of sacrifice and death. At this point Lucy does not know what action she can take to express her love and purge her fear, but she does know that any such action must be the work of man, not God. While she sits at the shore, her friend Mina brings no news from Jonathan, and she advises Lucy to "take comfort, the Lord will hear our prayers." "The Lord," Lucy replies, "is so far from us in the hour of distress." Lucy will soon realize that the traditional means for alleviating distress in her culture, though much "closer," offer no more help than the far-distant Lord. As she waits for news, and as her love and fear give way to longing and despair, Lucy is in danger of succumbing to stasis and becoming a still life, like the portrait Jonathan carries to Castle Dracula. It is almost as though Lucy's energy and state of wakefulness have been drained by an unseen vampire. The final image of Lucy before Nosferatu's arrival and Jonathan's return demonstrates her increasing lassitude. More beautiful than ever, Lucy stands behind a window; she is motionless except for the movement of her eyes from left to right. Only a mechanical, purposeless gaze remains—not her visionary ability to see. She is inside a building, enclosed by glass that is rippled and pocked with impurities, framed by curtains and by the bars of the window, and confined to only half of the image. When we see her in this way, we hear the repetitive chant that accompanied the film's opening images of the cave of the dead and the bat in slow-motion flight. In the bright daylight of Wismar Lucy is dying, and she does not awaken with a scream.

As Lucy gazes out the window, the reflection of a ship passes across the glass, like a foreshadowing of the *Demeter*'s imminent arrival in Wismar. This arrival, as in Murnau's *Nosferatu*, demonstrates the vulnerability and defenselessness of the city. The camera holds on another picturesque view of Wismar, seen from eye-level: still water fills the center of the image, with streets and buildings on both edges of the frame, and no motion until the *Demeter* glides slowly into the canal, entering from the lower right corner of the frame. After the ship has moved completely into our field of vision, it stops, its voyage complete. Nothing prevents the *Demeter*'s entrance. In fact, the ship fills the open space in the center of the image, thereby completing the design of the composition, and it fits so neatly into Wismar's empty waterway that this dock might have been custom-built for the *Demeter*.

Faced with this mysterious ship that has a dead man lashed to its wheel, the citizens of Wismar watch as two white-haired men in black frock coats begin their investigation. Except for a pair of small children, whom the camera pans down to observe, the groups of onlookers could be mannequins or background figures in a genre painting. Any action is left to the officials who lay down a gangplank to climb aboard the ship. (Ironically, the rats and the vampire come ashore on this same gangplank.) As in Murnau's film, these men remove the captain's corpse and his logbook, so that the investigation can be continued in a public meeting room, with doctors and a crowd of other, similarly well-dressed men in attendance. (In *Nosferatu the Vampyre*, the walls of this large room are lined from floor to ceiling with paintings and portraits; the art with which the male ruling class surrounds itself parallels and memorializes the picturesque yet stagnant still-life beauty of Wismar.) Even more explicitly than Murnau, and very much in keeping with the presentation of official and unofficial figures of authority in his earlier films like *Even Dwarfs Started Small* (1970) and

Every Man for Himself and God Against All, Herzog mocks the bourgeois gentlemen in this all-male assembly who put their trust in the "mystified" Van Helsing, then dash out of the building at the first mention of the plague—not unlike the rats who stream helter-skelter off the *Demeter*. With this action, what Philip Strick calls "the collapse of a smug and stifling bourgeois community" begins.[45]

Once these men, with the rest of the city's inhabitants, the onlookers, have scattered and disappeared, presumably into their own houses—"shut windows and doors!" one man yells as the meeting abruptly adjourns—the passengers onboard the *Demeter* can disembark with absolutely no difficulty and take possession of Wismar's deserted streets. As the rats begin to spread over the empty street in the daytime and as the vampire carries his coffin to its new resting place at night, we again hear *Das Rheingold*, which earlier accompanied our first glimpse of the ruined castle and the final stage of Jonathan's journey to his appointed meeting with Nosferatu. The distance between Wismar and the Carpathians has been bridged; the tenuous bonds that hold this quaint city together have been loosed. The camera pans over the rats until for a moment our field of vision is completely dominated by this disorganized mass that spreads over the street. What Herzog emphasizes is not that the rats are predatory or evil or diseased or possessed of extraordinary intelligence or physical skills (like, for example, the creatures that threaten London in James Herbert's *The Rats* or the rats that climb out of the pit in Edgar Allan Poe's *The Pit and the Pendulum*), but instead that these rats enter the city en masse, and Wismar lies before them ready to be overrun. Herzog's image of the rats disembarking has no direct source in Murnau's film, where the rats bearing pestilence follow the vampire out of the dark hold and then disappear into Bremen like evil emissaries from the underworld that cannot be seen to be combatted.

Herzog directly alludes to *Nosferatu*, however, in his depiction of the vampire's journey through the dark, vacant city to his new home, a building with boarded-up or broken windows that is almost identical to the property Jonathan sells Nosferatu in Murnau's film. (In *Nosferatu the Vampyre*, this deserted, rundown building is not shown during the opening sequence in Wismar; it is revealed only after the vampire's arrival.) As *Das Rheingold* continues, fully dominant over any natural sound, Nosferatu carries another coffin through a small, moonlit cemetery and into an abandoned church, in a scene that evokes not Murnau's suggestion about the absence of Christianity in Bremen, but Stoker's insistence on the decline of true faith in the selfish and skeptical modern world.

Only after the rats have moved into Wismar's vacant streets by day and Nosferatu into its vacant buildings by night is Jonathan transported back to his home. Lucy rushes to embrace her husband, but he pushes her away and demands to know "Who is this woman?" Lucy faints, and in the next scene when she reappears she seems to have lost her lethargy and gained a new independence and a determined resolve to take whatever action is necessary. Van Helsing diagnoses Jonathan's illness as "severe brain fever," though Jonathan's pallor and sensitivity to sunlight indicate that his transformation into a vampire is well under way. That Jonathan should not recognize Lucy is appropriate since he has ignored her "strange fears" and thus rejected her love by journeying to Castle Dracula. Jonathan never seems to know his wife. By the end of *Nosferatu the Vampyre*, he will have achieved the escape from Wismar and the isolation he seems to have desired from the first.

Even as Jonathan rejects Lucy, Nosferatu seeks her out. Soon after the vampire has entered Wismar, for example, Herzog shows Nosferatu looking in a window at Lucy, Jonathan, Van Helsing, Mina, and Mina's husband. Herzog presents this situation so as to emphasize what looks to be an irreconcilable split between the vampire alone under the bluish moonlight, casting his elongated shadow over the building, and the living gathered together as a group inside, illuminated by candlelight. Lucy and the others are unaware that they are being observed; Nosferatu is shut out, unable to hear their conversation.

Yet this distance can be bridged, even without the vampire receiving the invitation that traditionally precedes his entrance into his victim's bedroom. While Lucy, dressed in a white nightgown, sits before a mirror letting down her hair (she looks very much like she did earlier when she had her troubling dreams), the door behind her opens with a creak and Nosferatu enters. Their conversation has no parallel in Murnau's *Nosferatu* or any other vampire film I am familiar with. Count Dracula, we might say, speaks Lucy's language, for he confesses that "the absence of love is the most abject pain," and he proposes that she become his "ally" and provide "salvation" both for himself and for her husband by sharing the love she has "with" Jonathan. Although he casts no reflection when he enters the room, as Nosferatu speaks, he is reflected in Lucy's mirror, as if he is humanized in her presence. Even in the medium close-ups that isolate him in the frame (again like a talking head), Nosferatu's face is less chalky white and more wrinkled than it was at the castle. Unlike Jonathan, who in Castle Dracula is speechless after his host speculates about death and the futility of existence, Lucy responds to the vampire's appeal by declaring her own belief in the "cruel certainty" of death, the inviolability of her love for her husband, "even if Jonathan no longer knows me," and in the fact that "salvation comes from ourselves alone." Neither the letter nor the spirit of Lucy's statements could be uttered by Murnau's Nina or Stoker's Mina or any of the heroines in the retellings of *Dracula* that I discussed earlier. Without garlic or Christian talisman (although Lucy wears a gold cross, she does not use it as a defensive weapon), Lucy forces the vampire from her room, even though *The Book of Vampires* counsels those whom the vampire "doth approach" to "abandon all hope." Jonathan may no longer know Lucy, but she knows herself and stares at her own reflection in the mirror after she tells Count Dracula that "salvation" in the face of death and unrequited love "depends on ourselves alone." With whimpering moans of frustrated desire, the vampire departs.

Lucy's victory in this private confrontation with Nosferatu highlights by way of contrast the ease with which the plague overruns Wismar. Like Murnau, Herzog focuses on neither the disease itself nor the agonizing death it brings, but rather on its effects on the city and the citizens' futile attempts to maintain some type of order. The coming of the vampire in Murnau's *Nosferatu* reveals how confining and defenseless Bremen truly is. In lieu of the narrow residential street, barely wide enough for a procession of coffins, that become so central in Murnau's film, Herzog offers Wismar's expansive townsquare, which opens in front of what seems to be a large church and is bordered by rows of smaller buildings. An overhead shot reveals that this enclosed, paved area—with one statue in its center and no trees or fountains—is the heart of the city. We do not see the square until Nosferatu literally leads us into it at night, when it is completely empty because the people of Wismar have deserted the public streets to seek private refuge behind locked doors and windows. Later, the vampire will lope through the moonlit square, in a scene that indicates how completely Wismar has become Nosferatu's domain.

While Lucy sits at her dining table in the sunlight and reads *The Book of Vampires* (with Jonathan seated in a corner behind her—now the homebound invalid whose odd chuckles sound more and more like

Renfield's maniacal laughter), black-suited men in top hats carry simple wooden coffins through the townsquare, their footsteps keeping time with tolling churchbells. As in Murnau's film, in *Nosferatu the Vampyre* these pallbearers participate in a communal ritual (though we never see this ritual completed) that at first seems to embody order, dignity, and stoical acceptance—qualities that from a certain perspective define the difference between the living, on the one hand, and the undead and the pestilent rats, on the other. Yet such a definition of the living does not take into account the qualities that make Lucy unique, and Herzog, more than Murnau, exposes the mindlessness and absurdity of the pallbearers' futile gesture. From high above the square, we look almost directly down on these anonymous men who move, like ants, in symmetrical rows. Their footsteps again follow the slow rhythm of tolling churchbells; their identical black suits and the identical white pine coffins they carry give this procession the look of a solemn, choreographed spectacle that only the camera and God high above can see and appreciate.

The scene changes completely, however, when Herzog cuts to a more human, eye-level perspective inside the square. The pallbearers still walk in unison, but the larger sense of symmetry and order is lost. Most important, the lines of indistinguishable men are now contrasted with Lucy, who enters the square after having learned "the cause of all this evil" from *The Book of Vampires*. Lucy's movements betray her fear, excitement, frustration, and confusion, and the camera, now hand-held, follows her and not the pallbearers, who maintain their mechanical, uniform pace. The camera, which often seems mesmerized into immobility when it views the vampire, here chooses to enter the world by accompanying Lucy. Her journey through the square (the first of two such eye-opening journeys she will take) is thus linked to the exploration of the cave of the dead in the opening of the film and to Jonathan's nighttime trek through the Borgo Pass, sequences that also feature a moving hand-held camera. What Lucy—and the viewer—sees in the square is as frightening and nightmarish in its way as the mummies or the Carpathian landscape. However much Lucy has been isolated from the public life of Wismar and however much she believes that "salvation comes from ourselves alone," she still enters the square with the intention of taking the knowledge to Wismar's socially sanctioned male authorities. "I must speak to the council," she insists, or to "the mayor then." One quartet of pallbearers pauses only long enough to tell her that the "council no longer exists" and that the mayor is dead. Their advice is for Lucy to "go home quickly." They carry on with their task without listening to Lucy's explanation of the cause and the cure for the plague. Like Jonathan before his mission to Transylvania, these men pursue their work regardless of Lucy. Behind her, row after row of pallbearers pass by, as more pine coffins are piled near a wall inside the square. Order is suddenly revealed to be a mindless, purposeless uniformity; communal ritual is meaningless repetition that obliterates individuality—it is the last recourse of a male ruling class that can neither protect the living nor bury the dead. On the ground near the coffins lie a dead horse and an overturned, wrecked carriage, two objects that point toward both the coming outbreak of disorder and the impossibility of escape. Surrounded by her fellow citizens, Lucy is more alone than ever before. The camera mimics her movement as she spins in confusion with apparently nowhere to turn.

Proving herself to be still, to some degree, a product of a society that instinctively turns to male figures of authority for guidance, Lucy presents her case to Doctor Van Helsing, even after the men in the square have ignored her. By default, Van Helsing occupies the place in society and in Lucy's life that would have been reserved for the priest or wise elder. Dressed like the pallbearers, the aged, physically feeble doctor becomes the spokesperson for science, which is for him both a method for discovering truth and the basis for all that makes the modern world an enlightened age. In his closed-mindedness Herzog's Van Helsing, needless to say, is the opposite of Stoker's Dutch professor. The success of Van Helsing in *Dracula* or in films like Fisher's *Horror of Dracula* or Saville's *Count Dracula* is matched by the doctor's failure in *Nosferatu the Vampyre* to diagnose correctly what ails Lucy and Jonathan, to discover what killed the captain of the *Demeter* and later Mina (though close-ups reveal similar wounds on the necks of both corpses), to prevent the plague from infecting all of Wismar, or even to keep Renfield securely imprisoned in the asylum (the madman escapes and leaves the city bound for Riga on the orders of his Master, who is more than glad to be rid of him). For Van Helsing, Lucy is a child who suffers from the same disease so often found among children, women, and the unenlightened. "My child," he tells her as she paces the room, "all this is a product of your imagination . . . you need rest and quiet. Your husband's illness has exhausted you." The rest and quiet Van Helsing prescribes would return Lucy to the state of suspended animation, of still life, which Wismar fosters. Her refusal to take the doctor's advice is at once a commitment to independent action and an affirmation of her own imagination and what she calls her "inner knowledge" and "faith"—a faith based, Lucy asserts, on "what I see with my own eyes." "I'll destroy this monster myself," Lucy declares and ushers Van Helsing out the door of her house. She is left with her husband, who asks: "Dear lady, where have we met before?" Only Nosferatu seems to know and to value Lucy for what she is.

Lucy remains true to what she has seen by night and by day; her faith finally is in herself. She is liberated as well as isolated by her realization that neither Jonathan, God, the city fathers, nor Van Helsing can offer her comfort or assistance. Her ensuing action is taken in spite of the men in her life, though it will presumably benefit these men.

In contrast to Murnau, Herzog has his heroine venture into the plague-infested streets—first to give information to the city council, then to seek out the vampire's lair. Climbing up steps that are covered with rats, Lucy enters the deserted building where Nosferatu has placed one of his coffins. Only eerie electronic chords and the sound of rats are heard as Lucy moves alone through the inside of this vast, shadowy, rundown building, until she sees the black coffin. The dirt inside the coffin is alive with rats when Lucy pushes aside the lid and sterilizes the Transylvanian earth with pieces of the host. There is no comparable scene in Murnau's *Nosferatu*, for Nina never enters the vampire's domain or relies on Christian talismans. Lucy's search for Nosferatu's coffin has some affinity with the vampire hunters' journey to Carfax Abbey in Stoker's novel, but the crucial difference between these two excursions is that Lucy is by herself, without the protection of armed comrades and rat-killing terriers and without the guidance of a surrogate father. Her action is even more noteworthy when it is placed in the context of the other stories of the living and the undead that I have discussed, in which the isolated individual, particularly the isolated woman, is almost always an unsuccessful hunter or an easily taken victim.

The sound effects, the rats, and the set design (particularly the dark, forbidding blind spots in the room, from which something could at any moment emerge) link Lucy's journey into the old building with countless other horror stories in which a character chooses to enter an area that has become the domain of the monster. Herzog contrasts this familiar situation, which is dependent on suspense and on the potentially fatal violation of taboos about the exploration of forbidden areas, with the much more disturbing horror of the next sequence of *Nosferatu the Vampyre*. As Lucy moves away from the coffin after she sterilizes the rat-filled earth, Herzog cuts again to the townsquare, which the camera slowly pans from eyelevel: closed coffins rest on the ground and are propped against buildings along with thin wooden crosses; small bonfires burn unattended, spreading a smoky haze over the area; an elderly woman dressed in black sits motionless on a straight-backed chair, and other pieces of furniture are scattered around her; a sheep and two large pigs meander through the debris, and one of the pigs defecates on the cobblestones. During these panning shots, the music that was heard in the deserted building continues, adding to the dreamlike sense of unreality, of the city suddenly cut loose from its moorings. The anonymous pallbearers have disappeared leaving their coffins behind, and the townsquare looks like a refugee camp without any refugees. It is strewn with possessions that are no longer anyone's private property and with domesticated animals that seem to be lost in their new freedom. During this pan and the following stationary shot, Wismar looks very much like Basse-Terre, the city in Herzog's 1976 documentary, *La Soufrière*, which was evacuated because of the threat of a volcanic explosion, and like the courtyard of the institution after the anarchic inmates revolt in *Even Dwarfs Started Small.*

Wismar, however, is not yet a ghost town. The next shot in *Nosferatu the Vampyre* begins with the blue sky and tilts down the front of the church to take in the entire townsquare from high overhead. The same camera set-up was used earlier to reveal the orderly march of the pallbearers. Now the square appears as a disorderly field of random action, partly obscured by drifting clouds of smoke. If "the Lord is so far from us in our hour of distress," as Lucy believes, then perhaps these overhead extreme long shots approximate His point of view, as far above the human comedy in the square as it is above the *Demeter* as it carries Nosferatu to Wismar.

As he had done in the earlier sequence when Lucy confronted the pallbearers, Herzog again directly juxtaposes the distanced, overhead viewpoint with a moving hand-held camera that accompanies Lucy as she enters the square. The choral music that begins with the overhead shot continues while Lucy walks into the square, where we hear only this music, and no synchronous sound. The disjunction between sound and image adds to the disorienting strangeness of Lucy's journey through Wismar's dance of death, especially since some of the revelers are playing musical instruments, and many more are twirling to a much faster rhythm than the solemn choral melody we hear. As throughout *Nosferatu the Vampyre*, Herzog's emphasis in this important sequence is on what and how Lucy, in her isolation, sees. Spread before her is a swirl of human activity, played out amid the furniture, animals, fires, and identical closed coffins that were shown in the opening images of this sequence. Whereas Bremen's inhabitants in Murnau's *Nosferatu*, after being confined to their homes and helplessly falling prey to the plague, finally take to the streets in search of a scapegoat, the citizens of Wismar spill into the townsquare with the intention of enjoying life before their imminent, inevitable death.[46] Whatever black-suited men from the procession of pallbearers remain in the square now mingle with a diverse crowd composed of women as well as men and young as well as old. Drinking and smiling, these people dance to music we cannot hear and reach out for Lucy, trying to pull her into their futile celebration. In overhead shots we see her escape from one circle of dancers and spin away from the grasp of another man. The hand-held camera then moves with Lucy through the chaotic action that always seems about to engulf her, as she looks with bewilderment on the revelers, including one man who stands upon a table and attempts to mount a goat. Earlier, soon after Jonathan was returned home, Lucy looked out into the street and asked Van Helsing: "Is it possible we'vè all gone mad and will wake up one day in straitjackets?" In the townsquare she sees her fear come true. Once the bonds of order and decorum are loosed and the stagnant, picturesque beauty shattered, the newfound freedom of the citizens of Wismar explodes in a burst of communal madness, which is here associated with the acting out of private desires in a public, communal setting; there are no straitjackets because there are no attendants and because the plague will soon halt this saturnalia.

At the end of Lucy's journey through the square, after she has become a stranger in a land become suddenly strange, the choral music fades out and is replaced by natural synchronous sound, as if to signal a return to reality (as at the country inn, where Jonathan heard the warnings of the gypsies). Herzog cuts from the revelers to the rats, which climb up a small flight of stairs and swarm over a row of coffins, establishing their dominion over Wismar, as nature reclaims the paved and civilized bourgeois city. It is the rats' squeaking that replaces the choir on the soundtrack, as the camera slowly moves over one last group of doomed citizens who are seated at a large, elegantly set table (recalling the table of food that Jonathan finds at Castle Dracula). The men wear dark suits like the pallbearers, and the women are equally well dressed. These people are not dancing with drunken abandon or cavorting with animals; they are more normal, more sane, which is to say that they maintain standards of etiquette and decorum in their orderly last supper. This order could well be the maddest response of all, for rats crawl over the feet of these people, who smile, oblivious to the sound and the touch of the rats. The feasters, like the dancers, attempt to include Lucy in their final celebration. "Won't you drink with us?" one of the men asks her. "Be our guest. We have the plague so we rejoice at every remaining day." During her final journey through the townsquare, the danger for Lucy is that she will be captured and infected by these groups of celebrants, apparently the only type of community that can emerge in Wismar. Before Lucy can respond to the man's invitation with anything except bewilderment, Herzog cuts to the row of coffins, now covered with rats, and then back to the table seen from the same camera set-up as during the feast, but now the people are gone, and the table is alive with rats who also have spread over the ground and beyond the limits of this framed image. Wismar's short-lived festivities are over; the townsquare belongs to the rats, which are as oblivious to man's attempts at order as they are to man's displays of disorder.

Having survived her long journey through the city, Lucy is called upon to witness one more "horrible" sight, the corpse of her friend Mina, whose neck bears two bloody wounds. ("It is certainly not the plague," Van Helsing says with reassuring confidence.) "I know what I have to do," Lucy declares, and she follows the instructions of *The Book of Vampires*, which is, in Herzog's film as in Murnau's, a relic of the superstitious, premodern world.[47] The rituals enacted by Lucy and Nina differ, though both call for a "woman pure in heart" to keep the vampire by her side until he is destroyed by "the first light of day." Before Nosferatu's arrival in her bedroom, Lucy crumbles the host and sprinkles it on the ground around Jonathan, who still sits in his corner of the Harkers' home. Neither the host nor the small cross Lucy wears throughout *Nosferatu the Vampyre* are present in Murnau's *Nosferatu*. These objects identify Lucy as a Christian, yet it is not the cross, but Lucy herself and the beams of first light that destroy Nosferatu. She succeeds because she is pure of heart, not because she is armed with sacred weapons. In *Nosferatu* Nina's purity seems to be linked to her childish, virginal innocence. Lucy is not childlike, and her attitude toward Jonathan, for example, never suggests that she is technically a virgin. (Nina looks and acts as if she could well be.) So in what sense is she pure of heart? Lucy's purity, it seems to me, is reflected in the way she remains true to herself, to the love and fear she feels, to what she sees—without living solely in terms of her own ego and without shunning the earthly life. Lucy is pure in that she is uncontaminated by Wismar.

Lucy does not need to throw open her bedroom window as an invitation to the vampire, and Nosferatu as he approaches casts no ominous shadow that wrenches at her heart. Herzog presents the encounter of Lucy and the vampire in a manner that recalls certain details of Murnau's film (the physical appearance of Nosferatu; the position of the two figures as the woman lies on the bed and the vampire kneels next to her; and the sunlight that suddenly floods the room, for example), though these parallels in turn highlight significant dissimilarities. Lucy, unlike Nina, is awake. She guides the vampire to her throat, then draws him to her again when he is about to depart before dawn. When the sun does rise, Nosferatu does not disintegrate in the daylight as in Murnau's film. The rosy beams blind him, and he wheezes as if all the life is being sucked out of him, then collapses to the floor in convulsions before curling into a fetal position. Lucy sees the sunlight and begins to smile, then she gasps in surprise and pain and dies without having been reunited with her husband. Together, these details all work to render the vampire more human (even when we quite distinctly hear him sink his teeth into Lucy's neck and drink her blood) and the sacrificial victim more isolated and more conscious of her own actions.

As well as alluding to and commenting upon Murnau's film, this sequence in Lucy's bedroom also refers back in various ways to the opening of *Nosferatu the Vampyre*, clarifying the significance of certain motifs that are announced in the first sequence of the film and suggesting the distance traveled between Lucy's awakening and her death. For example, as in our initial sight of Lucy, at the end she is dressed in white, with her hair loose over the pillow of her narrow bed. In the beginning, she awakens with a scream and still sees "something horrible." At the end of the film, she finally returns to sleep, having taken Nosferatu instead of Jonathan as her husband and perhaps thereby finally having lived out what began as a terrifying dream. While the vampire drinks Lucy's blood, Herzog inserts three brief images of bats in slow-motion flight through a grainy blue expanse. As in the film's prologue, in which a similar bat appears, the origin of these images is not clearly identified, and the relationship, if any, between these bats and Nosferatu is not fully explained. According to *The Book of Vam-*

pires, "Nosferatu the Undead . . . can move through walls and doors. As a bat he flies into the chambers of the sleeping." John Badham, in his 1979 film adaptation of *Dracula*, shows right before our eyes the Count's physical transformation into a bat. Herzog's vampire, however, undergoes no such transformation, and the bats do not suddenly fly in slow-motion from the blue sky into Lucy's bedroom. As I noted earlier, Herzog's editing of the opening sequence suggests that the first image of slow-motion flight may be part of Lucy's dream. In this respect the bat does enter into the "chamber of the sleeping." The inclusion of similar slow-motion images at the end of the film further links the bat and the vampire, so that (perhaps) what Lucy sees in the beginning of the film are not only visions of isolation and death but also intimations of her coming encounter with Nosferatu. (Herzog inserts images of the bat in flight at one other point in the film, immediately after the captain of the *Demeter* ties himself to the wheel and before Nosferatu moves toward him in the darkness. Here Herzog explicitly associates the image of slow-motion flight with the vampire and the threat of his attack on the living.) At the end, long past being able to turn to Jonathan for help and comfort, Lucy herself directs the action and sets the scene—which is beautifully arranged to appeal to Nosferatu's desire for Lucy's love as well as her blood. As Bruce Kawin puts it, Lucy here "pursues her inner vision to the point of death" and thus vindicates her "autonomy."[48] To destroy the vampire, Lucy must face her fears and bring her nightmare to life.

Nosferatu's centuries of "experiencing the same futilities" are over. Through Lucy he finds death, if not salvation, or death that is his salvation. And in this death he takes on an expression strikingly similar to several of the mummies seen in the first sequence of the film. He has crossed from the undead into the dead—but, like the mummies, without the reassuring look of peace that signals "true death" in Stoker's *Dracula*. Ripped by pain, Nosferatu becomes fully human; like Lucy he knows that "only death is cruelly certain," a realization that belongs only to living human beings.

Lucy's fulfillment of the ritual, like Nina's, has immediate consequences for her husband and for society at large, though these consequences are very different in *Nosferatu the Vampyre* than in *Nosferatu*. As the cock crows, heralding the vampire's coming destruction, we see one brief exterior shot of Wismar. Again, as in the beginning of *Nosferatu the Vampyre*, the still canal water is part of a motionless tableau, an empty, picturesque, static world that is as oblivious to the sacrifice of the living as to the threat posed by the undead. Lucy's final action brings Wismar's citizens back into the streets and indirectly causes the life of the city to recommence. Immediately after her death we see a group of people gathered outside the Harkers' home. Upstairs in the bedroom, Van Helsing examines Lucy and sees the Count's corpse on the floor near her bed. "Now I know," the old man confesses, "if only I had listened to her before. A stake, a hammer! Quickly! I must destroy this monster once and for all."

Like his counterpart in Murnau's *Nosferatu*, Van Helsing in Herzog's film arrives too late. The young woman must die before this foolish man of science can be enlightened, and his traditional, violent actions with hammer and stake serve finally to free rather than destroy the monster. Armed with these weapons, Van Helsing climbs to the bedroom, then reenters the downstairs room dazed, with bright red blood on his hands and the stake he holds, more blood than is seen anywhere else in the film. Whomever Van Helsing has transfixed—for we do not actually see his actions—his bloody deed has been superfluous. Yet this action, does, ironically, help promote Wismar's return to normality. Two men enter the house, both dressed, as is Van Helsing, in black suits similar to those worn by the pallbearers. Without giving the doctor an opportunity to offer his "statement," one of the men declares: "You are under arrest, Doctor Van Helsing." Between Van Helsing and this authoritative speaker stands a second man, very old, small, and wizened, who holds what seems to be an oversized account book. (This old man resembles the official in Murnau's film who marks crosses on the doors of the infected houses in Bremen.) Suddenly the tone of *Nosferatu the Vampyre* shifts completely, and the conversation proceeds as follows:

First Man: Call the police.
Second Man: They are all dead.
First Man: Take him to prison then.
Second Man: The warders are all dead.
First Man: Arrest him anyway.
Second Man: How? I'm unarmed.
First Man: Arrest the man. You are a public official.
Second Man: I don't know.
Van Helsing: Take me where you want.

With this interchange Wismar returns to normal. The city does not require police or prison warders or armed protectors, but only one "public official"—any public official—and a citizen who believes in order and law and the need for public officials.[49] The official and the citizen are serious men whose conversation sounds like a bit of music-hall patter. In the context of what precedes this scene (Lucy's sacrifice, the destruction of Nosferatu) and what follows it (the emergence of a new vampire), the brief appearance of these representatives of Wismar's status quo becomes an absurd, black-comic interlude that hints at why the city reacted as it did to the spread of the plague. Unlike Murnau, Herzog does not indicate whether Lucy's action ends the epidemic, only that the beautiful city and its ruling class have survived.[50]

To make the irony of this penultimate scene of the film complete, Jonathan is present in the corner of the room behind these three men. It is Jonathan, in fact, who calls for help when Van Helsing climbs upstairs armed with hammer and stake. "Arrest him. He has killed the Count," Jonathan tells the two men when they enter the house, and his orders are soon carried out. Since they do not allow Van Helsing to make his statement, the citizen and the official do not know the truth about the situation. For them the evidence is clear-cut, and it is a criminal, not a monster, whom they are concerned with. Van Helsing, of course, is justly punished for his scientific close-mindedness and his condescending treatment of Lucy. The doctor is escorted out, clearing the room for Jonathan, who has witnessed this absurd confrontation with obvious satisfaction. After Jonathan has a maid sweep up the crumbled host that still imprisons him, he is free to leave the corner, for only we realize that his chalky pallor, long pointed fingernails, and ratlike teeth are proof that he has become Nosferatu, taking the Count's place much as the Count had taken Jonathan's place in the bedroom with Lucy.[51] Like Wismar, the vampire survives. What the world loses is Lucy, with her capacity for fear and love, her purity of heart, and her ability to see.

This new Nosferatu, unlike his predecessor, has not yet experienced centuries of futility, and Jonathan is impatient to begin his new undead existence. "Bring me my horse," he orders the maid, "I have much to do, now." Suddenly Herzog cuts to a flat expanse of shifting sand that stretches out from the camera until it meets the sky at a distant horizon. On horseback, Jonathan rides into the foreground of the frame and gallops away from the stationary camera into the distance until he eventually disappears into and merges with this environment (a landscape that resembles certain desert locations in Herzog's *Fata Morgana* [1970]). Above him, dark clouds move in fast-motion through a bluish sky, recalling the sky above the phantom castle beyond the Borgo Pass and the blue atmosphere through which the bat flies in slow-motion. The new Nosferatu, it would seem, can survive in this hazy, diffuse daylight. Embracing his new mission, Jonathan rides alone into this open wasteland, where earth and sky are in perpetual motion that does not, however, bring forth change or growth. On this second horseback journey Jonathan has truly escaped from Wismar.

By examining the way *Nosferatu* and *Nosferatu the Vampyre* unroll from beginning to end, I have tried to hold these films up for comparison and to reveal how they discover and explore certain possibilities in the story of the living and the undead, particularly in the confrontation between Count Dracula, the Harkers, and to a lesser extent, Professor Van Helsing. The feature that most immediately sets these two films apart from Browning's *Dracula*, for instance, or Fisher's *Horror of Dracula*, is the presentation of the vampire—the emaciated, ugly, predatory Nosferatu, who in Murnau's films is evil, phallic-shaped, and awkwardly rigid, and in Herzog's film at times appears to be physically fragile and at times contemplative and pathetic. However, the obvious distinctions between Max Schreck's Nosferatu and Bela Lugosi's Count Dracula or between Klaus Kinski's performance and Frank Langella's or Louis Jourdan's are finally not the most interesting or most significant of the distinctions between these retellings of Stoker's novel.

As I have noted throughout this chapter, *Nosferatu* and *Nosferatu the Vampyre* focus on the relationship between the public and the private, the city and the home, the townsquare and the bedroom. The three brief stories quoted in my introduction also depict the invasion of both home and village by the undead, and the moral community that forms in Stoker's *Dracula* is driven by civic as well as personal motives. But Murnau and, to an even greater extent, Herzog bring the relation between the public and the private to the fore. In their films Bremen and Wismar are not merely backdrops or settings; they are—with the foreign vampire and the pure-hearted woman—the subject of the film, in the sense that the western town of Hadleyville is the subject of *High Noon* or the California city of Santa Mira is the subject of *Invasion of the Body Snatchers* or London is the subject of *A Journal of the Plague Year*. Among the most memorable and cinematically impressive images in *Nosferatu* and *Nosferatu the Vampyre* are those that visualize the vulnerability and the deadliness of Bremen and

Wismar. Yet, in fact, it is Bremen and Wismar that survive, while Nina and Lucy are sacrificed and the Harkers' household destroyed. Whereas Stoker criticizes the selfishness and skepticism of the modern world and Fisher points out certain weaknesses in the patriarchal family, Murnau and Herzog question the price that must be paid for the survival of the bourgeois city and question also the values and institutions upon which such cities are based. *Nosferatu* and *Nosferatu the Vampyre* therefore serve as essential points of comparison for the works that I will consider in the next two chapters, novels and films like Matheson's *I Am Legend* and Romero's *Night of the Living Dead* that bring the undead into the heart of American culture.

The special emphasis given by Murnau and Herzog to Jonathan's isolated journey through the Carpathians and to his wife's premonitions and nightmares also sets *Nosferatu* and *Nosferatu the Vampyre* apart from other retellings of Stoker's *Dracula*, as does the redefinition by these German directors of the madman Renfield's place within the narrative and within the world of sane men epitomized by Van Helsing. Even more significant, however, is the difference between the work that the living must do in *Nosferatu* and *Nosferatu the Vampyre* and the wild work undertaken by the vampire hunters in *Count Dracula* and the other stories I have discussed. Like the holy crusaders in Stoker's novel, Lucy and Nina follow carefully prescribed rituals, but these women do not arm themselves with crosses and stakes or, for that matter, with Kükri knives or medieval pikes. In fulfilling these rituals, the pure-hearted seers in *Nosferatu* and *Nosferatu the Vampyre* cannot rely on the protection and guidance of Professor Van Helsing or any other elderly priest, doctor, father, or surrogate father. In this respect Nina and Lucy are the antithesis of the defenseless female victims in Franco's *El Conde Dracula* and Browning's *Dracula*, as well as of Le Fanu's Carmilla, who is protected by a battery of elderly men, including her father. As I have noted, the visionary heroines of *Nosferatu* and *Nosferatu the Vampyre*—because of the depth of their love and fear—are as much aliens in bourgeois civilization as is the vampire. Yet these women choose to offer themselves in solitary sacrifice, with no promise of heavenly or earthly reward and no possibility of being regenerated after traveling the "thorny paths" that they have undertaken. Their sacrifice is not recognized by the society at large, and they do not live to participate in the return of normality. Normality, particularly in *Nosferatu the Vampyre*, has become at best suspect and at worst more deadly and inimical to life than the vampire. Self-sacrificing, visionary maidens are not to be found in the works I will consider in the following chapters, for such women have no place and no mission in an America overrun by the stumbling zombies of *I Am Legend* and *Dawn of the Dead* or under attack by the satanic King-Vampires of *'Salem's Lot* or *Count Yorga, Vampire*. However, Murnau's Bremen and Herzog's Wismar could well be the nineteenth-century antecedents of the besieged, easily invaded, crumbling America that has become a primary subject of the contemporary horror story.

NOTES

1. For my research I have used a print of *Nosferatu* with titles prepared by Robert E. Lee. This print corresponds in almost all respects with the screenplay of *Nosferatu* that is included in *Masterworks of the German Cinema* (New York: Harper & Row, 1973). In her critical study, *Murnau* (Berkeley: University of California Press, 1973), Lotte H. Eisner published a translation of Murnau's annotated copy of Henrik Galeen's script for *Nosferatu*, as well as a list of variations from the script that are included in the final screen version. The characters in this original script (and presumably in early prints of *Nosferatu*) have the following names: Jonathan is Hutter; Nina is Ellen; Van Helsing is Professor Bulwer; Renfield is Knock; Count Dracula is Count Orlok. To preserve the clarity and continuity of my discussion and to keep in mind the relation between *Nosferatu* and the works discussed in the previous chapters, I have chosen to refer to these characters by names, borrowed from Stoker, that are used in prints of the film currently in release in the United States: Jonathan Harker, Nina Harker, Van Helsing, Renfield, and Count Dracula.

2. "Entretien avec Werner Herzog," *Ecran* 77 (Feb. 1979), 44. The most interesting of the many interviews Herzog granted after the release of *Nosferatu the Vampyre* is included in Hans Gunther Pflaum et al., *Werner Herzog* (Munich: Carl Hanser Verlag, 1979), pp. 59–86.

3. Ibid., p. 152. Herzog's prose screenplay for *Nosferatu* is included in Werner Herzog, *Drehbücher III: Stroszek. Nosferatu.* (Munich: Carl Hanser Verlag, 1979). Although this screenplay has not been translated into English, *Nosferatu the Vampyre* (New York: Avon, 1979), "a novel by Paul Monette based on Werner Herzog's screenplay for the 20th Century Fox film," is available. This novelization bears very little relation to Herzog's film.

4. Lotte H. Eisner, *The Haunted Screen: Expressionism in the German Cinema and the Influence of Max Reinhardt*, trans. Roger Greaves (Berkeley: University of California Press, 1969), p. 97, and Siegfried Kracauer, *From Caligari to Hitler: A Psychological History of the German Film* (Princeton: Princeton University Press, 1947), p. 86.

5. Carlos Clarens, *An Illustrated History of the Horror Film* (New York: Capricorn Books, 1968), p. 21.

6. Consider Ivan Butler's untenable conclusion that "Germanic mystic moralising was imposed upon the story [*Nosferatu*], but otherwise it followed the

story [*Dracula*] fairly closely" (*Horror in the Cinema* [New York: Warner Books, 1970], p. 42). Michael J. Murphy echoes this idea when he concludes that "the overall concept" of Murnau's film "was not significantly different from Stoker's *Dracula*" (*The Celluloid Vampires: A History and Filmography 1897–1979* [Ann Arbor, Mich.: Pierian Press, 1979], p. 9). Following an argument introduced by Kracauer in *From Caligari to Hitler*, Lane Roth discusses *Nosferatu* as "the product or symptom of moral malaise and social-psychological *Angst*" in "Dracula Meets the *Zeitgeist*: *Nosferatu* (1922) as Film Adaptation," *Literature/Film Quarterly* 7 (1979), 313.

7. *Nosferatu the Vampyre*'s relationship to *Nosferatu* is one of the clearest examples in film history of the sort of revisioning process that Harold Bloom finds in the major British and American poetry of the nineteenth and twentieth centuries. Using the terms Bloom introduces in *The Anxiety of Influence: A Theory of Poetry* (New York: Oxford University Press, 1973), we can say that in revisioning Murnau, Herzog employs the "ratios" of "*clinamen*" (a misreading that is a "swerve" away from the predecessor in the name of "creative correction" [p. 29]) and "*tessera*" (a "'completion'" that is "antithetical" to the precursor [p. 66]).

8. Donald M. Lowe offers a brief but insightful summary of "the family and private space" in bourgeois society. "Bourgeois society," he writes, "consolidated the privacy of the family. It promoted the separation of the workplace from the home," and at the same time "the differentiation of sex roles paralleled the separation of workplace and private family" (*History of Bourgeois Perception* [Chicago: University of Chicago Press, 1982], p. 70).

9. Robin Wood, "The Dark Mirror: Murnau's *Nosferatu*," *Film Comment* 7 (Summer 1971), 23–27, rpt. in *The American Nightmare: Essays on the Horror Film*, ed. Robin Wood and Richard Lippe (Toronto: Festival of Festivals, 1979), p. 45.

10. Eisner notes how *Nosferatu*, unlike almost all German films of the period, was filmed on location "with a minimum of resources." Using "real" images of the castle, the natural landscapes, and the "little Baltic townscapes," Murnau, she concludes, created the effect of supernatural horror in *Nosferatu* "without the aid of the least artifice" (*Haunted Screen*, pp. 99, 101, 102).

11. Wood, "Dark Mirror," p. 46.

12. Ibid., p. 47.

13. See Gilberto Perez Guillermo's perceptive comments on Murnau's style, in "Shadow and Substance: Murnau's *Nosferatu*," *Sight and Sound* 36 (Summer 1967), 150–53, 159.

14. Daniel Defoe, *A Journal of the Plague Year* (New York: New American Library, 1960), p. 153.

15. Montague Summers, *The Vampire: His Kith and Kin* (1928; rpt. New Hyde Park, N.Y.: University Books, 1960), p. 168.

16. Compare this sequence in *Nosferatu* with Defoe's *Journal of the Plague Year*, in which the narrator spends a great deal of time describing the dire effects of the lord mayor's attempt to "shut up" the infected households in London.

17. Wood, "Dark Mirror," p. 48.

18. René Girard, *Violence and the Sacred*, trans. Patrick Gregory (Baltimore: Johns Hopkins University Press, 1977), p. 79.

19. Geoffrey Marks and William K. Beatty describe several similar historical events. For example, during the fourteenth-century black plague epidemic, the citizens of Basle, possessed by the "wildest passions," blamed the plague on the city's Jewish population, and so "all the Jews in Basle, whose number could not have been inconsiderable, were enclosed in a wooden building, constructed for the purpose, and burnt together with it" (*Epidemics* [New York: Scribner's, 1976], p. 90).

20. See Eisner's discussion of acting in the German expressionist film (*Haunted Screen*, pp. 137–49).

21. Mircea Eliade describes several sacrificial rituals involving human victims in *Patterns in Comparative Religion*, trans. Rosemary Sheed (New York: Meridian, 1963), pp. 341–45. See also Sir James George Frazer, *The Golden Bough: A Study in Magic and Religion*, abr. ed. in 1 vol. (1922; rpt. New York: Macmillan, 1951), pp. 680–86, for a detailed description of the Aztec "sacred drama" of human sacrifice. Nina's act (like Lucy's in *Nosferatu the Vampyre*) is much different from the public sacrificial acts such as Eliade and Frazer describe and Girard analyzes (in *Violence and the Sacred*), again suggesting the separation of the public from the private in these two films.

22. Jack Kerouac, "*Nosferatu*," *New York Film Society Notes*, 9 Jan. 1960, rpt. in *Focus on the Horror Film*, ed. Roy Huss and T. J. Ross (Englewood Cliffs, N.J.: Prentice-Hall, 1972), p. 65. See also Wood's comment that "our sense that the greatest energies in the film are Nosferatu's intensifies the poignance of his helplessness and his destruction" ("Dark Mirror," p. 48).

23. Eisner, *Murnau*, pp. 114–16.

24. Guillermo, "Shadow and Substance," p. 159.

25. Ibid., p. 153.

26. Once we learn of the sexual threat Nosferatu poses to Nina and the contrast between the vampire and the naive, immature Jonathan, the phallic shape of the protruding tower at Castle Dracula takes on added significance. Murnau's use of the image of the leveled tower as a synecdoche for the end of the vampire's threat seems to support Wood's argument that Nosferatu embodies our "repressed animal natures, our sensuality" ("Dark Mirror," p. 49).

27. Defoe, *Journal of the Plague Year*, p. 237.

28. Ibid., pp. 238–40.

29. Albert Camus, *The Plague*, trans. Stuart Gilbert (New York: Random House, 1948), p. 278.

30. Bruce Kawin has proposed to me a different reading of this scene, which takes Nina's story as an "elevating tragedy" in which she is "spiritually justified" and ultimately "rewarded, however indirectly, by the audience's sympathy." I base my interpretation on the visual details of Nina's death and on a comparison of her fate with Mina Harker's in Stoker's *Dracula*.

31. For this sequence, Herzog filmed the mummies of Guanajuato, Mexico. These mummies are also featured in *Las Momias de Guanajuato* (1972) and two other Mexican horror films in which they return to life and battle popular superheroes.

32. This musical theme is called "Die Nacht Derhimmel" [*sic*] on the soundtrack album for *Nosferatu the Vampyre*, which is available on EGG records. The original music for the film was written by Florian Fricke, who records under the name Popul Vuh.

33. Compare the blue light in Herzog's film—that becomes, as I will suggest, associated with the vampire, the Carpathian mountains, and Lucy's dreams—with the "blue flames" that Jonathan sees during his coach ride to Castle Dracula in Stoker's novel. On the eve of St. George's Day, these flames are "seen over any place where treasure has been concealed" (D, 31).

34. Jacques Petat, Jean Roy, and Dominique Païni, "L'éternel retour de Nosferatu le vampire," *Cinéma* (Paris) 243 (March 1979), 12–13.

35. Bruce Kawin points out several other parallels between *Nosferatu the Vampyre* and Herzog's previous films. Kawin also begins to suggest the generic context for *Nosferatu the Vampyre* by noting that, in addition to Murnau's *Nosferatu*, Herzog draws upon the *Dracula*s of Stoker and Browning, "the folk backgrounds of the vampire mythos, and even some recent articles on horror theory" (Review of *Nosferatu*, *Film Quarterly* 33 [Spring 1980], 45).

36. Quoted in Beverly Walker, "Werner Herzog's *Nosferatu*," *Sight and Sound* 47 (Autumn 1978), 205. See also Janet M. Todd's comments on the fate of the bourgeois world and its "social order, propriety, and civic morality" in *Nosferatu the Vampyre* ("The Class-ic Vampire," in *The English Novel and the Movies*, ed. Michael Klein and Gillian Parker [New York: Ungar, 1981], pp. 201–7). Todd's essay is one of the few perceptive discussions of *Nosferatu the Vampyre* and of the relation between Herzog's film and other vampire stories, although she pays only passing attention to the relation between *Nosferatu the Vampyre* and Murnau's *Nosferatu*.

37. Petat, Roy, and Païni, "L'eternel retour," p. 11.

38. Quoted in "'I Feel that I'm Close to the Center of Things': Werner Herzog Interviewed by Lawrence O'Toole," *Film Comment* 15 (Nov.-Dec. 1979), 42.

39. As in the opening sequence of *Nosferatu the Vampyre*, Herzog here seems to subvert the traditional point-of-view shot. For an excellent discussion of this shot, see Edward Branigan, "Formal Permutations of the Point-of-View Shot," *Screen* 16 (Autumn 1975), 54–64.

40. Quoted in Mary Blume, "Shadowboxing with Werner Herzog," *Los Angeles Times*, 24 Feb. 1979, sec. 1, p. 9.

41. James Malcolm Rymer, *Varney the Vampyre or, The Feast of Blood* (1847; rpt. New York: Dover, 1972), p. 770.

42. James Ursini and Alain Silver, *The Vampire Film* (New York: A. S. Barnes, 1975), pp. 89–95.

43. Bernhardt J. Hurwood, *By Blood Alone* (New York: Charter Books, 1979), p. 210. Similarly, the vampire who is called back into existence during the first days of the French Revolution in Les Daniels's *Citizen Vampire* despairs because "there was no love in what he did, and no poetry" (*Citizen Vampire* [New York: Ace, 1983], p. 90).

44. Van Helsing is played by Walter Ladengast, the same actor who played Daumer, the paternalistic man of reason who unsuccessfully attempts to inte-

grate Kaspar Hauser into bourgeois society in *Every Man for Himself and God Against All.*

45. Philip Strick, Review of *Nosferatu the Vampyre, Sight and Sound* 48 (Spring 1979), 127.

46. Compare Thucydides's description of the actions of certain citizens when the plague raged in Athens for two years: "Men who had hitherto concealed their indulgence in pleasure now grew bolder . . . the pleasure of the moment and any sort of thing which conduced to it took the place both of honour and expediency. No fear of God nor law of man deterred a criminal" (quoted in Marks and Beatty, *Epidemics*, pp. 23–24).

47. Cf. Dreyer's *Vampyr*, in which the all-important book that describes the undead and the work the living must do to destroy the vampire is not specifically associated with the premodern world. In *Vampyr*, while the protagonist dreams, he is given the book—not by superstitious peasants, but by an elderly man whose daughters are threatened by the vampire. David Gray, the young man who receives the book of knowledge, is, in David Bordwell's words, "explorer and expiator, reader of the prophetic Word and dreamer who becomes prophet" (*The Films of Carl-Theodor Dreyer* [Berkeley: University of California Press, 1981], p. 111). As such, Gray shares much more with the visionary heroines of *Nosferatu* and *Nosferatu the Vampyre* than with the various incarnations of Jonathan Harker in the other versions of *Dracula* that I have discussed. *Vampyr*, however, differs substantially from the films of Murnau and Herzog in its image of evil, its portrait of the family and of patriarchal authority, and its lack of concern with the social implications explored in *Nosferatu* and *Nosferatu the Vampyre.*

48. Kawin, Review of *Nosferatu*, p. 46.

49. The confused official is played by Clemens Scheitz, who also plays the town notary in Herzog's *Every Man for Himself and God Against All.* This 1974 film ends with a scene somewhat similar to the conclusion of *Nosferatu the Vampyre.* After Kaspar, the enigmatic foundling, is murdered, a group of bourgeois gentlemen doctors perform an autopsy, and the notary records with pleasure that the abnormalities discovered in Kaspar's brain and liver account for his odd behavior. "Finally we've got an explanation," the notary declares, as he strolls down a street away from the camera toward the center of town.

50. Paul Monette ends his novelization of *Nosferatu the Vampyre* on a very different note: with Lucy's sacrifice, health returns to Wismar and "everyone's temperature dropped to normal." "Like brave survivors everywhere, the citizens of Wismar emerged from their houses into the sun and put the horrors of the past behind them" (*Nosferatu the Vampyre*, p. 169). Neither Murnau nor Herzog ever suggests that the bourgeois citizenry are "brave survivors."

51. By way of contrast with the transformation of Herzog's Jonathan Harker, consider the transformation of Jonathan in Stoker's *Dracula* from a "frank, happy-looking man, with strong, youthful face, full of energy, and with dark brown hair" to a "drawn, haggard old man, whose white hair matches well with the hollow burning eyes and grief-written lines of his face" (D, 307).

PART FOUR

Legions of the Undead

Increasingly, we cannot fight without an image of the enemy as totally evil, for whom any mercy or sympathy is incongruous, if not traitorous. Our wars are tending to become religious crusades once more.

J. Glenn Gray
The Warriors

It's repulsive at first: the sheer weight
of their numbers, how they gather themselves
along roadsides and fields near the river.
Until one gets used to it, the burning, too,
disconcerts. The tents smoke, their bodies
blacken and smell as they shrivel and fall.
But the torch is almost instant; a true
improvement. Watching them, the little ones first,
the young climbing for cover, the old
simply writhing, one thinks back
to flame pulsed into the bunkers on Iwo.
Or to the old burial pits in Poland.
One feels, at first, for the individuals
trying to escape. And some, of course, do.
But the hand-held torch is, for a fact,
clean: one learns to scorch the survivors
almost by rote. The least of them
would return to lay waste to the land.
Their numbers are fearsome.

Philip Booth
"Burning the Tents"

CHAPTER

7

The Invasion of America

ALMOST ALL OF THE WORKS I have discussed, from Stoker's *Dracula* to Herzog's *Nosferatu the Vampyre*, involve a journey to (even an invasion of) the modern, Western European world by the undead, though Herzog's film and several of the adaptations of *Dracula*—unlike Stoker's novel—are set in the past rather than the present. This journey to modern civilization is a recurrent motif in recent stories of the living and the undead.[1] In Clive Donner's farcical *Old Dracula* (1974), for example, the Count's trip to "swinging" London is played for laughs, as the modern metropolis offers attractions far stranger and more decadent than anything in Transylvania. A more effective modernization is Paul Morrissey's *Blood for Dracula* ([1974] also released as *Andy Warhol's Dracula*), in which an emaciated, dependent Count Dracula is driven to Italy by his valet because the stock of virgins has run out near his ancestral home. Unfortunately, the Count's luck is no better in Italy. He gags on the blood of women who only pretend to be virgins, and he is finally hacked to pieces by a virile peasant who, with a New York City accent, mouths quasi-socialist slogans. *Old Dracula*, *Blood for Dracula*, and parodies like Stan Dragoti's *Love at First Bite* (1979) all defang the aristocratic vampire and suggest in one fashion or another that the undead pose no threat to the modern world.

Quite the contrary is true in Stephen King's *'Salem's Lot*, Richard Matheson's *I Am Legend*, George A. Romero's *Night of the Living Dead* and *Dawn of the Dead*, and other recent stories that bring the undead into present-day America.[2] These and most of the other works that I will consider in this and the following chapter expand rather than diminish the threat posed by the undead. Such works, much more than films like *Old Dracula* and *Love at First Bite*, modify, extend, and at times subvert the conventions of the genre and thereby force us to re-assess our understanding of the story of the living and the undead.

To my mind, the most interesting and significant recent versions of this story are the apocalyptic nightmares like *Night of the Living Dead*, in which legions of the undead seem capable of overrunning a deeply flawed, perhaps irredeemably corrupt America. Of course, not all stories of the living and the undead, not even all American novels and films of the past fifteen years that involve the undead, follow the pattern of *Night of the Living Dead*. For example, as I noted earlier, both Dan Curtis's *Dracula* (1973) and John Badham's *Dracula* (1979) could be said to modernize Stoker's novel by altering in different ways the role of the vampire, the victims, and the vampire hunters. Yet these two adaptations are period pieces set primarily in England, and they share few of the thematic concerns found in *'Salem's Lot* or *Dawn of the Dead*. A number of recent vampire stories set in present-day America do, however, have the same narrow scope that characterizes Curtis's *Dracula*, a made-for-television film in which the confrontation between the living and the undead involves only a handful of participants whose life-or-death struggle has little, if any, bearing on the fate of society at large. Unlike Stoker's *Dracula* or F. W. Murnau's *Nosferatu*, in Curtis's film it makes no difference to the modern world whether or not the vampire is destroyed—what is under contention are the lives of a few isolated men and women and the existence of one troubled vampire, a creature who seeks only a bride, not a new order of undead followers.

In this regard Curtis's version of *Dracula* is of a piece with stories like Jory Sherman's *Vegas Vampire* (1980), a paperback original that is the fourth in a series of "occult adventure" novels. Here the solitary, European-born undead creature who murders Las Vegas showgirls is little more than a sort of exotic, dangerous criminal, not a King-Vampire or a Nosferatu. A professional "psychic investigator" destroys the Vegas vampire and thus saves the lives of other beautiful, young, potential victims—at least until another murderer takes to the streets. While there is no doubt that this vampire is destroyed, the novel also suggests that other undead creatures might well be lurking unrecognized in our midst, concerned not with conquest, but only with survival.

Emphasizing in a straightforward manner the process of crime, investigation, and eventual punishment, *Vegas Vampire* is structured very much like a mystery thriller.[3] So, too, is John Llewellyn Moxey's *I, Desire* (1982), a made-for-television film that begins with the same premise: among all its other dangers, the night also hides a vampire who preys on the unwary. Anne Rice's *Interview with the Vampire* (1976), Jan Jenning's *Vampyr* (1981), and Whitley Strieber's *The Hunger* (1981) in different ways develop this basic premise by suggesting that vampires have always existed in our world, feeding off us, watching our centuries come and go, and occasionally granting one of us immortality. All three of these novels are most concerned with detailing what Rice calls the "nuances of vampire existence"—the pleasures, the hunger, the isolation, the facts of night-to-night survival.[4] In these works the single human being (often quite explicitly designated as a surrogate for the reader) who encounters the strange, appealing realm of the undead finds his desire for knowledge mixed with an attraction to the unique possibilities offered by "vampire existence."

I, Desire focuses on a man who discovers that certain particularly vicious homicides are the work of a vampire. In *I, Desire* the truth sets no one free. The process of discovery changes David, the discoverer, from a clean-cut law student who is happily in love to an obsessed investigator, and then eventually to a would-be hunter who roams the dangerous nightworld of Hollywood Boulevard searching for the beautiful creature he both desires and seeks to destroy. The police and his girlfriend both suggest that David needs psychiatric help and that the deadly female vampire he pursues is a creature born of his own imagination. In one of the first scenes in *Dracula: The Vampire Play*, Van Helsing emphatically declares that "the strength of the vampire is that people will not believe in him" (DVP, 27). David also discovers the validity of this proposition. (Implicit in Van Helsing's statement is a more far-reaching indictment of modern man's inability to "believe" in anything; this indictment is also implicit in *I, Desire*.) Alone and tempted, David finally proves himself to be a "righteous man" by destroying the voluptuous vampire and her latest victim, a priest who failed in his quest to rid the world of the undead. David survives; he is even reunited with his plain, wholesome girlfriend. Yet the one reasonably intelligent and sympathetic police detective realizes that the facts of this case must be covered up—with lies that, in effect, maintain the illusion that our world holds no surprises.[5] In the final image of *I, Desire* the camera moves away from the reunited couple to reveal a new vampire watching from the shadows. David has accomplished nothing. He could just as well be insane as righteous. The world he lives in refuses to be enlightened, and thus it remains a safe hunting ground for the vampire.

Four films released by American International Pictures during the early 1970s, *Count Yorga, Vampire* (1970), *The Return of Count Yorga* (1971), *Blacula* (1972), and *Scream Blacula Scream* (1973), can be taken as the transition between stories like *I, Desire* and King's *'Salem's Lot*, in which a town in modern America is invaded by a European vampire who turns the local citizens into his undead slaves. Bob Kelljean's *Count Yorga, Vampire* brings the aristocratic vampire to the New World, as does William Crain's *Blacula*. Urbane and calculating, Yorga is similar in many respects to Hammer's version of Count Dracula. Crain identifies Blacula as Mamuwalde, an African prince who journeyed to Europe in the eighteenth century to protest the slave trade and was transformed into a vampire by the sadistic, racist Count Dracula. Particularly in the two Blacula films, the foreign vampire is a commanding, sexually attractive figure, an aristocrat who has no peers in America. In fact, much of *Blacula* and *Scream Blacula Scream* (also directed, like the two Yorga films, by Kelljean) is concerned with demonstrating Blacula's superiority both to the streetwise pimps and dandies he encounters and also to the successful middle-class black professionals and the white policemen who attempt to hunt him down. That the articulate, noble African is also a ferocious monster who tears at the throats of his victims would seem to endorse the most simple-minded of racist assumptions, but the two films insist that Mamuwalde became Blacula only because he was infected by a thoroughly corrupt European aristocrat. The black prince is actually a tragic victim who is fully conscious of his agonizing plight.

Count Yorga, by way of contrast, has no misgivings about his identity and his destiny. In southern California Yorga finds an isolated mansion perfectly suited to his needs. Here he keeps his brides, and Yorga's harem recalls Castle Dracula in Stoker's novel. However, the undead women in *Count Yorga, Vampire*—all stolen from their American lovers—are much closer to automatons than are Dracula's brides. These zombielike women are completely under Yorga's control. Sitting on his throne, the Count makes them rise from their coffins and do his bidding. The undead women are even more prominent in *The Return of Count Yorga*, where they appear dressed in flowing, pastel-colored nightgowns and resemble glazed-eyed, blood-stained Barbie dolls under the power of the almost Hugh Hefnerish Count Yorga. Blacula also is not alone, although he desires no harem. All of his victims, males as well as females, become slavish creatures who in turn seek out new victims. By the end of *Scream Blacula Scream* the would-be vampire hunters must destroy more than half a dozen vampires.

The undead creatures created and commanded by Yorga and Blacula lack the enticing sensuality and dissembling guile of the vampiric Lucy Westenra in Stoker's novel. Like Count Dracula's Transylvanian brides, these creatures fall on their prey in the manner of ravenous animals. The victims of the female vampires in *Count Yorga, Vampire* are their human lovers, who have tried to play the role of heroic vampire hunters. In *Blacula* and *Scream Blacula Scream*, the victims include friends, lovers, and innocent bystanders of both sexes. The undead women in *The Return of Count Yorga* quite literally emerge from their graves to follow Yorga's commands and invade the home of an utterly helpless, upper-middle-class family. In presenting this attack, Kelljean emphasizes the frightening fate of the victims, who fall prey to a force that easily overruns their comfortable world. The sense of carnage and chaos when the hungry undead attack this defenseless family is very much reminiscent of certain scenes in Romero's *Night of the Living Dead*, though Romero includes no aristocratic mastermind.

Blacula and *Scream Blacula Scream*, in contrast to *The Return of Count Yorga*, depict the undead as a much less organized force, although in the course of both of these films the monsters begin to multiply and gather together as if readying for a mass attack on normality. However, this attack never occurs. In the conclusion of *Blacula*, Blacula's undead slaves perish in flames, and in *Scream Blacula Scream* they are are run through with stakes. At the end of *The Return of Count Yorga*, the vampire women survive, after having murdered not only the unprotected family but also a psychiatrist, a minister, two policemen, and the rest of the men who have hunted them.

Blacula and *Scream Blacula Scream* both conclude by focusing on the fate of the masterful vampire prince, who has been unable to replace his beloved, long-dead wife or to remove the curse that enslaves him. In *Blacula*, for example, Mamuwalde cannot be destroyed by mortal men, yet he elects to end his accursed existence by walking into the sunlight. Because of this emphasis on the black vampire prince, *Blacula* and *Scream Blacula Scream* are particularly significant in the history of the so-called blaxploitation film of the late 1960s and 1970s, as well as in the history of that subgenre of horror that takes as its subject the sympathetic monster, the noble monster, and the monster-as-victim (*Frankenstein* [1931], *King Kong* [1933], *The Wolf Man* [1941], and *Peeping Tom* [1960] are particularly noteworthy examples.)

However, for my purposes, the Count Yorga films are the more interesting transitional works in the story of the living and the undead. To a greater degree than *Scream Blacula Scream*, these films contrast the one-of-a-kind aristocratic, Old World, self-styled classical vampire with the growing legion of undead creatures under his power. Yorga is creator and master, lover and father, but *Count Yorga, Vampire* ends with the destruction of the Count and the survival of his slaves, as if to signal a turning point in the genre. Though Count Yorga somehow "returns" in Kelljean's sequel, once again he is destroyed. And once again all the vampire hunters are killed as well, leaving only the undead American women to survive. Ultimately, in these two open-ended films, the joke is on the supremely self-confident Count Yorga, who is bested by a human being, and on the would-be hunters, who think they can recapture their stolen women. The joke is also on the viewer, who is tricked into assuming that the death of the aristocratic vampire signifies the end of the threat. (Recall that such is the case, for example, in *Dracula: The Vampire Play*, Browning's *Dracula*, *El Conde Dracula*, and Hammer's Dracula films of the 1960s.) In fact, the Yorga films leave us with the sense that the real carnage has yet to begin. Even having seen the massacre of a family in *The Return of Count Yorga* and the destruction of a squad of fully armed policemen in both *Blacula* and *Scream Blacula Scream*, we have barely glimpsed how vulnerable our world truly is to the threat posed by legions of the undead such as roam through America in *'Salem's Lot*, *I Am Legend*, *Night of the Living Dead*, and *Dawn of the Dead*.

Complacently nestled in the twentieth century, the small Maine township of 'salem's Lot is initially as far from the faith and glory of Jerusalem as it is from the superstition and communality (right or wrong) of Salem. Without any conscious effort in the name of traditionalism or nostalgia, this town has become increasingly isolated and therefore vulnerable and perhaps expendable. Well before the vampire arrives, the town is already dying of anemia—its young blood drained off generation by generation, its economic heart sorely in need of a massive transfusion. Yet while it may be the town's lot to be destroyed, King's omniscient narrator reveals a society that is no decadent Vanity

Fair or soap-opera Babylon of unbridled adultery and cutthroat ambition. The inhabitants of 'salem's Lot have settled into a life of routine marked by few public disturbances. Even the bizarre atrocities committed some thirty years before in the Marsten House, which "actually *looms*" high overlooking the town, have been conveniently forgotten or assimilated into child's games and local legend.[6] As Father Donald Callahan—one version of Van Helsing in the novel—ruefully admits, the townspeople apparently know "(evil)" and perhaps "evil," but not "EVIL" (SL, 150).

Like Stoker's England, 'salem's Lot begins as a world of isolated individuals who, while being more petty and dissatisfied with their lives than Lucy Westenra's suitors, are still placated by regularity and repetition. Personal habits have taken the place of group rituals; there are no American-Gothic lotteries (à la Shirley Jackson) in the Lot. Neighborly familiarity and party-line gossip superficially bridge this isolation and lack of community, but the veneer of social contact does not alter the fact that each citizen is alone with memories, dreams, and desires. These are secrets that remain private, if they are acknowledged at all. Secrets like Dud Rogers's supreme pleasure in running the town dump—burning garbage and shooting rats while he thinks of braless, "slutty little" Ruthie Crockett, who looks on him with amused disdain (SL, 51). And of the few families that King mentions, most are disintegrating with almost textbook predictability: for example, Susan Norton, an attractive and intelligent young woman, rebels against her mother's overprotectiveness and decides to leave home; Sandy McDougall, a witless teenage girl forced into marriage after she becomes pregnant, violently takes out her frustration on her infant son, while her blue-collar husband drinks with the boys and smashes up their coffin-shaped mobile home. And so it goes with almost every character, major or minor, as the distanced, all-seeing narrator moves from home to home and person to person, revealing secrets, amassing naturalistic detail, and creating a panorama that resembles a large jigsaw puzzle spread over a table with only a few pieces attached.

Unlike the peasant villages and nondescript towns in Hammer's vampire films or even the English cities in Stoker's *Dracula*, 'salem's Lot is for King the prize as well as the battleground when the living and the undead struggle. Yet this small American town seems no more worth the effort and the cost than Bremen in *Nosferatu* is worth the sacrifice of Nina Harker. And finally, like a vampire, 'salem's Lot must be destroyed before it can die a "true death." As a "sedentary small town" (SL, 119) destined only for death or undeath, 'salem's Lot has none of the picturesque, if stagnant, Old World beauty of Herzog's Wismar, though both environments are extremely vulnerable and easily overrun. In *'Salem's Lot* this vulnerability is largely the product of both the town's citizenry with their lack of communal ties and also the town's insularity and insignificance, economically and socially. The private citizens of 'salem's Lot, "stuffed" with "aggression and darkness" (SL, 236), inhabit the same America as the people of Milburn in Peter Straub's *Ghost Story* (1979) and the New Englanders in *The Picture in the House* (1924) and other stories by H. P. Lovecraft. Yet, paradoxically, the strength, ingenuity, and selfless bravery at times demonstrated by certain inhabitants of 'salem's Lot seem as distinctively American as their "aggression and darkness" and their weakness and self-centeredness.

In many respects King's novel, like a number of recent horror stories, is a response to saccharine, nostalgic images of small-town American life as stable, uncomplicated, and exceedingly safe.[7] Such stories reveal the sedentary small town to be a locus of horror, a sort of haunted house writ large (John Hancock's *Let's Scare Jessica to Death* [1971]), for example, or an inescapable trap in which the old feed off the young (Bernard McEveety's *The Brotherhood of Satan* [1971]) or a bastion of archaic, inhuman ritual (Thomas Tryon's *Harvest Home* [1973]). In Gary Sherman's *Dead and Buried* (1981), for instance, the seaside village of Potters Bluff gives the appearance of an almost unbelievably content and cohesive community, but only because the locals are all corpses who have been reanimated by an elderly coroner/mortician, who sees himself as an artist in the Henry Frankenstein tradition. King's novel differs from stories such as *Dead and Buried* because he suggests that while 'salem's Lot is a perfect hunting and breeding ground for vampires, it can also give birth to vampire hunters as well.

To this sedentary small town comes Kurt Barlow, an ancient foreigner whose attractiveness, suave "European manner" (SL, 353), and "friendly fatherliness" (SL, 292) mask his own corruption and help allow him to tap the corruption of others. Calculating and totally egocentric, Barlow is the "king vampire" of *'Salem's Lot* (SL, 293), who invades modern civilization in search of fresh blood and new disciples. King does not call his masterful vampire "Count Dracula," but Barlow is much closer in conception to Stoker's King-Vampire than are the Draculas in Curtis's *Dracula* and Franco's *El Conde Dracula*. This obvious correspondence is one major example of what King himself has called the "intentional similarity" between *'Salem's Lot* and *Dracula*.[8] Like Stoker's Count, Barlow is no pathetic victim of immortality or easily routed anachronism. He is unquestionably, unceasingly evil, or, more accurately, Evil—a satanic "Master," who in turn has his own "Dark Father" (SL, 319) to whom sacrificial rites must be performed. Unlike other vampire stories of the 1970s, such as Badham's *Dracula*, Rice's *Interview with the Vampire*, or Herzog's *Nosferatu the Vampyre*, *'Salem's Lot* insists on the reality of the awesome, tempting power of satanic Evil.

For this Evil to thrive by feeding off, liberating, and nurturing the "aggression and darkness" in 'salem's Lot, Barlow requires human attendants and accomplices. Dracula has his gypsies; Barlow has Richard Straker, a "human watchdog and bodyguard" (SL, 319) whose most important function is to buy the Marsten House and arrange for Barlow's arrival in modern-day America.[9] Like his Master, Straker is "very Old World charming" (SL, 198) and very much aware of his superiority to the citizens of 'salem's Lot. (There is even a suggestion in the novel that Straker is somewhat more than merely mortal, though he does eventually die a "human" death.) In Tobe Hooper's 1979 adaptation of *'Salem's Lot* as a mini-series for CBS television, Straker, played by James Mason, becomes an even more prominent character than he is in King's novel. Hooper often shows the fastidious, urbane, condescending Straker in his antique shop surrounded by costly European bric-a-brac and gawking local customers. As in Stanley Kubrick's *Lolita* (1962) and Alfred Hitchcock's *North by Northwest* (1959), James Mason here again plays the corrupt, manipulative representative of the Old World who is ultimately defeated in America.

In addition to expanding Straker's role, Hooper also significantly alters King's portrait of Barlow. For example, Hooper physically models his King-Vampire more on Murnau's Nosferatu than on Stoker's Count Dracula, so that his Barlow is never seen as a seductive fulfiller of dark fantasies. With two protruding ratlike teeth, the hissing, yellow-eyed Barlow in Hooper's television adaptation of *'Salem's Lot* is the Hyde to Straker's Jekyll. Yet the physically normal, cosmopolitan human is no less monstrous than his animalistic undead Master. Both of these Old World creatures, we soon realize, must be destroyed. As I have begun to suggest here, a comparison of Hooper's mini-series with King's novel—particularly in terms of their treatment of the King-Vampire—

helps to underscore certain affinities between King's story of the living and the undead and Stoker's *Dracula*, affinities that are not evident in Hooper's telefilm.

Count Dracula has no Straker, however. This human attendant's primary function in both the novel and the mini-series is to secure the necessary invitation that Barlow requires to enter 'salem's Lot. The conventional insistence in vampire stories that the living offer an invitation to the undead highlights both the importance and the fallibility of man's free will: the potential victim is granted a choice between life or undeath, but in most cases he is either not aware of the magnitude of the decision at hand, or he is completely subjected to the oftentimes irresistible, hypnotizing power of the vampire's will. In King's novel, however, Larry Crockett, the local realtor in 'salem's Lot, is not under the vampire's control when he sells Straker the Marsten House and thereby invites Barlow into the town. Even though Crockett has a fortune stashed away from shady business ventures and even though he senses that he is making "deals with the devil" (SL, 58), he cannot resist the multimillion dollar profit that Straker guarantees. This realtor, who reads *Satan's Sex Slaves* in his office while never daring to enjoy his wealth or even to proposition his secretary, is King's vision of banal, native American evil that with its avarice and repression provides an entree for the real thing. (This sense of mortal man's complicity with supernatural Evil is emphasized in several of King's novels, where it also serves to force the reader to draw distinctions between "evil," "[evil]," and "EVIL.") At least the more Faust-like Renfield in Stoker's *Dracula*—who admits the vampire into the building where Mina Harker sleeps—risks his life and his soul for the promise of immortality and of power second only to the King-Vampire's.

With the necessary assistance of Straker and Crockett, Barlow is able to begin his colonization of 'salem's Lot. As his victims themselves seek victims and converts, a new order of the undead is created such as Dracula can only dream of. With the vampire's embrace, private—even unspoken and unacknowledged—desires are fulfilled, for Barlow knows the secret measure of "aggression and darkness" that renders each person unique and isolated and dissatisfied. Thus Dud Rogers is promised Ruthie Crockett, and so he has her, "in enameled darkness within an abandoned freezer" (SL, 310). Oblivion, too, seems sweet, "green as still water at dark fathoms" (SL, 146), when the victims lock eyes with the ravenous undead—though the newborn vampires awaken not to oblivion but only to a gnawing hunger and a "need to serve the Master" (SL, 355). Reborn into the world of the night, the townspeople of 'salem's Lot ironically gain a unity that was lacking before Barlow's arrival. For example, in a macabre "family scene" (SL, 387), the undead Roy and Sandy McDougall now sleep in a crawl space under their mobile home with their no-longer-abused infant. When the sun sets, the undead rove alone or in packs—all equal, all slaves to one Master, all "children" of one father (SL, 393).

Barlow's new order has no parallel in the various retellings of *Dracula*, where the vampire seeks out a beautiful woman for his bride or for an addition to his Transylvanian harem. Yet as I noted in chapter 2, Stoker's Count Dracula does desire to be the "father or furtherer of a new order of beings" (D, 308), a quasi-feudal world reduced to just one father-king and the rest dependent children, one Master and a multitude of slaves or "jackals" (D, 312). ("What good are peasants," Dracula asks Jonathan early in the novel, "without a leader?" [D, 38].) The King-Vampire's colonization of England is, however, a very slow process that depends on his seduction of Lucy Westenra and Mina Harker, and he does not succeed in transforming the modern world into his domain. Only Renfield, driven by the mad desire to be a slave to an all-powerful Master, is allowed by Dracula to glimpse the "new order": "a dark mass spread over the grass, coming on like the shape of a flame of fire; and then he [Dracula] moved the mist to the right and left, and I [Renfield] could see that there were thousands of rats with their eyes blazing red—like his, only smaller" (D, 285).[10] More than any living peasants could ever be, the rats are a perfectly uniform mass, formed in the image of and unquestionably subservient to their Master.

In Stoker's novel Seward's scientific diagnosis is that Renfield suffers from "homicidal and religious mania" (D, 110), one more mark of insanity and abnormality, further proof that Renfield should be isolated and institutionalized. Yet by the standards of 'salem's Lot, Renfield is, in fact, no abnormal madman at all, but an average citizen. Like the willing converts to Barlow's new order, Renfield exemplifies the common notion that—in Hannah Arendt's words—"the instinct of submission, an ardent desire to obey and be ruled by some strong man, is at least as prominent in human psychology as the will to power" (OV, 39). Since there is none of "God's women" in 'salem's Lot, where the stars "gleam in beautiful indifference" (SL, 343), the Renfields of this world feel no pangs of conscience occasioned by the sight of incarnate spiritual good. These citizens of the modern world can satisfy their "ardent desire to obey" without suffering any guilt whatsoever. Except perhaps for Father Callahan, no one resists Barlow in the fashion that Renfield struggles against Dracula (and against his own human nature as well). Thus things are much easier for Barlow than for Stoker's King-Vampire—in keeping with a general tendency in post World War II horror stories as otherwise dissimilar as *Invasion of the Body Snatchers* (1956), *The Swarm* (1974 novel, 1978 film), and *Nosferatu the Vampyre* (1979) to emphasize how easily and how quickly the monster is able to overrun normality.

With no need to begin by capturing "God's women," Barlow can be much less selective than Count Dracula about his victims. Children and old men spread the gospel just as well as voluptuous young women, for once they become vampires, all the undead are equally hungry and equally single-minded. Chief among Barlow's "children" are children. A seven-year-old boy is offered as a sacrifice to the "Lord of Flies" (SL, 73), and the boy's older brother soon rises as one of the undead. In fact, the first of the novel's three sections concludes with Matt Burke, a decent, elderly schoolteacher, "paralyzed with fear" as he hears "the high, sweet, evil laugh of a child—and then the sucking sounds" (SL, 165). (Hooper's television adaptation of *'Salem's Lot* omits many of the peripheral characters in King's panorama, yet Hooper does retain these two young brothers, who assume an even more prominent place in the story.) In contrast, the few children in Stoker's *Dracula* are innocent victims who are "kissed" but not transformed into vampires by the undead Lucy Westenra.

Here again the difference between Stoker's *Dracula* and *'Salem's Lot* reveals the degree to which King is representative of the modern horror story, which often presents children, from infants to teenagers, not only as victims, but as "objects of fear and loathing," to use Edgar Z. Friedenberg's phrase.[11] The evil laughter of the undead schoolchildren in *'Salem's Lot* has its echo in *The Omen* (1976) and the many other "demon-child" stories, and also in the opening sequence of *Halloween* (1978). In these stories children do indeed become objects of extreme "fear and loathing," murderous creatures who cannot be reasoned with or disciplined, only destroyed, or, in the case of *Halloween*, institutionalized. (Romero's *Martin* [1977], as I briefly noted in my introduction, is the most perceptive exploration of the teenager-as-monster motif.) Such stories seem to speak to our uneasiness and confusion concerning the changing conditions of family life; the autonomous child, with rights and privileges of his or her own, becomes in these works, the monstrous child. For King, as for Romero in *Night of the Living Dead* and *Dawn of the Dead*, that there are children among the undead also becomes an effective means of demonstrating a more general proposition: all Americans have a place in the legions of the undead—each of us can become one of them.

Certain of the people in *'Salem's Lot*—though not the actual civil authorities, who are of no help at all—can also become vampire hunters, and therein lies the potential salvation of the living in King's novel. Unlike the human beings in Hammer films like *Horror of Dracula* and *Brides of Dracula*, these hunters must band together if they are to have any chance of surviving. However, no experienced, paternal foreigner is needed to instruct King's "Fearless Vampire Hunters" or to provide the special tools with which to combat the creatures of the night.[12] Books from the local library and, more interesting, the conventions of vampire films and novels supply the necessary information.[13] Stoker's *Dracula* becomes a sort of canonical text that tells what wild work must be done and provides consolation to the hunters. Thus the role of *Dracula* within *'Salem's Lot* parallels the way this text serves as King's narrative and thematic model.

What the hunters realize is that holy water is available from the deserted neighborhood Catholic church; stakes can be lathed out of backyard firewood and hammered in with a Sears Craftsman handtool; a cross can be formed from two tongue depressors. In the correct hands mundane objects become sacred implements in a heroic quest, much as every home in the town contains an attic, root cellar, or crawl space that seems custom-built to house the undead. When "the bestiality of the night rises on tenebrous wings" (SL, 343), 'salem's Lot is well prepared.

Like Franco, Badham, and Herzog, King does not put at the head of the living one wise elder who is both hunter and healer, scientist and Christian. In lieu of Van Helsing, *'Salem's Lot* offers three characters who in different degrees resemble Stoker's Dutch professor and who all ultimately fail to partake of the bittersweet, incomplete victory of the living over the undead: Matt Burke first recognizes the nature of the threat and becomes the group's "Researcher General," compiling traditional information about the undead (SL, 247); Jimmy Cody, a young general practitioner, shares Van Helsing's medical expertise and, more important, his open-minded awareness of mysteries that science cannot explain; and Father Donald Callahan, a middle-aged

Catholic priest, is the man of faith, fully conscious of the spiritual struggle at hand.

By error or by design, each of these men faces the monster alone, and neither the teacher nor the doctor nor the priest can by himself triumph over the vampire. After an encounter with the undead ruptures Matt's life of "sweet evenness" (SL, 159) and "careful academicism" (SL, 299), he suffers a heart attack that leaves him unable to participate actively in the search. He remains bedridden until a second seizure kills him. Cody is outsmarted by the cunning King-Vampire and dies an agonizing but "natural" death, impaled in a trap rigged up with kitchen knives. Callahan, the alcoholic priest "pining for a Challenge" with "EVIL" (SL, 150), is granted his wish, only to see his faith waver when he confronts Barlow face to face. Tainted like Mina Harker in Stoker's novel because he is forced to suck the vampire's blood, Callahan becomes a modern-day Cain, wandering isolated, neither alive nor undead, shunned by the Good as well as the Evil. Unlike Mina, Callahan undergoes no redemptive purification. In *'Salem's Lot* decency, righteousness, courage, and the willingness to sacrifice oneself do not guarantee success, and neither does the knowledge of tradition nor the unwavering commitment to communal action. We are far indeed from Browning's *Dracula* with its masterful Van Helsing and farther still from Le Fanu's *Carmilla*, in which knowledgeable and dedicated men have no difficulty in carrying out the "pious sacrilege" that will "subserve the vengeance of Heaven" and "relieve our earth of certain monsters" (C, 63–64).

In addition to the teacher, doctor, and priest, the group of vampire hunters in *'Salem's Lot* includes Ben Mears, a thirty-year-old writer who has returned to 'salem's Lot to face nightmares that haunt him from his childhood, and Mark Petrie, an imaginative and resourceful boy of eleven. (At the start, a young woman also is part of the group, and potentially part of a new family unit with Ben as husband and Mark as child, but she easily falls prey to the undead after she foolishly attempts, by herself, "to take positive action" [SL, 258].) No ceremony of collective worship ritualistically links these hunters into a circle of holy crusaders. Yet like the moral community that forms in Stoker's *Dracula*, those who seek to destroy Barlow's new order must shun the modern world by violating now-irrelevant laws and trusting in the validity of cross and stake. Ben, for example, not only discovers the comfort and protection offered by the cross, but also finds himself reciting prayers with a "sudden, eerie surety" (SL, 265) and submitting to the "alien ritual" of confession, which leaves him "out of joint with his time" (SL, 326). He is drawn—like so many vampire hunters—to Catholicism presumably because it is the old form of Christianity, closer to the ritualistic, primitive sources of all religion.

Initially, each of the vampire hunters is driven more by fear and the personal desire for revenge or confrontation than by a grand spiritual purpose, and as a group they are less unified than either Stoker's moral community or Barlow's minions. Frail because they are human beings, these hunters gain strength, if not security, in numbers, though they are continually under siege as the undead each night expand their domain. After the death of the teacher and the doctor and the failure of the priest, only Ben and Mark remain, and *'Salem's Lot*—as much as any disaster movie or World War II combat film—makes us ask why these particular characters survive when so many others do not.

Unlike most of the citizens of 'salem's Lot, Ben and Mark do not welcome death or undeath; they want to survive, whatever the cost, and they have the physical and psychological strength to persevere despite the fact that they witness life become a nightmare from which there is no awakening. They are willing and able to undertake any wild work that is necessary, even if such work means that they will be baptized in the blood of the undead. Above all, King implies, the novelist and the boy survive because they have not lost the taste of childhood fear and have not suffered the "ossification" of their "imaginative faculties" (SL, 243)—Ben and Mark do not have to be taught that there is Evil in the world.

By including a child among the group of vampire hunters—and also by showing children as victims and as vampires—King insists that children and childhood must be taken as significant elements in the story and in life, in a way that they are not in Stoker's *Dracula* or any of the films discussed in chapters 3–5. King argues in *Danse Macabre* (his critical study of the modern horror story) that the goal of horror stories is "to knock the adult props out from under us and tumble us back down the slide into childhood." This premise is based on the simplistic and commonplace contrast between adulthood as the tedious realm of "logic and rationalism" and childhood as the magic kingdom of intuition, imagination, and fear. For King, this contrast is, in turn, linked to the opposition between mind and emotions, and between the modern and the primitive.[14] In *'Salem's Lot* the living can challenge the undead only after modern man has been stripped of his routine assumptions and adult defenses by the taste of true fear, which "overspills logic and the bright Formica reasoning of the cerebrum" (SL, 261). This "childlike, dreamy" fear (SL, 87) emanates in waves from the "spinal cord, a much older network of nerves and ganglia" than the conscious mind (SL, 203). Thus Ben and Mark are not fearless; like Van Helsing in Fisher's *Horror of Dracula* or Browning's *Dracula*, they are inspired by their fear. Yet when Father Callahan and Matt Burke face the undead, these old men realize with terror that their long-repressed childhood fears had not been "staked," but "only tucked away in their tiny, child-sized coffins with a wild rose on top" (SL, 204). As a result, the teacher and the priest are paralyzed and helpless. Alone, confronting the vampire, each old man returns to the "dark turns and exhalations" of childhood "alienation" (SL, 293). (No such realm exists for Stoker's characters, who never were children in King's twentieth-century sense of the term.) In fact, given the definition of the function of horror stories in *Danse Macabre*, Callahan and Matt are models of the perfect reader, and the King-Vampire—with his skill at manipulating events and orchestrating effects and his sense of irony, surprise, and high drama—is an image of the teller of horror stories.[15] Ben, who is writing a novel about Evil, and Mark, whose hobbies are magic and monster movies, provide an informed audience for Barlow's extravaganza, until ultimately they are able to wrest control over the horror story that is their life.

Approaching the final confrontation with the King-Vampire, Ben and Mark "no longer saw themselves as doers or avengers or saviors . . . helplessly, they were only living" (SL, 404). Yet they are together—"it's got to be both of us," Ben tells the boy (SL, 405)—bound by fear, vulnerability, and mutual need. They risk their lives when they could easily escape from 'salem's Lot because they are moral human beings, not self-serving egotists, and because a true community of two is infinitely preferable to isolation and to Barlow's new order. Together, the man and the boy are the best the living can offer. As they break into the vampire's lair, Ben becomes "possessed" with "Power" born of "inevitable rightness, of *whiteness*" which seems to transform him into a divinely inspired avenger (SL, 408). But when they remove the lid from Barlow's coffin, Mark succumbs to the vampire's gaze, and Ben "was only Ben Mears again, and he was afraid" (SL, 411). Thus when he hammers the stake into the heart of the King-Vampire, Ben is no more and no less than "merely" human. He is a man who has risen to the occasion.

As a result of their ordeal, Ben and Mark become "father and son"

(SL, xi), but they are not washed clean in the dead vampire's blood, and God does not signify his presence with purifying beams of rosy light. For a year after they destroy Barlow, Ben and Mark wander cross-country, finally settling in a small Mexican village. Distance, confession, and the warm waters of the Pacific, however, cannot enliven the boy's "bleak inner horizon" (SL, xii) or purge the man's waking nightmares. Stoker's community of the good, rewarded with "happiness" for their sacrificial pain, make a final pilgrimage to Transylvania seven years after Dracula's death and find that "every trace of all that had been was blotted out" (D, 382). Knowing that the undead still roam the streets, now slaves without a Master, Ben and Mark return to 'salem's Lot and ignite a fire of "purification" as the first step in a project of systematic destruction that will be as "ugly" as it is "dangerous" (SL, 427).

Having disposed of Barlow, Ben and Mark, we might say, are prepared to enter the twentieth century. The heroic struggle is over, now the grim dirty work of mass murder begins with a fire that will burn 'salem's Lot to the ground and no assurance that a New Jerusalem will rise from the ashes. The only reward for these two vampire hunters is that they are together—"you and me" are Mark's last words in the novel (SL, 427). With its open ending, then, *'Salem's Lot* affirms the importance of community, even as it suggests that "thorny paths" still must be traveled and that the newborn family is incomplete and therefore incapable of generating new life.[16]

As I have suggested, one significant distinction between *Dracula* and *'Salem's Lot* is that King is much less optimistic than Stoker about man's ability to unite in a moral community that will triumph once and for all over the undead and so become the basis for a regenerated existence in the twentieth century. Yet like Stoker (and quite unlike *I Am Legend* and *Night of the Living Dead*, as we will soon see), King insists that the war against the undead be fought with stake and cross. Both Lucy Westenra's suitors and the vampire hunters in *'Salem's Lot* must learn the importance, the all-importance, of faith and ritual. And both must suffer even as they risk their lives to save a selfish and skeptical world that may not be worth saving. Most important, *'Salem's Lot* recounts the confrontation between Good and Evil that is so central in Stoker's *Dracula*. King presents this confrontation as a contemporary story, not as a circumscribed period piece like Fisher's *Dracula, Prince of Darkness* or Saville's *Count Dracula*.

Before his faith fails him when he challenges the King-Vampire, Father Callahan, King's flawed priest, wants to engage in a "pure" struggle, "unhindered by . . . politics," against true Evil (SL, 150). Ben Mears, too, comes to believe in the "recurrent power of evil" and in the existence of "evil men in the world, truly evil men" (SL, 111). For both Callahan and Ben the "truly evil" is opposed to the "mindless, moronic," dull evil of daily life (SL, 149), like child abuse, which can be countered, if at all, by counseling and not by transfixion. In the face of true Evil, King implies, human beings experience "real fear" and real horror. Thus as a local citizen of 'salem's Lot unknowingly transports Barlow to the Marsten House, the man feels "a strain of fear enter his heart that he had not even felt in Nam, although he had been scared most of his time there" (SL, 86–87). For this man, an encounter with the King-Vampire puts the Vietnam War into perspective, makes it, in some important way, less "real," less "true," surely less of a standard against which to judge all peacetime horrors. *'Salem's Lot* seems designed to put us in the position of this veteran. The Vietnam War, child abuse, and innumerable other social and political "problems"—problems that become the subject of documentary films—are not matters of Good and Evil. When man must struggle for his very existence against unmistakable Evil, then such problems become irrelevant, even inconsequential or not truly "real."

Of course, in the bifurcated, Manichaean world King presents in *'Salem's Lot* there is little room for neutral onlookers, and life is dangerous for those people who enlist in the "army" of "God, right, goodness" (all "names for the same thing," Callahan concludes [SL, 150]). What are gained by these recruits are a clear, righteous purpose and a certainty about the nature and the identity of their opponent. There may be no explanation for the ultimate origin of Evil, but nonetheless the world suddenly makes perfect sense, as all quotidian concerns, all puzzling human relationships, all insoluble problems are forgotten. While it requires the greatest courage, faith, and determination for King's vampire hunters to destroy the undead, there is never any doubt about the necessity for and the legitimacy of such violent action. More than any of the hunters in Stoker's *Dracula*, Ben and Mark are psychologically scarred by what they have done and have witnessed, yet they do not suffer the guilt that, for example, troubles the outcast sons who murder the primal father in Freud's scientific myth of the primal horde. Barlow elicits no ambivalent emotional response, and neither does Straker. They are Evil. So, too, is the undead Susan Norton (heretofore Ben's girlfriend), whose blood splashes over Ben as he pounds a stake again and again into her heart. If she weren't Evil, he would be a murderer, quite possibly what we would call a monster.

In its insistence on the reality of antihuman, superhuman Evil, as well as in its presentation of the violent struggle mounted against such Evil, *'Salem's Lot* shares a great deal with several of the most widely known modern horror stories, including *The Exorcist* (1971 novel, 1973 film), *The Omen* (1976) and its sequels, *Halloween* (1978), *Alien* (1979), and *Halloween II* (1981).[17] Demon or psychotic, Antichrist or extraterrestrial alien, the threat in each of these stories is, like Barlow the King-Vampire, "truly" Evil besides which all lesser evils pale. In return for frightening us, the story of Evil, of "unmixed malignity," offers its own consolation by bringing the terms of existence into clear, certain focus, ridding life of its impurities and its complications, removing man, for a time at least, from history. Man's most heroic act—indeed, his only alternative besides capitulation or defeat—is to challenge this Evil. For it must be destroyed; it cannot be cured or reformed or treated as a object worthy of scientific study. And if these stories demonstrate how easily our bodies, our homes, our cities, our country, and our universe can be invaded, they also show us the fitness of man and define what heroism has come to mean in modern America.

The particular shape that Evil takes in *'Salem's Lot* has direct affinities with Stoker's story of the living and the undead, for Barlow is more similar to Stoker's Count Dracula than are the aristocratic vampires in, for example, the retellings of *Dracula* by Browning, Fisher, or Curtis. Unlike Barlow, however, Stoker's Dracula is not able to create his new order. The roving mass of undead in *'Salem's Lot* can only be glimpsed in Stoker's *Dracula* as part of a madman's vision—possibly because Barlow's undead embody terrifying fears of dehumanization and the perversion of community that could only arise in the twentieth century, as we seek out monsters that draw upon and surpass those provided by our own history. For example, the ravenous undead in *'Salem's Lot* seem to me in some respects to be a nightmarish version of the already nightmarish phenomenon of totalitarianism. Barlow has no multileveled hierarchical organization, no secret police or propaganda ministry, yet certain basic features of totalitarianism, as Hannah Arendt describes it in *The Origins of Totalitarianism* (1958), are shared by Barlow's new order. In both cases, for instance, "atomized, isolated individuals" are linked by their absolute loyalty into a "completely heterogeneous uniformity," which seeks to abolish all "human spontaneity." The aspect of totalitarianism most clearly suggested in *'Salem's Lot*, however, is what Arendt refers to as the "Leader principle, according to which every functionary is not only appointed by the Leader but is his walking embodiment, and every order is supposed to emanate from this one ever-present source."[18] The undead follow with absolute loyalty the will of the King-Vampire and become quite literally the "walking embodiment" of Barlow. They are the progeny as well as the slaves of this foreign invader who seeks to establish his dominion over America.

Another parallel that is closer to home than European totalitarianism and more contemporary with *'Salem's Lot* is the Manson Family as depicted in Vincent Bugliosi's *Helter Skelter* (1974), which was adapted by Tom Gries as an impressive television mini-series in 1976. (Again, I am not concerned here with questions of direct influence or with cataloguing all modern representations of Evil.) For Bugliosi, the district attorney who prosecuted the Tate-LaBianca murder case, the sense of horror and monstrousness was evoked not only by Manson, the demonic guru, but also by his Family, which Bugliosi describes as a "real family in almost every sense of that word, a sociological unit complete to brothers, sisters, substitute mothers, linked by the domination of an all-knowing, all-powerful patriarch." Manson sexually initiated and rechristened newcomers to the Family, and they became, in Bugliosi's words, "robots, zombies, automatons" under the control of one Master.[19] Compare Ray Danton's *The Deathmaster*, a low-budget 1972 film in which a bearded vampire becomes the guru for a group of aimless, free-spirited teenagers and transforms their commune into a cult of zombielike undead. Inspired by their vampire Master, these devoted followers believe that they are "the pure, the strong," who alone will survive and who are fully justified in killing lesser beings. Like the undead in *'Salem's Lot* and *The Deathmaster*, the Manson Family in *Helter Skelter* is a new order, a "cancerous growth" that seeks the apocalyptic downfall of American society and seems to thrive on blood. Calling for the death penalty (in effect, calling for the sort of closed ending that is so rare in post-1968 horror stories), Bugliosi concludes his summation by telling the jury once again the story that "might have been the plot of a horror film": "As the helpless, defenseless victims begged and screamed out into the night for their lives, their lifeblood gushed out of their bodies, forming rivers of gore. If they could have, I am sure that Watson, Atkins, and Krenwinkel [three of the defendants] would gladly have swum in that river of blood, and with orgasmic ecstasy on their faces. Susan Atkins, the vampira, actually tasted Sharon Tate's blood."

Bugliosi can't help but tell a horror story in *Helter Skelter*, for what other type of story can be told about vampires and zombies, "human monsters" and "human mutations"?[20] The plural here is crucial, as it is in *'Salem's Lot*. Barlow and Manson are not alone; in America they find willing converts, slaves, followers. They create families made in their own image, as extensions of their will.

The notion that the monster and that monstrous Evil may take the form of the many as well as of the one—the sense of what I will refer to as a *multiple threat*—is crucial in recent stories of the living and the undead and in many other post–World War II horror stories. As much as the multiple threat in all its manifestations seems to be a form of the monster that has particular significance for the second half of the twentieth century, as much as it seems to be *our* monster, the one-of-a-kind psychotic killer, alien, shark, or vampire remains at least equally popular in horror stories of this period. The multiple threat such as is depicted in *'Salem's Lot* and *Helter Skelter* is by no means an image found only in our culture, or even in our century. The other side during wartime is always potentially just such a threat—a barbaric horde, an inhuman many-headed monster.[21] To cite one important example, American Indians have been pictured as an evil, multiple threat in countless stories from Puritan "captivity narratives" like Mary Rowlandson's *The True History of the Captivity* (1682) to nineteenth- and twentieth-century westerns.[22] Norman Cohn studies a much different image of the multiple threat in *Europe's Inner Demons* (1975), in which he exhaustively surveys the "age-old fantasy" of a "clandestine, systematically anti-human society" that practices "erotic debauches, infanticide, and cannibalism." Early Christian communities were described in these terms by Roman critics, and these same terms were in turn used by later Christians to characterize the witches' Sabbat and so to justify the European witchhunt. In this fantasy the monstrous threat is an Evil group "organized and headed by Satan," a group that preys on children. By its very existence, as well as its crimes, this "anti-human society" challenges and endangers normal society. The image of Evil Cohn describes is an important forerunner of twentieth-century stories of the cult and the coven and other versions of the multiple threat.[23] (Similarly, the plague of frogs and the plague of locusts in

Exodus are obvious antecedents for works like *The Birds* [1963], *The Swarm*, and *Came a Spider* [1978], in which masses of one animal threaten to overrun human civilization.)

I Am Legend, *Night of the Living Dead*, and *Dawn of the Dead*, with their images of stumbling zombies who are quite unlike the malevolent vampires in *'Salem's Lot*, take the idea of the multiple threat to one of its most significant—and most logical—conclusions. Yet this threat has assumed many forms in recent stories of the living and the undead (again suggesting the flexibility of this particular type of horror story and the cumulative development of popular genres). John Shirley's *Dracula in Love* (1979), for example, links the vampire story to a "demonological fantasy" of the sort described by Cohn. Dracula, "Lord of Vampires" in this novel, commands an elaborate hierarchical power structure that includes human servants, mindless, worm-eaten revenants, and even rats that are also an "embodiment of his hunger" and are "compelled by his will."[24] Dracula looses these creatures on modern America and simultaneously calls forth the barely repressed bloodlust of the living. In *Dracula in Love*, the Lord of Vampires' poisonous influence is only halted by the intervention of a superhuman power.[25]

On the other hand, the vampire cult of "chosen people" in Terry Becker's *The Thirsty Dead* (1974), a low-budget horror/sexploitation film shot in the Philippines, remains hidden in its jungle temple, waiting to make another foray into the city to kidnap beautiful young women who will be bled during elaborate, ceremonial rituals. The most ingenious variation on the motif of the cult is Rod Hardy's *Thirst* (1979), in which the vampires belong to a worldwide organization called the "Brotherhood." For these vampires, members of what they assume to be a "superior race," drinking blood is the "ultimate aristocratic act." Although the Brotherhood has its ritualized initiation ceremony, the group is more like a multinational corporation than a satanic cult. Its headquarters resemble an orderly, sanitary research facility equipped with the latest technological apparatus, as well with a sophisticated behavior modification program and a farm stocked with human victims whose blood is drained by machine. Aside from one woman whom the Brotherhood seeks as a convert, none of the living ever challenges these vampires, and finally even the unwilling woman embraces her new identity as one of the chosen people.[26]

The multiple threat in *Thirst*, which involves "nothing supernatural" and nothing Evil, is far indeed from King's portrait of the undead in *'Salem's Lot*. As my discussion in this chapter suggests, King's novel is ideologically linked to Stoker's story of the living and undead in ways that the works I have just mentioned are not. *'Salem's Lot*, in fact, might be taken as an attempt to retell *Dracula* as a modern American vampire story, and so too might Robert R. McCammon's *They Thirst* (1981), which tells fundamentally the same story as King's novel. A brief look at *They Thirst* can therefore serve as a summary of several major topics that have been covered thus far in this chapter, before we turn to the much different type of horror envisioned by Matheson in *I Am Legend*.

Prince Conrad Vulkan is the "king-*vampir*" in *They Thirst*, a creature who dreams of an "invincible vampiric army" and of a "new race" that he will sire.[27] Using human attendants and drawing upon man's reservoir of darkness and totalitarian tendencies, Vulkan transforms the diverse classes and races of Los Angeles into a unified whole that is at once like a superior army in its single-minded zeal and its orderly chain of command, and like a malignant cancer in its amazingly rapid ability to multiply by feeding off of the living. (As would be expected, cancer is an almost irresistible metaphor in recent stories featuring a multiple threat, though McCammon pursues neither the correlation between the microcosm and the macrocosm suggested by the comparison of vampirism and cancer, nor the ways that this metaphor points out one major function of horror stories—to conflate disease and the monstrous, and then to offer us a successful cure.) As in *'Salem's Lot* and in certain respects *Helter Skelter*, the cancerous multiple threat created by one supreme leader in *They Thirst* is unambiguously Evil. And this Evil finds a perfect breeding ground in modern America, which seems destined to suffer apocalyptic destruction, to be either dead or undead.

In McCammon's novel, Los Angeles is buried by dust storms, then finally ripped apart by earthquakes and cleansed by a tidal wave of "holy water blessed by God Himself." Since "*God is on the side of those who don't give up*," He steps in only after the living have proven their mettle by undertaking the wild work of destruction. For here it is man's responsibility to destroy Evil, regardless of the cost. The vampire hunters in *They Thirst* take the form of an alliance rather than an army: a middle-aged policeman, originally from Hungary, provides faith, experience, and knowledge of Old World traditions. He is accompanied, assisted, and saved by an ingenious eleven-year-old boy, a young woman reporter, a dedicated barrio priest, and a successful Hollywood comedian. These people all exhibit righteousness, bravery, endurance, and the willingness to die in the struggle. Through "the combination of their actions," they triumph against seemingly insurmountable odds.[28] Their victory proves the fitness of individual heroism, of human "combination," of stake and cross, and of the Good.

The novel ends with Gayle, a once cynical, selfishly ambitious journalist, heading to the East to warn the rest of America about the Evil that lurks unseen in its midst. She is wounded and about to die in the desert when a family of scared survivors stops to give her help. The man of the family warily approaches—he correctly realizes that every stranger is potentially a monster—and Gayle sees that "the object he held gleamed with dawn's faint light, and it was the most beautiful thing Gayle had ever seen. A crucifix."[29] As a representative inhabitant of the selfish and skeptical modern world, this reporter-become-prophet learns basically the same lessons as Lucy Westenra's suitors in Stoker's *Dracula* and the vampire hunters in King's *'Salem's Lot*: the need for help, the necessity for sacrifice, the possibility for redemption, the importance of faith and tradition, the reality of Good and Evil. She is enlightened; the terms of existence are clear. She has a mission; there is work to be done.

The new order of undead that is glimpsed by the insane Renfield in Stoker's *Dracula*, that is confined to a small Maine township in *'Salem's Lot*, and that overruns Los Angeles in *They Thirst*, inherits the earth in Richard Matheson's *I Am Legend*, a novel published in 1954, but set in the 1970s.[30] In *I Am Legend* there is no seductive, aristocratic Dracula, no wish-fulfilling Barlow, no King-Vampire at all, just the mindless undead, who "walked and walked about on restless feet, circling each other like wolves, never looking at each other once."[31] Among these anonymous crowds, a procession of groveling female vampires, "posing like lewd puppets in the night" (IAL, 14), takes the place of the voluptuous undead sirens so prominent in the various retellings of *Dracula*. All of the creatures in *I Am Legend* are capable of "demented fury" (IAL, 43) and "snarling and fighting among themselves" (IAL, 14) when their single-minded purpose is thwarted. But they almost completely lack even the rudimentary sense of animal cunning and the vestiges of individual identity found in the vampires in *'Salem's Lot*. Compared to the zombies in films like *White Zombie* (1932) and *Revenge of the Zombies* (1943), who are merely slaves controlled by the will of an all-powerful Master, and compared to the plague-carrying vampire bats in Martin Cruz Smith's *Nightwing* (1977), whose physiological perfection and "communal instincts" work in tandem to satisfy the need for blood, the undead in *I Am Legend* are stumbling, inept mutants, threatening only because of their persistence and their numbers.[32] In the world created by Matheson, the "return of corpses has become trivial in import" (IAL, 64), and "monotonous horror" (IAL, 110)—an oxymoron that Stoker and most of the other storytellers I have mentioned could not even imagine—covers all.

Isolation is the fate of the vampire and the pure-hearted seer in *Nosferatu* and *Nosferatu the Vampyre*, and it is the price paid in Stoker's *Dracula* and King's *'Salem's Lot* for living in a modern society that has unknowingly severed its life-giving roots. In *I Am Legend*, to be a human being is to be isolated, for Robert Neville, Matheson's protagonist, is the "last of the old race" (IAL, 171)—*our* race. Because of purely fortuitous circumstances, Neville is immune to the plague that transforms the living into the undead. Being "saved," however, renders him stranded and alien, a latter-day Robinson Crusoe on an island that might have been designed by Albert Camus. Neville's isolation is at once more complete and more dreary than Jonathan Harker's terrifying adventures in Transylvania. The last man on earth chooses to remain alive, but each ingenious step he takes to ensure his survival necessarily increases his "forced isolation" (IAL, 58). His boarded-up, air-conditioned, sound-proof home, for example, becomes a "gloomy sepulcher" (IAL, 11), a castle in which Neville, like Count Dracula, is tempted to indulge in a "nostalgic preoccupation with the past" (IAL, 78).

Even in the past, before the world had completely become the domain of the undead, there were no wise, selfless Van Helsings to provide explanations and to lead the living in their struggle for survival. Left to his own devices, Neville turns to Stoker's *Dracula*, just as the vampire hunters do in *'Salem's Lot*. Yet for the solitary man surrounded by a very different sort of new order than Stoker envisioned, the "melodramatics" and "driveling extrapolations" of *Dracula* (IAL, 25–26) offer neither practical advice nor spiritual consolation. Neville angrily tosses the novel aside, and in a sense his critical gesture summarizes the relationship of *I Am Legend* to Stoker's *Dracula*. Matheson, however, does not so much offhandedly dismiss *Dracula* as he consciously demythologizes certain assumptions about violence, heroism, faith, and ritual that inform Stoker's novel and other vampire stories that precede *I Am Legend*—assumptions, as I have suggested, that continue to inform many subsequent stories of the living and the undead, including *'Salem's Lot* and Hammer's series of Dracula films.

For example, in *I Am Legend*, ridding the world of the undead is a never-ending, unheroic task, described in prose as terse and matter-of-fact as Dashiell Hammett's: "After lunch, he went from house to house and used up all his stakes. He had forty-seven stakes" (IAL, 24). "A man could get used to anything if he had to" (IAL, 11), Neville concludes, even the ever-present stench of garlic and the "tiresome" work of lathing wood doweling into stakes (IAL, 12). The wild work of destruction has become here just a monotonous, demanding, Sisyphean task—a routine rather than a ritual. Thus for much of the novel Neville resembles another of the many alienated workers so often discussed in the fiction and nonfiction of the 1950s, who receive no pleasure and no challenge from their jobs, but can do nothing except continue the routine and take out their frustrations, as does Neville, in after-work drinking. (At times, Neville also seems to be a parody of the suburban homeowner, obsessed with do-it-yourself home repair projects like replacing broken windows and cleaning the front yard of corpses.) After months and months of daily slaughter, the undead still gather nightly around Neville's barricaded house. Stakes and garlic notwithstanding, life plods on in a stalemate of "monotonous horror." Driving a stake into a comatose body becomes for Neville not a dangerous, difficult, sacrilegious act, but merely a "method of disposal" (IAL, 12). Eventually he discovers that a deep cut on the wrist is an even more efficient method. In *I Am Legend* the violence carried out by the living is neither redemptive nor ritualistic; it is only a methodical and futile attempt at genocide. By this significant reversal of generic convention, Matheson makes us realize how almost all the stories I have mentioned take completely for granted the fact that the living *must* kill the undead.

As the vampire hunter, Neville is no more an embodiment of Good than the undead are an embodiment of Evil—"Morality," he realizes, "had fallen with society" (IAL, 59). Yet as we have seen, a great many stories of the living and the undead center on the clear-cut, categorical distinction between Good and Evil. In fact, several of these stories—Philip Saville's *Count Dracula* and Freddie Francis's *Dracula Has Risen from the Grave*, for example—emphasize the plight of skeptical modern men who must come to accept the reality of Good and Evil. Inverting Neville's maxim, we can say that the living in these stories discover true morality only after they have "died" to society. If the undead are irredeemably Evil, then the hunter has both the right and the responsibility to destroy all such creatures, even those who were once lovers or relatives, and to suffer no guilt when he is stained with the blood of the vampire. According to certain folk traditions summarized by Summers in *The Vampire: His Kith and Kin*, "The Vampire is one who has led a life of more than ordinary immorality and unbridled wickedness; a man of foul, gross and selfish passions, of evil ambitions, delighting in cruelty and blood."[33] In this appealingly simple, logical, and just scheme of things, only the sinful and corrupt in life become evil undead monsters. There is no such infallible justice in *I Am Legend* and no system of Good and Evil in Neville's world unless man feels the need to invent one.

The type of religious faith that for Stoker and King helps to transform desecration into a redemptive act and isolated people into holy crusaders cannot vindicate Neville's wild work or provide the meaning his world lacks. While he is searching for some explanation for the actions of the undead, Neville recalls a time when the plague was at its height and open-pit fires consumed diseased corpses by the thousands. As the fear of vampires spread, "people had turned to primitive worship" and "revivalism," searching for "quick answers" and for salvation (IAL, 114). (Similar scenes, given even more narrative and thematic prominence, are found in Ingmar Bergman's *The Seventh Seal* [1957] and Camus's *The Plague*.) Far from gaining strength and assurance through faith and communal worship, the terrified believers "had died as quickly as the rest of the people, but they had died with terror in their hearts" (IAL, 114). Repelled by the cross they had worshiped, the once-faithful became the most pitiful of all the undead.

Neville does not attempt to find solace and answers in faith, and he does not gain a new sense of purpose and identity from the methodical violence he commits. The options taken by the vampire hunters in Stoker's *Dracula* are either irrelevant or unavailable in *I Am Legend*, so Neville turns to science for "natural" explanations that do not rely on "blood-eyed vampires hovering over heroines' beds" and "bats fluttering against estate windows" (IAL, 86). He maintains his sanity by submerging himself in research and experimentation. And ultimately, medical textbooks, sophisticated microscopes, and rigorous logic provide answers for the novice scientist, "all without the supernatural" (IAL, 86)—as Matheson once again inverts certain of Stoker's most basic assumptions. (In this regard, Neville's success is almost exactly the opposite of Seward's failure as a scientist in Stoker's *Dracula.*) Neville's findings have the formal beauty of an ingenious, air-tight scientific explanation that blends physiological evidence with psychological insights: bacteria, spread by dust storms, insects, and human carriers, infect human beings, transforming them into vampires; the odor of garlic is an allergen to these diseased creatures; the stake hammered into an undead body allows air in which destroys the symbiotic relationship between bacteria and host; and the cross is feared because the vampire's inescapable need for blood conflicts so strongly with the vestiges of human consciousness and cultural training.

With this knowledge, and because he has devoted himself to creative work and not only to a routine of monotonous labor, life becomes "almost bearable" for Neville (IAL, 116), even though he fails to devise effective antibiotics or a vaccine for the disease. Science, he realizes, cannot explain the origin of the "vampiris" bacteria or why the plague appears when it does in human history. "There's no answer" to these questions, Neville concludes, "no reason" for the situation. "It just is" (IAL, 150). To accept the existence of the bacteria, and thus the ever-present possibility of the plague, as a fact of life is to realize that no supernatural force of Good or Evil can be held responsible, no wrathful God placated by prayers, no grand adversary staked.

By accepting his situation and living only in the "day-to-day" present (IAL, 120), Neville survives. Whereas at first he is obsessed with memories of his wife and child, eventually the desire for human contact—companionship, love, sex—fades, and he becomes "afraid" of the "sacrifices" and "responsibility" that inevitably accompany human relationships (IAL, 139). Just as "for him the word 'horror' had become obsolete" (IAL, 145), so, too, does the idea of community, the very idea that Stoker celebrates as man's saving grace in *Dracula* and King tenuously grasps as man's only hope in *'Salem's Lot*. Forever alone in his "dungeon" (IAL, 110), living only one day to the next in a completely secular world of corpses, vampiric automatons, and unanswerable questions, Neville is the existential man as permanent exile and prisoner-for-life, a man who has adapted to a situation even more "absurd" than that which is found in the quarantined city of Oran in Camus's *The Plague*.[34]

Once he has settled comfortably into his solitary existence, Neville's life is disrupted not by a new, more virulent form of the monster, but by an encounter with another person, a frightened young woman named Ruth. This woman, Neville discovers, is actually a "living" vampire, a human being impregnated with the disease. The distinction between the living vampires and the undead walking corpses whose bodies are totally activated by the bacteria is suggested at several points in the novel, but Neville continues to kill both types indiscriminately, for he discovers no effective cure for the disease. Like the reader, Neville does not place much importance on the distinction between the two different kinds of creature who come out at night; vampires, after all, are vampires. They may not be satanically inspired creatures of Evil, but they are the Other, a nuisance to be disposed of. "If I didn't kill them [the living vampires]," Neville reasons, "sooner or later they'd die and come after me. I have no choice; no choice at all" (IAL, 146).

Neville learns from Ruth that the living vampires have banded together and devised a drug that holds the disease in abeyance. Born of science, this group is attempting to create a "new society." In the eyes of this new society, Neville is not merely the "abnormal one," he is the "invisible specter" and "terrible scourge" (IAL, 173); he is the monster who alone roams the daylight hours, leaving bloodless corpses in his wake as he randomly murders the innocent, the living as well as the undead. When we are reminded that all definitions of the monstrous are relative and when we are forced to take this new society's point of view into account, Neville's scientific work in retrospect can no longer be seen solely as a testament to human ingenuity. For example, in his "experimental fervor," he pulled a woman from her bed, dragged her outside by her hair as she clawed and tried to escape, and then "stood there and watched her die," as she "lay twisting helplessly on the sidewalk" (IAL, 36). This "experiment" proves his hypothesis, just as later experiments enable him to discover a more efficient means of disposal and perhaps also to satisfy his own "repressed craving for violence" (IAL, 91) and his own unsatisfied sexual desires. (As Ruth realizes, "Men can learn to enjoy killing" [IAL, 171].) All such experimention in the name of science is legitimate, presumably, if the subjects are nonhuman creatures who constitute some sort of threat to the researcher. It seems to me that the scientific work of the decent, adaptable, ingenious Robert Neville is disturbingly similar in kind to the notorious experimentation conducted in Nazi concentration camps on Jews and other "subhuman" species, experiments carried out to "advance" scientific knowledge and to develop more efficient means of disposal.

Like Stoker's moral community or the vampire hunters in *'Salem's Lot*, the new, still primitive society that Ruth belongs to is in the process of "repossessing" the world "by violence" (IAL, 170). The living vampires hunt down and destroy the undead, who have no "union," only the motivation of individual need. With "a clumping of boots" (IAL, 164) and expressions of "vicious triumph" (IAL, 162), heavily armed, uniformed squads of "assigned killers" (IAL, 171) carry out this "methodical butchery" (IAL, 162) using razor-tipped pikes instead of wooden stakes—and the line between these holy crusaders and "gangsters" or stormtroopers becomes thin indeed (IAL, 162). *I Am Legend* suggests that in a world that does not contain Good or Evil, violence, even when it is directed against the undead and when it is undertaken in the name of survival, necessarily dehumanizes and creates monsters.

Regardless of Neville's ability to accept and to thrive in the isolated life of a hermit, it is the community that ultimately triumphs in *I Am Legend* as in Stoker's *Dracula*. The unorganized walking dead are easily destroyed, and Neville is wounded—in the chest, appropriately enough—then captured and imprisoned in a "real" dungeon. In the end, as he swallows the poison Ruth has given him so that he can escape the public execution the new society has planned for him, Neville looks out of his cell at the crowd gathered outside. Silently, with "awe, fear, shrinking horror" (IAL, 173), they confront their "anathema and black terror" (IAL, 174), a singular threat that has been subdued at last. And Neville realizes that for these people he is "legend"—the archvillain, the individualist, the destroyer, the monster who must be sacrificed before the new age can truly begin. Neville has tossed aside *Dracula* and replaced legend with scientific fact. *I Am Legend*, however, demonstrates that even in a new society that owes its existence to science, legends of Evil—horror stories—are essential, for they define by contrast the Good, offer justifications for our actions, provide much-needed explanations, and link human society with the supernatural. In a world where Dracula does not exist, Matheson implies, he must and will be invented.

As I have suggested throughout this study, a familiarity with the generic context greatly enriches and in some cases radically revises our reading of any individual story of the living and the undead. So does a familiarity with the way a given story has been adapted and retold. For example, a comparison of *I Am Legend* with *The Last Man on Earth* (1964), Sidney Salkow's film adaptation of Matheson's novel, highlights the treatment of science, violence, and legend in Matheson's story of the living and the undead.[35] In the opening sequences of his film, Salkow effectively evokes both the monotonous daily routine of the last man on earth (here called Robert Morgan instead of Robert Neville) and also the desolation of this gray, urban world, which at times resembles a bleak Antonioni-esque cityscape, dotted with corpses. However, the film is very clearly designed as a serious vehicle for Vincent Price, who came to the role of Morgan direct from starring in *House of Usher* (1960) and several other adaptations of Edgar Allan Poe's stories by American International Pictures in the early 1960s.

The Last Man on Earth is constructed around a series of scenes that depict Morgan as a pathetic and sympathetic victim of forces far beyond his control. And Price's performance in these scenes is as maudlin and overstated as Matheson's prose is unadorned and understated. Neville survives by accepting his isolation and channeling his energy into scientific research. He dies sharing our realization that, ironically, he has become legend. Morgan never loses his preoccupation with the past (the depth of his nostalgia is here the surest mark of his humanity), and he remains in a state of despair and dissatisfaction until his death. A long flashback sequence shows exactly what Morgan has lost: a clean, spacious home with framed art reproductions on every wall; a cute, affectionate young daughter who plays in the large backyard; and an elegant, devoted, blissfully domestic wife much younger than himself. In *The Last Man on Earth*, this household represents the best that man can hope to achieve. (It is also a vision of the good life that seems to me probably more appropriate for 1954 than for 1964.) After the plague strikes, Morgan's wife returns as a hungry, dirt-covered vampire, and his home becomes a cluttered, broken-down command post. His forced bachelorhood is his tragedy, particularly because Morgan is a scientist, and he still is unable to prevent the loss of his Eden. Finally, having fled from his home, Morgan is murdered in a church by the assigned killers of the new society. We learn that his pure blood could have "cured" all the infected survivors, but instead he lies dead on the altar with a spear in his chest, his arms spread as if he has been crucified. In the end Morgan is a martyr, not a monster.

Unlike *The Last Man on Earth*, Christian Nyby's *The Thing (From Another World)* (1951) is as accomplished and significant a work as *I Am Legend*.[36] In fact, I would argue that Nyby's film and Matheson's novel are among the most noteworthy American horror stories to appear in the decade after World War II. Both works modernize the vampire story and use it to address widely felt anxieties and topical issues: the fear of worldwide nuclear devastation in *I Am Legend* and the threat of a foreign invasion that would turn all Americans into slaves in *The Thing*. Since my major concern at this point is examining the place of Matheson's novel in the ongoing story of the living and the undead, I will not offer a complete analysis of *The Thing*. However, a brief discussion of the major elements of Nyby's film helps to bring into even sharper focus those qualities that make *I Am Legend* unique, qualities that would inspire Romero to film *Night of the Living Dead*.

Like a vampire, the alien creature that lands near the North Pole in *The Thing* thrives on blood and cannot be destroyed by bullets.[37] Though a wise-cracking reporter dubs it an "intellectual carrot," all such attempts to classify the creature fail. It is humanoid, yet composed solely of vegetable matter; intelligent, yet in the end easily outwitted. Its origin remains a mystery, as does the fact that it is highly radioactive. What finally is clear is that the Thing from another world is an enemy that threatens the lives of an isolated group of Americans at an Arctic research station, and by extension, endangers the existence of all mankind. When it is freed from its coffin of ice by human curiosity and human error, the alien proves to be "unpredictably dangerous" in its willingness to kill to survive. The real danger, however, becomes evident when the military men and civilians realize that the creature they have uncovered has begun reproducing itself by cultivating seed pods—in other words, when the prospect of a multiple threat emerges. Subsequently, the Thing is revealed to be a would-be conqueror, "growing some kind of horrible army" and planning to "turn the human race into food for it" much faster than Count Dracula or Kurt Barlow could ever dream of spreading their new orders.[38]

The alien is not a creature of satanic or supernatural Evil, but it is thoroughly malevolent and dangerous, quite unlike the stumbling undead masses in *I Am Legend*. While Robert Neville must learn to adapt to a world of "monotonous horror," the group of Americans in *The Thing* must realize that the universe contains enemies that must be destroyed as soon as they are encountered. In fact, Nyby's film concludes with the reporter broadcasting his account of the successful battle and exhorting, "Everybody, wherever they are" to "watch the skies! Everywhere. Keep looking. Keep watching the skies." By the end of *The Thing* war has been declared, and our survival depends on our vigilance, our fear, and our readiness to struggle against any "horrible army" that would enslave us.

Even as the reporter warns us that the threat remains an ever-present possibility, what we see in the final images of *The Thing* are those Americans who have just fought and won "one of the world's greatest battles." Nyby's film, of course, is at least at much concerned with the human beings from our world as it is with the Thing from another world. Like the vampire hunters in Stoker's *Dracula*, these humans can only survive and triumph if they pool their talents and together face the alien invader. Anyone who resists the group effort jeopardizes the entire operation. Thus almost as dangerous as the alien is the formal, impersonal, asocial Dr. Carrington, an eminent scientist who believes that "there are no enemies in science, only phenomena to study." Carrington has no need for friends, lovers, or workmates, only laboratory assistants, and his world, we could say, has no place for legends or for fear. Before the Thing smacks Carrington aside, he rushes up to it alone and unarmed and declares: "I'm not your enemy. I'm a scientist." Carrington's allegiance to science and his elitism masked as objectivity endanger not only his colleagues, but all of mankind. (Interestingly, the reporter reveals at one point that Carrington has also been associated with the development of the atomic bomb.)

Notwithstanding Carrington, science—particularly practical, technological science—plays an important role in defeating the Thing. Among the "handful of American soldiers and civilians" who together manage to destroy the alien is one of Carrington's former laboratory assistants, who, along with other scientists, has realized that there are indeed enemies in the universe. These scientists and the reporter work under the direction of an Air Force flight crew headed by Captain Pat Hendry. What soon becomes clear in *The Thing* is that all the elements of this newly formed alliance make important contributions—the civilians as well as the military, amateurs as well as professionals. Under the threat of death, the human beings in *The Thing* "naturally" become an effective unit, each member of which is essential. While Hendry, the ranking military officer, assumes the role of the leader who coordinates the combined effort, he takes suggestions from the civilians and enlisted men under his command (and even from one of the few women at the base) as often as he gives orders.

This group of Americans need not demonstrate any deep religious faith nor follow any prescribed ritual when they confront the alien. But they must violate orders from superior officers who remain at a safe distance from the action, and they must disregard "S.O.P." (the Air Force's code of "Standard Operating Procedure"). Free of these bureaucratic and often foolish restrictions, the group succeeds because of its combined expertise and ingenuity. Guns do not stop the Thing, and fire is only minimally effective, so the men construct an improvised, high-voltage trap that they use to electrocute the alien. Their triumph is at once the victory of technology, of human ingenuity, and of the newly formed, cohesive alliance of soldiers and civilians. Unlike *I Am Legend*, with its distrust of all groups and all efforts at communal action and with Matheson's emphasis on the solitary confinement of the individual in a world where the only monsters and the only comprehensive explanations are fabrications of man, *The Thing* offers us a bona fide enemy that must be destroyed and then demonstrates that Americans can meet the challenge if we work together and "watch the skies."

NOTES

1. Other recent stories of the living and the undead are structured around the journey from modern civilization to the superstitious, primitive domain of the vampire. In Karl Alexander's novel, *The Curse of the Vampire* (1982), for example, a Hollywood actress travels to Transylvania, while in Frederick Goode's film, *Beast of Morocco* (1966), a British architect encounters a vampiric siren in the ruins of an ancient palace in Morocco. Such stories share many of the features of Jonathan Harker's journey to Castle Dracula in Stoker's novel.

2. Contrast these stories with two films that mix the conventions of the vampire story and the western, *Curse of the Undead* (1959) and *Billy the Kid vs. Dracula* (1966), in which the aristocratic, European vampire invades nineteenth-century America.

3. This point was reinforced for me when I saw a 1976 episode of the television detective series *McCloud*, entitled "McCloud Meets Dracula," guest starring John Carradine as an old horror film actor obsessed with his role as Count Dracula. In this episode random killings by a "psycho" sniper are juxtaposed with a series of murders that look to be the work of a vampire. Nothing is made of this potentially interesting juxtaposition, except for a comment by the cynical, hard-nosed police lieutenant, who dismisses both types of homicide with a "takes all kinds" gesture. Like McCloud, we never know for sure whether the movie star in his cape and formal attire is truly a vampire, merely a good actor, or a madman victimized by his obsession with horror movies. (Contrast Sherlock Holmes's debunking of the supposedly undead threat in Arthur Conan Doyle's *The Sussex Vampire.*) The end of this show leaves open the possibility that the old man has not jumped to his death, but has instead flown away into the night. No matter—the sniper has been caught and the next episode will bring another, probably more menacing threat. Dracula—real or imagined, dead or undead—is just another case.

4. Anne Rice, *Interview with the Vampire* (New York: Ballantine, 1976), p. 45.

5. Both *I, Desire* and *Vegas Vampire* are direct descendants of *The Night Stalker* (1972), a made-for-television movie that similarly depicts the crimes of a classical, thoroughly evil vampire in modern-day Las Vegas and the very traditional means of disposing of this monster. *The Night Stalker* for many years had the distinction of having attracted the largest audience of any made-for-television film. It was directed by John Llewellyn Moxey (director of *I, Desire*), produced by Dan Curtis (director of *Dracula* [1973]), and scripted by Richard Matheson (author of *I Am Legend*), and it served as the basis for the television series, *Kolchak—The Night Stalker* that ran on ABC television during the 1974–75 season. *The Night Stalker* was adapted from Jeff Rice's novel of the same name, although the novel was not published until 1973 (New York: Pocket Books). In his version of the story, Rice particularly emphasizes the way self-serving government officials, law officers, and representatives of the media cover up the truth of this case for economic and political reasons.

6. Stephen King, *'Salem's Lot* (New York: New American Library, 1976), p. 330. All future references to *'Salem's Lot*, abbreviated SL, will be included parenthetically in my text.

7. "Adjacent" to these particular horror stories are, on the one hand, revenge dramas like *A Small Town in Texas* (1976) and *Moving Violation* (1976), which present the corrupt small town as a deadly trap that is inimical to youth, mobility, romance, and freedom, and on the other hand, blackly comic movies like *A Boy and His Dog* (1975) and *Cars That Eat People* (1974), in which the small town is at once a source of horror and an object of satire.

8. Stephen King, *Danse Macabre* (New York: Everest House, 1981), p. 38.

9. One important precursor for the role of Straker in *'Salem's Lot* is the role of the doctor in Dreyer's *Vampyr*. Titles identify this man as the "vampire's accomplice," who carries out the commands of his Master and so becomes one of the "living damned." In his screenplay for the film, Dreyer describes the doctor's face as being "marked by unctuous servility, coupled with relentless malignity" (*Carl Theodor Dreyer: Four Screenplays* [Bloomington: Indiana University Press, 1970], p. 88), a description that applies equally to Straker in *'Salem's Lot*. Interestingly, given the conventions of the genre, the destruction of the doctor (he is trapped inside a cage and slowly buried by falling white powder—destroyed by "whiteness," as it were) occurs after the destruction of the vampire in *Vampyr*, suggesting that his human evil is perhaps more threatening than the supernatural evil of the vampire.

10. Contrast Renfield's description of the rats to the images in *Nosferatu* and *Nosferatu the Vampyre* of the rats that accompany the vampire. It is interesting to note that the few times Stoker depicts a "mass" threat (as opposed to a singular evil creature) in his short stories, this threat takes the form of rats whose "blazing" eyes suggest a sort of demonic consciousness. See *The Judge's House* and *The Burial of the Rats* in *Dracula's Guest* (1914; rpt. New York: Zebra, 1978).

11. Edgar Z. Friedenberg, "Children as Objects of Fear and Loathing," *Educational Studies* 10 (1979), 63–65. For a recent example that bears some rela-

tion to the story of the living and the undead, see *The Children* (1980), a low-budget horror film in which a leak at a nuclear power plant causes a group of innocent children to become malevolent, radioactive, zombielike creatures who instinctively seek to destroy their parents and other adults.

12. King has stated that one "intentional similarity" of *'Salem's Lot* to Stoker's *Dracula* is "of course, the band of Fearless Vampire Hunters which forms in each book" (*Danse Macabre*, p. 38).

13. Cf. Rice's *The Night Stalker*, in which the cynical, old-style newspaper reporter turned vampire hunter also relies on *Dracula* and the literature about the undead. Rice's pseudodocumentary narrative becomes, like *'Salem's Lot*, a sort of verification of the reality of the fictitious.

14. King, *Danse Macabre*, pp. 106, 377. *Danse Macabre* is itself a horror story of sorts, with King as the protagonist always peering over his shoulder in fear of (and in fear of being mistaken for) academic literary critics, who come to embody analytical thinking and all the other worst qualities of adulthood.

15. This aspect of *'Salem's Lot* has parallels in a number of recent horror stories in which the fine art of murder is emphasized and the monster becomes analogous to the teller of horror stories. *The Exorcist*, *Halloween*, and *The Funhouse* are three of the more interesting examples.

16. King has indicated on various occasions that he plans to write a sequel to *'Salem's Lot*, pursuing the elements left open in this novel, including the fate of Father Callahan, the failed vampire hunter. He also suggests one possible direction that this sequel might take in *One for the Road* (1977; rpt. in *Night Shift* [New York: New American Library, 1979]), a story set two years after the burning of 'salem's Lot, when vampires still roam the area, preying on unwary travelers.

The end of King's novel differs substantially from the conclusion of Hooper's telefilm version of *'Salem's Lot*. In Hooper's adaptation, Ben pounds a stake into Barlow's heart and sets fire to the Marsten House, then drives off with Mark. A dissolve links the fire to a full moon, then another dissolve carries us to a church in rural Guatemala. Ben and Mark are on the run, armed with holy water and stakes. In the final sequence Ben must drive a stake into the voluptuous, undead Susan Norton, who has tracked the pair of hunters from 'salem's Lot. "There will be others," Ben tells Mark, and the two haggard fugitives leave. The camera then moves to show the same full moon that hangs over the Marsten House. In Hooper's ending, the vampire hunters have become hunted exiles, destined never to escape completely from the undead or the full moon. King's Ben and Mark, by way of contrast, choose to return after their self-imposed exile to become again crusaders in the service of the Good by completing the wild work they have begun.

A much more unambiguously closed ending is found in the version of Hooper's telefilm that was intended for theatrical release and was eventually shown on a cable TV movie channel. This retelling of King's novel concludes with the destruction of Barlow and the burning of the Marsten House, thus suggesting that the threat has been vanquished and the living have completed their work and need no longer concern us.

17. Robin Wood notes that in what he calls the "reactionary wing" of the

contemporary American horror film, the monster is presented as "*simply* evil" and as "totally non-human" (*The American Nightmare: Essays on the Horror Film*, ed. Robin Wood and Richard Lippe [Toronto: Festival of Festivals, 1979], p. 23). Wood's critique of *Halloween, Alien*, and other films he dubs "reactionary" offers a necessary contrast to King's argument that "the horror movie is innately conservative, even reactionary" (*Danse Macabre*, p. 173).

18. Hannah Arendt, *The Origins of Totalitarianism* (New York: World, 1958), pp. 323, 322, 405, 374.

19. Vincent Bugliosi, *Helter Skelter: The True Story of the Manson Murders* (New York: Bantam, 1974), pp. 655, 549.

20. Ibid., pp. 161, 552–53, 606. The opening page of the Bantam paperback edition of *Helter Skelter* (as of 1982 in its fortieth printing) warns the prospective reader: "The story you are about to read will scare the hell out of you." During his testimony at the trial, Manson himself seemed to seek a very similar effect. "What about your children?" he yelled at the people in the courtroom, "you say there are just a few? There are many, many more, coming in the same direction. They are running in the streets—and they are coming right at you!" (ibid., p. 530). It seems to me that any comprehensive study of the contemporary horror story needs to take into account the spate of nonfiction horror stories that have appeared since Truman Capote's *In Cold Blood: A True Account of a Multiple Murder and Its Consequences* (New York: Random House, 1965).

21. See J. Glenn Gray's excellent discussion of "Images of the Enemy" in *The Warriors: Reflections on Men in Battle* (1959; rpt. New York: Harper and Row, 1970), pp. 131–69. As W. Warren Wagar notes, a related image of the multiple threat appears in pre-World War I stories of a "coming *Rassenkampf*, a Darwinian battle to the death between the White Man and various contenders for his overlordship of the planet, chiefly the Yellow Man" (*Terminal Visions: The Literature of Last Things* [Bloomington: University of Indiana Press, 1982], p. 122).

22. See Richard Slotkin, *Regeneration through Violence: The Mythology of the American Frontier, 1600–1860* (Middletown, Conn.: Wesleyan University Press, 1973), pp. 94–145.

23. Norman Cohn, *Europe's Inner Demons: An Enquiry Inspired by the Great Witch-Hunt* (New York: New American Library, 1977), pp. 49, xiv, 17, 252.

24. John Shirley, *Dracula in Love* (New York: Zebra, 1979), pp. 117, 248.

25. In Scott Baker's occult-fantasy novel, *Dhampire* (New York: Pocket Books, 1982), the vampires belong to a satanically inspired, parasitic sect that seeks to extend its dominion over the earth. *Dhampire* is a rather pretentious tour through spiritual realms, magical kingdoms, and states of heightened consciousness that all demonstrate how inconsequential ordinary reality truly is. J. N. Williamson's *Death-Coach* (New York: Zebra, 1981) offers a comparable image of vampires and the occult.

26. Compare *Thirst* to Guy de Maupassant's *The Horla* (1887; rpt. in *The Dracula Book of Great Vampire Stories*, ed. Leslie Shepard [Secaucus, N.J.: Citadel Press, 1977]). In this story the isolated first-person narrator either

imagines or actually encounters the "Horla"—"invisible, though tangible beings, a species of vampire" that seeks to make man "his chattel, his slave and his food" (*Horla*, pp. 106–7).

27. Robert R. McCammon, *They Thirst* (New York: Avon, 1981), pp. 453, 295. Cf. William W. Johnstone's *The Devil's Kiss* (New York: Zebra, 1980), which also follows *'Salem's Lot* in its presentation of the life-or-death battle between a community of citizens turned faithful hunters and the collective forces of Evil, which include corrupt human beings, inhuman beasts, and undead creatures, all under the control of Satan's henchmen.

28. McCammon, *They Thirst*, pp. 496, 411, 518.

29. Ibid., p. 531.

30. Because it is set in the future and is concerned with the end of the world, *I Am Legend* is often classified as a science fiction novel. Other recent attempts to combine vampirism and science fiction include: Colin Wilson, *The Space Vampires* (New York: Random House, 1976); Tanith Lee, *Sabella or The Blood Stone* (New York: DAW Books, 1980); and David Bischoff, *Vampires of Nightworld* (New York: Ballantine, 1981). Among the science fiction films that involve vampiric creatures are Roger Corman's *Not of This Earth* (1957), Mario Bava's *Planet of the Vampires* (1965), and Christian Nyby's *The Thing* (1951), which I will consider later in this chapter.

31. Richard Matheson, *I Am Legend* (1954; rpt. New York: Berkley, 1971), p. 64. All future references to *I Am Legend*, abbreviated IAL, will be included parenthetically in my text. Matheson has had a long and very successful career both as a screenwriter and as an author of horror fiction. Among his many works are other vampire stories like *Drink My Blood Red* and *No Such Thing as a Vampire*, and a number of screenplays including *The Night Stalker* and *Dracula* for Dan Curtis. See the biographical sketch and interview with Matheson in John Brosnan, *The Horror People* (New York: New American Library, 1977), pp. 195–200.

32. Martin Cruz Smith, *Nightwing* (New York: Jove, 1978), p. 65. When Arendt describes the horror of the totalitarian regime's concentration camps, a horror that "can never be fully embraced by the imagination" (*Origins of Totalitarianism*, p. 444), she emphasizes how the inmates were methodically transformed into "living corpses" by the destruction of the "juridicial person" in them, then the "moral person," then any traces of individuality and spontaneity (ibid., pp. 444–57). After this process of dehumanization, "nothing then remains but ghastly marionettes with human faces . . . which all react with perfect reliability" (ibid., p. 455). Unlike the vampires in *'Salem's Lot*, the undead creatures in *I Am Legend* and Romero's films have far greater affinities with these victimized "living corpses" than with the totalitarian regime that is structured according to the "Leader principle."

33. Montague Summers, *The Vampire: His Kith and Kin* (1928; rpt. New Hyde Park, N.Y.: University Books, 1960), p. 77.

34. Albert Camus, *The Plague*, trans. Stuart Gilbert (New York: Random House, 1948), p. 79.

35. *I Am Legend* was also the source for Boris Sagal's *The Omega Man*

(1971). Matheson was not involved as a screenwriter with either adaptation of his novel.

36. As John Brosnan and a number of critics have noted, *The Thing*, a film produced by Howard Hawks, is similar thematically and stylistically to other films directed by Hawks. I refer to the film as Christian Nyby's *The Thing* for the sake of uniformity, since Nyby is credited as the film's director. See Brosnan, *Horror People*, pp. 87–88; and John Baxter, *Science Fiction in the Cinema* (New York: Paperback Library, 1970), pp. 104–6. In "The Mummy's Pool," *Dreamworks* 1 (Summer 1981), 292–94, Bruce Kawin contrasts *The Thing* with *The Day the Earth Stood Still* (1951) to distinguish between the horror and science fiction film. It should also be noted that any complete reading of *The Thing* would have to take into account its allusions to and revisionings of James Whale's *Frankenstein*.

37. In John Campbell's *Who Goes There?* (1938), the novella upon which *The Thing* is based, the evil, monstrous alien does not feed on blood and reproduce itself. Instead it assimilates and perfectly imitates the life forms it encounters on earth. While Nyby's film emphasizes man's capacity for creating new, effective communities in the face of the malevolent extraterrestrial, Campbell's story shows how quickly (and how justifiably) men come to suspect each other of being the monster. The isolated human beings in *Who Goes There?* must kill their possessed co-workers. In this regard, John Carpenter's 1982 remake of *The Thing* has much more in common with Campbell's story than with Nyby's film.

38. One important antecedent for *The Thing*—and for all twentieth-century stories of alien invasions—is H. G. Wells's *The War of the Worlds* (1897). For all their advanced technology, the Martian invaders in Wells's novel are vampiric monsters who "took the fresh living blood of other creatures, and *injected* it into their own veins" (*The War of the Worlds*, ed. Frank D. McConnell [New York: Oxford University Press, 1977], p. 245). For another use by Wells of vampirism, see his story, *The Strange Orchid* (1897).

CHAPTER 8

Land of the Living Dead

As in *The Thing*, in *Night of the Living Dead* we learn more and more as the film progresses about the nature of the monster—its particular strengths and weaknesses, its motivation, its origin, and the type of threat it poses to man. In this respect our situation approximates that of the besieged human beings in George Romero's film, to whom each new piece of information about the undead (beyond the simple information about how to destroy the monster) only prolongs the nightmare and lessens the chance that the living will survive. Unlike Stoker's *Dracula* and most other vampire stories, *Night of the Living Dead* does not assume that knowledge is power, at least not for the people in the film whose fate we are most concerned with.

Soon after the opening credits, the first of the living dead enters a sunlit cemetery alone. A young woman in her twenties, Barbara, and her cynical brother, Johnny, have driven 200 miles into the country to place a wreath on their long-dead father's grave. To them, the slow-moving figure in the distance is simply an odd, harmless, even pathetic or ludicrous stranger, dressed in disheveled but ordinary clothes. According to Romero, in the black-and-white images of *Night of the Living Dead* "there's nothing about the make-up that tips you right away" that this man is actually a monster.[1] At first glance, the lone man, as David Pirie notes, is "hardly a threat or even a curiosity."[2] As thunder provides Gothic sound effects, the man approaches and suddenly grabs Barbara, who is rescued by her brother. After Johnny is overpowered and apparently killed, Barbara flees and the killer pursues her, running with a lurching, pigeon-toed gait so that he seems almost a caricature of the creature in James Whale's *Frankenstein*.

The terrified woman takes refuge in a farmhouse, as her stumbling, glazed-eyed assailant approaches. There is no reason to doubt that he is a human being—a homicidal maniac, perhaps, or a feeble-minded sex offender or an escapee from some asylum (all common forms of the human monster in horror stories). There is also no reason to assume that Barbara has accidentally encountered some sort of multiple threat, since only one man chases her. Thus, as we enter the world of *Night of the Living Dead*, we seem to be in familiar, if still frightening terrain: the victim is an isolated, unlucky young woman; the monster is a single deranged man. Night, we soon realize, has not yet fallen.

When the sun sets and crickets chirp in the still rural darkness, several other figures appear outside the farmhouse, moving slowly from out of the black shadows. Ben, another human being on the run, seeks refuge in the house. Using a tire iron he beats to death three of the creatures that attempt to follow him inside. Yet the more of the living dead Ben destroys, the more of them arrive and gather outside, joining the growing crowd of men oddly dressed in bathrobes, T-shirts, or soiled suits. Each of the living dead is as physically unique as he was in life, though all move with similarly stiff, awkward gestures, and all are apparently interested only in getting the people who are inside the house (though we do not yet know why). Ben discovers that he is able to overpower any one or two of the creatures, that they are scared of fire, and that they can be destroyed by a bullet or a heavy blow to the head. Yet he quickly realizes that he cannot hope to kill them all, for each time he glances out the boarded-up windows, more of the things have gathered. Soon women are in among the rest, along with half-decayed walking corpses, old folks, and assorted figures in hospital gowns, neat work clothes, or no clothes at all. The living dead mill about without speaking, apparently without even noticing each other. These mute creatures, unlike the King-Vampire and his undead sirens, cannot use human language to deceive, tempt, or command the living.[3]

Inside the farmhouse, Ben, Barbara, and two other couples who had been hiding in the basement listen to a series of emergency radio and television broadcasts concerning the "epidemic of mass murder" that is spreading over the eastern United States. These news reports obviously extend the scope and the magnitude of the threat (from one woman in danger to a handful of people to a large area of the United States), and, as I will later suggest in more detail, they ironically demonstrate the incompetence and the failure of official government authorities. These broadcasts also attempt to make sense of what we have seen, if only by naming the monster. For example, a newscaster describes the "killers" as "ordinary looking people" who have become part of "a virtual army of unidentified assassins" that has thrown a third of America into chaos. In addition, we learn from a radio announcer that the "killers are eating the flesh of the people they murder," and a television newscaster informs us that "the unburied dead are coming back to life and seeking human victims." The only explanation even tentatively offered by the media is that this phenomenon has somehow been caused by NASA's destruction of "a recent Explorer satellite shot to Venus," a space probe that was returning to Earth with a "mysterious, high level of radiation."

In the long run, none of what they hear on these broadcasts helps the people in the isolated farmhouse survive. For them, experiencing the horror far surpasses being told about it. For us, Romero's images of the undead are more vivid, memorable, and immediate—more descriptive—than any newsman's verbal account could ever be. For example, after we hear incredulous warnings about flesh-eating killers, we see, as does Ben, a macabre sort of picnic under the moonlight, with the undead creatures feasting on the remains of a young couple whose escape attempt failed. Like the vampires in *I Am Legend*, the living dead snarl and fight among themselves, here not for blood, but for organs, intestines, and flesh-covered bones. Driven by hunger, these almost purely instinctive creatures could hardly be called "killers," much less an "army of assassins." The living dead remain, as R. H. W. Dillard realizes, "still recognizably ordinary." [4]

That they can easily be destroyed with a shot or a heavy blow to the head and that they are so clumsy, slow, and predictable obviously set the living dead apart from the tradition of cunning, malevolent, and in some respect superhuman monsters like Count Dracula or the Thing from another world. Yet the creatures in *Night of the Living Dead* pose at least an equal threat, for ultimately they cannot be kept out of the farmhouse. By sheer force of number and nonstop pushing and pounding, they break through the barricaded windows and doors, overturn the furniture, and pack the living room from wall to wall, like so many wind-up toys with no space to move. Included among the mass of creatures at the end of the film are the man who originally chased Barbara from the cemetery, the newly undead Johnny, who captures his sister, and a young child who has just killed her mother with a garden trowel and feasted on her father's corpse. These three once very different and now very similar figures remind us how much a multiple threat differs from a singular threat. Killing Johnny or the little girl will not suddenly restore the safety and comfort of the living. In contrast to the film's opening scene, in the conclusion escape is no longer possible. Like Johnny and the little girl, all people can join the classless ranks of the living dead and become driven by a hunger that cuts every family tie and makes existence simple indeed.

Romero's presentation of the living dead, which would have a major influence on the image of the monstrous threat in a great many subsequent horror stories, may have certain parallels with earlier films featuring zombies or zombielike creatures, including *Invisible Invaders* (1959) and *Plague of the Zombies* (1965).[5] But by far the most important antecedent for *Night of the Living Dead* is *I Am Legend.* On various occasions Romero has acknowledged that the original idea for his film was "inspired" by Richard Matheson's novel, and the resemblance between the two works is striking.[6] For example, both the vampires in *I Am Legend* and Romero's living dead cannot transform themselves into mist or animal form, for they are not one-of-a-kind, supernatural beings on the order of the aristocratic vampires in Philip Saville's *Count Dracula* and John Badham's *Dracula.* And where generic convention often demands that vampires must be invited into the homes of their victims, no invitation need be offered to the crowd gathered outside Robert Neville's house or to the creatures in *Night of the Living Dead.* Most important, while the undead as depicted by Matheson and Romero are undeniably threatening, they are not Evil in the sense that the vampires in *'Salem's Lot* and most Hammer films are Evil. The living dead and the true vampires in *I Am Legend* belong to our world. They are our fellow citizens who, with no leader and no motive besides hunger, have returned to feed on us, and, with no malice and no grand design, to reach out and pull us into their ranks.

Night of the Living Dead, however, is a retelling of *I Am Legend,* rather than simply an attempt to bring Matheson's innovative portrait of the multiple threat to the screen. Thus the vague speculations in Romero's film about the ultimate cause of the sudden outbreak that threatens America seem to be almost a parody of Neville's scientific explanation of vampirism in *I Am Legend* and of the emphasis on the saving power of explanation throughout the story of the living and the undead. To assert that "mysterious radiation" in some unexplained way causes the dead to roam the land in search of human flesh is finally little better than no explanation at all (especially since this is a quasi-official explanation and therefore likely in *Night of the Living Dead* to be a lie, distortion, or cover-up). Human error might be the cause, so might the space program, extraterrestrial forces, "natural" conditions in outer space, and so on.[7] Ben and the other people trapped in the isolated house do not have the time to search for explanations, which would make little difference in any case. These people are too busy trying to survive the night. Their situation has none of the "monotonous horror" that plagues Robert Neville.

In their struggle for survival the living in Romero's film cannot rely on garlic, mirrors, or religious talismans for protection, and here the hungry undead are not restricted to only a nocturnal existence. (Once all these restrictions have been lifted, we can see in retrospect how many flaws mar Count Dracula's superior mode of being and how many commandments restrict the King-Vampire's freedom to exercise his powers in Stoker's novel.) Whether we choose to label Romero's living dead as vampires or not—they are never called vampires in the film, though human blood is part of their diet—they are obviously undead creatures, similar to the walking corpses in *I Am Legend*, but several steps further removed from traditional images of the undead.[8] The major distinction between the living dead and the vampires I have discussed thus far is, of course, the fact that the creatures in *Night of the Living Dead* eat warm human flesh, a fact that Romero graphically records and never allows us to forget. The feeding habits of the living dead have nothing in common with the sexually charged, mutually pleasurable act of bloodsucking in, for example, *Dracula, Prince of Darkness*, for example. Quite unlike the experienced, masterful vampires who seduce their victims and unlike even the hissing, possessed brides of Dracula, Romero's living dead tear at their food and devour it like starving animals to whom all of existence is only a matter of hunting for food and eating.

After his first encounter with the living dead, Ben immediately begins to refer to the creatures outside the house as "things." And they are "things"—nonhuman beings of no value, for which we have no adequate name. The radio announcer who calls them "assassins" or "misshapen monsters" or "killers" obviously has not seen the living dead and has settled for available labels. Yet when Barbara recounts her terrifying experience in the cemetery, she refers to her assailant as a "man"—and she, too, is right. The first of the living dead that we see in the film is a man before he is a thing; he is one of *us* before we realize that he is one of *them*. He and all the rest of the living dead retain the physical appearance of human beings. They do not suddenly bare oversized canine teeth or stare with blood-red eyes. Even when they are eating the remains of the two teenagers, the living dead never cease to look like—and therefore in some fashion to be?—human beings. After all, most Americans are flesh-eaters, while none of us survives solely by drinking blood. The living dead, as Romero told an interviewer, are "the neighbors."[9]

Freud's comments in *Totem and Taboo* about repression and projection suggest one possible explanation for the popularity of Romero's *Night of the Living Dead* and other stories of the confrontation between the living and the undead. Primitive taboos concerning the dead, Freud argues, are rooted in the "*unconscious* hostility" and "evil impulses" that the living project onto the dead. "This process of projection, which turns a dead man into a malignant enemy" (TT, 63–64), seems also to be present in the stories I have discussed. Stoker's *Dracula*, no less than *Night of the Living Dead* or *'Salem's Lot*, exploits what Freud in a 1919 essay entitled "The 'Uncanny'" calls "the primitive fear of the dead [that] is still so strong within us and always ready to come to the surface at any opportunity. Most likely our fear still contains the old belief that the deceased becomes the enemy of his survivor and wants to carry him off to share his new life with him."[10] I would suggest that Freud's idea of the dead-as-enemy takes concrete form when the undead Lucy Westenra tempts Arthur Holmwood in Stoker's *Dracula*, when the newborn vampires attack their relatives and neighbors in *'Salem's Lot*, and when Johnny lunges forward to grab his sister Barbara in *Night of the Living Dead*.

Though Freud does not explicitly consider any fear or taboo that directly concerns what I have called the multiple threat, the new order envisioned by the King-Vampire in Stoker's novel has significant parallels with Freud's portrait of the primal horde, as I noted in chapter 2.[11] Embodiments of Evil like the Manson Family in *Helter Skelter* and the vampires in *'Salem's Lot* and *They Thirst* offer similar parallels. In these recent stories, the multiple threat takes the form of what Freud defines as the group in *Group Psychology and the Analysis of the Ego*: the members are all basically equal in their lack of freedom, and all desire to be ruled by a superior leader, who has a "masterful nature" and is "absolutely narcissistic, self-confident and independent" (GP, 71). When any "random collection" of people becomes a group, Freud concludes, we can see yet again the "survival" and the "revival" of the primal horde (GP, 70). Thus Freud rejects the argument that man is motivated to a great extent by a "herd instinct," an argument put forth by, among others, W. Trotter in *Instincts of the Herd in Peace and War* (1916). Instead, Freud defines man as a "horde animal, an individual creature in a horde led by a chief" (GP, 68). And the same definition applies to the vampires in *'Salem's Lot*.

The unconnected, leaderless undead in *I Am Legend* and *Night of the Living Dead*, however, are not a dark and threatening, evil manifestation of the primal horde that attacks modern civilization. The creatures depicted by Matheson and Romero constitute a very different form of the multiple threat, as different from the undead legions in *'Salem's Lot* as from, for example, the Viet Cong in John Wayne's *The Green Berets* (a film released in 1968, the same year as *Night of the Living Dead*). Wayne presents the enemy as a rampaging, faceless horde of sadistic murderers, led in their slaughter of the innocent by an egotistical, "superior" commanding officer. The Green Berets successfully kidnap this enemy leader, and the vampire hunters in King's novel destroy Barlow, but there is no such avatar of the primal father to slay in *Night of the Living Dead*. The living dead—without a leader—increase, press forward, force their way into the farmhouse like some sort of mob. Yet they are not an angry mob that is rioting, looting, or revolting against the status quo. Though the creatures in Romero's film do not emerge from any one specific social class, perhaps the living dead are our version of what in the past was called the "rabble."

I will not attempt here to survey the major nineteenth-century images of the mob as a dangerous, even monstrous threat to the status quo. However, two such images of the multiple threat are noteworthy as comparison points for *I Am Legend* and *Night of the Living Dead*. In James Malcolm Rymer's serial novel, *Varney the Vampyre* (1847), the threat posed by the mob almost surpasses the threat posed by the solitary vampire. Varney the Vampyre's "horrible appetite" for the "undefiled blood of a maiden's veins" places a number of beautiful, young virgins in danger, yet Varney is quite clearly a victim as well as a villain.[12] At several points in the novel, a "disorderly and vicious mob" sets out—unsuccessfully in every case—to destroy the vampire. Varney endangers maidens and upper-middle-class households; the mob, "a motley mass of human beings, wedged together, dark and sombre," threatens private property, law and order, and ultimately society itself. When the narrator of *Varney the Vampyre* pauses to speculate on group psychology and the "rabble" as a social phenomenon, he emphasizes the ignorance, destructive, "evil passions," and "wild, ungovernable superstition" of the mob.[13] At least equally significant are the narrator's metaphoric descriptions of the mob in action. "Resembling beasts of prey rather than any human multitude," the people who pursue the vampire are like "hungry wolves." Pictured in these scenes from *Varney the Vampyre* as a subhuman, animalistic force, the mob in Rymer's novel has other faces as well. For example, after setting fire to Varney's estate, the crowd "danced like maniacs round the fire; looking, in fact, like so many wild Indians, dancing round their roasting victims, or some demons at an infernal feast."[14] What an extraordinary confluence of images and of fears: the mob as insane revelers, bloodthirsty savages, demonic celebrants, in addition to being predatory animals—all at the same time, all in the heart of modern England. For Rymer, the multiple threat is at once animalistic, maniacal, primitive, and satanic. It endangers us physically, psychologically, culturally, and spiritually. Yet in *Varney the Vampyre* the mob can be contained, for the time being at least, by armed, orderly military forces.[15]

In Gustave Le Bon's *The Crowd* (1895; first published in English in 1896), an often-reprinted sociological study published two years before Stoker's *Dracula*, the mob is depicted as being less like a mass of demons or "wild Indians" than like a contagious disease or "microbes which hasten the dissolution of enfeebled or dead bodies." For Le Bon, the crowd is "only powerful for destruction," and its members are characterized by extreme impulsiveness, exaggerated sentiments, and an all-embracing "suggestibility" that eventually turns them into "automatons." Simultaneously, those people in the mob—all infected by the "contagion"—become "barbarians" who are ruled by "savage, destructive instincts," the "atavistic residuum of the instincts of the primitive man."[16] (Compare the "primitive" violence of the new society that demands Neville's execution in *I Am Legend*.) The diseased barbarians and destructive automatons who make up Le Bon's crowd and the mob in Rymer's *Varney the Vampyre* offer two nineteenth-century antecedents to the monstrous undead masses in the works I have been discussing and to other twentieth-century versions of the multiple threat.

Like Freud, Le Bon insists on the absolute importance of the leader in the structure and psychology of the mob, for he argues that "a crowd is a servile flock that is incapable of ever doing without a master."[17] Rymer is much more interested in the multitude than in the leader, though his mobs have their spokespersons, orators, and temporary commanders. In Le Bon's view, the leader's "magnetic fascination" attracts and satisfies the mob's blind, instinctive "turn to servitude" and their desire for submission to a "being supposed superior."[18] A horrifying, exaggerated example of this relationship is suggested in Stoker's *Dracula* and realized in King's *'Salem's Lot*. But in *Night of the Living Dead* the diseased, instinct-driven automatons walk the earth without a leader. They need no Master to seduce new recruits or to direct their assault on normality. The living dead are indeed like Le Bon's crowd in being "only powerful for destruction," and they are a contagion that spreads faster than any epidemic—killing, feeding off, and transforming the living into the undead. They are not, however, driven by any motive besides hunger—not revenge or the lust for power, not even the desire to destroy for the sake of destruction. The living dead do not require satanic cunning or superhuman strength to achieve their ends, and their simulacrum of immortality holds no promise of pleasure or privilege, just work and more work.

Like all monsters, the dead man become "malignant enemy" is to some degree a projection of our fears and hostilities. Such undead creatures, above all the figure of the aristocratic vampire, are also projections of our desires. Leonard Wolf, for example, finds Count Dracula to be "the willing representative of the temptations, and the crimes, of the Age of Energy."[19] Even horde creatures like the undead slaves in *'Salem's Lot* embody certain human desires, most notably those voiced by Renfield in Stoker's novel—the wish to be governed and to escape from freedom as well as from death. In the context of the stories I have discussed, Romero's living dead seem impoverished in this regard, for they apparently do not speak to our desire to be either masters or slaves, to rape or to command or to shatter sexual taboos. Perhaps the monstrous creatures in *Night of the Living Dead*, the "things" that are somehow still men, are the projection of our desire to destroy, to challenge the fundamental values of America, and to bring the institutions of our modern society to a halt.

The identifying features of the multiple threat in *Night of the Living Dead* become increasingly apparent when we examine these creatures in the context of the vampires in *I Am Legend*, *'Salem's Lot*, and Stoker's *Dracula*, and when we set Romero's film against other images of a multiple threat. Yet the creatures in *Night of the Living Dead*, as in all of the novels and films I have focused on, are defined to a great extent in relation to those human beings who serve as the victims, accomplices, or destroyers of the undead. And the undead, in turn, help define by contrast the strengths and weaknesses of the living. For example, in *Night of the Living Dead*, emotions such as fear, anger, hatred, and jealousy all come to seem quintessentially human, since they are expressed only by the living. Romero also suggests that the living have a certain propensity for murderous violence, territorialism, and irrationality—qualities that immediately surface during a crisis. As in any number of disaster movies or in westerns like *Stagecoach*, the flawed, would-be survivors in *Night of the Living Dead* embody a range of very different, clearly delineated human possibilities.[20] Each character, we could say, has his or her own story. The interaction between the living in the face of the undead is, in effect, a continual testing and redefining of these possibilities. In the course of the film, just as the principal characters all take refuge under one roof, so all these separate stories and the lives of all these separate characters become fully intertwined. In the fate of the living, we can see the fate of individual heroism, religious faith, communal action, romantic love, the nuclear family, and private property, and we can measure the fitness of man during the night of the living dead.

As I noted earlier, the film opens with Barbara and Johnny completing their annual journey far into the country to visit their father's grave. Their moving car is the first sign of life in the film; they could, in fact, be the only two people in the world. The distinction between brother and sister is immediately apparent: following the wishes of her mother, Barbara shows respect for her dead father by making this yearly pilgrimage and by kneeling and praying at his grave, an act that is at once a cultural, religious, and familial ritual. Johnny is quite obviously more concerned with his own life. He smokes and asks Barbara for some candy, and he is even dressed more stylishly than his sister. Johnny complains about wasting time and money, both better spent in Pittsburgh, and like a classic malcontent he cynically comments on the foolishness of this graveside ritual with its meaningless veneration for the dead and for one's parents. Johnny mocks Barbara's piety and her habit of churchgoing ("Not much sense in my going to church," he declares), and also her fear, for she is easily frightened. When the first of the living dead attacks in this rural cemetery, brother and sister both are extremely vulnerable, as if they have placed themselves in jeopardy by their journey away from modern civilization, like Jonathan Harker does in Stoker's *Dracula* or Herzog's *Nosferatu the Vampyre*. Later, however, we find out that Pittsburgh is probably no safer than the desolate countryside, and that civilization, home, and human company offer little protection to the living.

Given the distinctions between Johnny and Barbara, the fact that she survives and he becomes the first victim we see of the undead could be taken as a dispensation of justice: Johnny pays for being a self-centered, materialistic, cynical nonbeliever; Barbara, like the survivors in many other stories of the living and the undead, believes in tradition, demonstrates faith, and (therefore?) escapes from the monster. Such a tidy scheme—present, for example, in *Dracula Has Risen from the Grave* and *Taste the Blood of Dracula*, two Hammer films contemporaneous with *Night of the Living Dead*—is undercut by Romero. Though Barbara has been mocked and frightened by her brother, she survives only because Johnny comes to her aid. Traditional rituals offer her no protection, her veneration for the dead is pointless, and it makes no difference whether she demonstrates Christian faith. We realize by the end of *Night of the Living Dead* that Barbara's initial survival only guarantees that she will face a much more horrible and ironic fate at the hands of the undead.

After Johnny frees Barbara from the clutches of the monster, she is able to escape and seek refuge in an isolated farmhouse, the only potential haven in the open countryside. She has no keys for the car (Johnny was driving), and no destination in mind. Coming upon the house seems to be a bit of much-deserved luck. As terrified as she is, Barbara is not paralyzed by her fear until after she arms herself with a butcher knife and explores the modestly furnished two-story house. When she sees a half-decayed corpse lying at the top of the stairs, Barbara flees the house in a panic, and she is saved from the gathering undead only because she runs into Ben, who has just driven up in a pickup truck. An articulate and apparently middle-class black man, approximately thirty years old, Ben—like Johnny—offers an immediate contrast to Barbara. These paired characters at the beginning of *Night of the Living Dead* suggest the degree to which Romero structures this film around a series of sometimes overlapping oppositions that work to define the nature of both the living and the undead. For example, Barbara's passivity obviously contrasts with Ben's activity, particularly since both characters are often shown in the same image or in alternating shots. Once she has discovered the corpse, has felt the blood that drips from upstairs onto her hand, and has seen Ben kill three of the living dead, Barbara can offer Ben no assistance. She doesn't even respond to his simple inquiries, but instead asks him:

"What's happening?" While Ben works, she wanders through the house almost like a zombie, touching a tablecloth or a music box as if to reattach herself to some remnant of normality. Finally, Barbara does speak, recounting in childlike phrases what happened in the cemetery and hysterically demanding that they "go get Johnny!" Frantic and ready to run outside, she strikes Ben when he stops her. He slaps her across the face, and Barbara passes out. She does not fully emerge from her catatonic stupor until the end of the film.

Traumatized after she is forced to see the dead and the living dead, the killing of Johnny and the killing by Ben, Barbara is reduced to a state of helplessness, almost as if she has become chronically apathetic or has sought refuge in again becoming a young child. Whether or not her reaction is plausible by psychological standards, it is a common reaction in other stories in which human beings confront a life-or-death situation and must struggle if they are to survive. (In Paul Gallico's *The Poseidon Adventure* [1969], for example, most of those people lucky enough to survive the capsizing of the ocean liner are reduced to a state very much like Barbara's—and none of these shell-shocked people survives.) Barbara's fate in *Night of the Living Dead* demonstrates that survival has its price and that the person who witnesses horror is forever altered by what he or she has seen. That Barbara is a woman would seem to support certain sexist assumptions about female passivity, irrationality, and emotional vulnerability. Given the generic context of *Night of the Living Dead*, what is equally significant is that Barbara is clearly the character who most fully believes in the values of tradition and religion. In a different story of the living and the undead (perhaps a story written or at least set in another century), she might have found herself involved in a holy crusade, but in *Night of the Living Dead* stake and cross are of no use at all, and Barbara's faith only seems to make her awakening to her dilemma that much more rude and catastrophic.

In contrast to Barbara, Ben has no such faith and no such immobilizing fear. From the first moment he appears, he attempts to control events and to learn as much as he can about his situation. Like all hunters in stories of the living and the undead, Ben works to survive—first, by killing three of the creatures, then by boarding up the house. The wild work of destruction in *Night of the Living Dead*, however, is neither an act of ritualistic violence nor a monotonous chore. With a tire iron, Ben pounds and pounds at the bodies he straddles. What Romero emphasizes is both the sheer physical effort required to kill just one of the living dead and the utter lack of supernatural assistance for man. This solitary human being, armed with his blood-stained tool, could not look less like a holy crusader. After all his work, he fells the third of the creatures with a blow to the head, and the corpse topples forward only to reveal four more of the living dead approaching the house. Once he is safely back inside, Ben confidently tells Barbara that he "can handle" the things outside. But his killing ultimately makes no difference at all, even though he destroys more of the undead in this one brief sequence than the vampire hunters destroy in any one of the Hammer films I discussed in chapter 4.

While Ben is not regenerated by the violence he commits here, he is also not irreparably tainted by the blood that stains his hands. Quite the opposite of Barbara, Ben seems to become energized by the situation and the increasingly more difficult task he faces. If he is in some respects an image of the modern American hero-as-amateur, it is because Ben, like his namesake in *'Salem's Lot*, is able to act with ingenuity and purpose, even though his plain slacks and cardigan sweater do not suggest that he is a man of action or even a man who works with his hands. Once he has unluckily been thrust into this predicament, Ben is defined less by his knowledge and by the depth of his beliefs than by his actions, including his almost instinctive protection of Barbara, who is at times a hindrance to his own survival.

Ben's greatest achievement is to make the house safe, at least for the time being. Romero focuses on Ben's constant movement as he completes this physical work. (Ben's adeptness greatly contrasts to the clumsiness of the living dead.) We remain inside with the living and see the house transformed into a barricaded fortress. A hammer and nails are found in the kitchen; shelves and interior doors provide the necessary lumber. In one scene Ben dismantles a dining room table, then nails the table top over a window and wraps a curtain around one of the table legs to make a torch. He uses this torch to ward off the living dead, and he even sets fire to an overstuffed armchair for the same purpose. (Like wild animals, these creatures back away from the fire man controls.) As in *The Thing* and *'Salem's Lot*, the materials for self-defense are close at hand, if only we know how to use them. In retrospect, however, Ben's actions can be seen as the beginning of the destruction of this home, a piece of private property that can no longer serve as a refuge and repository of human values.

The isolated farmhouse that Barbara first enters is like a haunted house—dark, full of shadows and frightening sights, potentially a trap. When Ben has finished securing the downstairs, the windows and doors are boarded up, all the lights are on to reveal the drab (and somehow comforting) ordinariness of the decor, and the radio is broadcasting news reports. He has found a rifle, some ammunition, and even a pair of shoes to replace those Barbara lost. She sits quietly, and he assures her that "everything's all right for now." And so it seems to us as well, for the radio advises all citizens to "stay indoors at all costs . . . lock your doors and windows." Ben may not have single-handedly conquered an ancient, superhuman force of Evil (no such force exists in *Night of the Living Dead*), but he has quickly and resourcefully accomplished a great deal—all with only everyday objects at his disposal, with a helpless young woman suddenly become his responsibility, and with a mass of things gathering outside in the darkness.[21] As the news bulletin warns of the spreading "epidemic of mass murder," Ben tells Barbara that "sooner or later someone is bound to come and get us out." It seems as if he believes that other human beings will prove to be as competent as he has proven and that help will come to those who help themselves.

In an instant the entire situation changes. As Ben is upstairs pulling the decayed corpse out of sight (disposing of the horror, as it were), the threat outside becomes suddenly more monstrous, for the radio announcer declares that "in all cases, the killers are eating the flesh of the people they murder." Barbara sits alone near the radio. Across the living room from her, a small door that was previously hidden from view starts to shake, and hands emerge from behind the door as it opens. The intruders are not figments of Barbara's imagination (Romero's editing initially suggests that they could be) nor are they the living dead, but instead a middle-aged man, Harry Cooper, and a teenager, Tom, who have been hiding in the basement. Earlier, Ben startles both us and Barbara when he first appears in the film, suddenly looming forward diagonally in a disorienting close-up before he saves her life. The introduction of Harry and Tom is even more ironic. Although these men emerge from the inside rather than breaking in from the outside, their entrance indicates that perhaps this fortress is vulnerable and will again become the trap that Barbara originally perceives it to be. Harry and Tom first seem to be a threat of some sort, then are revealed to be merely two more people trying to survive. What *Night of the Living Dead* finally suggests, however, is that these human beings are indeed a threat to Ben's survival and that perhaps he would be better off in the sort of solitary confinement Robert Neville endures in *I Am Legend.*

Like Ben and Barbara, Harry and Tom are strangers who have sought refuge in the farmhouse. None of these people lives in the house, and their meeting is an accidental event that forces them to become, for better or worse, interrelated and interdependent. Furthermore, each of these men is accompanied by a dependent woman: Ben quickly claims Barbara as his responsibility; Tom has his teenage girlfriend, Judy; and Harry has both his wife, Helen, and his sick daughter, Karen. As soon as other people besides Barbara appear, Ben's simple struggle to survive becomes complicated by questions and conflicts about territoriality, authority, and responsibility—questions that quite obviously do not worry the living dead.

The most immediately apparent conflict inside the house is between Ben and the white, middle-aged Harry Cooper. Harry is no more of a professional man of action than Ben, but Harry, too, is in perpetual motion, as he paces and chainsmokes. Unlike Ben's work, Harry's clamoring and constant nervous activity accomplish nothing. Whereas Ben devises a plan for defense and later for escape, Harry endlessly complains about the fortifications—just a "lousy pile of wood," he says—and insists that the sole "safe place" in the house is the cellar, an enclosed area with only one exit. Harry would retreat, hide, and wait to be rescued. Ben, who deems the cellar a "death trap," would challenge the undead and defend himself upstairs where the living have at least a "fighting chance." By all counts, Ben is less cowardly, less self-centered, less obnoxious, and much more capable, inventive, and heroic than Harry. Yet Harry is correct about the cellar, which does prove to be the only safe place, and about Ben's barricades, which cannot keep the living dead out of the house. Like a harbinger of the film's conclusion, soon after Harry and Tom appear, several of the living dead thrust their hands through a boarded-up window and grab at Ben, who with Tom's help forces the creatures away for the time being. Among the most significant ironies in *Night of the Living Dead* is the fact that the insecure, egotistical coward offers the best plan for survival, while all of Ben's efforts ultimately are for naught. This situation has no equivalent in any of the stories of the living and the undead that I have discussed.

If the threat posed by the things outside the house initially calls forth Ben's admirable effort to protect himself and Barbara, the appearance of Harry and the other people thrusts Ben back into a social environment. When confronted by Harry's challenges and complaints, Ben claims the upstairs as his domain, the radio and other objects as his possessions, and Barbara as his ward. "I'm the boss up here," he yells at Harry, "if you stay up here you take orders from me." Ben's power grows partly out of the barrel of the rifle he now carries, a weapon he will eventually use to murder Harry. Armed with this weapon, Ben declares that the house is his private property and installs himself as the sole figure of authority. (Recall that in Browning's *Dracula* Van Helsing insists: "I must be master here or I can do nothing." Unlike Ben, once Van Helsing is recognized as master, he leads the living to victory.)

When faced with the King-Vampire in Stoker's *Dracula*, Van Helsing, Lucy Westenra's suitors, and the Harkers unite in a moral community, an alliance that is echoed, however feebly, in King's *'Salem's Lot*. The best that the living can hope for in *Night of the Living Dead* is that they will be able just to "stick together" long enough to survive the night. Tom, the "kid," becomes the spokesperson for the virtues of collective action. With reasonable arguments, he tries to settle the conflict between Ben and Harry, because "we'd be a lot better off if all three of us were working together." Tom is ready to risk his life in the communal effort. While his idealism and his optimism always seem more than a bit naive, Tom never goes so far as to assume the role of the youthful martyr who willingly sacrifices himself for the group. Yet the teenager cannot forge the new community, and when the living do attempt to mount a concerted effort, they fail and Tom dies in the process.

In addition to speaking for the value of working together, Tom and his girlfriend Judy are the embodiment of romantic love in *Night of the Living Dead*—in contrast to the Coopers, the nuclear family, and to Ben, the unattached individual. Tom and Judy are basically good kids, who, as Dillard notes, "would have been the romantic hero and heroine if this had been a 1950s teenage horror film."[22] What is interesting, given the 1968 release date of Romero's film, is that these young lovers, and Tom in particular, are more than willing to do whatever work is necessary and to follow without question the orders given them by Ben and the official experts who appear on the television broadcasts. Judy has her qualms and selfish (i.e., personal) concerns for her and Tom's safety, but he consoles her with an embrace and with his calm insistence that "we've got work to do." In normal times Tom would be the model citizen, the perfect draftee.

Like Tom, Ben also heeds the advice offered by official authorities. When the newscaster reads a bulletin from the National Civil Defense Headquarters in Washington that lays out a "definite course of action," Ben immediately proposes that they follow the instructions and travel to a civil defense rescue station, even though the earlier broadcasts had insisted that people remain in their homes. To escape, Ben and the others must unlock the gas pump behind the house and fill up the tank of the pickup truck. (With an odd prescience, Romero demonstrates how vulnerable Americans are when they are cut off from their fuel supply.) Ben is the leader of the operation, marshaling the meager troops and supplies at his disposal. The plan calls for all three men to work together, as Tom had earlier proposed: Harry, who remains pessimistic about the chances for success, will toss Molotov cocktails from an upstairs window (like some parody of a militant revolutionary), then Ben will rush outside and keep the living dead at bay with his rifle and a torch while Tom drives the truck to the pump. Just as Tom is about to drive away from the house, Judy rushes out to join him—love and fear prove to be more compelling than questions of safety and rationality. Once again in a story of the living and the undead, the human beings prove themselves to be all too human. With Ben's help, Judy gets into the cab of the truck. They reach the pump while a mass of creatures stagger after them. Through accident and human error (Ben lays the torch too close to the truck, and Tom spills gasoline as he rushes to fill the tank), fire spreads near the truck. Romero's editing is even more abrupt and disorienting than usual here, creating a sense of both urgency and chaotic action. Tom drives away, then stops when he sees that the truck is on fire. He is about to get out, but he leans back into the cab to help Judy, whose jacket is caught. Before they can escape, the truck explodes, and the young couple die like ill-fated teenage lovers in some maudlin rock and roll ballad. In "Teen Angel" or "Patches," however, no ravenous creatures feed on the corpses of the innocent victims of fate. Needless to say, romantic love is neither the means nor the prerequisite for survival in *Night of the Living Dead.* Again, as so often in the film, an overwhelming, blackly comic irony pervades the sequence: Judy's desire to remain by the side of her boyfriend helps cause both their deaths; Ben's plan and the entire attempt to "work together" fail, much as Harry predicted they would; the would-be escape leads only to a feast for the undead and to the inescapable confinement of the living inside the house.

Death, of course, is the great equalizer, yet by the end of Romero's film, after all the people who have taken refuge in the house are dead, we realize that Tom and Judy's instantaneous death in a fiery explosion is vastly preferable to the fate awaiting Ben, Barbara, and the Coopers. Unlike the death of the vampire hunters in *'Salem's Lot*, the sacrifice of the young couple in Romero's film does not assist or even inspire the living in their struggle for survival. These deaths that serve "no purpose" lead Dillard to conclude that "the real horror of *Night of the Living Dead* is that there is nothing we can do that will make any difference at all."[23] Yet what the film also demonstrates is that regardless of what they have experienced, human beings to the end will continue to act as if they can make a difference, as if action matters and life is worth preserving.

For example, both Ben and Harry are stunned when they see the truck explode, thereby canceling the already remote chance of escape, but Ben immediately fights his way back to the house through crowds of the living dead and kicks open the front door that Harry refuses to unlock. The short-lived communal effort having ended disastrously, Ben becomes for Harry an adversary who is better left outside, and Harry becomes for Ben a more detested and even more dangerous threat than the living dead. After they have again boarded up the door, Ben punches his cringing, cowardly fellow human across the room. This violent outburst is obviously more satisfying—and even more normal—than the act of destroying the creatures who are feeding outside. Here, as at several points in *Night of the Living Dead*, Romero's editing forces us to contrast the living and the undead, revealing that the monsters do not lack individuality, but rather personality, mixed motives, and primary emotions like the anger and hatred that Ben demonstrates, the fear that motivates Harry, and the love that binds Tom and Judy or Helen Cooper and her daughter.

As much as Ben detests Harry, he does not kill him, at least not yet, and he does not attempt to escape on his own. Ben, like Helen, is stuck with this selfish coward whose warnings, unfortunately, have proven entirely correct. With no means of escape—no exit from this hell—and with an increasing number of creatures gathered outside, the living wait for the next emergency telecast. Earlier I suggested that the media reports hardly correspond to what we and the people in the isolated farmhouse see, and that these reports often raise more questions than they answer. (The on-location, ostensibly live telecasts are inexplicably set during the daytime, making these reports seem all the more unreal and distant from the nighttime action in the farmhouse.) Still, the living—as all of us are conditioned to do in any sort of large-scale emergency—pay the greatest attention to the broadcasts. Presumably, even bad news is better than no news at all, and information of whatever variety at least reassures Ben and the others that life still goes on elsewhere. The living also seek guidance, in the form of expert opinion and authoritative directives, from the news reports. Yet the federal authorities we see on a telecast from Washington are foolish bureaucrats, already attempting to shift responsibility, and the advice from government agencies and scientists is of no help at all.[24] As Romero will insist much more completely in *Dawn of the Dead*, there is no hope of being rescued by outside agencies. In *Night of the Living Dead*, no God, father, or president, no military, scientific, political, or religious form of authority guarantees or in any way promotes the survival of the living.

What Ben, Barbara, and the Coopers last see on the television is a report from the scene of a "search and destroy mission" conducted by a heavily armed posse of local citizens. The leader of the posse is Sheriff McClelland, who is dressed in a pork-pie hat and a rumpled suit with a cartridge belt across his chest. NASA, the FBI, the Joint Chiefs of Staff, and the "Survival Command Center at the Pentagon" all may be puzzled and panicked, but McClelland sees "no problem" with the living dead: "Get yourself a club or a torch. Beat 'em or burn 'em. They go up pretty easy," he tells a reporter, as he deploys his civilian troops in what looks to be a simple, successful operation. McClelland's volunteer hunters are not a crack, professional rescue team or a galloping cavalry troop, but they are help on the way, help that is relatively close to the besieged farmhouse. Ironically, whatever hopes this television report raises are extinguished when the power suddenly goes off, and the farmhouse is plunged into darkness. Ben earlier had successfully illuminated the house by switching on the lights and linked the survivors with the outside world through the radio (which we see him tuning) and the television (which he finds and sets up). The power failure negates these achievements. And almost immediately after the power fails, the living dead begin their attack on the barricades that once seemed so formidable.

In the newscast McClelland's posse, loaded down with guns and ammunition and equipped with trucks and guard dogs, seems to have

Ben (Duane Jones) mans the barricades in *Night of the Living Dead* (1968), as the private home proves to be more of a trap than a refuge and as all Ben's ingenuity and heroism ultimately go for naught. (Museum of Modern Art/ Film Stills Archive)

The socially sanctioned forces of order in *Night of the Living Dead* (1968) prepared to restore control. The task undertaken by the unemotional and almost cynically matter-of-fact Sheriff McClelland and his posse is simply work and not a holy crusade against the forces of Evil. (Museum of Modern Art/Film Stills Archive)

The living dead in Romero's *Night of the Living Dead* (1968)—things that are still recognizably, undeniably human beings. Romero pictures the multiple threat as a leaderless mass composed of our fellow citizens who have returned to feed on us and pulls us into their ranks. (Museum of Modern Art/Film Stills Archive)

an easy time with their work. Their mission is conducted in the daylight, and these hunters are never cornered and outnumbered by an "army of things" that press mindlessly, inexorably forward. The attack on the farmhouse by the undead is, in contrast, a mass attack.[25] From inside the house we cannot see beyond the hands and faces that crowd at every crack in the boarded-up windows. In the end torches and rifles cannot keep this mass at bay. In fact, the table leg that Ben earlier used as a torch is picked up by one of the living dead, who methodically pounds it against the front door. Another of the creatures uses a rock to shatter a window pane (similar to the way the first of the living dead had broken the window of Barbara's car). However rudimentary, these objects are weapons, and their use reminds us one final time that the living dead are neither utterly alien, nonhuman monsters nor enviable creatures possessing superhuman powers.

During the final attack the rifle will be of little use against the living dead, but inside the house it remains a prized possession that is, at least for the emasculated Harry Cooper, the means to gain power and control. As Ben attempts to shore up a barricaded window, Harry grabs the rifle and orders his wife into the cellar. She refuses, and Ben knocks Harry aside, recaptures the rifle, and fires it at almost point-blank range into Harry's chest. Ben's act is not a matter of self-defense, for he has regained the gun. In fact, the shooting of Harry seems absurdly superfluous, since it only hastens what looks to be inevitable. The shooting is more than a testament to Ben's potential for violence; it is, Romero suggests, a uniquely, definitively human act, for the living dead do not kill each other out of anger or the desire for vengeance. As in *I Am Legend*, morality has again fallen with society. In the darkness as the creatures close in, Ben becomes judge and executioner—one of his final acts as a human being is to settle accounts by killing Harry. If the victim were an evil vampire and the rifle a stake, then Ben's act would be a heroic, ritualistic triumph instead of a cold-blooded murder. In either case, however, man is defined by the violence he commits.

Mortally wounded, Harry staggers down into the cellar and collapses near where his daughter lies; his would-be refuge becomes his tomb. Upstairs, the living dead reach through the splintered front door to grab Helen. She screams and struggles to escape, for these monsters do not lovingly caress their victims or cast them into a hypnotic trance. Barbara suddenly comes alive to help free Helen, who does not return the favor, but instead runs downstairs in search of her daughter. In the cellar, Helen sees that one of her unspoken desires has been satisfied—with Harry's death, her loveless marriage is over. She also sees her worst fears realized. Karen kneels next to her father's corpse, with dark stains on her mouth and a piece of what looks to be bloody flesh in her hands. "It's mommy," Helen pathetically declares, as her daughter advances toward her with outstretched arms. Backed into a corner, Helen falls to the ground, defenseless and terrified as Karen picks up a garden trowel and repeatedly stabs the body of her mother. The staccato rhythms of the music and editing in this sequence clearly recall the murder of Marion Crane in *Psycho*, though the differences between these two scenes are telling indeed. Romero, like Hitchcock, focuses on the eyes of the helpless victim, eyes that in *Night of the Living Dead* see not a psychotic stranger (a deranged, overprotective "mother"), but a beloved child armed with a weapon more mundane and—we could say—more "unweaponly" than a butcher knife.

Helen's fate seems all the more bitter and horrifying when we recall that Romero initially shows her in the film ministering to her daughter. Helen is first and foremost a mother: "She [Karen] is all I have," Helen tells Judy. In fact, only because Helen is Karen's mother does she remain with Harry, a man she obviously detests. Particularly when juxtaposed with Tom and Judy's teenage romance, the Coopers' marriage—the *only* marriage we see in *Night of the Living Dead*—appears as an endless round of arguing and backbiting, of Helen's whining criticism and Harry's ill-fated attempts to assert masculine dominance. Yet like romantic love, marriage does not guarantee survival. Harry and Helen die separately, each having lived out a very personal nightmare. If the explosion of the pickup truck signals the death of the devoted couple (as well as canceling the possibility of escape), in the cellar we see the death not just of husband and wife, but of the family, as Karen feeds on her father's corpse and hacks at her mother with a garden trowel. That she acts without malice or passion makes her butchery more disturbing than any frenzied act of rage or madness. For Robin Wood, the death of the Coopers concludes Romero's "analysis" of the "'typical' American family," and Karen's destruction of her parents "represents the film's judgement on them and the norm they embody."[26] Whether or not the Coopers are truly typical or are the embodiment of a particular norm, they are the sole family in the film and as such are not just a family, but *the* family, one more fundamental aspect of American life that will not survive the apocalyptic night of the living dead.

Barbara, too, will not survive the final attack. After lapsing into an infantile state of dependency and passivity soon after she encounters Ben, Barbara becomes an independent, active adult again when the living dead begin to break into the house. The fear of imminent death revives her and returns her to sanity. As Johnny had earlier rescued her, now Barbara rescues Helen. Once again, however, a pervasive sense of irony and futility surrounds and ultimately undercuts any heroic action that the living are capable of. Barbara saves Helen from the hands of the living dead, yet Helen suffers an even worse fate in the cellar. And no one is able to come to Barbara's aid, though she screams for help when her now-undead brother grabs her. Barbara would have been better off if she had not emerged from her state of shock. Being conscious, she recognizes the undead creature who hours before was Johnny, and she realizes her fate as she and Johnny disappear into a crowd of hungry undead creatures outside the front door. Now, as he clasps her in what under normal circumstances would verge on an incestuous embrace, Barbara has a real reason to be frightened of her brother. Like Helen, she is the victim of what looks like her own flesh and blood. Ben stands only a few feet away from Barbara as she is carried off, but he can no more save her than he could prevent the death of Tom and Judy. Barbara's fate underscores the futility of the attempt by these people to keep the living dead at bay, and it begins to suggest the hopelessness of all of man's attempts to survive.

Finally, of the seven survivors who sought refuge in the farmhouse, only Ben remains alive when the living dead crowd in through the windows and the front door. As he backs into the center of the living room, Karen appears behind him—still hungry it seems—and he has to toss her aside. He does not have a "fighting chance"; he cannot struggle or escape, but only hide in the cellar, the very place he earlier had labeled a "death trap." He bars the cellar door and descends into the windowless, underground room that seems part cavern, part fallout shelter, part tomb (oddly enough, a fit resting place for a classical vampire). Except for the rifle, Ben has lost all the objects he claimed upstairs by right of first possession. As soon as Ben has descended into the cellar, Harry starts to rise to a new undead existence, and Ben shoots him three times at close range. Having shot the living Harry once, Ben must repeat the murder, as if he is condemned forever to kill and kill again. Then Ben shoots Helen as well, after her eyes snap open. (No Dracula need command nor Christ call forth the dead Coopers.) During this night, to live is to kill, for humans as well as monsters. In disgust Ben knocks over a table and throws the rifle aside. Yet as he hears the muffled sounds of the living dead from upstairs, he retrieves the gun from the shadows. Ben strikes a vigilant pose, down on one knee, his rifle drawn ready to fire, his eyes looking toward the room above. Trapped in a cellar with corpses around him, he is, for all we know, the last man on earth, ready for some final stand at the end of this long night—even though his bullets can make no difference whatsoever. Ben deserves to be facing a King-Vampire, but upstairs the living dead tramp through the living room and pound on the walls. They are grotesque, absurdly inept, and comical, but they fill the room and all of the image. The world is theirs.

At the very moment when the living dead overrun this vulnerable outpost, they fade from our sight, and a dissolve carries us outside the house into the morning light. The noise of shuffling feet and pounding gives way to the chirping of birds, for this dissolve, it seems, has transported us almost magically to a peaceful, harmonious setting that is not disrupted by either the living or the undead. A string of brief images records the still beauty of this picturesque rural scene, which shows few traces of the previous night's struggle. Then a helicopter flies across the sky, heralding the return of normality, which here is not synonymous with peacefulness and the natural order. The camera pans to follow it. A helicopter figures prominently in *Dawn of the Dead* as a vehicle for escape from society as well as from the living dead. In *Night of the Living Dead*, however, the helicopter carries us back to the world we lost touch with when the power went off at the farmhouse—the world, that is, of the "search and destroy mission." The same fields and farmland seen in the opening sequence of the film appear again at the end, but now they are dotted with civilian hunters and policemen restraining snarling dogs. We accompany the posse as it sweeps through the area destroying the living dead. "Everything appears to be under control," remarks the news reporter seen on the earlier telecast. As far as he and we can see, the emergency has ended, anticlimactically.

In the cellar Ben awakens to the sound of dogs and gunshots. He has been saved as much by accident as by being forced to follow Harry Cooper's strategy of holing up instead of fighting. By cutting several times from Ben to the posse, Romero makes clear how much simpler their work is than Ben's. The men outside, equipped with more than enough vehicles, weapons, and ammunition, have not even been tested, much less trapped and overpowered. Whereas Ben had to fight his way through a crowd of the living dead after the pickup truck exploded, the sheriff's forces far outnumber the few creatures who stumble across the fields, feebly attempting to flee. The hunters are not engaged in a life-or-death struggle for survival; they are merely taking target practice, for the living dead are all killed at a distance, not shot at close range or beaten to death. Here the monsters seem to pose no threat at all. As they stagger and are shot down, they are incapable even of self-defense. Thus the living dead finally appear in *Night of the Living Dead* as the antithesis of the traditional vampire of folklore and fiction, who, as Montague Summers notes, has "strength and agility more than human."[27]

What initially seems most ironic about the concluding sequence of *Night of the Living Dead* is that the posse has actually been very near the farmhouse—help was on the way. The deaths of Tom, Judy, and the others thus seem even more purposeless and more a matter of bad luck. One group of men approaches the farmhouse, and the sheriff, glancing at the burned-out shell of the pickup, casually notes that "somebody sure had a cookout here." The dead are the dead; McClelland justs wants to finish the job at hand.

Still carrying the rifle, Ben unbars the cellar door and warily crosses the living room so that he can look out the window. Outside, one of the men standing with the sheriff sees "something" move in the house, so McClelland tells him to "hit 'em in the head, right between the eyes." The man's aim is true, and Ben falls backward, a bullet hole in his forehead. "Okay, good shot," McClelland concludes, "he's dead. Let's go get him. That's another one for the fire." In a film full of ironic reversals and subverted expectations, Ben's fate is the final turn of the screw. Mistaken for one of them, just as the creature in the cemetery is mistaken for one of us, Ben dies in the daylight after having survived the night of the living dead. Both *Night of the Living Dead* and *I Am Legend* conclude with the death of the single survivor at the hands of the group. In the eyes of the new society, Robert Neville is a terrifying monster who must be destroyed. Yet for McClelland's posse, Ben is just "another one" of them, another "messed up" thing to be disposed of. (Though the posse cannot see that Ben is a black man, this murder evokes American racism at its deadliest and most virulent, a topic Romero will return to in the opening sequences of *Dawn of the Dead.*) What we realize is that, however flawed and unsuccessful he has proven himself to be, Ben remains the closest any of the human beings in *Night of the Living Dead* come to being a resourceful, brave, principled man of action, to being the sort of hero that is found in stories as diverse as Stoker's *Dracula*, *The Thing*, and *'Salem's Lot*. Romero has written that *Night of the Living Dead* "moves progressively toward absolute despair and ultimate tragedy."[28] Ben's death is the final stage in this movement, after Romero has shown us the failure of tradition and religious faith; the incompetence of the federal government, civil defense authorities, and the news media; the inadequacy of communal action and romantic love; the self-consuming destructiveness of familial ties; and the vulnerability of the private home.

For an instant following Ben's death, it seems as if *Night of the Living Dead* itself fails, as Romero, in Dillard's words, "abruptly shatters the film's smooth forward motion."[29] The men who will cart Ben's body to a bonfire appear in a grainy still image. Then follows a series of similar stills, all resembling poor-quality news photographs. The camera provides the only motion by zooming in to point out significant details in the photographs, such as Ben's face as he lies dead on the floor of the living room, the group of hunters as they enter the same farmhouse that the living dead had entered the night before, and the meat hooks that these men stick into Ben's body so that he can be carried off. When Ben is laid on the pile of wood, he does not look much different from the other corpses; the dead are the dead. Yet in these grainy still images, no one is alive. We hear the sounds of a crackling police radio, the helicopter's motor, and McClelland's voice, but on the screen the sheriff's men, with sunken eyes, stare at us, looking like corpses propped upright, like the living dead, in fact. These images suggest that the hunters, too, will die and that perhaps they also will rise and roam the countryside in search of victims.[30]

After the series of stills, motion resumes for the concluding seconds of *Night of the Living Dead*. McClelland orders a deputy to "light those torches over there," and suddenly the pile of wood and corpses bursts into flames that rise to fill the right half of the image, as the chief moves off screen to the left. McClelland is unemotional and almost cynically matter-of-fact. He is concerned not with explanations, but only with getting his job done. The work he is engaged in is just work and not a mission, much less a holy crusade. Somewhat similar in physical appearance to Harry Cooper and more successful than Ben at being the boss, McClelland is the final human being we see in the film—the survivor. What is left at the end of *Night of the Living Dead* is the bonfire McClelland has called for. The aborted Christian graveside ritual with which *Night of the Living Dead* opens—a vestige of what Donald M. Lowe calls the bourgeois "sentimentalization of death for the benefit of the bereaved"—is answered by the final bonfire, an unsophisticated means for the disposal of refuse.[31] Unlike the fire ignited by the vampire hunters at the conclusion of *'Salem's Lot* or the fire that consumes Count Dracula in the final images of *El Conde Dracula*, the bonfire in *Night of the Living Dead* is not a fire of purification or just punishment. It is less like a funeral pyre for a fallen hero than a pile of flammable rubbish.[32]

McClelland and his men have gotten used to killing anything that moves, to carrying corpses with meat hooks, and to smelling burning flesh. It's all in a day's work. The fact that "everything appears to be under control" is a small consolation indeed.

Well before Romero released *Dawn of the Dead* in 1979, *Night of the Living Dead*—like all commercially successful genre films—was imitated, borrowed from, and exploited by other storytellers. (One obvious example of this process was the publication in 1974 of the novelization of *Night of the Living Dead* written by John Russo, co-author with Romero of the original screenplay.) The American International vampire films featuring Count Yorga and Blacula that I mentioned in chapter 7 incorporate certain aspects of Romero's portrait of the living dead, and so do a number of otherwise very different horror films, including *Horror Express* (1972), *Fear No Evil* (1981), and *One Dark Night* (1982). In these three films, as in *'Salem's Lot*, the mass of walking corpses that threaten the living are under the control of a single malevolent master. The parallels to *Night of the Living Dead* are also immediately apparent in Alan Ormsby's *Children Shouldn't Play with Dead Things* (1972), in which an egotistical would-be movie director half-seriously recites black magic incantations to summon the corpses buried in an island cemetery. Responding to the call, the dead, in various stages of decomposition, crawl out of their graves and attack the director and his companions, who attempt—like Ben, Barbara, and the Coopers—to take refuge in a deserted, isolated house. Looking very much like Romero's living dead, these creatures also feed on human flesh. *Children Shouldn't Play with Dead Things* ends with the victorious, masterless undead on board a small boat floating back toward the mainland, as the lights of Miami flicker in the distance. According to David Pirie in *The Vampire Cinema*, a film even more closely modeled on *Night of the Living Dead* is Jorge Grau's *The Living Dead at the Manchester Morgue* ([1974] also released as *Don't Open the Window*). This "compellingly apocalyptic study of mass vampirism" pictures the undead as the "machine-like product of radiation sickness,"[33] while in Lucio Fulci's equally apocalyptic *Zombie* (1979) voodoo curses cause the dead to rise on a Caribbean island. The creatures in *Zombie* stalk both natives and visitors, and in the end they are unknowingly transported to America by boat. For his version of the open-ended, worst-fears-realized, xenophobic finale, Fulci concludes with an image of the leaderless undead crossing a bridge into Manhattan while a terrified newscaster announces: "The zombies are taking over . . . they're coming in!"[34]

Set against the context of Romero-influenced films like *Zombie*, the accomplishment of *Dawn of the Dead* becomes immediately apparent, for this second film in a projected trilogy is at once a continuation and an elaboration of *Night of the Living Dead*, a reconsideration of the major themes and assumptions of the earlier film, and an informed, ambitious, innovative expansion of the story of the living and the undead.[35] At the end of *Night of the Living Dead* American society seems to get a reprieve, for the authorities—McClelland's posse—have the situation under control. In *Dawn of the Dead*, however, the process of disintegration continues, until finally there are no authorities to turn to, no United States of America, in fact, but instead an open and dangerous land that is part war zone, part wilderness.[36]

The confident television news reporter at the end of *Night of the Living Dead*, who is satisfied that "everything seems to be under control," gives way in the opening credit sequence of *Dawn of the Dead* to a television station where little, if anything, is under control. Like a traditional exposition scene, this sequence provides a great deal of information. As the credits roll, an announcer interviews Doctor Foster, an expert who describes the threat posed by the living dead, insists that these creatures be "exterminated," and repeats federal government orders that citizens must leave "private residences" and gather in "central areas of the city" during this state of martial law. The doctor—who offers himself as the sole voice of reason, knowledge, and authority—is challenged at every turn by the announcer conducting the interview and by the jeering crowd of technicians and onlookers. At the same time, Romero repeatedly cuts away from the expert to show us brief details of the disorganized, frantic activity in the studio. For example, he quickly cuts from the control console to people fleeing the building and then to the station manager insisting that the crew keep broadcasting the names of rescue stations that have long been closed down. (Romero himself appears playing a harried operator at the control console. Appropriately, since he edits his own films, he casts himself as the director-as-editor, not as the station manager.) Questions about the ethics of extermination and about the individual's moral and social responsibility during a time of crisis are raised and left unanswered. Though no chalky white undead creatures break into the television station, this opening sequence that shows us only the living succeeds in evoking a sense that the fabric of American society is unraveling and ripping apart right before our eyes—here, in a communications center that is a monument of sorts to technology and control. As one of the young employees of the station succinctly puts it: "We're losing."

For Dr. Foster, who would have us concentrate only on "facts" and forget "issues of morality," the sole option left for the overly emotional, helpless citizenry is to follow martial law edicts and trust in "specially equipped squads of the National Guard." As if in response to Foster's advice, the film abruptly shifts to an exterior nighttime scene, where an official paramilitary operation is underway. Armed with automatic rifles and tear gas, these men dressed in blue jumpsuits look like a police S.W.A.T. team, although we later will see uniformed National Guardsmen involved as well. The official forces surround a public housing project occupied by blacks and Hispanics, kill the armed militants in a shoot-out reminiscent of a 1960s urban riot, storm the building, and herd the residents outside. The troops move from floor to floor, shooting the undead creatures they encounter, then methodically destroying a room full of zombies who have been locked in the basement. However, even with all the graphically recorded acts of extermination, we never see if the apartment house is successfully cleaned out or if civil order is reestablished. And we never see where the authorities take the frightened survivors. The entire operation seems like a futile gesture, and the official fighting force itself is at best suspect. Amid the carnage, Romero inserts several images that demonstrate, for example, how easily the troopers can be routed in hand-to-hand struggles with the living dead. In the face of the horror it confronts, this group of trained, supposedly disciplined men is always on the verge of fragmenting into separate individuals who will forsake their duty to run or to commit suicide or, like one deranged racist trooper, to slaughter indiscriminately the living as well as the undead.

In these two opening sequences Romero, like many other storytellers who offer what W. Warren Wagar calls "terminal visions,"[37] emphasizes just how quickly the institutions of society and the preconceptions of the citizen can be short-circuited. As daylight—and with it the dawn of the dead—approaches, martial law seems to have failed. There is no accurate list of rescue stations to be broadcast and no one alive to respond to the radio at the police dock. The only sane alternative is to flee the city—to escape from Philadelphia, birthplace of the United States.

What the rural countryside offers are small, deserted airports and open fields through which roam undead creatures just as hungry as the things in the inner-city projects. At least part of the rural world, however, is under the control of a posse of hunters larger and rowdier than the one McClelland heads in *Night of the Living Dead*. The riot police and army troops (complete with heavy artillery) stationed in the area seem as much concerned with the armed civilians as with the slow-moving zombies. After all, the living here far outnumber the undead, who stumble about in groups of two or three, easier to gun down than targets in a shooting gallery. Even more than the images of the "search and destroy mission" in *Night of the Living Dead*, this sequence in *Dawn of the Dead* presents extermination as a game that any trigger-happy redneck can play, apparently without fear of losing. Drinking and whooping it up, the members of the posse have no conception of the extent of the threat they face. The hunters and soldiers will be dangerous and unpredictable indeed when they fully realize that the social contract has been nullified and that they are not just playing at self- and civil defense.

The four people whose story Romero chooses to tell fly over the posse in a helicopter without ever considering the possibility of landing and joining the party. Once these people have escaped from the city, they know that they must make their way alone and that the armed civilians and soldiers could well prove to be a greater threat than the undead. Although *Dawn of the Dead* begins with a very different portrayal of the threat than does *Night of the Living Dead*, both films focus on the attempt of a small group of people to survive. Through their actions, these people exemplify the strengths as well as the weaknesses of the living. There are no children or teenagers among the group in *Dawn of the Dead*, and no middle-aged married couple like Harry and Helen Cooper. All four of the central characters are approximately the same age as Ben in *Night of the Living Dead*, and all four are articulate, intelligent inhabitants of the city, who flee after witnessing society collapse around them.

The only woman in the group, Fran, is the first person we see in *Dawn of the Dead*. She sleeps huddled against a wall in the television studio, then awakens with a start after the title of the film appears on the screen. Fran's awakening, as if from a bad dream (of the dawn?), calls to mind the opening of Werner Herzog's *Nosferatu the Vampyre.* In *Dawn of the Dead,* however, we and Fran have no trouble distinguishing dream from terrifying reality. While other people leave the studio or jeer at Dr. Foster, Fran attempts to assume responsibility and to do her job as part of the station management. For example, she even runs an abandoned camera at one point, and, against the orders of her boss, she stops the telecasting of a list of inoperative rescue stations. In the pandemonium of the studio Fran is the sole voice of morality. Watching Foster and the other people around her, Fran realizes that "we're blowing it ourselves"—referring, it appears, not only to Foster and the employees of the station, but to all of the living, who are failing this most important test. The hopelessness of the situation seems to immobilize her. When Stephen, Fran's lover and co-worker (we later discover that she is pregnant with his child), insists that she escape with him in the station's helicopter, Fran starts to object in the name of responsibility, yet eventually she follows his instructions. As a result, she becomes, for a time, almost completely dependent on Stephen, for whom the situation is perfectly clear: "We've got to survive, somebody's got to survive."

The two people who accompany Fran and Stephen in their flight are members of the S.W.A.T. team that storms the public-housing project. Roger, a white man in his mid-twenties, and Peter, a slightly older black man, flee after they effectively and efficiently carry out their part in the futile official operation. From the first, these two men are defined as skilled professionals, particularly adept with firearms. In different ways both Peter and Roger will prove to be trapped by this role as well, for *Dawn of the Dead* continues the examination of the image of the heroic man of action begun with the presentation of Ben in *Night of the Living Dead.* Like Peter and Roger, Stephen seems to be a determined figure of action and authority—a potential leader—when he first appears, but Romero soon informs us that Stephen is, after all, only a "traffic watch" helicopter pilot, dressed in a stylish imitation of a World War II leather flight jacket.

The initial distinction among the three men is not only that Stephen is a poor marksman and an amateur obviously inexperienced and untested in life-or-death crisis conditions but also that he has not lived through the raid on the housing project. Thus, unlike Roger and Peter, Stephen has not seen the true horror of the situation. During the raid the two troopers witness how easily the living become innocent casualties, suicidal victims, and insane murderers. In fact, Peter and Roger meet only after they each have dissociated themselves from the other men and escaped alone to the basement.

Most important, Peter and Roger see—as we do—the living dead, who fill a storage room where they have been placed by their relatives and neighbors in a futile, if humane, attempt to deal with this catastrophic situation. None of these zombies poses any sort of immediate threat: some are tied up in makeshift straightjackets and body bags; others are busy gnawing on bones. Taking careful aim, Peter shoots them in the head one by one, until he must stop to reload, then Roger helps continue the job. Horror films are rife with acts of butchery, murder, and wild work, but I know of no scene comparable to this methodical destruction of these monstrous, pathetic, somehow still human things caged in the basement of the apartment house. This work is without question an act of extermination rather than of ritualized struggle or heroic self-defense. These creatures must be destroyed, even though the act of destruction requires no particular faith or skill or even courage, and it is not likely to alter the basic situation that the living face. All that will be altered are the hunters themselves, who may come to take extermination as a type of sport or may themselves become emotionless zombies as they carry out their work. Roger, in particular, seems to loathe the role he is here required to play, disgusted with undertaking a job that will never be finished. The sequence in the housing project ends with Peter firing yet another bullet at point-blank range. The next time we see the two troopers, they are about to escape in the helicopter. In deserting what remains of human society, Peter and Roger—who are introduced to us as armed agents of the status quo—are not so much running away from the threat posed by the living dead as moving toward a place where their actions will matter.

One thing soon becomes clear, however. There is no place in the America of *Dawn of the Dead* where the living can survive without killing the undead—surely not in the city of brotherly love. When the helicopter lands to refuel in a deserted rural airport, for example, Stephen must beat a zombie to death with a hammer, and Peter must fire round after round into two children who attack him. Day breaks when the group is in flight, and Peter, Roger, Stephen, and Fran see below them a convoy of Army trucks and a large posse spread over the rural landscape. "It's everywhere," Roger declares—referring, it would seem, both to the invasion of the living dead and to the general sense of mobilization and civil disorder. From the air they also see a car explode into flames after it is shot (with only a few zombies roaming the fields, the hunters are ready to shoot at almost anything), just as the pickup truck explodes in *Night of the Living Dead.* This allusion suggests how much better off these four people are than Ben, who had no means of escaping from either the living dead or the posse. Yet as safe as they are in the air, the group still must land for food, fuel, and water, and so must return to the world of the living and the undead.

Dawn of the Dead does not offer a single example of a person who attempts to survive alone. All the living belong to groups of one sort or another. Stephen asks Roger and orders Fran to accompany him; Roger asks Peter. This group initially shares very little with the unified, harmonious community of vampire hunters in Stoker's *Dracula,* and certain distinctions among the four would-be survivors are immediately apparent. Fran and Stephen are civilians, and she seems at times to be as helpless as Barbara in *Night of the Living Dead.* Roger and Peter are more confident and capable, individually and as a team. For the time being, the group has no leader. Though Stephen flies the helicopter, they have no set destination, and it is Peter who most accurately assesses the situation: "We're thieves and we're bad guys. That's exactly what we are, and we gotta find our own way." Fran is more openly pessimistic than the rest about their chances without food, water, a radio, or a destination, but none of the group seems to realize at this point the degree of freedom that their situation could possibly offer.

The flight ends when the helicopter lands on the roof of a large shopping mall, which suddenly appears like some ugly, imposing fortress in the morning light. Fran and Stephen look down at the zombies who move through the empty parking lot, while Roger and Peter immediately begin to "check it out," with weapons drawn as if they are on a reconaissance patrol. Quickly and efficiently, the two troopers assess the terrain, break through a skylight, and search several connected rooms that are separated from the mall's shopping area. This suite of rooms, which will become the group's apartment, is empty save for cartons of civil defense supplies—a detail that suggests, on the one hand, the exceedingly good luck of this group, and, on the other, how far removed they are from the civil world, which they have given up defending.

While Stephen sleeps and Fran nervously paces, Roger and Peter continue to make the decisions. The troopers embark on a "hit and run" foray into the two floors of stores—a potential "gold mine," Roger calls it. Both men are obviously delighted at the opportunity, for this mission promises to be much different from the raid on the housing project. Here they must do more than merely exterminate the undead. Moving into the machinery room (where they discover the "keys to the kingdom"), then to the mall proper, Peter and Roger are a confident, effective team who speak the same language, share ideas, and perfectly complement each other. For example, when Peter takes out a tiparillo (à la Clint Eastwood in Sergio Leone's spaghetti westerns), Roger provides a light with his Zippo. The raid is dangerous—more so than it first appears—and thus even more exhilarating. Once they escape from the living dead by locking themselves inside a Penney's, Roger kicks a zombie in the face and casually shoots it in the head. He obviously is enjoying himself, yelling with glee as he begins the shopping excursion by sliding down the railing of a stopped escalator. Among all the other things the mall provides and contains, it offers Roger the opportunity to play at being the trooper and the child in an unsupervised, exciting world of action.[38] Peter, too, comes to life now that they have a concrete chance to find their own way, free of other human beings. Both men here resemble the heroes of a high-adventure buddy movie that depicts uncomplicated, surmountable dilemmas and celebrates male camaraderie.

Meanwhile, Stephen has awakened, taken the remaining rifle, and ventured alone in search of Roger and Peter. Romero cross-cuts between the troopers' high-spirited action inside Penney's and Stephen's movement through the machinery room. Again, the contrast is very much to Stephen's disadvantage, for he is not only nearly overpowered by a single zombie (appropriately, a security guard who pursues this trespassing "bad guy"), but almost shot by his own errant bullets that richochet around the room. This sequence parodies the many recent horror movies that use a moving hand-held camera to approximate the monster's point of view as it stalks its often helpless potential victim through a dark, mazelike setting. Stephen has, as it were, stumbled into the sort of chilling but predictable type of horror story that Romero's films always challenge and subvert.

At the last moment Stephen saves himself by firing his only remaining bullet into the head of the undead security guard. Having survived the monster's attack, Stephen joins the other two men inside Penney's.

"You did all right this time, flyboy," Peter tells Stephen, who has now run the gauntlet, so to speak, and is welcomed with smiles and laughter into this exclusive fraternity. Stephen immediately proves his worth by helping to devise a plan whereby they can return unnoticed to the upstairs rooms that will now serve as their living quarters.

However, while the men celebrate their victory and return with their booty, a single zombie retraces Stephen's route and corners Fran, who has been left without a gun. This sequence poses an illuminating comparison with Dracula's attack on Mina Harker in Stoker's novel, for in both cases the woman is excluded from the men's collective efforts and thus becomes an easy target for the undead. Like Mina, Fran is rescued by her male companions. In both stories the women must henceforth be included in the community of the living, though Fran will never be worshiped as one of "God's women." In fact, Romero and Fran herself will directly challenge the assumptions about women that inform Stoker's novel and most other stories of the living and the undead, including *Night of the Living Dead.*

Mina Harker is attacked by the superhuman King-Vampire; Fran is attacked by an undead Hare Krishna disciple wearing wire-rimmed glasses, a frail-looking young man who still has a tambourine tied to his orange robe. Therein lies much of the difference between *Dracula* and *Dawn of the Dead.* Because *Dawn of the Dead* is a color film that is almost always set in brightly lit exteriors or fully illuminated interiors, the diversity and individuality of the living dead are even more apparent than in *Night of the Living Dead.* For example, close-ups shot under these lighting conditions single out the unique faces of the living dead, and Romero's use of color calls attention to the many individual differences in dress. Only a few of the creatures actually look monstrous, with gaping wounds, disfigured faces, or missing limbs. Like the Hare Krishna, the rest—of all shapes and sizes, ages, sexes, races, and occupations—are physically intact and normal save for a dull, greyish pallor to their skin and a slow, puppetlike clumsiness in their movement. When the living dead are seen from a distance (as in many of Romero's long shots), these shared characteristics tend to cancel out individual distinctions and to make the creatures—inner-city blacks as well as suburban whites—all part of one homogeneous mass.

What is most apparent, of course, is that the Hare Krishna who stalks Fran is a ridiculous, absurdly comic figure (not least of all because many Americans are apt to consider real, living Hare Krishna disciples as mindless zombies who pester and stalk us). All of the creatures in *Dawn of the Dead* are clumsy and stupid—one unwittingly climbs onto a crate and has the top of his head lopped off by the helicopter's whirling blades—but the zombies who gather in the mall are initially made to seem the most harmlessly comic of all. When Roger and Peter switch on the fountains, escalators, window displays, and sound system of the mall, the living dead begin their ballet, tottering around as if to the beat of the Muzak, toppling into fountains, and being carried willy-nilly up the escalators. Later they will grab at mannequins in display windows, get tangled up in a hockey net at an indoor skating rink, and paw at closed glass storefronts. An official scientific spokesperson on an emergency television broadcast has no explanation for the entire phenomenon, but he describes the actions of the living dead as the product of "pure motorized instinct" and "remembered behavior from normal life." And such is the case with the creatures we see here, who act out of hunger or "remembered behavior," each one oblivious to the rest. Stephen is apparently correct when he concludes that the living dead are drawn to the mall by "some kind of instinct, memory of what they used to do. This is an important place in their lives." In their fashion the living dead aspire for the restoration of normality.

The creatures in *Dawn of the Dead*, who with their "mechanical inelasticity" and "automatism" embody much of what Henri Bergson defines as the comic in his classic study, *Laughter* (1900),[39] stand far apart from other versions of the multiple threat in horror stories of the 1970s, including many of the novels and films I have discussed, which depict the legions of undead as utterly malevolent, even satanically Evil. *Dawn of the Dead* is, for instance, the antithesis of deadly serious stories that show people at war with killer bees, sharks, or some other form of "natural" threat that is, in certain important ways, superior to human beings. In Martin Cruz Smith's *Nightwing* (1977), one of the best such stories, the colonies of vampire bats are not clumsy mutations, but "miracles of evolution," frighteningly efficient creatures "whose every organ and sense were so designed and attuned solely for the taking of sustenance."[40] Stories like *Nightwing* are in part humbling reminders that human beings are also creatures of the natural world, not the masters of it, for even if man does win, the evolutionary process, red in tooth and claw, will continue, repaying us for our pride and challenging our confident sense of superiority. In *Dawn of the Dead*, however, man, in the person of Stephen, Fran, Peter, and

Roger, is unquestionably superior to his opponent in every way except numbers.

Yet perhaps the most surprising aspect of *Dawn of the Dead* is that, for all of their readily apparent flaws, the living dead are still a threat. Indeed, all four members of the group during their first hours in the mall barely escape from the clutches of the clumsy undead. Fran is saved from the harmless-looking Hare Krishna, and Stephen fires his last bullet into the approaching security guard. Even Roger and Peter come close to being bitten, when they—like the viewer—are surprised by a zombie's sudden attack. From the opening of the film, in fact, Romero makes the danger of the situation clear. In the public-housing project a mass of mindless (and therefore fearless) undead creatures overpower several armed troops in the basement; while upstairs, one of the living dead rips mouthfuls of flesh from the shoulder and arm of a screaming victim. The living must always remain cautious of the threat posed by the undead, no matter how ludicrous the zombies look or how easily they are outmaneuvered. And if the living dead cannot be eluded, they must be killed—with hammers and screwdrivers if no automatic firearms are within reach.

Roger dispatches the Hare Krishna with the butt of his rifle, swinging down toward the camera, which has for the moment assumed a point of view approximating that of the zombie. Variations of this image appear several times in the film, most notably when Peter fires his final shot at the living dead in the basement of the housing project and when Roger kills the zombie that has followed him inside Penney's. In each such case the camera set-up equates us with the living dead. We can become the target because, as in *I Am Legend* and *Night of the Living Dead*, the living can all potentially become the undead. For example, this fate awaits both Stephen and Roger, who later in the film die and rise again and so must be destroyed.[41] After the group has captured the mall, Fran asks: "Who the hell are they [the zombies]?" and Peter responds: "They're us, that's all." Like the living dead (and like the stereotypical American consumer), the living also prove to be creatures very much governed by "remembered behavior," creatures who are drawn to the mall and all the things it contains and the values that it embodies and promotes. (Obviously, shopping malls are likely to be familiar places for most viewers of *Dawn of the Dead* as well.)[42]

The group lands at the mall in hopes of finding a safe place where Stephen, in particular, can sleep after the long flight from Philadelphia. Following the first successful raid of the "gold mine" below them, the men decide that they will stay. Peter argues that they have "got a good thing going here" and so should "hold out" at the mall, while listening over the radio for news of the situation outside. Stephen is even more enthusiastic, as he tells Fran: "This place is terrific. It really is. It's perfect," full of "great stuff" such as the booty that the men have already brought upstairs. (Quite clearly, one likely reason that Stephen finds the mall so "terrific" is that here he has been accepted as an equal by Roger and Peter.) Fran sees the mall neither as a convenient, well-stocked hideout nor as an earthly paradise. "You're hypnotized by this place," she tells Stephen, "it's so bright and neatly wrapped. You don't see that it's a prison too." Yet the only alternative Fran can offer is that they "keep going" toward Canada (like latter-day draft dodgers); and, in any case, she has no say in the decision. Romero will explore and test all three of these conceptions of the mall through the remainder of *Dawn of the Dead*, in a manner comparable to his examination in *Night of the Living Dead* of the private home as refuge, fortress, and trap.[43]

Fran is more successful at forcing the men to reconsider their relationship to her than in convincing them to fly to Canada. Immediately after she is saved from the Hare Krishna, Fran becomes quiet, frightened, withdrawn, and apparently entirely dependent on Stephen—similar to Barbara in *Night of the Living Dead*. And, like Barbara, Fran takes no part in the planning. She lies down by herself, while the men sit in an adjacent room, passing a bottle of Jack Daniels. Stephen informs Roger and Peter that Fran is almost four months pregnant. "It doesn't change a thing," Peter calmly tells Stephen, "do you want to abort it? It's not too late, and I know how." The line is chilling because Peter so completely leaves Fran out of the picture, implying that the decision is solely Stephen's, and also because it reminds us that these people are entirely on their own, medically and morally.

The next morning Fran indirectly responds. Unlike Barbara, Judy, or Helen Cooper in *Night of the Living Dead*, Fran demands to be considered an equal member of the group, not merely an accessory or a sheltered dependent: "I don't want to be treated any different than you treat each other, and I'm not going to be den mother for you guys. I want to know what's going on, and I want to have something to say about the plans. There's four of us." Fran also insists that she be taught to fly the helicopter in case something happens to Stephen and that she never again be left without a gun. Stephen is embarassed and angered at what he perceives to be a personal attack on him, but Peter immediately agrees with Fran, since, potentially at least, her honesty and her willingness to accept responsibility will strengthen the group. Peter's only proviso is that Fran "learn how to handle herself" before she accompany the men outside the apartment. He is not threatened by her demands, for they are "fair enough." This encounter foreshadows and helps to define the relationship between Fran and Peter in the concluding sequence of *Dawn of the Dead*.

Once the group has decided to remain where they are, the men begin the process of transforming the mall into a secure refuge, much as Ben responds to his plight in *Night of the Living Dead* by barricading himself inside the deserted farmhouse. (In another, more obviously ironic allusion to *Night of the Living Dead*, one of the first radio broadcasts we hear in *Dawn of the Dead* reminds us that citizens should "no longer seek occupancy in private residences, no matter how safe or well-protected they may be.") In both films this work does not reveal man's ability to follow ritual, endure suffering, and demonstrate faith, but rather his ingenuity and his competence at something other than killing. In *Dawn of the Dead* the operation is an elaborate group effort that eventually includes Fran as well as the three men. Initially, however, she watches from the roof while Roger and Peter hotwire large trucks they find nearby and park them in front of the mall's entrances. Stephen follows the action in the helicopter.

We see all four characters in this sequence and at times share each one's point of view, but the primary focus is on Roger, who comes most alive outside in the bright sunlight, with a difficult task at hand. The pace and rhythm of Romero's editing run parallel to the loud, uptempo rock music soundtrack here, and the editing seems almost to mimic Roger's infectious enthusiasm and adolescent bravado in the face of an adventure more exciting and dangerous than any make-believe war game. Joking over the CB radio, hotwiring a semi, tripping a zombie, Roger gets more animated as the operation continues, until suddenly the stakes in the game are raised. While hotwiring a second truck, Roger is trapped in the cab, unable to kill a female zombie who climbs on top of him. All he can do is hold up the young woman's head so that Peter can shoot her from his position in an adjacent truck. The zombie's blood and brains splatter over Roger's face and his uniform. After this horrifying baptism, his high-spirited enthusiasm changes in an instant to maniacal, destructive obsession. He drives over several zombies in the parking lot, smearing their blood across the windshield, then pauses to shoot others after he climbs out of the truck. Roger is saved from being bitten only because Peter rescues him and Fran shoots the creature that grabs at Roger's leg. In his desire to destroy as many of the zombies as he can, Roger accidentally leaves his bag of tools behind. When he returns for them, he is bitten and so is destined to become one of the living dead. In this world, killing is inevitable—thus Fran must learn to shoot—but Roger endangers himself and the entire group as soon as he begins to kill for the sake of pleasure or revenge, for the sake of killing itself.

Roger's fate is potentially the fate of all the men in *Dawn of the Dead*—the S.W.A.T. troops and redneck hunters as well as Peter and Stephen. Even the best marksman can fall prey to the hungry undead or lose control when he comes face to face with these creatures. Each man can also become the victim of his own fantasies of action and adventure. For with the fall of society and law and with the end of routine, everyday obligations, these fantasies can possibly be lived out. The mall is an environment perfectly suited for the enactment of any number of such fantasies. For example, in preparing for the second stage of their operation to secure their domain, Peter and Stephen load up on weapons and ammunition at a gun shop that has piped-in jungle sound effects. Romero depicts the men arming themselves in a series of brief images. Like a paean to the cult of the gun, the fetishistic objects flash by: high-powered rifles, derringers, revolvers, western-style handguns and holsters, cartridge belts, shotgun shells, and more. These are not merely weapons necessary for survival. They are the central icons in the so-called male action genres of popular culture; they are the elements of style, the props for a grand performance.

When the entire group next appears, all of them are armed with weapons and cartridge belts. They burst into motion like a commando team or a cadre of urban guerrillas. The second stage of the plan calls for them to lock the doors and set alarms near all the entrances, so that no more zombies can enter the mall. As in war movies about the covert operations of a small group (like *The Guns of Navarone* [1961], for example) or stories of a "big caper," in *Dawn of the Dead*, the plan is logical, imaginative, and difficult to carry out.[44] And it is in many respects the opposite of what Montague Summers calls the "ancient and approved methods" by which human beings rid the world of vampires.[45] Yet like the holy crusade against the King-Vampire in Stoker's *Dracula*, the operation against the living dead requires the effort of all the members of the team. It is Fran, for example, who suggests that they use a car on display in the mall to drive from entrance to entrance without being caught by the living dead.

Romero has called this sequence "high adventure." "All those guns and weapons and using the car in it—it's *The Dirty Dozen* coming to Monroeville," he told an interviewer.[46] The generic context for the "high adventure" in *Dawn of the Dead* is not only *The Dirty Dozen* and its many imitators, but a range of popular stories in the Vietnam and post-Vietnam era, including westerns like *The Wild Bunch* (1969) that center on a group of professionals, and simple-minded tales of vigilante justice and revenge like Don Pendleton's *Death Squad* (first published in 1969, now in its twenty-third printing as part of the best-selling paperback series, *The Executioner*).[47] Such stories often define the all-male group of professionals in opposition to the status quo, the family, and the appointed guardians of society, who are corrupt, emasculated, or impotent. In Pendleton's novel, for example, a group of Vietnam veterans, all expert specialists, band together to form a "small but highly professional army" that wages war on the Mafia.[48] For the "death squad" and other such groups, camaraderie and professional expertise replace the communal rituals and shared faith that unite the moral community Stoker presents in *Dracula*.

One other recent version of the commando-style, highly skilled group is the S.W.A.T. team seen earlier in *Dawn of the Dead*.[49] This group seems to accomplish nothing by its raid on the housing project. Peter, Roger, Stephen, and Fran, in contrast, successfully seal off the mall and carry out the final stage of their operation—the destruction of the zombies that are trapped inside. Romero shows no details of what Peter calls the "hunt," except for the aftermath. Looking up toward the second floor, the camera pans past the decorative pseudo-jungle foliage in the foreground to bring the hunters into clear view. From their superior perspective they look down on the conquered, "pacified" territory, strewn with corpses. The scene looks less like a battlefield than the site of a massacre. Fran backs away while the men survey their domain. The mall—refuge or promised land or prison—belongs to the living. However, in making it safe and habitable, they have, figuratively at least, closed themselves in and surrounded themselves with corpses. Even the waist-high railing in front of the men in this image has the look of bars.

The only work remaining to be done hardly qualifies as wild work or as "high adventure." Fran tries to minister to Roger's wounds as best she can. Finally, all she can do is give him morphine. Peter and Stephen build a wall to hide the entrance to the apartment, then haul the corpses of the undead into a large meat freezer. Half-delirious, Roger yells: "We got it all!" And so they do. Like the winners of some fabulous free shopping spree, Roger and the others have the run of the mall and the choice of all its seemingly endless variety of products. The fast-moving sequence that depicts this spree is a celebration of conspicuous consumption. The survivors all select new outfits and shop for candy and gourmet foods. Fran ice skates, Peter shoots basketball inside a department store, Roger and Stephen test their skills at arcade games—for a time they all play like free and irresponsible children. Romero plays in the same spirit by including quick close-ups of now-irrelevant cash register totals, for example, and by showing us the view through a bank's surveillance camera as Peter and Stephen pose with smiles after they have "stolen" stacks of worthless bills.

The spree ends with the group once again surveying its domain from the second floor, though now the corridors of the mall are empty and clean, and the living have exchanged their cartridge belts for fur coats. Outside, the living dead snarl and claw at the closed doors, for they are still "after the place," as Peter realizes. The group of survivors is in no immediate danger, but the facts of existence have not changed. Peter, Stephen, and Fran will soon be reminded of these facts in a much more dramatic manner when Roger dies.

Roger's death and his resurrection as one of the living dead are as important in *Dawn of the Dead* as the fate of Lucy Westenra in Stoker's *Dracula*. Roger does not die in battle, and he is not an innocent victim or a heroic, selfless martyr. His friends live in the same apartment with him during his gradual deterioration, and they can do little to help him. Roger's death thus makes Fran, Stephen, and Peter that much more aware of their own mortality and of the limits of what they can accomplish—even here, in the mall overflowing with "great stuff." Worst of all, they know that Roger will become one of the living dead, however much he vows "not to come back."

As his friend nears death, Peter sits against the wall in Roger's bedroom, drinks whiskey, and waits, gun in hand. Fran and Stephen remain in the next room watching a television broadcast. After all that Peter has accomplished and all the zombies he has destroyed, a more horrible task remains. When the undead Roger starts to sit up, we share Peter's point of view, then shift to the reverse angle as Peter aims his gun directly at us. Once again, the camera set-up is a reminder that the living dead are indeed "us" and not merely disembodied targets in the scope of a high-powered rifle. The ashen, sunken-cheeked thing Peter is about to shoot in the head at close range is still recognizably his friend and partner, Roger. As in most of the retellings of *Dracula*, as well as in *I Am Legend*, *'Salem's Lot*, and many other stories of the living and the undead, in *Dawn of the Dead*, one of the most disturbing requirements in the struggle for survival is that a human being can and will be called upon to kill an undead creature who in life was his closest friend, his fiancée, or his lover. However, unlike the "fearful ordeal" of transfixing Lucy Westenra (D, 221), which for Stoker's Arthur Holmwood is a privileged act that spiritually redeems the monster, the equally necessary destruction of Roger is simply a "fearful ordeal."

Before Peter actually pulls the trigger, Romero cuts to the other room, where on the television a harried scientist proposes that the living be "reasonable" and attempt to survive by feeding corpses of the newly dead to the zombies or by dropping nuclear bombs on "all the big cities." As in the beginning of the film, people in the television studio shout down the scientist, and Fran says, almost to herself: "It's really all over, isn't it?" As if in response, she hears Peter's single shot and the scientist's repeated demand that "we've got to remain rational, logical." Fran is correct. It really is all over—Roger's suffering and Peter's awful responsibility to his friend, as well as the life that the group has heretofore led, the faint hope for a solution granted God-like from outside, and the feeble attempt of society to preserve order and save itself.

Protected from the living dead and insulated from whatever elements of human society have survived outside the mall, Peter, Stephen, and Fran settle into an unadventurous life of leisure and domesticity. In one image, Fran sits on the floor of a clothing store surrounded and almost covered up by a pile of new outfits; shopping has become a tedious, deadening routine. The two men also fill their endless hours of leisure with purposeless activity: Stephen takes snapshots and pecks at a typewriter; Peter hits tennis balls against a wall on the roof. When such action ceases, these survivors slide into a stasis that parallels the still life of Wismar in *Nosferatu the Vampyre*. For example, Romero begins one image with a close-up of Stephen in bed, then pulls the camera back to reveal Fran next to him, as both lie motionless, staring vacantly in different directions. This still life could almost be an advertisement for designer sheets. In fact, the entire apartment resembles a display in a fashionable department store, with state-of-the-art stereo equipment, hanging plants, elegant liquor decanters, a battery of kitchen appliances, and informal, color-coordinated furniture.

Just as the apartment can be decorated using the objects on hand in the mall, so Fran, Stephen, and Peter are free—within the limits of this environment—to choose the roles they wish to play now that their work is apparently over. Initially they choose the type of roles that the mall caters to and helps to create and perpetuate, as if they are seeking in this way to reestablish normality. (The living dead, as I noted earlier, follow a very similar course of action.) Thus in one sequence, Peter, like an accomplished waiter, serves wine and a dinner by candlelight to Stephen and Fran, who are stylishly dressed for the occasion. In this "romantic" setting, Stephen proposes marriage to Fran by offering her a wedding band. When he is not being the consumer or attempting to be the husband, Stephen has a very difficult time filling his leisure hours. Fran becomes the housewife: she cooks, waters plants, and marks off the days of her pregnancy on a calender. However, in one brief scene, she breaks out of this monotonous round of simple tasks: she sits before a vanity mirror at what seems to be a cosmetics counter. Her face is heavily made-up, and she puts on fake eyelashes and spreads lotion on her neck. Striking "provocative" poses with a six-gun, Fran resembles a painted mannequin or a poor imitation of a gangster's moll or a child costumed as an adult. Over the mall's loudspeakers, a voice calls all "shoppers" to pay attention, and Fran looks up as if she realizes the extent to which she has become the willing, predictable "shopper"—the prisoner who can no longer see the bars of her prison. In the next sequence Fran sets the table in the apartment while the two men play poker with worthless currency. They suffer through an uncomfortable meal during which Peter, like an awkward guest, quietly listens to Fran and Stephen argue about whether the television should be left on now that there hasn't been a broadcast in three days. This re-creation of "normal" domestic life—defined here by its facile comforts and its limiting roles—is nearly fatal. Fran knows this earlier in the film when she looks at herself in the vanity mirror and when she refuses Stephen's offer of the wedding band because the pseudo-marriage "won't be real." She knows it best of all at the dinner table when she asks Peter and Stephen: "What have we done to ourselves?" This question gives credit where credit is due. For unlike the automatistic zombies who still fill the parking lot and press against the entrances of the mall, the well-fed, safe, comfortable human beings in-

The living dead in Romero's *Dawn of the Dead* (1979)—of all shapes and sizes, races, ages, sexes, and occupations. These comic yet dangerous automatons seek only food and the restoration of normality.

The four would-be survivors in *Dawn of the Dead* (1979) strike suitably "high-adventure" poses in this publicity still. Ironically, the shopping mall they capture will prove to be a trap, and ultimately their weapons will not save them.

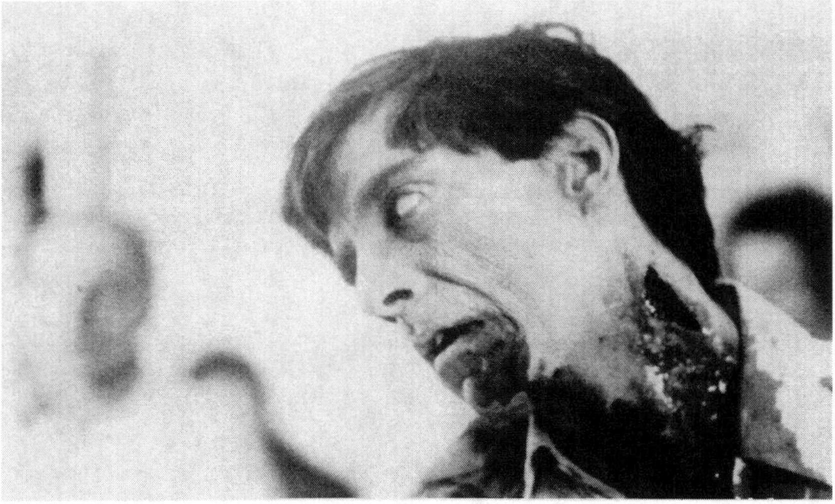

The victim of his own greed and materialism, Stephen (David Emge) in *Dawn of the Dead* (1979) rises from the dead to join the zombies as they reclaim the mall.

side this fortress have the freedom to choose, now that "it really is all over."

In the subsequent sequence, choosing life instead of the slow death of purposeless leisure and empty domesticity means becoming concerned again with survival in the world outside the mall. In the bright sunlight Stephen loads the helicopter with boxes of supplies and teaches Fran how to fly it. When she succeeds, Fran snaps out of her lethargy and once again becomes animated. But the choice of life will not be nearly this simple. Directly after Fran's lesson, a roving gang of heavily armed survivors spot the helicopter and prepare to raid the mall. The juxtaposition of Fran's flight lesson and the first glimpse of the threatening band of survivors suggests that the decision to resume life inevitably leads Fran, Stephen, and Peter back into a situation in which they must struggle in order to survive.

To a degree, the gang that attacks the mall—Peter calls them "raiders"—are analogous, as Wood suggests, to McClelland's posse in *Night of the Living Dead.* Both groups ultimately pose a threat to the heroes that is at least equal to the threat posed by the undead.[50] The distinctions between the raiders and the posse, however, are immediately apparent. The posse is a quasi-official group of citizens and lawmen who act in the name of civil authority. In fact, their presence in *Night of the Living Dead* is proof that society still exists, whereas the arrival of the raiders on motorcycles in *Dawn of the Dead* verifies that "it's really all over" and that there are no longer any effective civil authorities.

Better than any emergency television broadcast, the raiders give us some sense of the shape of the new America beyond the mall's parking lot. Unlike the S.W.A.T. team, the National Guard, the Army, or the redneck hunters, the raiders have thrived in the land of the living dead. That they are still alive attests to their fitness and their ability to take advantage of whatever new opportunities are available. This large, mobile group, which arrives on customized choppers and in vans, has very little internal organization, no single leader, and no goals except to kill, loot, and raise hell. Though the raiders in their rather predictable leather and denim "biker" outfits are an exaggerated, almost comic-book version of an outlaw motorcycle gang that has been given free reign, they still have significant affinities with Roger, Peter, Stephen, and many of the other human beings in *Dawn of the Dead.*[51]

Not only have the raiders fully embraced the opportunity of being "bad guys" who are now responsible for making their own way through the new post-United States world, but they have turned the necessity of killing into a source of pleasure. Peter suggests that the gang is a sort of "professional army," yet no S.W.A.T. team or National Guard unit is armed with sledgehammers, daggers, cutlasses, and maces, in addition to rifles, machine guns, and hand grenades.[52] Romero's montage of brief images when the raiders' weapons are being distributed directly parallels the sequence I described earlier of Stephen and Peter outfitting themselves in the mall's gun shop. Similarly, the high-spirited camaraderie of the raiders echoes the response of Stephen, Roger, and Peter after their first successful foray into the mall. The motorcyclists may not take on the appearance of a commando unit, but the raiders also live out a "high adventure" scenario of their own. In this scenario they often seem to embody—in an extreme form—certain qualities also present in the male heroes of *Dawn of the Dead*, qualities like Roger's adolescent bravado and love of action.

It is also Roger who becomes obsessed with killing the living dead and derives the most satisfaction from this work (that often seems for him to be play). Fran seldom uses weapons, but even she, in a moment of frustration and rage, curses and fires down from the roof top at the zombies. And before the first hunt, Peter seems to relish the chance to pick off the creatures one by one with his high-powered rifle. In these moments, the violence Fran and Peter commit is not a distasteful responsibility or a piece of routine, necessary work, it is a gratifying act—even though it does not suddenly rid the world of monsters or assure the victory of the living over the undead. Roger, once he has left the city, consistently finds this sort of gratification in killing the living dead. He smiles as he demonstrates over and over again his skillful marksmanship. For Roger, the destruction of the zombies becomes more and more like a game, a new sort of sport (like it also is for the redneck hunters). When Roger's life is actually threatened by the living dead, he retaliates by seeking out victims, as if he foolishly believes that somehow he can settle the score.

Like Roger, the raiders seek out the living dead and kill not for social or spiritual reasons, but for fun or revenge. Life has become for the raiders an extended gang war or barroom brawl in which the opponent is all but defenseless. After reopening the doors of the mall and thus allowing the living dead back inside, the raiders machine gun, burn, run over, pound, decapitate, stab, and shoot the zombies with a gleeful, sadistic exuberance. With its nonstop, bloody mayhem, this sequence resembles an animated cartoon come suddenly to life or even a silent film comedy, particularly when the raiders begin to throw cream pies into the zombies' faces and squirt them with seltzer bottles. For the raiders, slamming a machete deep into the head of an undead teenager is no different than smashing an overripe tomato onto the face of an undead shopper. So much for sacred weapons and the ritualized wild work of destruction that will cleanse the world, redeem the victim, and regenerate the hunter. Thus, following *I Am Legend* and *Night of the Living Dead*, *Dawn of the Dead* demythologizes the role of violence in the genre and so comments on previous portrayals of the living as well as the undead. The pleasure that the morally and spiritually justified Jonathan Harker and Quincey Morris feel in destroying the King-Vampire in Stoker's *Dracula* is only quantitatively different from the pleasure of the raiders armed with sledgehammers, machine guns, and cream pies in *Dawn of the Dead*.

While the raiders' slaughter of the living dead echoes in an exaggerated manner Roger's actions as a hunter, their looting of the mall is a parodic repetition of Fran, Stephen, Peter, and Roger's shopping spree. Romero clues us in to this latter analogy by showing the raiders loading up on guns and ammunition and "stealing" money from the bank, just as Peter and Stephen had done earlier. Yet while Fran and the three men most often shop for the clothes and appurtenances of a stylish, leisurely good life, the raiders grab cheap jewelry and silver cups, armfuls of tennis shoes, and even a bowling ball (almost the only things they intentionally leave behind are a portable television set and a shirt and tie). Finally, the motorcycle gang seems to be looting for the sake of looting—an activity that looks to be as much fun as swinging down from the second floor of the mall buccaneer-style to bash yet another zombie. Like the plague-ridden citizens of Wismar in Herzog's *Nosferatu the Vampyre*, the raiders are saturnalian revelers celebrating the end of civilization or at least the lifting of all extrapersonal sanctions on behavior.

In contrast to the four people who arrive by helicopter and then set about recapturing and pacifying the mall, the raiders do not seek possession of this comfortable, well-stocked fortress. All the work Peter and his companions do in cleaning up the mall and turning it into a fascimile of normal existence is undone in an instant. If the raiders are like pirates, shoplifters, or revelers, they are also like teenage vandals given the opportunity to trash the centerpiece of the community. To the accompaniment of a bugle's cavalry charge, the cyclists roar into the mall, circling the fountains, knocking over the inane displays, and driving through the aisles in Penney's. At times, we and the camera even ride with the motorcyclists. After the increasing stasis and the slide into domesticity following Roger's death, the raiders' anarchic energy and high-spirited vandalism might well offer an exhilarating and thoroughly appealing return to some form of "high adventure"—if these mock-adolescent survivors were not so obviously sadistic, stupid, and inept.

The raiders' attack forces Peter and Stephen to return to purposeful action, to the work of survival. The change is most apparent in the case of Peter, who discards his cumbersome jewelry and empties his pockets of worthless currency, picks up his rifle, and then zips up the regulation jumpsuit he had worn earlier in the film. Peter's plan is to lock the security gates in front of the stores and let the raiders fight it out with the living dead. As the gates descend, the two men look to be confined behind bars, reminding us of Fran's description of the mall as a prison. It is Stephen who has been most trapped by this environment, for when he sees the looting and the gratuitous destruction, he declares: "It's ours. We took it." Stephen shoots at the trespassing vandals, thus forcing a confrontation in which he will be wounded and, appropriately enough, trapped inside an elevator. Before Peter can rescue him, Stephen falls prey to the living dead. If Roger is undone when his own exuberance becomes a fanatic preoccupation with killing, Stephen's flaw is his obsession with the "great stuff" in the mall and with the limited set of values fostered by this "perfect" sanctuary. Before he himself entered the mall, Stephen remarked that the living dead were gathered here because "this is an important place in their lives." Eventually, this refuge is just as important for Stephen, and after he rises from the dead, he joins the zombies as they reclaim the mall.

Once Stephen has blown their cover, Peter again proves to be the most skillful and intelligent of the living. Like a sniper, he picks several of the raiders off their motorcycles, causing the rest to flee in confusion. The real victors, however, are the living dead, for no matter how many of them have been shot, beaten, or hacked to death, more and more of the creatures appear, returning to this most "important place." For example, a crowd of zombies converge on one of the raiders whose machine gun offers him no protection at all. The wounded gang members and the stragglers on foot are ripped apart and devoured by the living dead, who a moment before seemed to be merely pathetic, defenseless targets of the raiders' fun, incapable of posing any sort of threat. The close-up views we get of this feast—more colorfully detailed and graphic than even the images of the zombies in the public-housing project—make us, like the raiders, aware of the hunger and the collective strength of the living dead. This horrific feast is indeed an appropriate finale to a film that forces us to keep revising our sense of the monstrous and of the particular pleasures of safety and of destruction, a film that constantly plays tricks with our expectations about "high adventure," for example, and about the violent confrontation between the living and the undead.

Romero then goes one step further by cutting directly from the zombies devouring the bloody remains of their victims to a series of images that present the living dead as inept, comic automatons ludicrously (and pathetically) attempting to return to a sort of normal existence. To the sounds of piped-in Muzak, the zombies in all their variety stumble across the ice-skating rink, wander through the gunshop, and move down the aisles of the department store. In other words, they retrace the earlier actions of Fran, Stephen, Peter, and Roger, and Romero thereby underscores the parallels between the living and the undead. Through this sequence, he raises one last time all the unresolved questions in *Dawn of the Dead* about the nature of these creatures and about the relationship between the monstrous and the normal.

While the living dead feed on the raiders and browse through the mall, Fran and Peter wait upstairs in the apartment. This hidden, comfortable refuge is no safer now than it was when Fran was almost killed by the undead Hare Krishna, for Stephen leads a crowd of his fellow zombies through the camouflaged entrance and up the stairs to the apartment. The bloody, crippled creature who both is and is not Stephen enters first, and Peter—who earlier killed Roger—now must kill Stephen. This time, however, we see the act and so does Fran, as Stephen's blood splatters over the wall, staining forever this stylish, domestic haven. A crowd of zombies then enters the apartment in a scene that is almost a reprise of the attack on the farmhouse in *Night of the Living Dead* (so too Peter's destruction of Stephen parallels Ben's shooting the undead Coopers). Once again the clear impression is that no private residence can protect the living from the undead.

Although Fran and Peter, unlike Ben, have a means of escape, Peter refuses to climb to the roof where the loaded helicopter awaits them. After sending Fran up the ladder, he goes into his bedroom and waits with a derringer held to his head. Peter offers no explanation for his actions here except to tell Fran unemotionally that "I don't want to go. I really don't." Presumably by committing suicide he will save himself from the fate of Roger and Stephen, and he will end what seems to be a futile struggle against the undead. Yet when the first of the zombies enters the room, Peter shoots the creature instead of himself. Like a halfback, he fights his way through the zombies who now occupy the apartment and mill about the roof. To climb aboard the helicopter that hovers several feet off the ground, Peter must leave his rifle in the hands of one of the living dead. "How much fuel do we have?" he calmly asks Fran after he is safely seated next to her. Just as calmly, she answers, "Not much." "All right," Peter replies, and the helicopter takes off into the dawn, moving toward the brightest patch of blue in the open sky. From the roof we briefly watch these two survivors depart.[53] Then the final credit sequence begins. To the accompaniment of a piped-in polka, the end credits roll over a series of brief images of the mall, now filled with the living dead—business as usual. Ironically, the mall's clock chimes over and over, marking the hour for a crowd of shoppers who will never again worry about the passage of time.

The end credit sequence in *Dawn of the Dead* (a very effective parody of an uptempo promotional film or a local television advertisement) returns us to the absurdly comic rather than the graphically horrific, yet this sequence still emphasizes that the living dead, who dominate the mall in the final images of the film, also dominate, we assume, the world at large. To the extent that the monstrous threat in this film is able to withstand man's best efforts, Romero's ending resembles the conclusion of other stories of the living and the undead, like *The Return of Count Yorga* and *I, Desire*. *Dawn of the Dead*, however, ends with no unexpected, frightening revelation of the ability of the undead to survive. By this point in the film, we are already familiar with the particular sort of power the zombies wield and with the fact that life as it once was "really is all over."

Unlike *Night of the Living Dead*, which ends with the apparent restoration of "control" and the dubious triumph of the living, *Dawn of the Dead* shows us the victory of the living dead. But it is the sequel that offers what Romero calls a more "optimistic perspective," because Fran and Peter "finally opt to survive, instead of just giving up."[54] Both of these characters choose to resist the temptation of "just giving up," unlike Stephen and Roger, who never feel such a temptation. Ben in *Night of the Living Dead* has no such freedom to choose. Like Robert Neville in *I Am Legend*, Ben ironically becomes the monster and dies so that social order—such as it is—can be reestablished. We might say that Fran and Peter manage to escape or defy the sense of irony that is so apparent when Roger, Stephen, and the raiders meet their appropriate, if not entirely just, desserts. Because they survive, Fran and Peter qualify as being in some way the fittest of the living. And deservedly so, for Fran—carrying within her the prospect of new life—has been the most perceptive of the group, and Peter has been the most skillful and the most inclined to regard her as an equal.

In the end Peter must "opt to survive" and literally surrender his rifle to climb aboard the helicopter. This act marks the final humanization of Peter, who initially appears in the film wearing a gas mask and holding an automatic rifle—an anonymous, faceless trooper ready to kill the living as well as the undead. After destroying the zombies, the raiders, Roger, and Stephen, Peter is ready to kill himself. Perhaps by killing them he has always been killing himself, and suicide is the alternative to becoming one of the living dead or futilely attempting to restore normality or living in the manner of the raiders. When Peter leaves his rifle behind he seems to be heeding the advice given to him and Roger by an old Puerto Rican priest in the public-housing project. The frail, crippled, understatedly courageous priest emerged like a specter in the basement when the two troopers were discussing whether or not to "run." Instead of admonishing the men to have faith and to follow the ways of tradition, the priest cryptically warned Peter and Roger that "we must stop the killing or we lose the war." As far as we can tell, the living cannot completely escape the burden of killing in order to survive, but in the conclusion of *Dawn of the Dead* Romero suggests that the rifle must be discarded like a vestige of a previous existence. Considered in the context of the ongoing story of the confrontation between the living and the undead, this action summarizes Romero's rejection in *Night of the Living Dead* and *Dawn of the Dead* of the idea of sacred weapons and ritualized violence that can redeem and regenerate.

The couple that survives in *Dawn of the Dead*—a black man and a pregnant white woman—is not the traditional heterosexual couple (Fran and Stephen come closest to filling the role of the new Adam and Eve) or the pair of male buddies (like the team of Peter and Roger), but potentially a new type of partnership. As the helicopter lifts off into the dawn, Fran and Peter are escaping not only from the immediate threat posed by the living dead, but also from the mall and from a life that was itself becoming a sort of living death. Perhaps since Fran is piloting the helicopter and Peter has left behind his rifle, this couple is also escaping from the limiting roles fostered by a racist and sexist society that has now been destroyed. Unlike the vampire hunters in *'Salem's Lot*, who return to complete the wild work they have begun, or the moral community in Stoker's *Dracula*, who succeed in re-creating an extended patriarchal family, Fran and Peter have no set itinerary and no destination in mind. If they move away from the camera as homeless, isolated exiles, their flight is at the same time a liberating entrance into a world of possibility as well as of danger and horror.

NOTES

1. Dan Yakir, "Morning Becomes Romero," *Film Comment* 15 (May-June 1979), 62.

2. David Pirie, *The Vampire Cinema* (London: Hamlyn, 1977), p. 143.

3. In "The Mummy's Pool," *Dreamworks* 1 (Summer 1981), 291–301, Bruce Kawin discusses the distinction between the verbal and the mute creatures in *The Mummy* (1932) and its sequels, films that I have chosen not to examine in this book. These films (as well as Hollywood's zombie movies of the 1930s and 1940s) offer another—to my mind less interesting—version of the story of the living and the undead, one that is adjacent to the stories I consider. Kawin's essay makes the best case for the Mummy films. See also Drake Douglas, *Horror!* (New York: Collier's, 1969), pp. 130–58; and R. H. W. Dillard, "Even a Man Who Is Pure at Heart: Poetry and Danger in the Horror Film," in *Man and the Movies*, ed. W. R. Robinson (Baltimore: Penguin, 1969), pp. 75–78.

4. R. H. W. Dillard, *Horror Films* (New York: Monarch, 1976), pp. 68–69.

5. See Rose London, *Zombie: The Living Dead* (New York: Bounty Books, 1976), and Douglas, *Horror!*, pp. 158–74, for a survey of films featuring zombies.

6. George A. Romero, Preface to John Russo, *Night of the Living Dead* (New York: Warner Books, 1974), p. 10. See also, for example, Mike Wilmington and Barry Brown, "Interview: George Romero, Knight of the Living Dead," *High Times* 71 (July 1981), 36.

7. In an interview with Dan Yakir, Romero offers this interesting comment: "The radiation scenario that people feel is an explanation in *Night of the Living Dead* was actually one out of three that were advanced in the original cut of the film, but the other ones got cut out and people have adopted that radiation thing as the reason why the dead are coming back. I really didn't mean that to be" (Yakir, "Morning Becomes Romero," p. 60).

8. Writing before the release of Romero's *Martin* and *Dawn of the Dead*, Herzog's *Nosferatu the Vampyre*, and Badham's *Dracula*, Pirie deemed *Night of the Living Dead* "the only truly modernist reading of the vampire myth"

(*Vampire Cinema*, p. 141). I am not sure if the film can be called "modernist" (or even exactly what Pirie means by the term), but *Night of the Living Dead* can be taken as a revisioning—by way of *I Am Legend*—of the vampire story, as I attempt to demonstrate in this chapter.

9. Yakir, "Morning Becomes Romero," p. 62.

10. Sigmund Freud, "'The Uncanny,'" in *On Creativity and the Unconscious* (New York: Harper and Row, 1958), p. 150. Sir James George Frazer argues that it is "the fear of the human dead" that has been "probably the most powerful force in the making of primitive religion" (*The Golden Bough: A Study in Magic and Religion*, abr. ed. in 1 vol. [1922; rpt. New York: Macmillan, 1951], p. vii).

11. Discussing a thesis put forward by Rudolf Kleinpaul in 1898, Freud in *Totem and Taboo* links "the malevolence of the dead" to the image of the vampire: "Originally, says Kleinpaul, *all* of the dead were vampires, all of them had a grudge against the living and sought to injure them and rob them of their lives" (TT, p. 59).

12. James Malcolm Rymer, *Varney the Vampyre or, The Feast of Blood* (1847; rpt. New York: Dover, 1972), p. 708.

13. Ibid., pp. 341, 234, 839, 220.

14. Ibid., pp. 376, 231.

15. Compare Rymer's portrait of the rabble with Thomas Carlyle's images of the demonic, animalistic, "continually increasing multitude" in *The French Revolution: A History* (1837; rpt. New York: Modern Library, 1934), pp. 140–50.

16. Gustave Le Bon, *The Crowd: A Study of the Popular Mind* (1896; rpt. London: Ernest Benn, 1952), pp. 18, 30, 32, 57, 51.

17. Ibid., p. 118.

18. Ibid., pp. 132, 55, 73.

19. Leonard Wolf, *A Dream of Dracula: In Search of the Living Dead* (New York: Popular Library, 1972), p. 302.

20. These would-be survivors are very often examples of what Lawrence Alloway, borrowing the term from E. R. Curtius, calls "maximized" characters, "figures that embody in terms of contemporary references maximum states of age, beauty, strength, revenge, or whatever" (*Violent America: The Movies, 1946–1964* [New York: Museum of Modern Art, 1971], p. 12). Alloway also correctly insists on the extent to which in genre movies "the conventional"—such as the "maximized" character—"becomes physically convincing" (ibid., p. 61).

21. For two extremely interesting variations on a similar theme, see Sam Peckinpah's *Straw Dogs* (1971) and the novel upon which it is based, Gordon M. Williams's *The Siege of Trencher's Farm* (1969).

22. Dillard, *Horror Films*, p. 66.

23. Ibid., pp. 80–81.

24. Vivian Sobchack effectively argues that Romero's "mordant" portrait of the "telecasts' uselessness, their inappropriateness, [and] their capacity for exploitation" should also be understood as mocking the "prevalent function of the media in most traditional SF films" (*The Limits of Infinity: The*

American Science Fiction Film, 1950–1975 [New York: A. S. Barnes, 1980], pp. 190, 188).

25. For Dillard, the "artistic antecedent for *Night of the Living Dead* is most clearly Hitchcock's *The Birds*" (*Horror Films*, p. 78). The similarities between these two works is most apparent in the scenes of mass attack on the barricaded private residence. As I note later in this chapter, the murder of Helen Cooper has interesting parallels with the murder of Marion Crane in *Psycho*.

26. Robin Wood, "Apocalypse Now: Notes on the Living Dead," in *The American Nightmare: Essays on the Horror Film*, ed. Robin Wood and Richard Lippe (Toronto: Festival of Festivals, 1979), p. 93.

27. Montague Summers, *The Vampire: His Kith and Kin* (1928; rpt. New Hyde Park, N.Y.: University Books, 1960), p. 181.

28. Romero, Preface to *Night of the Living Dead*, p. 12.

29. Dillard, *Horror Films*, p. 77.

30. This all-male, all-white posse, dressed in civilian clothes and carrying their own weapons, at times looks very much like a vigilante group. And they do, after all, kill an innocent black man in their attempt to restore order in this part of rural America. The "indigenously" American tradition of vigilantism—considered as one form of collective violence—was of great topical interest in the period when *Night of the Living Dead* was filmed and distributed. See, for example, the emphasis given to vigilantism in Hugh Davis Graham and Ted Robert Gurr's "Report to the National Commission on the Causes and Prevention of Violence," entitled *Violence in America: Historical and Comparative Approaches* (New York: Bantam, 1970), which includes Richard Maxwell Brown's long essay, "The American Vigilante Tradition."

31. Donald M. Lowe, *History of Bourgeois Perception* (Chicago: University of Chicago Press, 1982), p. 48.

32. Contrast the posse's bonfire with the fires traditionally lit on Halloween, which, according to Frazer, were remnants of "an ancient pagan festival of the dead." Frazer suggests that these fires were built by the living "throughout Europe" for "the souls of the departed [who] were supposed to revisit their old homes in order to warm themselves by the fire" (*Golden Bough*, pp. 734–35).

33. Pirie, *Vampire Cinema*, p. 169. Since the release of *Zombie* and *Dawn of the Dead*, a spate of low-budget, Italian-made films about flesh-eating zombies has appeared, including, for example, Umberto Lenzi's *City of the Walking Dead* (1983).

34. Donald C. Willis, in *Horror and Science Fiction Films II* (Methuchen, N.J.: Scarecrow Press, 1982), discusses several other films of the 1970s that seem to have been directly influenced by Romero's presentation of the living dead in *Night of the Living Dead*, including *Garden of the Dead* (1972), *Shock Waves* (1975), *Horror of the Zombies* (1976), and *The Child* (1977). Romero's *Martin*, as I have noted, is also a reworking of certain elements of *Night of the Living Dead*, as is *The Crazies* (also released as *Code Name: Trixie*), a 1973 film that Romero also wrote and directed, in which an accidentally released chemical causes the citizens of a Pennsylvania town to become crazed killers.

35. In "Knight of the Living Dead," *Village Voice* 24 (23 Apr. 1979), 1,

44–46, Tom Allen offers an informative survey of Romero's career, focusing on the financing, production, and distribution of *Dawn of the Dead.*

36. One important point of comparison for Romero's living dead films (and for all apocalyptic fictions) that I will not explore in my discussion is the vast sociological literature on disaster. See, for example, *Man and Society in Disaster*, ed. George W. Baker and Dwight W. Chapman (New York: Basic Books, 1962). Of particular interest is Gideon Sjoberg's essay in this volume which examines, among other topics, the effect on "interpersonal cooperation . . . when a social order is shaken to its very roots by disaster" ("Disaster and Social Change," in *Man and Society in Disaster*, p. 370).

37. See W. Warren Wagar's illuminating and comprehensive critical study, *Terminal Visions: The Literature of Last Things* (Bloomington: Indiana University Press, 1982).

38. Roger's unrestricted play inside Penney's—like several later scenes in *Dawn of the Dead*—calls to mind the department store scenes in *Modern Times* (1936) and *The Public Enemy* (1931). Intentional or not, these parallels suggest the way Romero continually evokes the conventions of other popular genres in his idiosyncratic horror film.

39. Henri Bergson, "Laughter," in *Comedy: Plays, Theory, and Criticism*, ed. Marvin Felheim (New York: Harcourt, Brace & World, 1962), pp. 215–19. Note also that Bergson begins his study by affirming that "the comic does not exist outside the pale of what is strictly *human*" (ibid., 214). If this is true, then the fact that the zombies are at times comic creatures serves to reinforce Romero's general point about the relationship between the living and the undead in *Dawn of the Dead.*

40. Martin Cruz Smith, *Nightwing* (New York: Jove, 1978), pp. 36, 65.

41. The transformation of Stephen and Roger from the living into the undead is also a transformation of the hunters into the hunted (who are in turn hunters as well). In *Horror of Dracula* (but not in Stoker's *Dracula*), Jonathan Harker undergoes a comparable ironic transformation, as does Robert Neville when he becomes legend in Matheson's novel. John Hayes's *Grave of the Vampire* (1972) is based entirely on this motif: a young man tracks down and destroys his undead father, a vampire who had raped the young man's mother. After driving a stake into the heart of his antagonist, the hunter himself becomes a vampire—the son becomes his father, ready to prey on the woman he risked his life to protect moments before. Well-intentioned but ultimately futile violence in *Grave of the Vampire* only serves to perpetuate a fatalistic, circular process.

42. Consider, for example, the prominence of the shopping mall in recent comedies like *Fast Times at Ridgemont High* (1982) and especially in *The Blues Brothers* (1980), which, with its celebratory destruction of an antiseptically clean mall, recalls several sequences in *Dawn of the Dead.*

43. In Romero's living dead films, the private home and the shopping mall are both defined in opposition to traditional images of the haunted house, as it appears, for example, in Stephen King's *'Salem's Lot* and Stanley Kubrick's *The Shining* (1980; adapted from King's 1977 novel). *Dawn of the Dead* and

Kubrick's horror film are similar, however, in that both explore the role of work and play, labor and leisure, in contemporary American culture.

44. For a discussion of the "big caper film," see Stuart Kaminsky, *American Film Genres: Approaches to a Critical Theory of Popular Film* (New York: Dell, 1977), pp. 100–29.

45. Summers, *Vampire: His Kith and Kin*, p. xxi.

46. Yakir, "Morning Becomes Romero," p. 63.

47. See Will Wright's discussion of the "professional plot" in *Sixguns and Society: A Structural Study of the Western* (Berkeley: University of California Press, 1975), pp. 85–122. According to Wright, westerns that utilize this plot focus on a "group of strong men, formed as a fighting unit, [that] comes to exist independently of and apart from society. . . . the social values of justice, order, and peaceful domesticity have been replaced by a clear commitment to strength, skill, enjoyment of the battle, and masculine companionship" (ibid., p. 86).

48. Don Pendleton, *Executioner #2: Death Squad* (New York: Pinnacle, 1969), p. 48. In 1982 Pendleton launched two new paperback series, *Able Team* and *Phoenix Squad.* Both of these spin-offs from *The Executioner* feature a "crack paramilitary team" that wages an ongoing, illegal war against terrorists, "the new enemy."

49. *S.W.A.T.* ran on ABC television as a prime-time series in 1975–76. Harry Castleman and Walter J. Podrazik argue that *S.W.A.T.* portrayed Los Angeles as "one huge battleground populated by raving lunatics, crazed maniacs, and helpless citizens," with only the heavily armed S.W.A.T. team capable of protecting the populace. "*S.W.A.T.*, in effect, restaged the Vietnam war and the riots in the streets, but returned ultimate control to the righteous forces of law and order for a satisfying conclusion" (*Watching TV: Four Decades of American Television* [New York: McGraw-Hill, 1982], p. 260).

50. Wood suggests that both the posse and the raiders dramatize "the possibility of the development of Fascism out of breakdown and chaos" ("Apocalypse Now," p. 95).

51. In *Knightriders* (1981), the non-horror film Romero wrote and directed after *Dawn of the Dead*, a group of traveling entertainers stage medieval jousts on motorcycles. Romero offers the group of motorcyclists and their entourage in *Knightriders*—unlike the raiders in *Dawn of the Dead*—as a positive, if flawed, embodiment of the possibility for the development of an alternate community in contemporary America.

52. See Lewis Yablonsky's description of the "violent gang" as a "moblike collectivity" that lacks the "features of an organized group" and that commits violence "in search of kicks" (*The Violent Gang* [Baltimore: Penguin, 1966], p. 5).

53. This image of the helicopter flying away toward the dawn is a particularly resonant image that seems to me to evoke and comment on the westerner's ride into the sunset and away from civilization, for example, as well as the prominent role of helicopters in the Vietnam War and in media coverage of that war. Ronald Neame's *The Poseidon Adventure* concludes with a compa-

rable image (as do less well-known disaster stories like *Fer-de-Lance*, a 1974 made-for-television movie). However, in Neame's film, unlike *Dawn of the Dead*, the weary survivors are being rescued by experts, and the helicopter's take off signals the return to normality.

54. Yakir, "Morning Becomes Romero," p. 62.

CONCLUSION

If the nexus between a genre and a single work is rather puzzling, we need not be reminded of the virtues, and even the necessity, of studious puzzlement.

Claudio Guillén
Literature as System

CHAPTER

9

Resolution, Violence, Survival

LIKE ALL STORIES of the living and the undead, *Night of the Living Dead* and *Dawn of the Dead* present us with images of death and of life unnaturally prolonged, and they address our understanding of, desire for, and apprehensions about closure and resolution. *Dawn of the Dead*, which depicts the end of American society, provides an open ending that answers and even qualifies the closed ending of *Night of the Living Dead*, which concludes with the restoration of official order. The distinction between the open and the closed, however, only begins to explain the differences between the concluding sequences of these two films. In his endings, as in his presentation of man and monster, George Romero varies and cross-examines generic conventions and thereby complicates and enriches our understanding of the ongoing story. Following the guide of *Night of the Living Dead* and *Dawn of the Dead*, we can offer some observations on the various strategies of closure and on the range of open and closed endings in stories of the living and the undead. Such stories, I believe, further our understanding of what Thomas Schatz correctly calls "the most significant feature of any generic narrative"—its "resolution."[1]

Night of the Living Dead has several possible points of conclusion: the zombies' successful takeover of the farmhouse, the coming of dawn, the arrival of McClelland's posse, the murder of Ben, and the bonfire. Each of these very different images could provide an end to the night of the living dead and a different sort of resolution to the film. As these images follow one another, each possible ending replaces and comments on its predecessors. For example, the dissolve that introduces the dawning of a new day also makes us question what looked to be the triumph of the living dead. Thus the final image of the bonfire gains additional significance because we see other ways that *Night of the Living Dead* could have ended—not merely hypothetical paradigmatic alternatives, but literally other endings. Whatever else the bonfire may signify, it is not the dawn, not the grainy still images of the posse, not the victorious living dead, and not the wary human survivor alone in the basement.

By leading us past this series of potential endings until we finally stop with the bonfire, Romero demands that we see his film through, beyond the credit sequence and beyond any conventional expectations about where it ought to end. Seeing *Night of the Living Dead* through means that we alone become privy to all-important information, like the fact that McClelland is wrong about the "thing" he spots in the farmhouse and that there is a striking similarity between the sheriff's men and the living dead. The men of the posse obviously do not realize the error they have committed. (What is worse is that in all likelihood it would make little difference if these men did realize their error.) Nor do they see their own likeness to the monstrous undead creatures. Yet in this sequence Romero cuts from Ben to the hunters and zooms in to details of the still images in order that we may see. This privileged sight is a revelation that we alone are allowed to witness. Since the revealed knowledge in the concluding sequence of *Night of the Living Dead* deepens the film's sense of irony and futility, the revelation becomes a burden of sorts, a price we must pay for desiring to know the truth and to discover what happens next.

Somewhat comparable to the revelation at the end of *Night of the Living Dead* is the privileged perspective we are given in the conclusion of John Badham's *Dracula* and Sheridan Le Fanu's *Carmilla*. In Badham's film we share Lucy's point of view as Count Dracula apparently undergoes his final, liberating transformation. In *Carmilla* we share Laura's recollection of Carmilla's "ambiguous alternations" (C, 85). For Lucy and Laura, the seductive vampire survives (even if only in "fancy"), and so, too, for us, since *Carmilla* and *Dracula* (1979) end by drawing us into the point of view of these women, a point of view distinctly apart from that of the male vampire hunters. (Compare Brian De Palma's *Carrie* [1976], in which the "monster" survives in the nightmare of the young female survivor.) The concluding image in *Night of the Living Dead*, in contrast, separates us from any particular character's perspective and reveals information that no character shares.

The simplest and, by the 1980s, the most common use of the concluding revelation is found in vampire stories like John Russo's *The Awakening* (1983) and John Llewellyn Moxey's *I, Desire* (1982). In Russo's novel the police detective who tracks down and destroys his undead antagonist has few, if any, doubts that his work has been successful. Yet we realize the hunter is wrong, for the omniscient narrator describes for us the vampire's regeneration. Furthermore, the final lines of *The Awakening* let us know that the vampire and his new bride have left America and arrived in London, unbeknownst to the detective and to all of the living. In *I, Desire*, as I noted in chapter 7, the concluding revelation appears at the end of a single image in which the camera pans away from the reunited couple toward a figure in the shadows, and then moves to face the figure when it bares its outsized canines. The vampire hunter has just agreed to lie about his harrowing experience with the undead, but the camera movement does not allow us to share the safety of his falsehood or to dwell on the joyful reunion. Thus both of these works in their conclusions provide us with privileged information that alters the way we read the entire story, information that clearly indicates that the confrontation between the living and the undead is far from over. Possessing this information sets us apart from and makes us superior to the potential victims and hunters, to whom the truth of the situation is not revealed. The living are safe in their ignorance, while we are granted knowledge that only reminds us of our own impotence as mere spectators, knowledge that seems to mock our curiosity and our desire to be frightened—to mock our role as viewers or readers of horror stories.[2]

The final act of revelation is, I think, much more apparent in *I, Desire* than *The Awakening* because the camera movement in Moxey's film (as in the concluding sequences of *Citizen Kane* and *Psycho*) underscores the process of being led and forced to see the revealed detail. One of the most effective examples of this particular type of conclusion in the films I have discussed is the final credit sequence in Philip Saville's *Count Dracula* (1977). What is revealed at the end of this retelling of Stoker's novel, as I noted in chapter 5, is a negative, slow-motion, black-and-white image of the vampire staring directly at the camera as it moves in toward his eye. None of the living shares our point of view here; they are last seen offering a prayer of thanksgiving after the destruction of Count Dracula. Concluding revelations like those in *I, Desire* and *Count Dracula* should remind us not only that we are being cast into the role of witnesses, but also that we are assigned a very specific viewpoint from which to witness the end of the story, a point-of-view that can be completely distinct from the perspective of the characters. (Of course, we also can literally share the viewpoint of a character like Lucy in Badham's *Dracula* or the female protagonist in *The Return of Count Yorga*, who, believing she is at last safe, is surprised to find her now-undead fiancé moving to attack her.) These examples from stories of the living and the undead begin to suggest how one important variable in the end of all stories is the precise narrative perspective assigned to the viewer or reader. This perspective not only helps to determine our relation to the characters, but it also reminds us of the sort of pleasures we seek when we read or view the works I have discussed and other horror stories.

Revelations such as those provided by Moxey, Russo, and Saville almost always give us information about the fate of the undead that inevitably casts a new light on the fate of the living. In *I, Desire* or *The Awakening* what we alone can see is that the threat posed by the undead still somehow persists, regardless of what the living may assume and regardless of the heroic efforts of the vampire hunters. This knowledge, *our* knowledge, transforms the ending into a potential beginning and qualifies or even negates any victory the living have achieved. In *Night of the Living Dead*, however, the final revelations do not focus on the undead, and the information Romero reveals about Ben and the posse does not constitute the beginning of a new story or the beginning of a new episode in an ongoing story. This information—above all the ironic fact that the latest victim of the "search and destroy" mission is not one of the living dead—serves to reinforce the sense of closure in *Night of the Living Dead*: Ben's story is complete; the sheriff and his men are securely in command of the situation; the living dead are nowhere to be seen.

If the monster has been vanquished and "everything's under control," what makes the ending of *Night of the Living Dead* so different from the closed endings of Stoker's or Browning's *Dracula*? Through Mina Harker's first-person account in Stoker's novel, we learn of the unquestionable victory over the King-Vampire and of the purifying beams of rosy light; her husband's epilogue then celebrates the "happiness" of the moral community seven years later.[3] The conclusion of Stoker's *Dracula* is very similar to the happy ending of classical fairy tales. Bruno Bettelheim, in *The Uses of Enchantment*, argues that fairy tales like *Hansel and Gretel* end with the "punishment of the evildoer," the formation of a harmonious "union," and the restoration of the "right order of the world." The absolute defeat of the threat is not by itself sufficient to create a happy ending, even if the child perceives this defeat to be a form of just punishment. Bettelheim argues that the fate of the hero, which is inextricably linked to the fate of the "evildoer" and the world, must enact and evoke the experience of "recovery and consolation." The happy ending thus satisfies the child's desire for justice as well as for a sense of psychological, social, and moral integration that will continue forever. Once "happily ever after" has been pronounced, there can be no more to tell.[4]

As in the fairy tales Bettelheim analyzes, any consideration of closure in the story of the living and the undead must take into account the fate of the world, the monster, and the living. Even though Stoker's *Dracula* lacks a guarantee about life in the "ever after" (at least ever after the epilogue), it concludes with a dispensation of just punishment and well-deserved rewards, with a restoration of the "right order," and with an achievement of a new, fulfilling integration—elements of closure that parallel the happy ending of a classical fairy tale. Hammer's series of Dracula films during the 1960s provide somewhat tempered and weaker versions of this type of resolution, as does Browning's *Dracula* with its final image of the bethrothed couple's ascent into the light. Stephen King's *'Salem's Lot*, while it leaves unfinished the punishment of the evildoer and the complete restoration of the "right order," affirms the union of its two surviving heroes, a union that offers the hope for a more complete "recovery and consolation."

King may not grant his audience a fully realized happy ending, but he never challenges or questions our desire for a fairy-tale resolution. Other works I have discussed do challenge this desire. Borrowing Bettelheim's terminology, we can say that F. W. Murnau's *Nosferatu* offers just punishment (for the vampire and for Renfield) and restoration (in the form of renewed health) without the harmonious union that should provide the Harkers and the viewer with a complete sense of "recovery and consolation." In this film the fate of the hero(ine) is made distinct from the fate of the world; the price exacted for justice and for the restored health of society is precisely the sacrifice of private consolation. Lucy Harker in Werner Herzog's *Nosferatu the Vampyre* also gains none of the benefits of integration and recovery. And, by allowing the new Nosferatu to escape punishment, Herzog goes further toward openness than Murnau. More important, *Nosferatu the Vampyre* forces us to question the values of the restored order and to acknowledge that the "right order" is, in fact, a specific form of social and cultural order.

By distinguishing the living dead from traditional notions of the evildoer, Romero dispenses with the possibilities for just punishment, unless the shooting of Ben could be taken as fit retribution for his murder of Harry Cooper. (It cannot, of course, and neither can it be taken as the defeat of the hero.) In lieu of justice, the conclusion of *Night of the Living Dead* offers an almost hopeless sense of irony and futility. The destruction of the living dead does not result from the formation of a new, harmonious union, nor does this destruction give birth to such a union. Without justice and without integration, all that the ending of *Night of the Living Dead* shares with the type of endings Bettelheim describes is the restoration of order—everything at last is "under control." Like Robert Neville in his prison cell, who sees how his own just punishment will provide a happy ending for the new society's legend of the struggle against evil, we remain separate from and superior to the order that is restored in *Night of the Living Dead*.[5] The "assigned killers" of the new society in *I Am Legend* are fully aware of their own role and of the special significance of the act of restoring order. McClelland and his men never seem to realize that their world truly has been threatened and that they are, for all purposes, the means of restoration. In *Night of the Living Dead*, the murder of Ben, the extermination of the zombies, and the disposal of corpses in a bonfire do not so much resolve the confrontation between the living and the undead as attempt to render it insignificant, even routine.

By the absences implicit in its ironic resolution, *Night of the Living Dead* reminds us of the particular pleasures that a closed ending can offer, pleasures that are perhaps most fully embodied in the conclusion of Stoker's *Dracula*, with its affinity to the happy ending of classical fairy tales. *Night of the Living Dead* and Stoker's *Dracula*, along with, for example, the vampire films of Murnau and Browning, begin to suggest the range of variation possible in stories that conclude with the triumph of the living. Not only does the definition of order and of restoration differ in each of these works, but so does our perspective on and our role in the movement toward closure.

Open-ended stories of the living and the undead offer a comparable range of variation. In the simplest terms those stories in which the living do not gain an unequivocal victory over the undead can be deemed open-ended. For example, in the final images of *Vampire*, a 1979 made-for-television movie, the vampire escapes into the night, taking the same path out of the story as Lord Ruthven does in John Polidori's 1819 story, *The Vampyre*. In a related form of this ending, such as is found in *The Awakening*, the escaping vampire has a precise destination in mind. In chapter 7 I described another popular variation on this type of ending, one in which the aristocratic, classical European vampire is destroyed, but his undead slaves and progeny still pose a threat. *Count Yorga, Vampire, The Return of Count Yorga, 'Salem's Lot*, and *They Thirst* all provide this type of conclusion, although the Yorga films place the final emphasis on how little the would-be hunters have accomplished, while for King and Robert McCammon, the destruction of the King-Vampire testifies to the selfless heroism of the outnumbered vampire hunters. The sole living witness is doomed in the final image of *Count Yorga, Vampire*. Ben and Mark in *'Salem's Lot* and the young reporter in *They Thirst* fully realize that there is still work to be done, for they share our knowledge about the monstrous threat and our sense of an open ending. In these two novels, no final revelation alters our reading of the story and reminds us of our superiority to the characters. With the reporter, we see the gold crucifix; with Ben and Mark, we see the fire of purification—and we realize that the struggle of the living continues.[6]

Our certain knowledge that the undead have survived in *Vampire* or *'Salem's Lot* ensures that we will take these stories as open-ended. Lack of certainty about the fate of the monster can create a similar effect. For example, Dan Curtis's *House of Dark Shadows* (1970), a feature film derived from *Dark Shadows*, Curtis's extremely popular late 1960s soap opera, concludes in the following manner: Barnaby Collins, the vampire, is about to possess a beautiful young woman who lies mesmerized in a mist-filled cryptlike area. With a smug air of superiority, the vampire insists that the girl's boyfriend serve as a "witness" to this perverse marriage ceremony (thereby reminding us of our role as spectators). Yet the young man manages to thrust a stake into the vampire's back and carry his beloved away. As they move off screen, he repeats the final words of awakening and assurance that so often signify the achievement of closure: "It's all right. Everything is going to be all right now." Then, quite literally, we are granted an "overview," as the camera zooms out to an overhead shot of this room.[7] Far below lies the vampire's corpse half-shrouded in mist. The end credits roll superimposed over this image. After "The End" actually appears on the screen, a bat flies up from out of the mist near the body and quickly moves out of the frame. This concluding sequence is not simply the "trick reverse ending" that R. H. W. Dillard dubs it.[8] Curtis employs the immediately recognizable, undeniably satisfying elements of a closed ending (with particular reference to Browning's *Dracula*, it seems to me)—the defeat of the monster, the reunion of the couple, the awakening and escape from the vampire's domain, the almost incantory words of reassurance—not merely to trick us, but to make us aware that we are privileged witnesses. As long as we can look, we must look, for even after "The End" the truth can be revealed to us alone. In *House of Dark Shadows*, the revealed detail is a bat that flits by in almost the wink of an eye. Whether or not the bat is actually the vampire reborn, its escape disturbs our sense of certainty (is "everything," as the young man assured us, still "all right?") and mocks "The End."[9]

As I noted in chapter 3, Badham concludes his retelling of *Dracula* with what could be taken as the Count's triumphant transformation and escape. The degree of ambiguity about whether or not the vampire does indeed survive inevitably opens up the end of the story. That we cannot fully believe our eyes or see with absolute certainty reminds us that we also belong to the world of the living, however privileged our point of view. Unlike *House of Dark Shadows*, Badham's *Dracula* does not grant us a final overview that is superior to the characters and then force us to witness what can be seen from on high. Instead, it links our point of view with Lucy's and separates us from Van Helsing, who is dead, and from Jonathan Harker, who no longer attempts to see. The distance between the two hunters and the woman they have "saved" is not bridged and can never be bridged because of what she and we alone are able to see.

Our familiarity with other stories of Jonathan, Lucy, and Van Helsing—in particular with Stoker's *Dracula*, *Dracula: The Vampire Play*, and Browning's *Dracula*—makes the absence of union, integration, and restoration in Badham's film that much more apparent and so underlines the lack of resolution or, more precisely, the lack of *a* resolution that would return Lucy to her "rightful" place. (Earlier, I proposed that Lucy's story is one of escape and fulfillment apart from the world of her father and her fiancé.) Badham's *Dracula*, like all the open-ended stories I have mentioned, makes us begin to realize what we expect of closed endings. To a greater degree than *House of Dark*

Shadows, for example, Badham's vampire film not only undercuts but also challenges our expectations about resolution.

This challenge is posed in a different fashion in *Dawn of the Dead*. In Romero's film it is not the vampire (or the black cape) that escapes from our sight, but the helicopter carrying Fran and Peter. And here there is no ambiguity at all about the fate of the monster. The living dead triumph and reoccupy the mall to the accompaniment of a celebratory Muzak polka. They have achieved the restoration of normality, and, interestingly enough, we are stuck with them for the final images of the film. By the standards of Stoker's *Dracula* or King's *'Salem's Lot*, the living have failed in *Dawn of the Dead*. Yet Fran and Peter's escape from the mall as well as from the living dead is best taken as a liberating movement into an uncertain future that promises no "happily ever after." These survivors, after capturing and closing off the mall, have already sampled the dubious pleasures of a closed ending.

If Badham's *Dracula* denies us the traditional reunion of the young couple (and thus, by extension, the formation of the family), *Dawn of the Dead* depicts the destruction of the potential nuclear family (with Stephen's death) and the creation of a new union for a new world: the black trooper, who has discarded his rifle, accompanying the pregnant, liberated white woman, who pilots the helicopter toward the dawn. After final images of the extended family (Stoker's *Dracula*), the betrothed couple (Browning's *Dracula*), the reunited married couple (*Horror of Dracula*), the victorious pair of young men (*El Conde Dracula*), and the father and son (*'Salem's Lot*), and after the pessimism about all the ties that bind human beings in *Night of the Living Dead*, Romero concludes *Dawn of the Dead* with the glimpse of a freely chosen new union that is not dependent on or emblematic of the restoration of normality.

Romero ends both his living dead films with sequences that are "confrontational" in that they "deliberately thwart reader expectations," to borrow a phrase from Marianna Torgovnick's *Closure in the Novel.*[10] *Night of the Living Dead* and *Dawn of the Dead* lack and even challenge the deeply satisfying, reassuring pleasures of what Bettelheim calls "recovery and consolation"—pleasures that in stories of the living and the undead are the product and the reward of bloody wild work. *Night of the Living Dead* offers us the grim and ironic prospect of restoration without recovery and consolation. *Dawn of the Dead* begins to suggest the pleasures of discovery and continuation, free from the burden of restoration. And this is quite an achievement given that horror stories almost always teach us that discovery is a dangerous form of transgression and that continuation is a prolonging of the nightmare.

Any discussion of how stories of the living and the undead end must necessarily involve a discussion of the nature and function of violence in these stories.[11] Victor Roman effectively demonstrates this point in *Four Wooden Stakes*, a story I mentioned in chapter 2. Roman's story concludes with a description of four coffins that once housed the undead; each coffin now contains a wooden stake, a "horrible tool" "bearing the fingerprints" of the hunters and "stained a brownish hue" with the blood of the vampire.[12] Similarly, the final object we see in Freddie Francis's *Dracula Has Risen from the Grave*, one of Hammer's vampire films, is the large gold cross, dripping with blood, on which Count Dracula has been impaled. After the confrontation between the living and the undead in these two works, and after protagonists and antagonists both disappear from our sight, the bloodstained weapon remains. Stake and cross here are more than reminders of life-or-death struggles and spilt blood. These traditional objects signify the efficacy of that form of ritualistic violence that Stoker's Van Helsing calls wild work.

The violence carried out by the living is no less apparent and no less significant when Kukri knives, automatic rifles, or meathooks replace stake and cross, or even when the weapons wielded by the living are hidden from view during the conclusion—as in Browning's *Dracula*, where the camera in the final image looks up toward John and Mina ascending into the light. The young couple's ascent would never occur, however, without Van Helsing's wild work in the crypt, an act so successful that it leaves no visible trace or bloodstained reminder. To look at Browning's *Dracula* and Roman's *Four Wooden Stakes* in the context of the other stories I have discussed is to see the narrative and thematic centrality of violence in the story of the living and the undead (even when it is almost completely absent as in Murnau's *Nosferatu* and Herzog's *Nosferatu the Vampyre*) and at the same time to be struck by just how many different opinions this genre offers, explicitly as well as implicitly, concerning the nature and function of violence.

For example, even *Four Wooden Stakes* and *Dracula Has Risen from the Grave*, which share a final emphasis on the bloodstained weapon and on the traditional wild work of destruction, vary considerably in their depiction of this justified and necessary violence. In Roman's story, the narrator and his threatened friend, Remson, carve the stakes and alone enter the family crypt to destroy the vampires. Acting in self-defense, they free Remson from his parasitic undead relatives. Here the bloody, dangerous, private actions of the living carry little, if any, religious significance and have no social effects. In Francis's film, by way of contrast, the bloodstained weapon testifies to the grand spiritual and moral issues involved when the living battle the undead—reminding us of the redemptive value of suffering and sacrifice, the necessity for Christian faith, and perhaps also the quality of divine justice.

Each of the stories I have discussed, from major works like Stoker's *Dracula* to minor ones like *Four Wooden Stakes* and *Dracula Has Risen from the Grave*, offers an internally coherent and complete definition of the nature and function of the violence undertaken by the living and the undead. (Similarly, each story, as I have noted throughout my study, also offers its own definition of the monstrous and of the status quo.) And we may discover in one or more of these stories a presentation of violence that suits our fancy or addresses our fears or corroborates our understanding. However, the genre itself—as it develops in response to the individual storyteller, the marketplace, and the cultural environment—inevitably qualifies, complicates, and even undermines all that the individual work attempts to present as perfectly clear and complete. Taken as a group, the series of texts that make up the story of the living and the undead offer, in their play of repetition and variation, an unsystematic and necessarily unresolved exploration of the nature and function of violence and a sampling of several important ways we have of making sense of violence.[13]

Much of my discussion has been an attempt to chart and comment on the course of this exploration by focusing on the presentation of the violent work of man and monster in a wide range of stories. The brief concluding remarks I offer here are less a summary than a survey of certain questions about violence raised by these stories and a preliminary attempt to situate these questions in the context of other inquiries into the nature and function of violence.

In an essay written for a 1968 anthology entitled *Violence and the Mass Media*, Walter M. Gerson proposes that empirical studies of violence as an "American value theme" begin with the commonplace distinction between "illegitimate" violence that is "contrary to the mores or against the law" and violence that is "positively sanctioned" and is thus "legitimate." Of the latter, we must ask, according to Gerson, "legitimate *according to whom*?" and also distinguish between "*offen-*

sive" and "*defensive*" violence.[14] To what extent do stories of the living and the undead dramatize or validate these distinctions and, in so doing, consider the "value theme" of violence?

The distinction between offensive and defensive violence in Stoker's *Dracula* and in the various retellings of this novel would seem to be perfectly clear: the aristocratic vampire initiates the confrontation, invading the modern world and the bedrooms of young women; in defense, the living retaliate. Terence Fisher, in *Horror of Dracula*, complicates this apparently simple formula by depicting Jonathan Harker, the innocent solicitor in Stoker's novel, as being from the first a committed hunter who journeys to Castle Dracula in order to destroy the vampire. Jonathan's actions are offensive, though his ultimate goal is the defense of the living. In fact, the stories I discussed in chapters 2–5 offer few situations in which the living commit acts of violence literally in self-defense. (The concluding struggle in Badham's *Dracula* is an exception, though even here Jonathan and Van Helsing initiate the final confrontation with Count Dracula by boarding the ship that is carrying the vampire away from England.) Most often, the living must seek out and attack the vampire, and so become hunters—recall the quasi-military offensive conducted by the moral community in the concluding sections of Stoker's *Dracula* and Saville's *Count Dracula*. Finally, the distinction between offensive and defensive legitimate violence in the retellings of *Dracula* is no more clear-cut than this distinction is in twentieth-century warfare, where all violent acts can be justified as ultimately defensive in intent. (Thus the notion of preemptive strikes and pacification.)[15]

No single act better expresses the paradoxical and potentially troubling relationship between offensive and defensive violence than the premeditated transfixion of a sleeping, completely passive, (and for the moment) defenseless female vampire. On the one hand, this act resembles a rape—a crime of unquestionably offensive, illegitimate violence. On the other hand, the staking of the undead, possessed siren is presented in these stories as a legitimate defensive measure—an act that protects innocent children and susceptible young men—that often serves as a means of granting salvation to the victim.

Like the stories involving Count Dracula, *Carmilla*, from the 1870s, and *'Salem's Lot*, from the 1970s, also clearly distinguish between the offensive violence of the undead and the defensive actions of the vampire hunters, who are free of the taint of being unjustified aggressors. *Night of the Living Dead* offers what initially looks to be another sort of unambiguous distinction—between the defensive action of the people trapped in the farmhouse and the posse's offensive "search and destroy" mission. Yet this mission (like all posses) is defensive in the sense that it seeks to defend the status quo by forestalling future threats. In both *Night of the Living Dead* and *Dawn of the Dead* Romero makes us take note of the difference between instinctive acts of violent self-defense and the premeditated defensive measures of searching and destroying undertaken by a posse or by a group of vampire hunters. Furthermore, Romero contrasts the offensive violence committed by the living dead, which is easily understood as simply an attempt to satisfy hunger (these creatures are quite unlike the aristocratic vampires who seek power and pleasure and, at times, revenge) and the violence of the living, which is disturbingly problematic. Ben's retaliatory murder of the unarmed Harry Cooper, for example, or the posse's purposeless, "accidental" murder of Ben complicates any simple notion of the relationship between offensive and defensive violence.

More important, these killings in *Night of the Living Dead* force us to reconsider what we understand to be the distinction between legitimate and illegitimate violence. Gerson correctly notes that the "degree of legitimacy" is a "continuum" ranging from the "fully legitimate" to the "completely illegitimate" and that there may be no social consensus about the legitimacy of any given act of violence.[16] One way to resolve this problem of definition is to equate illegitimacy with illegality and legitimacy with legality. Stories of the living and the undead shatter these equations.[17] The actions of the undead are *more* than merely illegal (is it simply illegal to desire to father a "new order of beings" or to tear the intestines out of a screaming victim?). Vampire hunters—except perhaps those in *Carmilla*—are lawbreakers. In fact, the relationship between the legal and the legitimate is a recurrent motif in the story of the living and the undead, as it is in a great many westerns and detective stories.

Hunters of the undead quickly realize, as Van Helsing points out in *Dracula: The Vampire Play*, that in their terrible task, "the police, all the powers of society, are as helpless as the doctors" (DVP, 29). Thus Stoker's moral community never appeals to legally sanctioned authorities. In Romero's films the authorities slaughter both the living and the undead. In *'Salem's Lot* the sheriff leaves town as soon as he realizes the nature of the threat. In *I, Desire* the police detective covers up the truth. Obviously, these and other similar details reflect our basic fear that the authorities will not be able to protect us in our hour of need.

That in so many stories of the living and the undead the police and those men in recognized positions of legal and social power are so often absent as to be for all purposes nonexistent also suggests that in these stories the state does not even satisfy the minimal requirements of what Robert Nozick calls the "classical liberal" notion of the "night-watchman state" with its "monopoly" on the use of force.[18] Not just the "bad guys" in *Dawn of the Dead*, but all hunters of the undead, to some extent, live with Richard Matheson's solitary hero, Robert Neville, in a world in which the legal and the illegal are empty, inapplicable concepts.

As in *I Am Legend*, in almost all stories of the living and the undead we are made to consider and to decide which acts of violence can be deemed legitimate when the relationship of these acts to legality and social mores is not a binding criterion. Often, the decision poses no difficulty, and our surety matches the confidence of Van Helsing in Stoker's novel and *Dracula: The Vampire Play* and of the Van Helsing figure in stories like *Vampire* and *'Salem's Lot*. These characters assess the situation from a position of wisdom, courage, and faith. They fully realize the implications of the urgent situation at hand, for they know their opponent, who is, in effect, their potential victim. The wise elder instructs the mystified, skeptical modern men in the nature of the confrontation and convinces them of the necessity for a specific form of legitimate violence. This common situation in stories of the living and the undead calls to mind J. Glenn Gray's observation in *The Warriors* that "the basic aim of a nation at war in establishing an image of the enemy is to distinguish as sharply as possible the act of killing from the act of murder by making the former into one deserving of all honor and praise."[19]

In Stoker's novel, for example, the complete legitimization of gruesome, barbarous acts of killing depends to a great extent on the "image of the enemy" that Van Helsing paints for Lucy's suitors and that Stoker paints for us through the collection of first-person accounts. The illegal, violent actions of the moral community in *Dracula* are legitimate because they are directed against the animalistic undead Lucy Westenra, who is trapped in an unnatural vampiric existence, and against Count Dracula, the "devil in callous" (D, 243). Because Van Helsing and his young allies "work to a good end" (D, 173), their violent means are justified as the highest form of duty. The hunters come to see themselves as holy crusaders, "instruments of ultimate good" (D, 321). Stoker suggests that their acts of mutilation and desecration are unquestionably legitimate because of the nature of their undead opponents, because no nonviolent recourse is possible and immediate action is required, because these violent acts bring about a "good end," and because the living selflessly undertake their wild work "for the safety of one we love—for the good of mankind, and for the honour and glory of God" (D, 326).[20]

Thus Stoker's *Dracula*, like *Carmilla*, *The Thing*, *'Salem's Lot*, and a number of other texts I have considered, offers an unadulterated, unambiguous version of what John Cawelti, in an essay on "Myths of Violence in American Popular Culture," calls the recurrent theme of "the moral necessity of violence." As Cawelti notes, there are several major, and often interrelated, forms this "narrative pattern" can take, reflecting different ways that "legitimated violence" can be justified and explained. For example, violence can be presented as a morally necessary act of personal revenge that satisfies the demands of *lex talonis*—retributive justice.[21] The young men whose wives and fiancées have been attacked or seduced or stolen by the vampire have a personal score to settle when they hunt their antagonist. They are seeking personal satisfaction and just punishment. Yet if Jonathan Harker, the naive would-be revenger in *Dracula: The Vampire Play* and Browning's *Dracula*, is to succeed, he must remain subservient to Professor Van Helsing, the figure of authority who acts on the basis of more impersonal, dispassionate motives.

Badham's retelling of *Dracula* alters this balance of selfish and selfless motives by having Van Helsing's daughter be the vampire's first victim in England. After this old man has been forced to confront his now-undead daughter and then cut out her heart to save her soul, he pursues Count Dracula, seeking personal revenge as well as more selfless "good ends." *Carmilla* also addresses the relationship between legitimate violence and personal retribution. In Le Fanu's story, unlike Badham's *Dracula*, the vengeance sought by the two elderly fathers whose daughters have been victimized by the vampire perfectly coincides with the desires of society at large—the destruction of Carmilla satisfies both the public and the private sense of justice. However, the desire for revenge that spurs on these injured men is little different from the desire that motivates the passionate warrior-vampire in Curtis's *Dracula*, who seeks to avenge the loss of his beloved, and the resurrected Count Dracula in Alan Gibson's *Dracula, A. D. 1972*, who attempts to make Van Helsing's granddaughter pay for her ancestor's exploits. (Like Jonathan Harker and Arthur Holmwood, Count Dracula in Stoker's novel also has a personal score to settle: "My revenge is just begun!" he threatens after he has attacked Mina [D, 312].) Curtis's and Gibson's films could be said to complicate Le Fanu's appealing image of complete accord between public justice and private vengeance, because these films depict the vampire's desire for revenge as an egotistical obsession that can only harm the living. As one story answers, challenges, or "corrects" another, we are left with no simple explanation of the relationship between private retribution and the common weal and between legitimate, just punishment and illegitimate, egotistical obsession. In this manner the genre raises questions, displays contradictions, and poses dilemmas.

In certain stories the violence undertaken in the name of "good ends" can provide other benefits to the hunter in addition to satisfying a personal desire for revenge. For example, Roger, Peter, and Stephen in *Dawn of the Dead* gain a sense of comradeship in the face of danger. Gray convincingly argues that such comradeship is one of the "enduring appeals of battle."[22] The newfound communality of the vampire hunters in stories of the living and the undead takes on a variety of forms, from Stoker's moral community, to the successful alliance of Jonathan and Quincey in *El Conde Dracula*, to the bond that links Ben and Mark as father and son in *'Salem's Lot*. The genre offers counterexamples as well, like *Night of the Living Dead*, in which the fate of the people in the besieged farmhouse proves that the confrontation with the undead does not necessarily foster comradeship among the living. Furthermore, in various stories the undead also have their unions, alliances, and communal bonds, all of which are to some degree disturbing reflections of and often appealing alternatives to the comradeship of the living. Thus the genre, as it discovers the possible clauses and provisions in the story it tells, presents us with new examples that qualify the general rule (in this case, concerning the comradeship born of violent confrontation) and exceptions that question the rule itself.

The danger posed by the undead and the desire to avenge personal injury mobilize the young men in Stoker's novel and the assorted hunters in *'Salem's Lot*; the witnesses to horror become participants.[23] In hunting the vampire and carrying out the terrible yet necessary wild work, these modern men are themselves transformed, matured, even regenerated. Cawelti includes the "myth of regeneration through violence" as one of the common "patterns of action which justify or explain the moral necessity of the hero's violence."[24] The most complete analysis of this "myth" is provided by Richard Slotkin in *Regeneration through Violence: The Mythology of the American Frontier 1600–1860* (1973). According to Slotkin, seventeenth- and eighteenth-century captivity narratives, with their images of the Puritan woman torn from her home and held captive in the wilderness by bestial, satanic Indians, are stories of the "ritual exorcism of projected evil." Such captivity narratives have clear analogies with stories of the living and the undead. The female victims in *Carmilla* and most retellings of *Dracula* are also versions of the captive, and the vampire—like all monsters—is a "projected evil" to be exorcised. What Slotkin refers to as the "myth of the hunter" is more directly concerned with the possibility of regeneration through violence. As with captivity narratives, there are immediately apparent links between the works I have discussed and this myth of the hunter who "embarks on a quest . . . into a primitive world," and through the hunt and the killing of the quarry is initiated into a "new life, a new world, a new stage of manhood."[25] What stories of the living and the undead insist on, unlike the stories and legends about Daniel Boone and Davy Crockett that Slotkin describes, is that regeneration is possible, if at all, only when existence becomes a life-or-death struggle for survival. The pursuit of the vampire is much more of a holy, entirely necessary crusade than a solitary quest or a journey of exploration into the wilderness. For the vampire hunters in Stoker's *Dracula*, Saville's *Count Dracula*, Hammer's vampire films, *'Salem's Lot*, and *They Thirst*, to be regenerated means to suddenly awaken to the reality of Good and Evil, to mature and assume responsibility (and often to discover a new father), to be initiated into a new life that is in fact an old life, stripped clean of the selfishness and skepticism that render modern man vulnerable, corrupt, or corruptible.

Even in these stories (not to mention Romero's films), the notion of regeneration through violence is not quite so simple, for the undead are nourished by the blood of their prey and so are also regenerated by the violence they commit. Stoker's Count Dracula, for example, actually becomes younger in appearance with each successful attack. For the King-Vampire, the blood is the life. Leonard Wolf, among other critics, argues that the vampire, "reduced to his essence," is a "baleful imitation of Christ."[26] And the King-Vampire in Stoker's *Dracula* forces Mina to drink his blood in a perverse form of communion, an act Van Helsing repeatedly refers to as a "terrible baptism of blood" (D, 347) that could very well transform Mina into a vampire. According to Mircea Eliade, "Immersion in water as an instrument of purification and regeneration" is an "immemorial and oecumenical" ritual,[27] and St. Paul speaks of baptism as man's death and resurrection "in the likeness" of Christ (Romans 6: 2–9). The victims of the undead, in a "terrible baptism of blood" rather than of water, are killed and reborn in the likeness of their monstrous assailant, and from that time forward they continue the violent process of generation and regeneration.

Often the vampire hunters undergo a corollary baptism—becoming immersed in or in some fashion stained by the blood of the undead creatures they kill. When Ben in *'Salem's Lot* drives a stake into Barlow's heart, "blood splashed upward in a cold gush, blinding him momentarily" (SL, 412). Ben does not actually drink the blood or consume the flesh of his enemy, but he is regenerated by the act, blinded so that he can gain a clearer sight.[28] However, when Roger in *Dawn of the Dead* is splashed with the blood of a zombie, he is unalterably stained, possessed by a sort of primal bloodlust, and eventually he rises as one of the undead. Through these images of baptism as a moment of triumph or defeat and these images of blood that nourishes or purifies or stains, stories of the living and the undead embody, vary, and challenge the "myth of regeneration through violence."

In addition, these stories make us realize that a distinction must be drawn between violence that regenerates the hunter and violence that regenerates or restores society. (In stories like Stoker's *Dracula* and *Horror of Dracula*, the violence of the living also purges the undead victim, exorcising all that is vampiric.) For example, in *Carmilla* and Browning's *Dracula*, the violence of the living purges society of the vampire, though the elderly hunters are not regenerated by the wild work they must commit—indeed, they have no need for regeneration. Just as the image of what constitutes the status quo can vary a great deal from story to story, so can the specific type of restoration that results from purgative violence. By destroying the undead, the living can reclaim what has been stolen (Mina in Browning's *Dracula*), reintegrate what has been broken apart (the Holmwoods' marriage in *Horror of Dracula*), or reaffirm what has been challenged (the authority of the patriarchal ruling class in *Carmilla*). The story of the living and the undead also leads us to distinguish the violence that purges and thereby restores the status quo from the violence that creates new bonds among the living. In the face of the monster and in the course of its violent destruction, a new community is created in Stoker's *Dracula*, *Count Dracula*, and *The Thing*.[29] As I noted in chapter 2, Freud's myth of the primal horde offers a comparable view of creative violence.

And once again, the undead pose a dark reflection of the living, for the monster's violence can create new bonds and new orders as well.

René Girard's *Violence and the Sacred*, one of the most ambitious and provocative studies of violence published in recent years, also addresses the role of creative or restorative violence. Like almost all stories of the living and the undead, Girard's study of primitive culture, religion, myth, and Greek tragedy insists that we acknowledge the "dual nature of violence":[30] maleficent violence that is terrifying in its potential to destroy human life and human culture; and beneficent, generative violence that is a "source of peace, strength, and fecundity" (VS, 277). According to Girard, maleficent violence is contagious, infectious, and staining. It is a product of the "violent impulses of society" (VS, 17) and the desire for personal vengeance, which threatens to initiate a "vicious circle of reciprocal violence, wholly destructive in nature" and apparently inescapable (VS, 144). Only "ritual violence," in the form of the sacrifice of a surrogate victim, can replace reciprocal violence. Originally, this sacrificial murder was a spontaneous, collective, unanimous action, undertaken to purge and expulse maleficent, reciprocal violence, and so to create "a new or renewed cultural order" (VS, 255). For Girard, "there can be nothing in the whole range of human culture that is not rooted in violent unanimity—nothing that does not find its source in the surrogate victim" (VS, 297).

What Girard calls a "sacrificial crisis" occurs when the difference between pure (ritualistic, beneficent) and impure (reciprocal, maleficent) violence disappears along with other "cultural distinctions" upon which all "order, peace, and fecundity" depend. "Contagious," reciprocal violence then spreads, or threatens to spread, "throughout the community" (VS, 49). The plague, twins, "enemy brothers," perpetrators of incest or patricide, monstrous creatures that are both man and beast—all can symbolize the "violent abolition of distinctions" that marks the sacrificial crisis (VS, 98). Myths, Girard concludes, "are the retrospective transfigurations of sacrificial crises" (VS, 64), and "ritual is the imitation and reenactment of spontaneous, unanimous violence" that was initially directed against a surrogate victim (VS, 99).

The concept of the surrogate victim is central in Girard's understanding of the cultural role of violence and of rites of sacrifice. The original surrogate victim was arbitrarily chosen from inside the community and served as the substitute for the community's own "burden of violence" (VS, 278). (Girard, like Freud in *Totem and Taboo*, insists that this collective murder was a "real event" [VS, 309].) In sacrificial rites designed to prevent the spread of reciprocal violence and to end the sacrificial crisis, a ritual victim, chosen from outside the community—yet in some manner a double of those people inside the community—is substituted for the original surrogate victim. Whether this ritual victim is "actual or figurative, animate or inanimate" (VS, 18), it is modeled on the original scapegoat, who is both a source of contamination and a means of purification—at once the "most beneficial" and the "most evil" (VS, 86), the transgressor and the redeemer. The murder or the expulsion of this victim in a communal act of violence is, Girard argues, the "exemplary guarantor of cultural stability" (VS, 280).

Since stories of the living and the undead share Girard's assumptions about the centrality of dual-natured violence in the life of man, we can ask to what extent these stories—indeed all stories of the confrontation between human beings and monsters—are transfigurations of what Girard calls the sacrificial crisis and the "surrogate-victim mechanism." The undead creature, especially the aristocratic, classical vampire, is repeatedly associated with incest, contagion, and the obliteration of all-important distinctions (between life and death, for example), as well as with the monstrous and the double, all details that are linked in *Violence and the Sacred* with the sacrificial crisis. In Stoker's *Dracula* the destruction of the King-Vampire and his female progeny is an example of what Girard calls "a form of violence that will put an end once and for all to violence itself" (VS, 27). Dracula and his brides are similar to Girard's scapegoat in that both are seen as "polluted objects" (VS, 95), who are outside human society, yet still bear an important resemblance to the members of society. However, Count Dracula and the undead Lucy Westenra are not arbitrarily chosen victims. They threaten society, and so the living in self-defense must destroy them. Furthermore, the various retellings of *Dracula* (unlike *'Salem's Lot*, for example, or *Taste the Blood of Dracula*) rarely suggest that the living are undergoing a crisis that stems from their own aggressive impulses and their own potential for reciprocal violence. Maleficent violence in these stories is generally associated only with the undead, who are wholly maleficent. That these creatures can offer immortality and the pleasures attendant upon "beautiful, fundamental nourishment" does not qualify them as beneficent (though in these transgressions, the King-Vampire acts out the more or less unacknowledged desires of the living and so is a surrogate for the vampire hunters).

The vampire stories of Stoker, Hamilton Deane and John L. Balderston, Browning, and Fisher do not depict the type of sacrifice described in *Violence and the Sacred.* Instead, these stories offer what Girard dismisses as a "Manichaean confrontation of 'good guys' and 'bad guys'" (VS, 150). However, the collective violence directed against the "bad guys" in Stoker's *Dracula,* like Van Helsing's solitary violence in Browning's *Dracula* or Fisher's *Horror of Dracula,* does have the generative or restorative effect of a sacrifice. Through the "true death" of the undead, the living maintain or restore or create their world—the destruction of the vampire serves as a wholly justified and necessary resolution to a confrontation that the vampire hunters themselves did not initiate.

In *I Am Legend* Matheson brings the role of sacrificial violence and the surrogate victim to the fore and thus helps us to see the importance of this motif throughout the entire genre (as well as in other horror stories from *Frankenstein* [1931] and *The Wolf Man* [1941] to *The Howling* [1981] and *Cat People* [1982]). In demythologizing Stoker's *Dracula,* Matheson presents sacrifice from the point of view of Robert Neville, the human being who becomes a legendary monster and eventually a would-be sacrificial victim. Matheson implies that violence is inevitable, both for the last man on earth and for the primitive new society that will inherit his domain. But this violence is never truly generative or beneficial for the hunter or for the world.

In various ways several other stories of the living and the undead challenge the notion that violence can be regenerative, restorative, or creative. In Badham's *Dracula,* for example, Van Helsing dies with a stake driven through his chest, and Jonathan Harker remains isolated and half-dead after his apparently unsuccessful struggle with the vampire. No new community has been forged, no domestic tranquillity regained, no spiritual order restored. Here the wild work of the living—like all violence, according to Hannah Arendt in *On Violence*—creates nothing.

A similar situation is found in Murnau's *Nosferatu,* where the only violent activity undertaken by the living is the mob's irrational destruction of a scarecrow. This attack on the "monster" is the last recourse of the frustrated, victimized townspeople. Murnau makes clear that such violent action cannot purge the infected society or create a new form of community. At the end of *Nosferatu the Vampyre,* Herzog introduces the ritualized wild work that was missing in Murnau's film, but only to mock Van Helsing and the bourgeois society he attempts to protect with his primitive, unscientific, traditional methods (and indirectly to mock the assumptions about violence and patriarchal wise men in films like Browning's *Dracula*). Ironically, Van Helsing's bloody deed in *Nosferatu the Vampyre*—taken by the other residents of Bremen for a homicidal crime rather than a heroic ritual slaying—does help to revive the status quo and the rule of law and civil authority in the city. For Badham, Herzog, and to a lesser extent, Murnau, the critique of creative violence is linked to a critique of the status quo that such violence seeks to restore. In this regard, these films are comparable to *Night of the Living Dead* with its portrait of McClelland's triumphant posse.

Romero, following the lead of Matheson's *I Am Legend*, dispenses with stakes and crosses and substitutes seemingly innumerable and interchangeable acts of extermination for rare, individually meaningful acts of transfixion. If the danger in *I Am Legend* is that Robert Neville will unthinkingly accept genocidal violence as merely a monotonous daily necessity, the danger in Romero's living dead films is that the living will be corrupted by the violence they must commit. Ben in *Night of the Living Dead* and the four survivors in the mall in *Dawn of the Dead* prove their capabilities in the struggle against the undead, but they all would also do well to heed Friedrich Nietzsche's advice in *Beyond Good and Evil*: "Whoever battles with monsters had better see that it does not turn him into a monster."[31]

Because of the many references to infection and contamination and the fact that the living can quite literally become the undead, the stories I have discussed always keep us aware of the potential danger to the hunter of monsters that Nietzsche describes. Yet before Roger rises as one of the living dead and so literally becomes the monster, he is corrupted by the violence he commits, as are the motorcycle raiders and certain of the S.W.A.T. troops. Given the opportunity to kill, free of the requirements of ritual and the restrictions of the law, these men are like certain warriors described by Gray, who take such "delight in destruction" that they become "berserkers and mad destroyers."[32] Such destruction is a completely personal, selfish form of violence that is degenerative rather than regenerative—so much so that ultimately the "berserkers" themselves must be killed. Peter in *Dawn of the Dead* and Ben in *Night of the Living Dead* are affected by the corrupting power of violence to a somewhat lesser extent. As well as killing the zombies in an act of legitimate self-defense, Ben murders Harry Cooper in an act of anger and vengeance. Peter relishes the hunt, though, when he finally chooses to remain alive, he must discard his rifle, which suggests that violence cannot regenerate the individual or create the new community. Romero's depiction of violence in *Night of the Living Dead* and *Dawn of the Dead*—like the variations he plays on our sense of open and closed endings in these films—transforms the genre and alters our understanding of all other stories of the living and the undead.

What the incomplete, unsystematic, open-ended exploration of the nature and the function of violence in the works I have discussed offers is not consensus, but contradictory claims and qualifications upon qualifications. Instead of definitive categories, the process of repetition and difference in the story of the living and the undead leaves us with a network of overlapping oppositions that rarely prove to be as clear-cut as we perhaps would desire or as any single story would have us believe. In light of the genre as a whole, basic distinctions between, for example, violent acts that are legitimate or illegitimate, offensive or defensive, necessary or gratuitous almost always come to seem differences of degree and not of kind. Furthermore, these distinctions become inseparable from a consideration of the myriad functions of violence in these stories as a means of, for example, subjugation or liberation, purification or contamination, personal vengeance or civil defense. Just as in each individual story the bloodletting of the living must be seen in the context of the bloodsucking of the undead, so, if we are to follow and participate in this ongoing exploration of violence, each story is best understood in relation to the entire series of works I have discussed—in the context of the creative, communal violence in Stoker's *Dracula*, the genocidal and sacrificial violence in *I Am Legend*, the restorative violence in Browning's *Dracula*, the liberating violence in *El Conde Dracula*, the irrational mob violence in Murnau's *Nosferatu*, and on through the genre's still-transformable inventory of options.

All the acts of violence in the stories I have chosen to focus on are part of a life-or-death confrontation that is, in effect, a struggle for survival between the living and the undead. "You must struggle and strive to live" (D, 297), Van Helsing tells Mina after she has suffered Count Dracula's "vampire baptism" in Stoker's novel. This dictum also holds true for the human beings in the various retellings of *Dracula* and in other stories of the living and the undead as well. Under such conditions, all that is unrelated to the struggle becomes inconsequential and is quickly forgotten. Every action becomes meaningful, every decision urgently important, and life appears purified, distilled, unexpectedly fraught with danger, terror, and vitalizing conflict, and with opportunities for freedom, purposefulness, and failure. The endings of these stories, as I have insisted throughout my discussion, provide a resolution or lack of resolution to this struggle for survival and in so doing identify the fittest and complete the process of defining what it takes and what it costs to survive—what fitness consists of.

Novels and films that depict the confrontation between the living and the undead are one version of a much more inclusive type of popular narrative, the story of an inescapable, literally life-or-death struggle for survival—a story surely as entertaining, flexible, durable, and ideologically significant as any tale that is told and retold.[33] Adjacent to Stoker's *Dracula*, Romero's living dead films, and the series of works I have discussed are other versions of the story of the struggle for survival: recent works of horror as dissimilar as *The Exorcist* (book, 1971; film, 1973) and *Friday the 13th* (1980); stories of invasion from *Invasion of the Body Snatchers* (1956) and *The Birds* (1963) to *The Swarm* (book, 1974; film, 1978) and the television mini-series *V* (1983–84); accounts of wartime combat, like *Objective, Burma!* (1945), and of wartime resistance, like *Edge of Darkness* (1943); apocalyptic fiction like *Alas, Babylon* (1959) and *The Stand* (1978); and celebrations of human endurance and ingenuity in the face of disaster, like *The Poseidon Adventure* (book, 1969; film, 1972) and *Alive* (1974). Climbing up through the treacherous debris inside an overturned luxury liner is hardly the same as battling extraterrestrial invaders or marching to safety through the jungles of Burma or driving a stake into the heart of a vampire, yet in all stories of the struggle for survival, the ever-present prospect of death and defeat makes us—like the would-be survivors—acutely aware of the quality of life. The story of survival is well-suited to embody our anxieties and our beliefs in all their depth and breadth, for with its emphasis on crisis and confrontation this genre displays our points of vulnerability and memorializes the world that we are in danger of losing.

With H. G. Wells's *The War of the Worlds* (1898) and Stoker's *Dracula* ushering it into the twentieth century, the story of survival has without question become one of our most popular and meaningful stories, particularly since World War II (or, more precisely, since the Japanese attack on Pearl Harbor and the U.S. bombing of Hiroshima—two events that dramatically altered our ideas about survival and confrontation). It is a story that immerses us in what Wells's narrator calls the "dark and terrible aspects of life" and has us experience, as human beings, a "sense of dethronement."[34] And this genre reminds us, as a character in James Dickey's *Deliverance* (1970) realizes, that "the world is easily lost."[35] The terror and the chastising warnings of this story, however, are in most cases tempered by first, our safe position as spectators to a struggle that very often insists that all would-be spectators must become participants if they hope to survive, and second, the sense of reenthronement or regeneration or simply victorious survival in so many of these stories. For every *Dracula* (1979) or *I Am Legend* there are ten works that depict man's much-deserved victory in the "battle for existence." Even the fearful and yet in some fashion desirable stripping away of all that protects us from the "dark and terrible" is advantageous in that it provides the occasion for the testing of man, whose frightening, unexpected fall may ultimately prove to be fortunate indeed.

The story of survival offers an urgent, potentially fatal contest that pits man against monster, nature, time, or other men. And in the face of this contest, which has life as its prize, all regulated sporting events or bloodthirsty fictional "deathsports" pale. Each new version of the struggle for survival and of the emergence of the fittest is inevitably an exploration and a definition both of struggling and of fitness. Throughout the twentieth century this ongoing exploration has reflected and shaped our understanding of individual heroism and sacrifice and of the ties—beyond familial and social roles—that bind one person to another. Stories of survival express and help to create our sense of civilization, and they allow us to witness—with pity, fear, and satisfaction—the process of shedding, stripping away, destroying, or defending civilization. There is, I believe, no better introduction to the story of survival and to the particular pleasures and the ideological significance of popular narratives than the series of works I have examined in this book—stories of the violent struggle between the living and the undead from Le Fanu and Stoker to Herzog and Romero.

NOTES

1. Thomas Schatz, *Hollywood Genres: Formulas, Filmmaking, and the Studio System* (New York: Random House, 1981), p. 30. Although I have limited my comments in this section almost exclusively to stories of the living and the undead, many of the distinctions I draw are also valid for a great number of other horror stories.

2. There are any number of variations in the way the final revelation is used

in stories of the living and the undead to create an open ending. For example, not until the final paragraphs of Marc Lovell's 1974 novel, *An Enquiry into the Existence of Vampires*, do we know for certain that the researcher who inquires into the "disease" of vampirism is himself a vampire. Lovell's rather predictable open ending (which suggests the degree to which the "surprising" final revelation can itself become a conventional and expected form of closure) may be contrasted with the concluding sequence in Roman Polanski's *The Fearless Vampire Killers* (1967): having rescued the heroine from the vampire's castle, the two vampire hunters escape with her in a sled. Professor Abronsius—a dedicated, comic, unwise elder who is the antithesis of Peter Cushing's Van Helsing—drives and so cannot see what occurs in the seat behind him. First we, then Abronsius's young assistant, discover that the beautiful heroine has become one of the undead. As the sled disappears around a bend, a voice-over narrator makes sure that we realize the implications of this revelation: "That night, fleeing from Transylvania, Professor Abronsius never guessed he was carrying away with him the very evil he had wished to destroy. This evil would at last be able to spread across the world." So ends Abronsius's "sacred mission" to rid the world of the undead. The superior, for all purposes omniscient, off-screen narrator, traditional discloser of "happily ever afters," here underlines the comically ironic open ending.

3. Marianna Torgovnick derives her definition of the epilogue from Russian formalist Boris Eikhenbaum. The epilogue, Torgovnick writes, "sets the perspective by a shift in time-scale or orientation; it provides some element of *nachgeschichte* (after-history) for the major characters" (*Closure and the Novel* [Princeton: Princeton University Press, 1981], p. 11).

4. Bruno Bettelheim, *The Uses of Enchantment: The Meaning and Importance of Fairy Tales* (New York: Vintage, 1977), pp. 143–50. J. Hillis Miller argues that it is impossible ever to demonstrate "whether a given narrative is complete," for "if the ending is thought of as a tying up in a careful knot, this knot could always be untied again by the narrator or by further events, disentangled or explicated again. If the ending is thought of as an unraveling, a straightening of threads, this act clearly leaves not one loose thread but a multitude, side by side, all capable of being knotted once more" ("The Problematic Ending in Narrative," *Nineteenth-Century Fiction* 33 [June 1978], 5–6). Miller is correct, though I believe that we can acknowledge this obvious "problematic" and still retain open-ended and closed-ended as useful and necessary critical concepts. I would suggest that in discussing stories like Stoker's *Dracula*, Browning's *Dracula*, and Romero's *Night of the Living Dead*, we can speak of degrees of closure.

Other studies of narrative closure by literary critics include: Alan Friedman, *The Turn of the Novel* (New York: Oxford University Press, 1966), and David H. Richter, *Fable's End: Completion and Closure in Rhetorical Fiction* (Chicago: University of Chicago Press, 1974).

5. In thinking about the type of closure in films like *Nosferatu* and *Night of the Living Dead*, I have profited greatly from Walter C. Foreman, Jr.'s *The Music of the Close: The Final Scenes of Shakespeare's Tragedies* (Lexington: University of Kentucky Press, 1978). In particular, see his discussion of "tragic

death" and "dull survival," in which he considers the relationship between the "destructive energy of the tragic figures who die" and the surviving "new order" that is "duller, more mundane, and dramatically less vital" (p. 19). See also Frank Kermode's comments on the "exhausted survivors" in *King Lear* who face an end that "is not an end" (*The Sense of an Ending: Studies in the Theory of Fiction* [New York: Oxford University Press, 1966], p. 82); and Schatz's discussion of "resolution," the "sense of loss," and "compromise" in Hollywood genre films (*Hollywood Genres*, pp. 30–33).

6. See chapter 7, note 16, for a discussion of the very different conclusions in both versions of Tobe Hooper's adaptation of *'Salem's Lot*.

7. Torgovnick concludes that in an "overview ending, the author's or narrator's understanding (and hence the reader's understanding as well) is often superior to that of the characters," although she admits that there are novels in which "the protagonist shares the author's overview" (*Closure in the Novel*, p. 15). I have also discussed certain uses of overview endings in film in "Seeing It Through: Closure in Four Horror Films," *Proceedings of the Purdue Conference on Film* 7 (1983), 17–24.

8. R. H. W. Dillard, *Horror Films* (New York: Monarch, 1976), p. 80.

9. In all likelihood, the open ending in *House of Dark Shadows*, as in a great many modern horror stories, also reflects a commercial decision to leave open the possibility for a sequel. This fact should not, however, stop us from paying close attention to the precise ways such works deny closure and resolution.

10. Torgovnick, *Closure and the Novel*, p. 18. Flaubert's *L'Education sentimentale*, which "refuses to offer either climax, or moral, or insight, or comfort," is Torgovnick's major example of a "confrontational" ending (ibid., p. 118).

11. Andrew Tudor goes so far as to argue—without a great deal of evidence—that not only the horror film but also the western and the gangster film as well all share one basic element: "the use of violence as the ultimate necessary solution to crucial problems." In these three genres, he concludes, "violence resolves all problems and tensions"—"in terms of plot, in terms of emotion, in terms of morality"; these movies thus "repeat" a "pattern of culture" found elsewhere in our culture (*Image and Influence: Studies in the Sociology of Film* [New York: St. Martin's Press, 1975], pp. 213–14).

12. Victor Roman, *Four Wooden Stakes*, in *The Dracula Book of Great Vampire Stories*, ed. Leslie Shepard (Secaucus, N.J.: Citadel Press, 1977), pp. 260–61.

13. A close study of the story of the living and the undead makes me even more inclined to agree with John Fraser, who begins his *Violence and the Arts* (London: Cambridge University Press, 1974) with the admission that "there is in fact no one thing, no chemically insolatable and analysable substance, that is violence." Just as there are a varied, broad range of "yearnings and fears that get catered to or played upon in works involving violence," so, Fraser argues, the "functions of violence are also numerous—violence as release, violence as communication, violence as play, violence as self-affirmation, or self-defence, or self-discovery, or self-destruction, violence as a flight from reality, violence as the truest sanity in a particular situation, and so on" (pp. 9–10). Fraser offers several interesting, if brief, comments on the characterization of the vic-

tim in horror stories and on the violence perpetrated by the monster, but he does not consider the violence undertaken by the human beings threatened by the monster.

14. Walter M. Gerson, "Violence as an American Value Theme," in *Violence and the Mass Media*, ed. Otto N. Larsen (New York: Harper and Row, 1968), pp. 154–55. There are, of course, other categories and other distinctions employed in the vast number of sociological, psychological, and historical studies of violence. To cite three diverse examples: Monica D. Blumenthal, Robert L. Kahn, Frank M. Andrews, and Kendra B. Head distinguish between "expressive" violence, which is the product of "hate or rage," and "instrumental" violence, which is used either to maintain "social control" or to "change the existing institutions and power structure" (*Justifying Violence: Attitudes of American Men* [Ann Arbor, Mich.: Institute for Social Research, 1972], pp. 13–14). Such distinctions come into play in works like Romero's living dead films, in which all of society is threatened by the undead (who ironically become creatures of "instrumental" violence). Lewis Yablonsky bases his sociological study on a different set of categories, closer to Gerson's: legal versus illegal, sanctioned versus non-sanctioned, rational versus irrational (*The Violent Gang* [Baltimore: Penguin, 1966]), pp. vii–ix). Questions about the "rationality" of ritualized wild work are linked to the presentation of madness in the retellings of *Dracula* I discussed in chapter 3. In "Historical Patterns of Violence in America," Richard Maxwell Brown attempts to distinguish "positive" violence from "negative" violence—a distinction that proves to be arbitrary indeed, since Brown defines as "negative" the act of violence that "seems to be in no direct way connected with any socially or historically constructive development" (In *History of Violence in America: Historical and Comparative Perspectives*, ed. Hugh Davis Graham and Ted Robert Gurr [New York: Bantam, 1970], p. 45).

15. Gerson refers to "a peculiar kind of American doublethink [that] emphasizes that the best defensive position is a strong offense—as indicated by U.S. skirmishes [!] in Korea, Vietnam, and the Dominican Republic—and that we must seek peace 'offensively'" ("Violence as an American Value Theme," p. 156).

16. Ibid., p. 154.

17. In their Introduction to *Violence in America*, Hugh Davis Graham and Ted Robert Gurr argue that while "'legality' and 'legitimacy' are words that we use to pass judgement on the desirability of violence, force, and protest," such distinctions are never "clear cut." This problem, for Graham and Gurr, reflects "the complexity of the American conflict between legitimacy and legality of actions" (*Violence in America*, pp. xxx–xxxi).

18. Robert Nozick, *Anarchy, State, and Utopia* (New York: Basic Books, 1974), pp. 23–25. Max Weber argues that "the use of force is regarded as legitimate only so far as it is either permitted by the state or prescribed by it. . . . the claim of the modern state to monopolize the use of force is as essential to it as its character of compulsory jurisdiction and of continuous organization" (*The Theory of Social and Economic Organization*, ed. Talcott Parsons [New York: Free Press, 1964], p. 156).

19. J. Glenn Gray, *The Warriors: Reflections on Men in Battle* (New York: Harper and Row, 1970), pp. 131–32.

20. Behind the moral community's crusade against the undead in Stoker's *Dracula*, we can trace the tradition of the Christian "holy war" or "just war." See Sue Mansfield, *The Gestalts of War: An Inquiry into Its Origins and Meanings as a Social Institution* (New York: Dial Press, 1982), pp. 127–43; and Lynne B. Iglitzen, *Violent Conflict in American Society* (San Francisco: Chandler, 1972), pp. 125–43, for a discussion of the theory of the "just war."

21. John G. Cawelti, "Myths of Violence in American Popular Culture," *Critical Inquiry* 1 (1975), 526, 529–30.

22. Gray, *Warriors*, pp. 39–51. Stephen Crane calls this "mysterious fraternity born of the smoke and dangers of death," the "subtle battle brotherhood" (*The Red Badge of Courage* [1895; rpt. New York: Harper and Brothers, 1957], p. 40).

23. Many studies of violence and popular culture focus on the effects of violence on the audience (particularly on children in the audience). See, for example, Larsen, ed., *Violence and the Mass Media*, pp. 33–54, 115–51; Robert M. Liebert, John M. Neale, and Emily S. Davidson, *The Early Window: Effects of Television on Children and Youth* (Toronto: Pergamon Press, 1973); and H. J. Eysenck and D. K. B. Nias, *Sex, Violence, and the Media* (New York: Harper & Row, 1979). As I have suggested throughout my discussion, stories of the living and the undead often include images of spectators—from Jonathan Harker in Stoker's *Dracula* to Lucy Harker in *Nosferatu the Vampyre*—who respond in different ways to the horrors that they witness.

24. Cawelti, "Myths of Violence," p. 530.

25. Richard Slotkin, *Regeneration through Violence: The Mythology of the American Frontier, 1600–1860* (Middletown, Conn.: Wesleyan University Press, 1973), pp. 174, 308, 539.

26. Leonard Wolf, *A Dream of Dracula: In Search of the Living Dead* (New York: Popular Library, 1972), p. 128. See also, for example, Linda Bayer-Berenbaum, *The Gothic Imagination: Expansion in Gothic Literature and Art* (Rutherford, N.J.: Fairleigh Dickinson University Press, 1982), pp. 35–36. As a point of comparison, consider Slotkin's comments on the Puritan's response to what they called the "Black Eucharist" or the "cannibal Eucharist" of the Indians (*Regeneration through Violence*, pp. 112–14, 124–25).

27. Mircea Eliade, *Patterns in Comparative Religion*, trans. Rosemary Sheed (New York: Meridian, 1963), p. 196. In *Countess Dracula* (1972), based very loosely on the life of Countess Elisabeth Bathory, the aristocratic female vampire keeps her youth by bathing in the blood of virginal peasant girls.

28. See Wolf, *Dream of Dracula*, pp. 109–10, for a brief survey of rituals that involve drinking the blood or eating the flesh of a slain enemy.

29. An additional context for these particular stories are sociological studies like Georg Simmel's *Conflict* (1923) and Lewis A. Coser's *The Function of Social Conflict* (1956), which consider the positive functions of conflict in, for example, binding and preserving group relationships and in furthering social change.

30. René Girard, *Violence and the Sacred*, trans. Patrick Gregory (Baltimore:

Johns Hopkins University Press, 1977), p. 37. All future references to *Violence and the Sacred*, abbreviated VS, will be included parenthetically in my text.

31. Friedrich Nietzsche, *Beyond Good and Evil*, trans. Marianne Cowan (Chicago: Gateway, 1955), p. 85.

32. Gray, *Warriors*, p. 51.

33. Of course, the phrases "struggle for existence" and "survival of the fittest" are, as Richard Hofstadter notes, the "most popular catchwords of Darwinism" (*Social Darwinism in American Thought*, rev. ed. [New York: George Brazillier, 1959], p. 6). See "Struggle for Existence," chapter 3 of Darwin's *The Origin of Species*. The stories of survival I refer to here could be taken in one respect as a response to the idea promoted by conservative Social Darwinists that competition leads to "continuing improvement" in the "slow and unhurried" process of evolution (Hofstadter, *Social Darwinism*, pp. 6–7).

34. H. G. Wells, *The War of the Worlds*, ed. Frank D. McConnell (New York: Oxford University Press, 1977), pp. 252, 264.

35. James Dickey, *Deliverance* (New York: Dell, 1971), p. 13.

Appendix: Précis of *Dracula: The Vampire Play*

Because I make many references thoughout my study to Hamilton Deane and John L. Balderston's stage adaptation of Stoker's *Dracula*, a play that is not readily available, I offer the following act-by-act summary of *Dracula: The Vampire Play*:

ACT I: Library in Seward's Sanatorium. Dr. Seward and Jonathan Harker discuss their inability to help Seward's daughter and Jonathan's fiancée Lucy, who is ill. Having been summoned by Seward, Professor Van Helsing arrives and is informed about Lucy and about Mina Weston, who has died of a similar, mysterious illness. After escaping from his cell, Renfield intrudes into the library. He pleads to be taken away from the Sanatorium, until the appearance of a bat crashing against the window causes him to stop. Renfield is taken back to his cell after he is questioned by Van Helsing. Van Helsing then examines Lucy, who describes her "horrible" dreams. Count Dracula enters, graciously pays his respects to Lucy, then leaves to wait in another room of the house. Van Helsing explains about vampires to Seward and Jonathan, and they agree to "stamp out this monster." Van Helsing sets up a trap using Lucy as bait, but the unidentified intruder escapes in the form of a bat. The curtain falls as Dracula asks: "The patient is better, I hope?" and Renfield's "wild" laughter sounds from off-stage.

ACT II: Lucy's boudoir. Dracula hypnotizes Lucy's maid. Van Helsing and the two men relate the information they have gathered about Dracula, then plan a course of attack. Renfield enters, ready to reveal Dracula's whereabouts, when the sight of a large bat in the window again causes him to quake before the "Master." All except Van Helsing exit, then Dracula enters and the two foreigners meet in a battle of wills. Using wolfsbane and the host, Van Helsing repels the Count, who flees with a "long, satirical laugh." Van Helsing gives Lucy a crucifix for protection, then he and Seward seal Lucy's room with wolfsbane. But the maid, under Dracula's hypnotic power, removes the talisman and opens the window. The curtain falls as Dracula holds Lucy in his arms, bares her throat, and leans to bite her.

ACT III.1: Library in Seward's Sanatorium. Van Helsing describes how he and Seward have discovered all but one of Dracula's coffins. Renfield enters and must be escorted off by the two men, leaving Jonathan alone on stage with Lucy, who suddenly manifests a dangerous, vampirish "vitality." Just as she is about to bite Jonathan's throat, Van Helsing rushes in, forces the snarling woman away with a crucifix, and Lucy becomes once again "herself." Van Helsing tells how he destroyed the undead Mina; Lucy describes being forced to drink Dracula's blood. Using Renfield as bait, Van Helsing attempts to lure Dracula into the library. Armed with crucifixes, Van Helsing, Seward, and Jonathan block the vampire's exit as sunrise approaches. But Dracula, with a "loud burst of mocking laughter," escapes through a secret passageway an instant before "God's daybreak."

ACT III.2: Dark vault in Carfax Abbey. Van Helsing, Seward, and Jonathan descend into the vault and open Dracula's coffin. Seward watches as Van Helsing positions the stake and Jonathan hammers it into the vampire's heart. Both Renfield and Lucy are suddenly released from Dracula's control. Lucy calls for her father and her fiancé. Van Helsing scatters a handful of dust from the vampire's corpse and says: "Dust to dust—ashes to ashes."

In a final curtain speech, Van Helsing appears alone on stage and warns the audience that their fears about vampires and madmen are justified, for in fact "there are such things."

Index

GREGORY A. WALLER is professor and chair of the department of communication and culture at Indiana University, Bloomington. His books include *Main Street Amusements: Movies and Commercial Entertainment in a Southern City, 1896–1930*, *Moviegoing in America: A Sourcebook in the History of Film Exhibition,* and other works.

The University of Illinois Press
is a founding member of the
Association of American University Presses.

University of Illinois Press
1325 South Oak Street
Champaign, IL 61820-6903
www.press.uillinois.edu